SURVEYS IN ECONOMICS

Macroeconomics

SURVEYS IN ECONOMICS
Series editors: Robert Millward, Michael T. Sumner and George Zis

Public sector economics
Macroeconomics

Forthcoming:
Economics of empire
Industrial economics
International economics
Labour economics
Microeconomics
Monetary economics

DAVID DEMERY
NIGEL W. DUCK
MICHAEL T. SUMNER
R. LEIGHTON THOMAS
W. NEIL THOMPSON

Macroeconomics

LONGMAN
London and New York

LONGMAN GROUP LIMITED
Longman House, Burnt Mill, Harlow
Essex CM20 2JE, England
Associated companies throughout the world

Published in the United States of America
by Longman Inc., New York

First published 1984

BRITISH LIBRARY CATALOGUING IN PUBLICATION DATA
Macroeconomics.
1. Macroeconomics
I. Demery, David
339 HB171

ISBN 0-582-29570-X

LIBRARY OF CONGRESS CATALOGING IN PUBLICATION DATA
Main entry under title:
Macroeconomics.
(Surveys in economics)
Includes bibliographical references and index.
1. Macroeconomics. I. Demery, David. II. Series.
HB172.5.M335 1983 339 83-710
ISBN 0-582-29570-X

Printed in Singapore by
Kyodo Shing Loong Printing Industries Pte Ltd.

Contents

Editors' preface

The aim of this series is to survey the primary literature on selected economic topics at a level designed for intermediate and advanced undergraduate students. Few textbooks contain an adequate perspective on the development of their subject, and still fewer portray the focus of current research; but is has become progressively more difficult to supplement textbooks by selecting journal articles which provide a satisfactorily comprehensive, coherent and self-contained treatment of a topic, at a length and level of technique within the capacity of a student. The widening gap between the pedagogic and the professional literature stems partly from the increasing volume of the latter, the consequent pressure to abbreviate manuscripts, and the dissemination of research in a growing number of more specialised journals. It also reflects the increasing technical sophistication of the subject in all spheres of application, and particularly the integration of theoretical and empirical analysis which characterises much recent research, in marked contrast to the teaching of economics and econometrics in separate compartments of most undergraduate courses.

The surveys have been written for those who are studying or have completed intermediate courses in economic theory and quantitative methods. They aim to guide the reader through the professional literature, paying particular attention to the introduction of empirical work and to synthesising relevant contributions from different areas of specialisation. The major issues are explained and attention is directed towards the most useful sources for further study. By providing a comprehensive overview of its subject, each survey enables users to pursue particular aspects of the topic in greater depth through the medium of primary sources, within a frame of reference which enables the significance of those individual contributions to be assessed in their broader context.

The subjects of the surveys have been selected for their economic importance and for the extent and inaccessibility of the literature in journals and monographs devoted to them. Each is complete and self-contained, and can be read without reference to the surveys of related topics which appear in the same volume. The volumes themselves are not intended to replace textbooks by providing comprehensive coverage of their area, but to supplement textbooks by conveying the current flavour of the state of the art.

The series as a whole has been designed for second- and third-year undergraduate students at universities and polytechnics, but individual surveys will also appeal to postgraduate students and to practising economists in government, nationalised industries and the private sector who wish to update their knowledge of the subject. Economics has developed rapidly in the last two decades, and even active members of the profession have experienced difficulty in keeping pace with progress outside their own field of specialisation. It is hoped that the series will prove useful to this wider readership of continuing students as well as those beginning their education in economics.

Robert Millward
Michael T. Sumner
George Zis

Acknowledgements

The burden of typing the manuscript and eliminating inconsistencies was carried with remarkable efficiency and incredible cheerfulness by Susan Mullins, Shirley Woolley and Kath Bacon.

We are grateful to the following for permission to reproduce copyright material:

The Controller of Her Majesty's Stationery Office for figs 4.1, 4.2, 4.3 from pp 41–3 (Spencer & Mowl, 1978); Lexington Books, D.C. Heath & Company for Table 2.2 from p 260 (Ash & Smyth 1973); Princeton University Press for Tables 3.1, 3.2 from pp 44–5, 62 (Friedman, 1957); Martin Robertson & Co Ltd for Table 2.1 from pp 165, 170, 173, 175 (Lewis & Ormerod, 1979); Williams & Glyn's Bank for Table 5.2 derived from article p 33 (Marin, 1973).

CHAPTER ONE

Introduction

Michael T. Sumner and George Zis

> It is a sign of the maturity of a discipline that its main problems are not drawn from immediate, changing events. A genuine and persistent separation of scientific study from the real world leads to sterility, but an immediate and sensitive response to current events stultifies the deepening and widening of analytical principles and techniques. The leading theoretical chemists are not working on detergents or headache remedies and the leading economic theorists need not be concerned with urban renewal or oil embargoes. . . . It may be (though I somewhat doubt it) that Keynes's General Theory was the product of the Great Depression, but if so it is one of the very few great events that have affected the basic theory (Stigler 1960: 38–9)

Whether or not it indicates immaturity, the concern with contemporary circumstances and events which arguably inspired the publication of Keynes's *General Theory* has remained a characteristic of macroeconomics. One reason is that changing events have a significant and highly visible impact on macroeconomic performance. Inflation and unemployment are more easily measured than, say, the extent and consequences of microeconomic resource misallocation. Their average levels differ substantially in different countries, and their movements over time display clear trends and marked fluctuations. The explanation of these systematic patterns poses a formidable intellectual challenge.

Macroeconomic phenomena are of more than purely intellectual interest. Explanation, a necessary but insufficient condition for control, stimulated policy experiments which in turn generated additional data and new phenomena to be explained. Policy prescription has occupied a central role in this interactive process, and the market for macroeconomic diagnosis and advice has remained more open and less fragmented than its microeconomic counterparts, some of which are conspicuous only by their absence. For example, households are assumed to maximise utility without any external guidance, and the exceptions who fail to discover their tangency solution are more likely to consult a psychiatrist or citizen's advice bureau than a microeconomist. The latter can afford to maintain a detached perspective, secure in the knowledge that their aberrant behaviour, whether 'random' or 'inert', does not affect his fundamental law of demand (Becker 1962). Where there is an advisory role for the microeconomist, entry is often restricted by the confidentiality of data. Moreover, if it is still true that 'there is, in any large corporation, a full-time job for an economist in undoing the work of the accountant' (Alexander 1959: 21), it seems unlikely that the incumbent will have time to revolutionise the theory of the firm. Even in the realm of public policy, the resolution of problems posed by interaction among firms and households, problems involving industrial structure, externalities, consumer protection or the relief of poverty, is more likely to require the tedious process of collecting new data than to raise any new issue of principle.

The pivotal role in macroeconomics of the policy response to contemporary problems is reflected in the literature concerned with its assessment and evaluation, a literature surveyed by David Demery and Nigel Duck in the first of their contributions to this volume. In view of the stringent requirements which they identify for successful intervention it is not entirely surprising that stabilisation policy has produced disappointing results. Altruistic intentions on the part of government are not sufficient to ensure that their attempts to reduce or offset the impact on the economy of exogenous disturbances will actually do so. Moreover, it is not only the technical capability of their advisers and the adequacy of macroeconomics for their purpose that have been called into question but also the altruism of the policy-makers themselves, whose electoral aims may conflict with the stabilisation objective. Demery and Duck conclude by examining the most contentious issue in modern macroeconomics: would a stabilisation policy confined to the passive role of not creating disturbances, which would be consistent with both recent theoretical developments and a widely held interpretation of past performance, produce better results than active intervention?

Macroeconomics is not merely more closely oriented than microeconomics towards policy problems but depends on them for its very existence. It is a commonplace that in a world which functioned as smoothly as a Walrasian general equilibrium system, the demand for money would be less significant than the demand for peanuts; indeed, it is difficult to visualise any demand for money as such. There would be no difficulty in determining current investment, since future demands for consumption needs would be declared in advance. The consumption function, a fundamental component of all macroeconomic models, would make no sense because current income, instead of acting as an exogenous constraint on consumers' expenditure, would be determined endogenously along with the demands for goods as the outcome of utility-maximising choices by individual market participants. A statistical relationship between consumption and income would still exist, but it would be devoid of any economic significance. It is only when the conditions assumed in the fullest development of microeconomics do not hold that macroeconomic problems emerge and the central relations of macroeconomics become proper subjects for study.

The voluminous literature, surveyed by Leighton Thomas, on the consumption function was inspired not by doubts about its logical coherence but by dissatisfaction with its predictive performance. It is worth remarking that Keynes himself was characteristically vague on this point, initially stating 'the conclusion that in a given situation the propensity to consume may be considered a fairly stable function' (Keynes 1936: 95), but later inferring from Kuznets's data 'both a lower figure and a more stable figure for the investment multiplier than I should have expected' (pp. 127–8). Whatever Keynes's expectation may have been, the consumption function proved insufficiently stable to produce reliable forecasts, a necessary component of active stabilisation policy. Post-Keynesian developments have concentrated on modifying the central role of current income as the constraint on consumption, not because current income is an endogenous variable when all markets clear on Walrasian lines, but because consumers can augment their current income by drawing on past savings or by anticipating future receipts. Thomas underlines the uncertainty which still attaches to consumer behaviour, despite the effort devoted to its study, by emphasising the difficulty of discriminating between competing hypotheses, and by documenting the revision of conventional wisdom in response to the unexpected developments of the 1970s.

The consumption function is only one, albeit the most intensively studied, of the behavioural relations which constitute the standard model of macroeconomics. In parallel with the exploration of its individual equations, the model as a whole has been extended and estimated for the purposes of forecasting and policy analysis. These activities now constitute a separate branch of the literature, distinguished by its technical content and unprepossessing format. The real sector of macroeconomic models has remained a disaggregated version of their textbook parent. The financial sector, however, which scarcely existed a decade ago, has undergone radical change in recent vintages of the models, and it is this development which forms the focus of Neil Thompson's survey of the channels of monetary influence. Whereas the textbook model, reinforced by a battery of single-equation studies of the demand for money, treats the money market as the core of the financial sector and the market for non-monetary assets as a residual, this ordering has been reversed in the large-scale models, none of which includes an explicit demand function for 'broad' money. Their treatment of money as the residual asset reflects the indirect method of monetary control exercised by the UK authorities through the so-called 'supply-side counterparts', viz. the public sector borrowing requirement, sales of gilt-edged securities, changes in bank lending to the private sector, and net external flows. The wisdom of subordinating fiscal and debt-management policies as well as the exchange rate to the requirements of monetary control is the substantive and highly contentious question which underlies this modelling procedure.

Not all the behavioural relations of macroeconomics resemble the consumption function in the frailty of their micro foundations; indeed many, like the Phillips curve which links unemployment and inflation, are borrowed directly from microeconomics. The abstract question of consistency is then replaced by the more mundane but no more tractable question of whether relationships derived from the behaviour of the individual firm or household can legitimately be translated to the aggregate level. The standard solution to the aggregation problem is to ignore it, since it is seldom possible to incorporate distribution effects in macro functions even when their theoretical role is well established. For instance, an individual faced with an imperfect capital market will exhibit marked discontinuities in his marginal propensity to consume as his current income declines (Flemming 1973); but in the absence of detailed information about the distribution of income changes, the economist must fall back on the hope that aggregation across dissimilar individuals, whose consumption functions are kinked at different income levels, will smooth the function at the macro level.

The literature on wage inflation is unique in its concern for aggregation across micro-labour markets and in the availability of data which provide proxies, at least, for distribution effects. The Phillips curve remained inconsistent with microeconomic theory, however, until the belated correction of its originator's failure to recognise that the textbook response of price to excess demand in a competitive market, on which he based his influential study of wage changes (Phillips 1958), is a *ceteris paribus* relation which requires augmentation when other prices are also changing. The controversies surrounding the theoretical foundations of the Phillips curve and the empirical validity of its augmented form, which have dominated the inflation literature since the later 1960s, are the major themes of Michael Sumner's survey, but he is also concerned to place earlier developments in perspective.

The corrected version of the Phillips curve is augmented by the expected rate of price change, a correction which is more easily described than implemented. While expectations feature prominently in all macroeconomic relations, the strong prediction of a unit coefficient on the expected inflation term of the augmented Phillips curve provided a more powerful challenge to econometricians than the less precise relation between, say, consumption and permanent income. Moreover, the issue surfaced when the acceleration of price change was making the rules of thumb formerly invoked to proxy expectational variables manifestly inefficient, in the sense that they produced systematically inaccurate forecasts. Such an outcome is inconsistent with the rational expectations hypothesis, originally formulated by Muth (1961) to explain price movements at the micro level but clearly applicable to the augmented Phillips curve, among other macroeconomic relations.

The speed and range of its application and the powerful results claimed by some of the advocates of rational expectations have attracted the label of 'revolution'. In the final survey Demery and Duck justify that description while discounting some of the more dramatic results attributed to the hypothesis. In a wider perspective, however, 'evolution' would be a more appropriate term, for the rationalisation of expectations is part of a continuing process of development which has transformed macroeconomics from a collection of *ad hoc* hypotheses to a systematised and tested, if still incomplete, body of knowledge. By the standards of microeconomics it may still be immature, but the work surveyed in this volume demonstrates the rapidity of recent progress in the most significant branches of the subject.

References

Alexander, S. S. (1959) Economics and business planning, in *Economics and the Policy Maker*, Brookings Lectures 1958–59, Brookings Institution, Washington, DC.

Becker, G. S. (1962) Irrational behaviour and economic theory, *Journal of Political Economy*, **70**, 1–13.

Flemming, J. S. (1973) The consumption function when capital markets are imperfect: the permanent income hypothesis reconsidered, *Oxford Economic Papers*, N.S. **25**, 160–72.

Keynes, J. M. (1936) *The General Theory of Employment, Interest and Money*, Macmillan, London.

Muth, J. F. (1961) Rational expectations and the theory of price movements, *Econometrica*, **29**, 315–35.

Phillips, A. W. (1958) The relation between unemployment and the rate of change of money wage rates in the United Kingdom, 1861–1957, *Economica*, N.S. **25**, 283–99.

Stigler, G. J. (1960) The influence of events and policies on economic theory, *American Economic Review*, **50**, 36–45.

CHAPTER TWO

Stabilisation policy

David Demery and Nigel W. Duck

1. Introduction

The term stabilisation policy refers in macroeconomics to the measures taken by governments to ensure that the actual values of a set of macroeconomic variables fluctuate around or deviate from their desired values as little as possible. The normative issues in macroeconomic policy concern which variables the government wishes to stabilise and what priority it attaches to each. In fact the set of variables in which most governments are interested has changed little this century though the priority attached to each variable within that set may have altered. For example, in elaborating the major objectives of monetary policy the MacMillan Committee (1931) placed great emphasis on foreign exchange stability and attached a lower priority to 'the avoidance of the credit cycle, and the stability of the price level' (p. 18). In the years after the Second World War much greater emphasis was, until recently, placed on avoiding fluctuations in output and employment, although the state of the balance of payments, the foreign exchange rate and the rate of inflation were still considered important. In more recent years, particularly with the election of the Conservative government in May 1979, the reduction in inflation has been given top priority. For example, the Chancellor of the Exchequer in February 1980 wrote that 'the main objectives of the government's economic strategy are to reduce inflation and to create conditions in which substantial economic growth can be achieved', adding that 'overriding priority must be given to reducing inflation and to strengthening the supply side of the economy'. Once the normative issues of which variables the government desires to stabilise, at what levels and the priority it attaches to each have been settled, the positive issue remains of how these desired values can be achieved. For the purpose of narrowing the focus of this survey we shall usually, though not always, restrict the term stabilisation policy to mean the attempt by governments to minimise fluctuations of output (or employment) around a steadily rising trend, and to achieve stability in the price level.

How can such attempts be made to succeed? The answer clearly depends upon how the economy works and hence involves an examination of macroeconomic theory and the relevant empirical evidence. It is nonsense to argue, as it sometimes is, that in the practical running of macro-policy theory should be abandoned and 'common sense' substituted, for 'common sense' is a particular view of how the economy works, which may or may not be correct. In Keynes's famous and often quoted words at the end of the *General Theory*, 'Practical men, who believe themselves to be quite exempt from any intellectual influences, are usually the slaves of some defunct economist. Madmen in authority, who hear voices in the air, are distilling their frenzy from some academic scribbler of a few years back.' (Keynes 1936: 383).

In this survey we shall examine major macroeconomic theories and their implications for the design of stabilisation policies. We begin in section 2 with the Keynesian view of macroeconomics and the form of stabilisation policies it implies. In section 3 we consider the empirical questions of whether the government has sufficiently powerful policy instruments to apply Keynesian policies successfully and whether, in fact, governments have applied such policies successfully. In section 4 we discuss why governments might fail to apply Keynesian policies successfully with a view to assessing whether such failure is inherent in the Keynesian approach. Section 5 outlines the theoretical basis for an alternative approach to stabilisation policy and briefly describes that approach.

2. Keynesian macroeconomics

In this section we develop a standard[1] Keynesian model of the economy and illustrate, at a very simple level, the approach to policy contained in Keynes's *General Theory* (1936).

The model we construct is an aggregate supply (AS) aggregate demand (AD) model which we hope is fairly familiar and can therefore be derived briefly. The AD curve shows the quantity of aggregate real output demanded at each price level and can be derived readily from a conventional IS–LM model. The IS curve shows all combinations of real output or real income and the rate of interest on bonds which are consistent with an equality between injections into the circular flow of income (investment and government expenditure in simple versions of the model) and withdrawals from it (usually savings and taxation). Since investment expenditure is generally viewed as being a negative function of the rate of interest on bonds whilst savings and taxation are both viewed as positive functions of income, the IS curve is normally drawn as downward sloping. Its position is determined by the value of certain exogenous variables: primarily the level of government expenditure, g, and the level of autonomous spending, A (i.e. that part of spending which is independent of the interest rate and income). The IS curve IS_0 in Fig. 2.1 is drawn for a level of government expenditure g_0, and a level of autonomous expenditure A_0. If either g or A were higher the IS curve should be drawn further to the right.

The LM curve shows combinations of real income and the interest rate on bonds for which the demand for money is equal to the supply. Since the demand for money is considered to be a positive function of income and a negative function of the rate of interest on bonds, this curve is drawn upward sloping. More importantly for our purposes, its position is determined by the real quantity of money in circulation. The higher the real quantity of money in circulation the

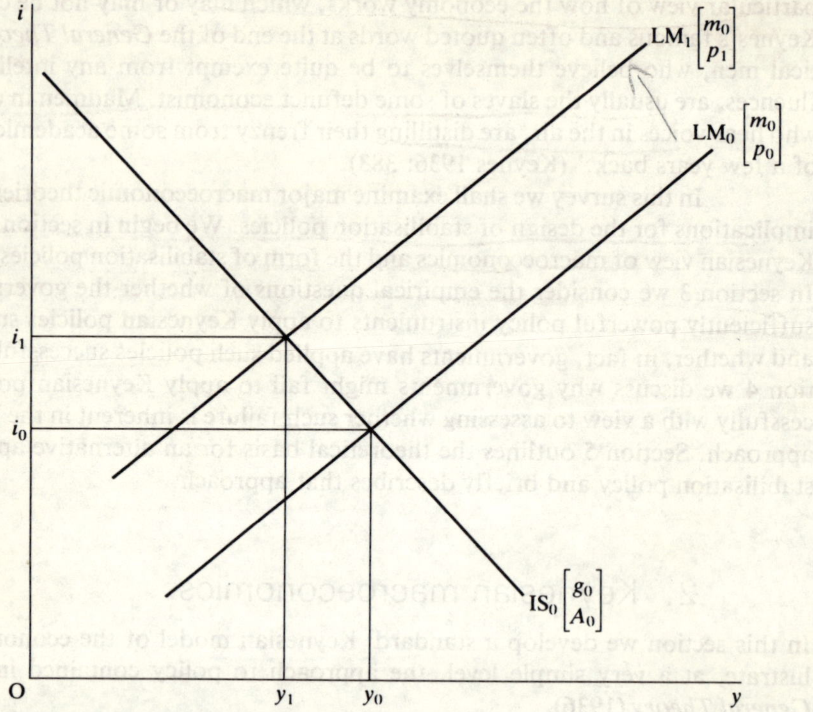

FIG. 2.1 Derivation of aggregate demand curve

higher, for any given interest rate, must the level of real income be for the demand for money to equal the supply. Hence the higher the real quantity of money the further to the right is the LM curve. And since a higher real quantity of money can arise from either a higher nominal supply of money with the price level remaining the same or from a lower price level with the same nominal supply of money, it follows that both a higher nominal supply of money and a lower price level shift the LM curve to the right. Two LM curves are shown in Fig. 2.1. Both are drawn for a given nominal supply of money m_0, but in LM_0 the price level is assumed to be p_0, whereas in LM_1 the price level is assumed to be higher at p_1. The combination of IS_0 and LM_0 yield a 'solution' for the interest rate, i, and real income y of i_0 and y_0. The solution for y (which is really what concerns us) is to be interpreted as follows: given the levels of g, A, m and p assumed in the construction of the two curves, the level of demand for real output which can be sustained is y_0; any other level of demand cannot be sustained for any length of time. In this sense y_0 is the equilibrium quantity of output demanded. It should be obvious from the above that it is possible to construct, on the basis of the IS and LM curves, another composite curve, an aggregate demand curve. From Fig. 2.1 it is clear that if the price level assumes a value of p_0, and if government expenditure, the nominal money stock etc., take the values assumed in Fig. 2.1 then aggregate demand in the sense defined above will be y_0. Hence p_0y_0 is one combination relating the price level to the level of real aggregate demand and so is one combination of p and y on an aggregate demand curve. Another such combination is p_1y_1 where p_1 is higher than p_0, and y_1 is lower than y_0. A whole set of such combinations could be derived to produce the aggregate demand curve AD_0 which, it should be remembered, is drawn for given values of g, m, and A.

Such an aggregate demand curve is shown in Fig. 2.2. An intuitive explanation of the slope of this aggregate demand curve is as follows: a lower price level implies, *ceteris paribus*, a higher value for the real money stock. A rise in the real money stock implies, *ceteris paribus*, that economic agents are holding more money than they want. Their attempt to reduce these excess money balances results in a higher level of aggregate demand (in this case through interest rate effects on expenditure).

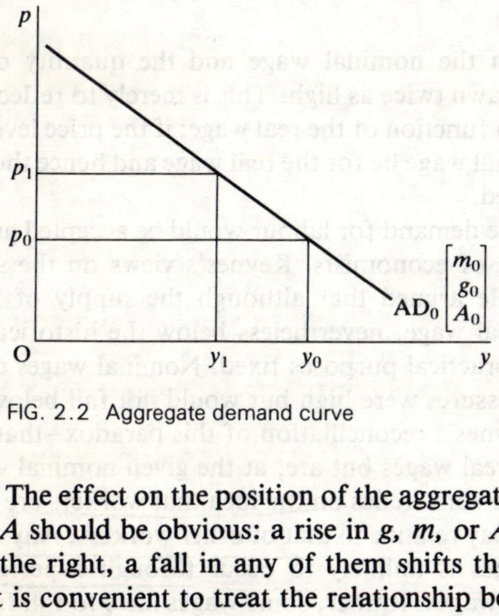

FIG. 2.2 Aggregate demand curve

The effect on the position of the aggregate demand curve of a change in g, m, or A should be obvious: a rise in g, m, or A shifts the aggregate demand curve to the right, a fall in any of them shifts the curve to the left.[2] For what follows it is convenient to treat the relationship between aggregate real demand and the price level as a logarithmic one, so p, y, m, etc. are best seen as the natural logs of the relevant variables.

The Keynesian aggregate supply curve can be derived from an analysis of the labour market in the following way. According to conventional microeconomic theory, the demand for labour will be a negative function of the real wage, that is the nominal wage divided by the price level. (Strictly the relevant wage for the producer is the nominal wage divided by the selling price of the product (i.e. the 'product wage'), but if we assume no relative price movements then the price of each product will move in line with the general price level and hence we can 'proxy' the one with the other.) The higher the real wage, whether because of a higher nominal wage or a lower price level, the less labour will be demanded. Although the crucial variable is the real wage, it is diagrammatically convenient to draw the demand for labour curve as a negative function of the nominal wage. We draw one such relationship in Fig. 2.3. There will of course be one such curve for every general price level. If, for example, the value of the price level were to double

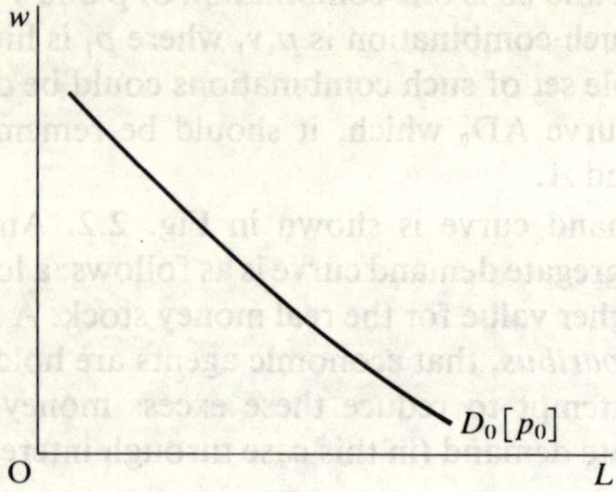

FIG. 2.3 Demand for labour

then the relationship between the nominal wage and the quantity of labour employed would need to be drawn twice as high. This is merely to reflect the fact that the demand for labour is a function of the real wage: if the price level is twice as high then so must the nominal wage be for the real wage and hence the demand for labour to remain unchanged.

This derivation of the demand for labour would be accepted as more or less accurate by a wide range of economists. Keynes's views on the supply of labour were less orthodox. He argued that although the supply of labour is generally a function of the real wage, nevertheless below the historically given level, *nominal* wages are for practical purposes fixed. Nominal wages could rise above this level if demand pressures were high but would not fall below it if demand pressures were low. Keynes's reconciliation of this paradox–that workers are generally concerned with real wages but are, at the given nominal wage, unwilling to accept nominal wage cuts–relies on the idea that workers are reluctant to accept any erosion of their pay relative to that of other workers. Any fall in the general level of nominal wages is unlikely to occur through a perfectly synchronised and equal fall in all wages. Rather, some wages have to fall first, to be followed by others. But no group of workers wants to be the first to accept wage cuts and it is this unwillingness, based on concern with pay differentials, which leads to nominal wages being, for practical purposes, fixed or at least downwardly rigid at their existing level, even though generally it is the real wage which determines the supply of labour.

These two strands of the Keynesian theory of the supply of labour are shown in Fig. 2.4. There w_0 is the log of the historically given level of nominal wages. If the log of the price level is p_0 then the supply of labour curve facing the firm is that labelled S_0 $[p_0]$. If the price level was twice as high then the supply of labour curve facing the firm would be the one labelled S_1 $[p_1]$.

In Fig. 2.5 we combine the demand for and supply of labour curves to determine at each assumed price level the equilibrium quantity of labour. So, given a price level of p_0, the equilibrium quantity of labour is L^f. (The fact that this equilibrium happens to be where the relevant supply curve kinks is of no real significance.) Given an explicit production function ($y = F(L)$) with labour as the

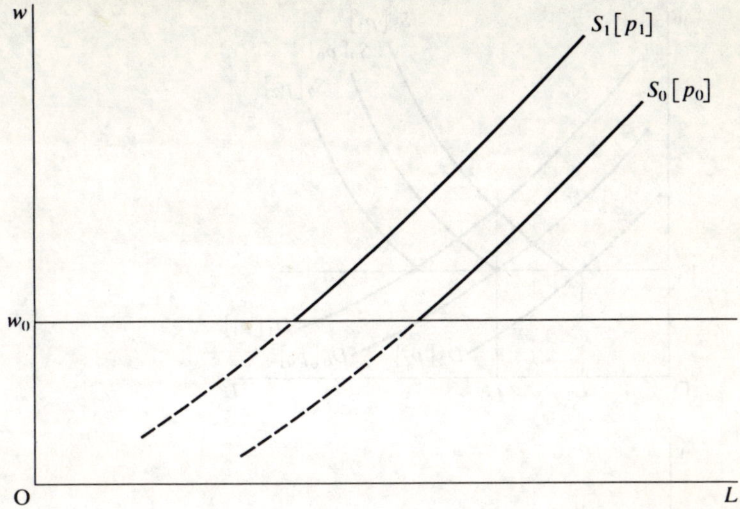

FIG. 2.4 Keynesian supply of labour

only variable input, the output level can be derived from the level of employment (as in Fig. 2.5). If the price level is p_0 the quantity of output supplied will thus be y^f. This combination $p_0 y^f$ is one point on an aggregate supply curve. Other points can be derived by assuming different price levels. Thus, if we assume that the price level is p_1, then since both the supply of and demand for labour shift up by the same percentage, they will intersect at the same level of employment, L^f, and hence a price level of p_1 will produce the same level of output y_f.[3] However, if we assume a lower price level, p_2, then since nominal wages are fixed at w_0, the new intersection of labour supply and demand curves will be at L_2 and output will be y_2. The aggregate supply curve will thus be upward sloping below p_0 but vertical above p_0. Its shape is illustrated in Fig. 2.6. It should be clear that the lower the historically determined level of nominal wages, the lower the aggregate supply curve. In Fig. 2.7 we combine the AD and AS curves to obtain a compact, though necessarily simplified, version of the Keynesian model. In that figure it is clear that given the historically determined level at which nominal wages are fixed and given the exogenous values of *m, g,* etc., the equilibrium value of y is y^f and the equilibrium price level is p_0.

The essence of the 'Keynesian revolution' is that the equilibrium solution for y need not be at y^f; that is, in our terms, the intersection of the AS and AD curves need not be y^f. In particular, if the AD curve intersects the AS curve below y^f, there is no *self-regulating mechanism* to push the economy back to y^f. The major policy implication is that if aggregate demand does sharply decrease—because of, say, a fall in autonomous expenditure—the government should increase its own expenditure or increase the money supply to ensure a level of aggregate demand compatible with full employment. And of the two policy instruments—government expenditure and changes in the money stock—the former was thought by Keynesians to be the more reliable and direct method of stimulating demand. Indeed one

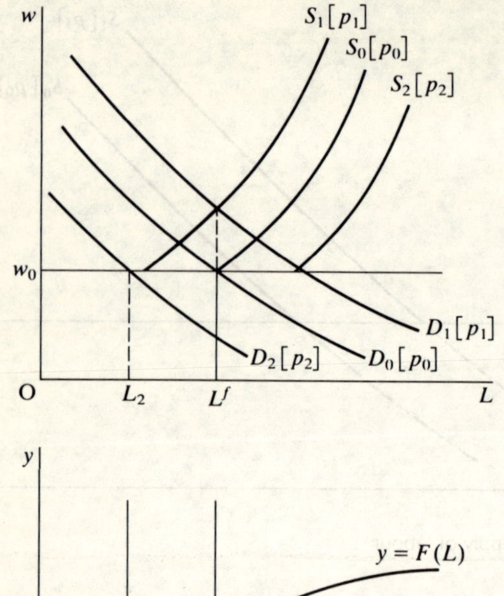

FIG. 2.5 Keynesian labour market

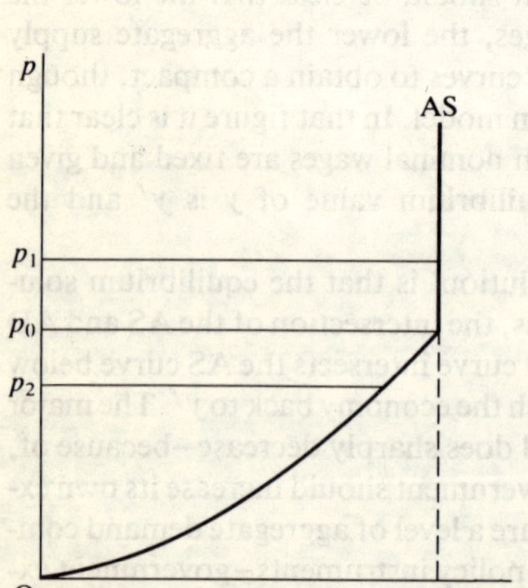

FIG. 2.6 Keynesian aggregate supply curve

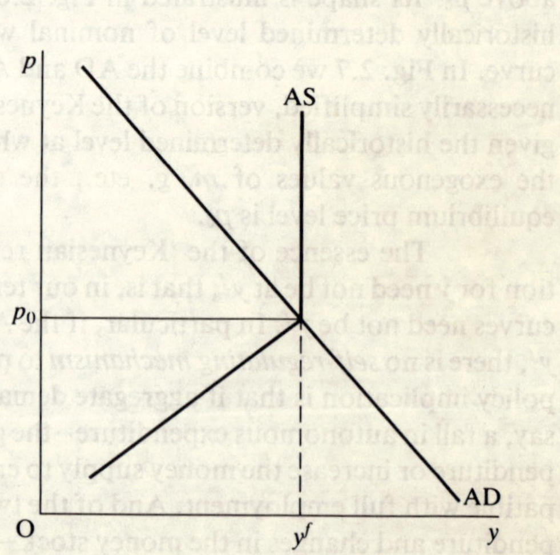

FIG. 2.7 Full employment in the Keynesian model

feature of Keynesian thought has been the belief that variations in the money stock might well have no impact at all on aggregate demand.

Keynes himself (1936) raised doubts about the ability of changes in the money stock to stimulate output. For example, he says on p.173, 'If, however, we are tempted to assert that money is the drink which stimulates the system to activity, we must remind ourselves that there may be several slips between the cup and the lip.' But by the time of the Radcliffe Report (1959) such doubts had become almost certainties about the inability of variations of the money stock to affect the economy. In para. 391 for example the Report says

> It is possible . . . to demonstrate statistically that during the last few years the volume of spending has greatly increased while the supply of money has hardly changed: the velocity of circulation has increased. We have not made use of this concept because we cannot find any reason for supposing, or any experience in monetary history indicating, that there is any limit to the velocity of circulation.

This Keynesian view of the economy dominated UK policy-making until fairly recently. As we shall see, its practical application to the problem of stabilising the economy involved a considerably greater degree of sophistication than the above analysis suggests, but the essence of the approach is contained in that analysis. To repeat, in a Keynesian view of the economy, booms and slumps (the latter being particularly important for Keynes writing in the 1930s) are likely to arise from the volatility of the spending plans of the private sector. A slump in private sector spending is likely to have persistent or long-lasting effects on output and employment because there is no self-regulating mechanism to ensure that such decreases in spending are quickly reversed. The government can and should combat these decreases in private sector spending by increasing its own spending. This will ensure a high enough level of spending to generate full employment.

Before considering some problems with this approach to stabilisation policy we outline a simple algebraic version of the Keynesian model. This allows us to make some of the points made above more sharply and will be useful later in distinguishing Keynesian and monetarist macroeconomic models.
The aggregate demand curve can be written as follows:

$$y_t^d = a_0 + a_1(m_t - p_t) + a_2 g_t + z_t \qquad [1]$$

where y_t^d is the log of the level of aggregate real demand at time t.
m is the log of the nominal money supply.
p is the log of the price level.
g is the log of real government expenditure.
z is a shock variable. Its normal or mean value might be considered to be zero. A negative value represents a shift downwards in aggregate demand, a positive value represents a shift upwards.
a_0 is a constant.
a_1 and a_2 are positive constants.

The aggregate supply curve is:

$$y_t^s = b_0 + b_1(p_t - w_t) \qquad [2]$$

where y_t^s is the log of aggregate real supply at time t.
w is the log of the nominal wage.
b_0 and b_1 are constants. b_1 is positive.

We are interested in the level of y and p at which the aggregate supply and demand are equal, that is where

$$y_t^d = y_t^s \qquad [3]$$

And finally we distinguish two 'regimes': the first where the economy is characterised by excess supply of labour (employment is determined by labour demand); the second where the economy is at full employment. The first regime implies [4] and the second [5].

$$w_t = \bar{w}_0 \qquad [4]$$

$$y_t = y^f \qquad [5]$$

where $\bar{w}_0$ is the log of the historically given level of nominal wages.
y^f is the log of the full employment level of output.

The first regime produces the following solutions for y and p (i.e. combine equations [1], [2], [3] and [4]):

$$y_t = \frac{b_1a_0 + a_1b_0}{a_1 + b_1} + \frac{b_1a_1m_t}{a_1 + b_1} + \frac{b_1a_2g_t}{a_1 + b_1} - \frac{b_1a_1\bar{w}_0}{a_1 + b_1} + \frac{b_1z_t}{a_1 + b_1} \qquad [6]$$

$$p_t = \frac{a_0 - b_0}{a_1 + b_1} + \frac{a_1m_t}{a_1 + b_1} + \frac{a_2g_t}{a_1 + b_1} + \frac{b_1\bar{w}_0}{a_1 + b_1} + \frac{z_t}{a_1 + b_1} \qquad [7]$$

The second policy regime implies the following (i.e. combine equations [1], [2], [3] and [5]):

$$y = y^f \qquad [8]$$

$$p_t = \frac{a_0}{a_1} + m_t + \frac{a_2g_t}{a_1} - \frac{y^f}{a_1} + \frac{z_t}{a_1} \qquad [9]$$

The first regime is the one of immediate interest. Consider a government which has a target value for y of y^T. This target may not equal y^f if, for example, the government regards the risk of inflation as being less if output is held somewhat below its full employment value (although such a risk is not allowed for in our simple model). If the government takes w and z as given at $\bar{w}_0$ and $\bar{z}_0$ then it can achieve this target value for y of y^T by an appropriate mix of fiscal and monetary policy. Setting y at y^T and w and z at $\bar{w}_0$ and $\bar{z}_0$ respectively, we can use equation [6] to obtain what the appropriate policy mix shall be as follows:

$$y^T = \frac{b_1 a_0 + a_1 b_0}{a_1 + b_1} + \frac{b_1 a_1 m_t}{a_1 + b_1} + \frac{b_1 a_2 g_t}{a_1 + b_1} + \frac{b_1 a_1 \bar{w}_0}{a_1 + b_1} + \frac{b_1 \bar{z}_0}{a_1 + b_1} \qquad [10]$$

i.e.

$$\frac{b_1 a_1 m^*}{a_1 + b_1} + \frac{b_1 a_2 g^*}{a_1 + b_1} = y^T - \frac{(b_1 a_0 + a_1 b_0)}{a_1 + b_1} - \frac{b_1 a_1 \bar{w}_0}{a_1 + b_1} - \frac{b_1 \bar{z}_0}{a_1 + b_1} \qquad [11]$$

where m^* and g^* represent the appropriate values for m and g respectively.

If the government takes the view that in fact monetary policy is unimportant in the determination of aggregate demand (i.e. it considers the value of a_1 to be zero), then equation [11] can be used to derive a unique value for g^* which will achieve the target value for y. This value for g^* will, from equation [11] (and the assumption that $a_1 = 0$) be

$$g^* = \frac{y^T}{a_2} - \frac{a_0}{a_2} - \frac{\bar{z}_0}{a_2} \qquad [12]$$

If the government thinks that both monetary and fiscal policy have significant effects on aggregate demand, then equation [11] provides them with a series of combinations of m and g which will achieve their objective and they can select which combination they prefer. Their choice of m and g in achieving this objective may be influenced by side effects of using each. For example, the higher the level of g the higher the interest rate is likely to be, and possibly therefore the lower will be the ratio of investment expenditure to consumption. For this reason a government which desires a high level of investment expenditure may prefer a lower level of g and a higher level of m to achieve the same level of aggregate demand. Alternatively, as we shall see in a later section, once allowance is made for the fact that countries trade with each other a higher interest rate may imply a greater growth in foreign exchange reserves and on those grounds be preferable for a government which considers its foreign exchange reserves are too low.

One extension to this analysis which it is convenient to discuss here has been made by Poole (1970) and concerns the choice of policy instrument in an economy in which there is uncertainty. Poole's analysis centres on the instrument of monetary policy, and although his analysis has wider implications we too will concentrate on that specific issue. We have so far discussed monetary policy in terms of variations in the supply of money. But often monetary policy is discussed in terms of the manipulation of interest rates. Poole discusses the problem of whether the monetary authority should set interest rates or the supply of money if the aim is to achieve as small a variation as possible around a target level of aggregate demand. Consider, as in Fig. 2.8, a simple IS/LM model where prices are fixed and the monetary authority which takes the IS curve as beyond its control wishes to stabilise aggregate demand at y_0. In a world where all the relationships which underly the IS and LM curves are known with perfect certainty it makes no difference whether the monetary authority determines the money stock at m_0 and lets the market determine the interest rate i_0, or sets the interest rate at i_0 and supplies whatever quantity of money is demanded – which will be m_0. In both cases aggregate demand will be y_0. But assume the relationships underlying the IS curve are stochastic, i.e. they contain random elements, such that the IS curve has a mean or expected position of IS_0 but can fluctuate between IS_1 and IS_2. Then setting an interest rate of i_0 and supplying whatever quantity of money is demanded could generate fluctuations around y_0 between y_1 and y_2. But setting a money stock of m_0 and letting the market determine the interest rate would lead to fluctuations in y anywhere between y_3 and y_4. Since the latter band is smaller the setting of the money stock is preferable to the setting of interest rates. Moreover it should be easy to see that if we had assumed that it was the LM curve rather than the IS curve which was stochastic the result would be reversed. In general the greater the stochastic element in the IS curve relative to the LM curve, the more likely it is that a policy of setting the money stock will be preferable to a policy of setting interest rates. So, for example, the greater the unpredictability of the demand for money function the less sensible it is to conduct monetary policy through control of the money supply and the more sensible it is to operate through the setting of interest rates. Poole (1970) develops and elaborates these general results.

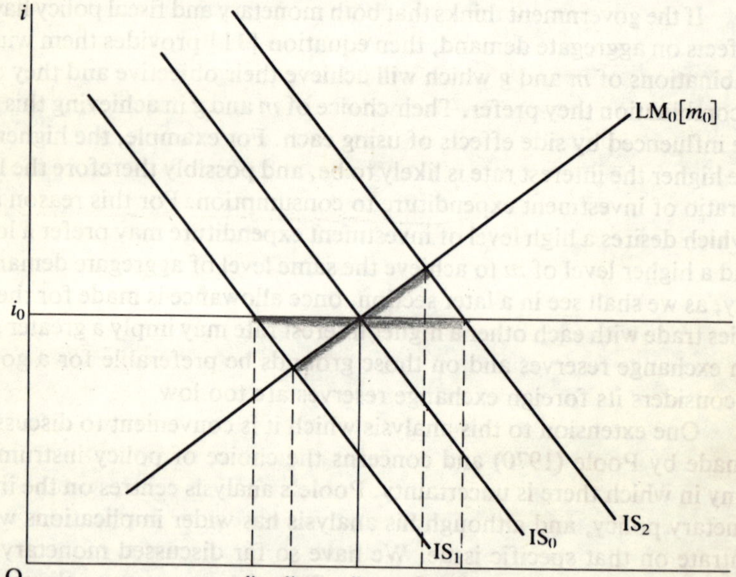

FIG. 2.8 Choice of policy instrument under uncertainty

3. Empirical issues

The Keynesian theory of macroeconomics, as the previous section showed, offers scope for monetary and fiscal policy to effect changes in and stabilise real output and the price level. In this section we turn to the practical foundations for stabilisation policy by asking two related questions.

1. Is there empirical support for the view that monetary and fiscal policies are sufficiently effective to enable governments to deploy them in a fashion that will stabilise the economy?
2. Have governments achieved, in their use of policy instruments, the principal objectives of stabilisation policy?

THE EFFECTIVENESS OF POLICY

Equations [6] and [7] above show how, in a Keynesian model, output and the price level can be influenced by monetary and fiscal policy. In what follows, in the interests of brevity, we shall concentrate mainly on the influence of policy on output. The degree to which output is influenced by policy changes clearly depends on the parameters of the aggregate demand and supply curves (a_1, a_2, b_1), and these in turn are determined by the 'structural' parameters underlying the two relationships. For example, the actual value of a_1, which partly determines the effectiveness of monetary policy, is related to the interest elasticity of the demand for money. If the demand for money is highly interest elastic, i.e. the LM curve is very flat, then a_1 will be low. In the limit it will be zero and hence the coefficient attached to m in the output equation will also be zero and therefore monetary policy will be ineffective. By a similar argument, a_1 will be zero if investment expenditure is wholly interest inelastic, and a_2 will be zero and hence fiscal policy will be ineffective if investment expenditure is perfectly interest elastic or if the demand for money is wholly interest inelastic. These results should be familiar. Laidler (1977) gives a particularly clear explanation of them.

Obviously any sensible government which wishes to use monetary and fiscal policy to affect output has to establish the effectiveness or otherwise of the instruments. If they are ineffective (i.e. if $a_1 = 0$ and $a_2 = 0$), then there is no point in manipulating them, at least as far as stabilising the economy is concerned. As the argument above suggests, there are two general approaches to determining empirically the effectiveness of monetary and fiscal policy. First, econometric studies of the underlying structural equations can be undertaken and their implications for the parameters a_1, a_2, etc. derived. For example, one can estimate the economy's demand for money function and quantify the interest elasticity. If the estimate is low then it suggests that monetary policy may be effective, if it is high it suggests that it may not be. Or one could estimate the investment expenditure or consumption function and from the estimates of the interest sensitivity of the two types of expenditure form some view of the value of a_1 and a_2, etc. On the basis of the estimates of individual equations, one could either come to some informal conclusion about the effectiveness of various policies, or, more ambitiously, one could incorporate such estimates into a larger model of the whole economy and this model could be used to estimate the effects of policy changes–an increase in government expenditure for example, or a cut in taxation. The main drawback of this second approach, apart from the complex and unwieldy models which it tends to produce, is that no model, however large, is likely to capture all the mechanisms by which monetary and fiscal policy work. In practice model builders exclude possible transmission mechanisms either because they do not, a priori, consider them likely to be important, or because the data with which one might estimate their quantitative importance are not available. For example, Keynes argued that one mechanism which may thwart the expansionary intentions of a rise in government expenditure is the effect of such measures on 'confidence'. 'With the confused psychology which often prevails, the Government programme may, through its effect on 'confidence', increase liquidity preference or diminish the marginal efficiency of capital, which, again may retard other investment unless measures are taken to offset it.' (Keynes 1936: 120.) But 'confidence' is a notoriously nebulous concept and practically impossible to measure. Therefore most models which purport to estimate the importance of fiscal policy will simply ignore this confidence mechanism altogether.

The exclusion of important transmission mechanisms prevents a complete answer to the question of policy effectiveness. Despite these drawbacks an enormous amount of research has, in the last thirty years or more, gone into the empirical estimation of individual structural equations and the estimation of large-scale models of the economy. We cannot here give a complete survey of all this work; instead we refer interested readers to Thompson's survey in this volume, and make two very general points. First, partly as a result of all this work and partly as a result of other empirical work to be discussed later, most economists probably would consider monetary policy more powerful and fiscal policy less powerful than they would have done thirty years ago. This is not true of every economist but is illustrated by the incorporation of a monetary section into models of the economy (e.g. the UK Treasury model) which previously treated it as irrelevant, and by such statements as the following by the American Keynesian, Modigliani: '... (T)he monetarists have made a valid and most valuable contribution ... in rehabilitating the role of money as a determinant of aggregate demand' (Modigliani 1977: 17). The greater prominence given to monetary policy by the authorities of various governments can also be seen as a reflection of the greater importance placed on it by professional economists and economic advisers. The second general comment we would make is that professional opinion has by no means swung wholly to the view that fiscal policy is ineffective.

To illustrate these two general comments we consider the evidence from the econometric model that the UK government itself employs for both forecasting and policy evaluation.[4] The model is naturally very large and complex – the March 1978 version of the model contained 810 variables of which 230 were exogenous—and in it policies have delayed as well as initial or impact effects on real output. A detailed exposition of the Treasury model can be found in a technical manual published by the Treasury but its essential features are conveniently summarised in Chrystal (1979), Laury *et al.* (1978), and Chapter 4 of this volume. Evaluation of policy effectiveness using the model entails simulation methods, in which the model is 'run' with and without a policy change and the contribution of this policy change is evaluated in terms of real output. Lewis and Ormerod (1979) have published the results of fiscal policy simulations using the Treasury model. In principle this model allows evaluation of the effects on the economy of a number of fiscal instruments (public authorities' current expenditure, nationalised industries' investment expenditure, changes in both personal tax allowances and the standard and higher rates of tax, corporation tax changes,

TABLE 2.1 Treasury simulation results

	Multiplier after number of years				
	1	2	3	4	6
Simulation 1 Government expenditure per quarter increased by £100 m. (interest rate, earnings, exchange rate fixed)	1.1	1.06	1.02	0.98	0.99
Simulation 2 As Simulation 1 but earnings endogenous, floating exchange rate	1.1	1.04	0.9	0.8	0.8
Simulation 3 Income tax reduced by £100 m. per quarter (interest rate fixed; earnings endogenous, floating exchange rate)	0.4	0.55	0.9	1.15	1.4
Simulation 4 Balanced budget: increase of both taxes and government expenditure of £100 m. per quarter (interest rate fixed, earnings endogenous, exchange rate floating)	0.75	0.4	0	−0.4	−0.6

Source: Lewis and Ormerod (1979)

VAT adjustments and duty on petrol, beer or tobacco). Lewis and Ormerod, by way of illustration, considered the effect on the level of GDP of a change in government expenditure under alternative assumptions about earnings and the exchange rate. These simulations are reported in Table 2.1.

All the simulations reported assume a fixed interest rate which implies an accommodating monetary policy. In this respect it could be argued that the results reported overstate the Treasury model's estimate of fiscal policy effectiveness. Despite this the results suggest strongly that fiscal policy is not as effective as textbook Keynesian models might suggest. These simple models, where the ratio of the change in GDP to the change in government expenditure is portrayed as equalling $1/1-c$ where c is the marginal propensity to consume suggest that as a plausible estimate of c is roughly 0.66, the multiplier is approximately 3.00. But as Table 2.1 shows, when earnings and the exchange rate are allowed to vary, the ratio of the change in GDP to a change in government expenditure is only slightly above one in the first two years and below one in the next three. Thus while fiscal policy changes have some effect on real output, the Treasury model suggests a much less significant role for them than early Keynesians would have expected.

Of course as we have already noted this method of evaluating fiscal policy effectiveness (and where possible the strength of monetary policy as well) is open to the objection that if the model is incorrectly specified (i.e. if it contains incorrect economic relationships and/or omits important ones), or if there are significant biases in the estimates of the model parameters (as there would be, for example, if there were unknown measurement errors in some of the variables used), the exercise is strictly invalid and could be highly misleading.

The second method for evaluating the effectiveness of monetary and fiscal policy which, at least on first consideration seems more appealing, is the 'reduced form' or 'St Louis approach' (named after the Federal Reserve Bank of St Louis under whose auspices a number of studies of this type have been carried out, e.g. Andersen and Jordan 1968 and Andersen and Carlson 1974). The characteristic feature of this approach is that no attempt is made to derive the parameter estimates of the structural model (e.g. the interest elasticity of the demand for money, etc.), but equations like [6] and [7] are estimated directly by regressing output on monetary and fiscal variables. By this technique, estimates of the composite coefficients (e.g. $b_1a_1/(a_1 + b_1)$) are derived but not individual estimates of b_1, a_1, a_2 and still less the *structural* parameters which lie behind a_1, a_2, etc. But since the aim of the approach is to find out how effective monetary policy and fiscal policy are, then it is the composite coefficients that are of interest and so, it is argued, estimates of structural parameters are of limited concern.

The major advantage of this approach, apart from its obvious simplicity, is that it does not restrict the influences of monetary and fiscal policy changes to operate via any specific and therefore possibly erroneous transmission mechanism. However, it does have considerable disadvantages of its own. Before considering these we present a very brief outline of the major results of this sort of study. Andersen and Jordan (1968) found, using US time series data, that fiscal expenditure had an immediate positive effect on nominal income (which is the usual dependent variable in these studies) over two quarters, but this effect was exactly offset by a negative effect over the next two quarters. Monetary policy, in contrast, had a lasting effect on nominal income. Similar results were obtained for the UK by Matthews and Ormerod (1978) who, using quarterly time series data between 1964 and 1974, report a significant effect for monetary policy on nominal income but an insignificant effect for their fiscal policy variable. Results for the UK, though, are generally less favourable to monetary policy than are results for other countries. See for example Artis and Nobay (1969) and Goodhart and Crockett (1970).

This is clearly nothing like an exhaustive survey of this type of study but it does give the flavour of the general result–namely that monetary policy is effective in determining nominal income whereas fiscal policy is at best effective in the very short run and possibly has no effect in the medium or long run.

These reduced form results have been criticised on a number of grounds. First, the measures of monetary and fiscal policy used may not be unaffected by output. Consider, for example, the case of a monetary authority which, in order to keep interest rates low, accommodates increases in nominal income (or expected future changes in income) by making appropriate adjustments to the money supply. Then rises in nominal income which occur quite independently of rises in the money supply will generate increases in the money supply. A St Louis equation would find a positive significant relationship between nominal income and money growth, and this result might be misinterpreted as evidence that changes in the money supply exert a strong influence on the economy. Or consider an economy in which fiscal policy is effective and is used by the government perfectly to offset movements in a variable like z in equation [6] so that income is constant. Then a St Louis equation in which real output was regressed on fiscal policy would show no significant role for fiscal policy since, despite fiscal policy changes, no changes in income were observed.

A second problem is that fiscal and monetary policy variables may be used in conjunction. For example, part of government expenditure may be financed by methods that affect the money supply and hence their separate effects may be difficult to isolate statistically. The high coefficient on the monetary policy variable in St Louis equations may be 'picking up' fiscal policy influences. Thus the reduced form evidence may be difficult or impossible to interpret in a fashion that will assist in determining policy effectiveness.

In view of the difficulties in assessing the evidence on monetary and fiscal policy effectiveness any conclusions must be treated cautiously. However, we conclude that from the various sources of evidence there is a fairly strong case for regarding both fiscal and monetary policy as having significant effects on real income and prices, and therefore at least a prima-facie case for regarding them both as possible instruments for stabilising the economy. This conclusion naturally leads to a further question: have governments *in practice* so deployed the instruments at their disposal to stabilise the economy or have their actions destabilised?

HAVE GOVERNMENTS STABILISED THE ECONOMY?

This important question turns out to be an extremely difficult one to answer. The source of this difficulty is clear: to answer it we need to be able to say what would have happened to the economy had the government not carried out the stabilising policies but instead had carried out other more 'neutral' policies. We need, in other words, a precise model of the economy in which we have confidence. But any available model has faults and inadequacies, and we can never be sure that the answer provided by any one model would not be different if these faults and inadequacies were eradicated. Nevertheless, several attempts, with differing degrees of subtlety, have been made to answer the question.

Assessments of UK policy are provided in Beckerman (1972), Blackaby (1979), Bristow (1968), Brittan (1971), Dow (1964), Hansen (1969), Little (1962), Matthews (1969), Musgrave and Musgrave (1968) and Posner (1978). Similar studies have been carried out for the US economy by, for example, Modigliani (1964), Kmenta and Smith (1973) and Taylor (1979).

Some of these studies, e.g. Dow and Brittan, examine in detail the policies different governments have carried out and the pressures on them to adopt such policies, and try to assess somewhat informally, but with the advantage of hindsight, their advisability. Others, e.g. Bristow, Hansen, Kmenta and Smith, employ models of the economy to predict what would have happened had government policies been in some sense neutral and thereby assess the success of actual government policies in stabilising the economy. Not surprisingly the conclusions of the various studies differ considerably. Dow (1964) states that 'As far as internal conditions are concerned, then budgetary and monetary policy failed to be stabilising, and must on the contrary be regarded as having been positively destabilising' (p.384). Similarly Brittan (1971) has argued that 'official economic management was actually destabilising and thus aggravated the fluctuations it was meant to correct. This is indeed suggested both by the general history of the period and from the timing of the most notable government interventions–the deflationary crisis measures of Thorneycroft in 1957, Selwyn Lloyd in 1961, Wilson in 1966, and the reflationary budgets of Heathcoat Amory in 1959 and Maudling in 1963' (p.450). Musgrave and Musgrave (1968) in similar vein, have written: 'Destabilising changes in fiscal and monetary policy have resulted from the failure to heed this relation (i.e. the lag between movements in unemployment and movements in output) so that restrictive policies have taken hold only after the growth of aggregate demand has slackened' (p.489).

Hansen (1969), who used a relatively simple model to determine the likely behaviour of the economy in the absence of stabilisation policies, found that, in the UK, governments positively destabilised. His conclusions are worth quoting at length:

> The United Kingdom is a country where one would expect to find well-designed budgetary policies. Institutional restrictions on the government's freedom of budgetary action are almost non-existent. There is a consensus in favour of policy intervention through the budget to influence both the level of activity and its fluctuations. And the administration has a relatively long experience both in making the forecasts on which such interventions must be based and in managing the resultant policies. Nevertheless, during the period 1955–65 the total effects of budgetary changes in the United Kingdom were almost systematically destabilising with respect to domestic demand, production and employment in the sense that fluctuations were reinforced or simply created by budgetary and other policies. (p.443).

Hansen's study was restricted to the use of fiscal policy for stabilisation purposes; he found that no other OECD country destabilised to quite the same degree as in the UK. However, other studies which include monetary policy suggest that policies have been destabilising in other countries. Kmenta and Smith (1973) and Taylor (1979), for example, use sophisticated models of the US economy and find that in the period they each consider monetary policy (and fiscal policy in the case of Kmenta and Smith) was destabilising.

Such conclusions have been challenged in the USA by Modigliani (1977) and others, and in the UK by Little (1962), Bristow (1968) and Worswick (1971). Little (1964) agrees that UK fiscal policy has at times been unwise but from his reading of Dow's evidence and that of his own study (1962) he is not convinced that it has been destabilising. Bristow (1968), in a study of UK taxation policy, found that without the tax changes that were actually put into effect output growth would have been lower and less stable. However, he also finds that stabilisation policy might have been even better if the tax changes had occurred one year earlier. Worswick (1971) criticises the techniques used by some of the authors of the above studies and concludes that 'If judgement of policy has to be made, there does not seem therefore any substitute for a careful examination of each move made by the authorities in the light of the situation as it was seen at the time . . . . But in the nature of things, any generalisations emerging from such a programme are bound to be impressionist and there is ample scope for subjective valuations' (p.52).

Perhaps the strongest view on the question of the actual performance of stabilisation policy with which most researchers would agree is that of Matthews (1969), who has argued that 'it cannot be denied that government policy did differ considerably from what it ought to have been if the object had been to maintain activity at a stable and consistent level' (p.130).

If Matthews's summary is correct then it is important to know why actual policy performance has been so disappointing. For if the fault is easily traced and rectifiable, then there is no need to change the approach to policy, but if it is incurable then perhaps a change may be called for. There are in fact a number of possible explanations for the poor performance: first, the government may have been pursuing incompatible objectives; second, the economy may be too subtle and complex a mechanism for the government to manipulate with precision; third, the government's actions may be determined by short-term and electoral considerations; fourth, the fact that any economy is but one (usually small) part of a world economy may prevent the successful implementation of Keynesian policies; and fifth, the theory on which the government is operating may be seriously flawed. We shall consider each of these in turn but the last one will be considered in a separate section since it is best examined as part of an alternative view on stabilisation policy.

4. The sources of failure

INCOMPATIBILITY OF OBJECTIVES

The problem of incompatible objectives is a simple and obvious one: policies adopted to secure a desired value for one target variable may push another further away from its desired value. To illustrate this problem and see how it can be resolved in theory, we shall make use of the AS/AD diagram developed above. Assume that the economy is initially in the position indicated by AS_0 and AD_0 in Fig. 2.9. If the target value for y is y^T, then the policy implication for the government is that it should increase aggregate demand by, say, increasing government expenditure in order to shift the AD curve to AD_1. If it does adopt such a policy it will however raise prices from p_0 to p_1. If the government is aiming for zero inflation (as most governments at least claim to), then the policy adopted to secure one target variable clearly hampers the achievement of another. There are a large number of similar examples of incompatible objectives in macroeconomic policy and the problem is therefore a general one.

Provided the government has at least as many effective and independent policy instruments as it has policy targets or objectives, the simultaneous achievement of all policy targets is at least theoretically possible.[5] To illustrate this with reference to our example: if the government had some method of directly reducing

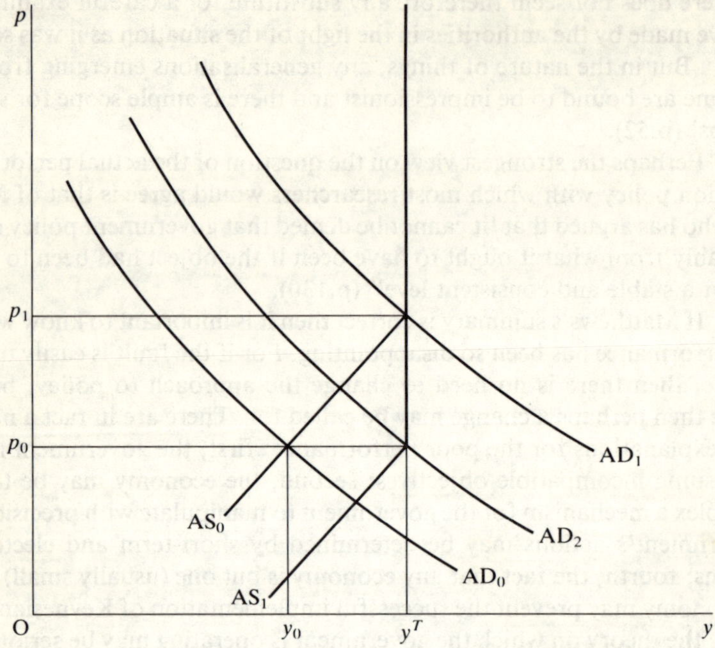

FIG. 2.9 Price stability and full employment with two policy instruments

nominal wages–for example, through an effective incomes policy–then by an appropriate policy mix it could ensure an increase in output from y_0 to y^T with no change in prices. This policy mix would require an incomes policy strong enough to cut nominal wages so that the AS curve shifts to AS_1, and an increase in government expenditure sufficient to shift the AD curve to AD_2.

The point can be brought into sharper focus by consideration of the algebraic model developed in section 2. In particular consider equation [12] which solves the optimum value for g, on the assumption that w and z are given at $\bar{w}_0$ and $\bar{z}_0$ and that money is unimportant in the AD curve ($a_1 = 0$). This value for $g(g^*)$ implies a value for y equal to its target y^T. But inserting this value for g into the price equation, equation [7], yields (assuming again that $a_1 = 0$) a price level as shown below:

$$p = \frac{a_0 - b_0}{b_1} + \frac{a_2 g^*}{b_1} + \frac{\bar{z}_0}{b_1} + \bar{w}_0 \qquad [13]$$

There is no reason why this should equal the target price level p^T. If it does not and if the government cannot manipulate any of the other variables on the right-hand side of equation [13] either directly or indirectly, then it must either accept the value of p as given or trade off divergences of y from y^T with divergences of p from p^T (that is, it can reset g so that y diverges from y^T but p diverges from p^T by less than before). Presumably there will be some new optimum value for g which generates an optimum combination of divergences, say $(y - y^T)^* (p - p^T)^*$. Clearly this value depends upon the government's 'losses' in being away from each objective.

However, if the government can manipulate the level of wages, then from equation [13] it can, given g^* and hence y^T, set w at whatever level is consistent with p^T. In general then, if the government has sufficient policy instruments, multiple goals can be achieved by an appropriate and co-ordinated setting of the different policy instruments. Numerous extensions have been made to this basic analysis of the manipulation of policy instruments to achieve policy goals. For example, Phillips (1954, 1957) examined stabilisation policy in a dynamic model rather than the static one presented here. Brainard (1967) considered the problems posed by assuming more complicated forms of uncertainty. Theil (1958, 1964) has considered what optimal stabilisation policy might consist of and how it might be achieved. These extensions and others are compactly explained in Turnovsky (1977).

One other extension considers the problems for stabilisation policy when policy instruments are deployed in an unco-ordinated fashion. This lack of co-ordination might arise because different sections of government administration are in charge of the various policy instruments. For example, the Bank of England might be considered as responsible for monetary policy, the Treasury in charge of fiscal policy. If each considers itself responsible for the achievement of one particular target and sets its policy instrument accordingly without consideration of the likely response of the other, then the actions of the two authorities might destabilise the economy. One solution to the problem is to ensure that both government agencies co-ordinate their actions. However, this is not necessary. Provided both agencies are assigned the 'correct' policy target, co-ordination is not required. And the 'correct' policy target is the one in which the particular agency has a 'comparative advantage' (i.e. the target upon which the agency's policy instrument has a relatively large effect).

So the existence of multiple goals provides no serious problem in theory to Keynesian stabilisation policy even if the authorities do not act in a co-ordinated manner. However, this does not imply that *in practice* the multiplicity of objectives has not been a source of instability. It may be, for example, that the government has only used a small range of instruments to pursue a large number of objectives, switching its attention from one, say output stability, to another, say balance of payments equilibrium, as and when it feels the target variables are seriously out of line. Brittan (1971) has so described the behaviour of the British authorities:

> During most of the period under consideration Chancellors behaved like simple Pavlovian dogs responding to two main stimuli: one was 'a run on the reserves' and the other was '500,000 unemployed' – a figure which was later increased to above 600,000. On the whole (although not invariably), it was officials who became alarmed on the first stimulus, and ministers on the second, although each side usually managed to communicate its alarm to the other. A response system as crude as this was pretty well bound to generate instability. (p.455).

Such an unsophisticated switch of attention between policy targets is especially likely to be destabilising in the case Brittan cites since both changes in reserves and changes in unemployment are what is known as lagging indicators, which means that movements in these two variables tend to lag behind movements in the real economy. So, for example, measured unemployment may continue to rise for a number of months after the economy has begun to move out of a recession, in which case gearing policy changes to the unemployment figures may involve, for example, boosting the economy when it is beginning to boom anyway.

Hansen (1969) also explains the destabilising effects of the UK authorities in terms of multiple goals: he blames 'the recurrent balance of payments crises which have accompanied each upswing and forced the government to shift from expansive to contractive policies' (p.71).

Why might governments have used policy instruments in this destabilising way? Is it purely accidental that politicians in the period of Keynesian stabilisation policy might have been prone to nervous and erratic changes of policy, or is it an inherent feature of political life? This is an important question because if such government behaviour is likely to persist, then it suggests a potentially serious weakness in the Keynesian approach to policy. In the view of Brittan (1971):

> A response system as crude as this was pretty well bound to generate instability. But from a political point of view it was perfectly rational. During the period there was a strong relationship between unemployment and political popularity. Equally, however, exchange rate variations were not free of both economic and political costs. The idea was unpopular and the effects were regarded as highly uncertain and possibly dangerous. Therefore it seemed rational to governments (a) to keep unemployment as low as possible for as long as possible but (b) to deflate, whenever necessary to preserve the sterling exchange rate, **provided that there seemed a good chance of being able to bring unemployment down again early enough before the next election.** (p.455, original emphasis)

We shall elaborate upon this in the next section.

THE POLITICAL INFLUENCES ON GOVERNMENT BEHAVIOUR

An implicit assumption in our discussion of Keynesian stabilisation policy is that governments have the long-term 'interests of the economy' at heart. Once a government understands the structure of the economy and is aware what needs to be done, it will proceed to carry out the necessary programme as swiftly as possible. As Buchanan (1978) has put it: 'Your economists, and notably Lord Keynes, along with their American counterparts, continued to proffer policy advice as if they were talking to a benevolent despot who stood at their beck and call' (p.4). One criticism of Keynesian stabilisation policy is that its view of politicians is hopelessly naive. Casual observation of the behaviour of politicians and governments suggests that the desire in them to win elections is seldom dormant, and that policies tend to be dominated by short-term and transitory crises. Such a view of political behaviour can be gleaned from reading the memoirs and diaries of politicians. For example, Richard Crossman in his diaries wrote in July 1969: 'It [the postponement of the increase in the BBC licence fee until after the election] was a terrible decision, and shows how tired we all were, but at all our Cabinet meetings it is becoming clearer that from now on nothing will be decided except in terms of electoral advantage' (Crossman 1977: 602).

A more sophisticated and relevant view of the formulation of stabilisation policy would surely recognise that governments often act, not necessarily in a corrupt or mischievous fashion, but in an almost fevered atmosphere where the needs to overcome daily crises, to satisfy the insistent voices of powerful pressure groups and to ensure a chance of winning the next election are dominant. Such a view of politicians is not a new one; it pre-dates Keynes as the following quote from J.S. Mill (1861) illustrates: '... the very principle of constitutional government requires it to be assumed, that political power will be abused to promote the particular purposes of the holder; not because it always is so, but because such is the natural tendency of things, to guard against which is the especial use of free institutions' (p.505). However, it is only fairly recently that economic theories of political behaviour have begun to be developed and their empirical relevance examined. These theories are 'economic' in the sense that they recognise that governments can be viewed as maximising a 'utility function'. The utility function is generally considered to include a 'popularity' variable which indicates their prospect of winning the next election (e.g. Nordhaus 1975, Gordon 1975). Such models, which are, it should be emphasised, still at a fairly elementary stage, provide some theoretical support for the view that politicians will exploit any shortsightedness in the electorate for their political advantage and may well, in so doing, exacerbate rather than moderate the business cycle. Consider, as a simple illustration of such models, an economy where an expansion of aggregate demand leads to a rapid rise in real output but only a sluggish rise in prices (that is, the AS curve of the economy is different from the one assumed in section 2 where the real output and price effects of a rise in aggregate demand occurred simultaneously). Further, assume that the higher the level of output and the lower the rate of inflation, the more 'popular' is the government. A government faced with an imminent election is likely to be tempted to expand aggregate demand, reap the electoral benefits of the higher level of output and attempt to reduce the rate of inflation, when it occurs after the election. (If the election has been lost of course then the new government can deal with the problem.) If the government succumbed to this temptation, it would create a cycle in economic activity which would not otherwise have existed. The government would therefore have exacerbated the very problem it was supposed to solve.

A small number of econometric tests of this approach have appeared in the literature recently. Two which relate to the UK are by Frey and Schneider (1978) and Moseley (1978). They both find that government popularity (as measured by opinion poll data) is significantly affected by the behaviour of economic variables—like the unemployment rate and the inflation rate—and that the temptation for governments to manipulate policy instruments to gain electoral advantage is a real one. They also find that governments have manipulated policy in response to their standing in the opinion polls. Of course this does not necessarily imply that governments have destabilised the economy—for the measures the government takes when say unemployment rises may be both popular and stabilising. However, the apparent significance of the government's popularity in determining policy raises suspicions that governments may destabilise the economy for electoral reasons. This suspicion is particularly aroused by Moseley's study in which the electorate's view of the seriousness of a problem (such as unemployment) is suggested to be subject to sharp changes as the particular problem variable reaches a 'crisis' level. It must again be stressed, however, that these studies are at an early stage of development and many of their results are open to econometric criticisms (see Pissarides 1980).

THE COMPLEX NATURE OF ECONOMIC RELATIONSHIPS

Our exposition of the Keynesian macroeconomic model and of the policy approach with which it is associated, and our brief account of the evidence on whether fiscal and monetary policies are effective determinants of aggregate demand and could therefore be used to stabilise the economy, obscure a particularly severe problem for practitioners of Keynesian policies. This problem is that if Keynesian policies are to be successfully applied, detailed knowledge of the workings of the economy is required. This detailed knowledge is needed for two reasons: first, given that there are inevitable delays in the formulation and implementation of policy, the government needs to *anticipate* future developments (e.g. a slump in private sector spending), rather than wait until they occur. The more accurately informed it is about the true nature of the economy, the more able it will be, for example, to distinguish between a drop in private sector spending that is likely to persist and one that is likely to be reversed very quickly. The former requires offsetting increases in government expenditure more urgently than the latter.

The second need for detailed knowledge arises from the simple fact that the government must make some estimate of the *size* of the effects of any policy change on the variable to be stabilised. It is not enough to know that government expenditure needs to be increased; the government must know the *size* of the required increase and *when* it will have its effect. But as we showed in section 2 this knowledge requires accurate estimates of the relevant structural equation of the economy. In the example given, the government needed to know the values of a_0, a_1, a_2 and $\bar{z}_0$ before it could derive the optimum values for g and m.

If such knowledge is not available or if the estimates of the key coefficients are in fact inaccurate, then governments may well not only mistake the need for policy changes but implement excessive changes in monetary and fiscal policy. Clearly, in either event, government policy aimed at stabilising the economy might well destabilise it. A number of economists have argued that in fact we do not have the knowledge necessary for the successful application of Keynesian policies, and that this lack of knowledge (especially when combined with an unawareness of it) has been the main reason why the performance of Keynesian policies has been disappointing and why such policies should be avoided in the future. In our view this argument has considerable force. The enormous quantity of empirical research into the nature of the economy mentioned earlier has revealed, not surprisingly perhaps, that the behaviour of the economy is very complex and difficult to understand, particularly over short periods of time (like one or two years–the sort of time horizon which dominates policy-makers). There are at least two important dimensions to this problem: first, the existence of time lags in almost all economic relationships; and second, the fact that the true nature of major economic relationships is always, to a certain extent, unknown and that these relationships are subject to large and unpredicted shifts.

The first of these does not by itself necessarily pose special problems for Keynesian stabilisation policy but does suggest that policy instruments will need to be reset continuously and subtly if policy is not to be destabilising. If there are significant delays in formulating and implementing policy and such continuous and subtle policy changes are not in fact feasible, then Keynesian policy may well be destabilising.

To illustrate the importance of time lags *per se*, consider the enormous amount of work on the consumption function–one of the key relationships underlying the IS curve and hence the AD curve–which strongly suggests that current income alone does not provide a satisfactory explanation for current consumption expenditure over a period as short as a year or a quarter. Much more satisfactory explanations of current consumption expenditure can be obtained by allowing for the effects (*inter alia*) of past income and consumption levels (see Davidson *et al* 1978, and Chapter 3 of this volume): whether the presence of past income levels is due to economic agents taking time to adjust their expenditure from one income level to another, or whether it is due to past levels of income determining expected long-term income–to which current consumption is itself linked–is not important here. For whatever the reason the implication for policy is the same: measures taken to raise aggregate demand and current income will have effects not merely on this period's but also on subsequent period's consumption and income. Furthermore the impact effect of a policy change may be quite different from the longer-term effect. To illustrate this argument we rewrite equation [6] for simplicity as

$$y_t = \pi_0 + \pi_1 m_t + \pi_2 g_t - \pi_3 \bar{w}_0 \quad [14]$$

To capture the idea that lagged income effects are an important determinant of aggregate demand, we add to the above equation a lagged income term and thus obtain:

$$y_t = \pi_0 + \pi_1 m_t + \pi_2 g_t - \pi_3 \bar{w}_0 + \pi_4 y_{t-1} \quad [15]$$

Consider now an increase in government expenditure with m and w remaining constant. A higher value for g will initially raise income by $\pi_2 \Delta g_t$ where Δg_t is the change in g. But in the subsequent period if the higher level of g is maintained income will be raised by a further $\pi_4 \pi_2 \Delta g_t$ through the effect of y_{t-1} in [15]. Further changes in future periods will also occur and in fact income will finally be $\pi_2 \Delta g_t/(1-\pi_4)$higher than it was before the increase in level of expenditure. Higher order (i.e. longer) lags in equation [15] would complicate the response of output to a policy change but would add little to the policy implications of admitting the importance of time lags. These are that even in the absence of continuing exogenous aggregate demand shifts originating in the private sector governments may have to vary the values of their own policy instruments frequently if not continually. In the algebraic example just developed, where only one time lag was assumed, a government wishing to set income at y^T would need, if it takes m and w as given at m_0 and w_0, to set government expenditure initially at g_0^* where

$$\pi_2 g_0^* = y^T - \pi_0 - \pi_1 m_0 + \pi_3 \bar{w}_0 - \pi_4 y_{-1} \quad [16]$$

But in the next period even if nothing else had changed the level of y_{t-1} would be y^T rather than y_{t-1} and a new value of g^* would be required to keep y at y^T, i.e.

$$\pi_2 g_1^* = y^T - \pi_0 - \pi_1 m_0 + \pi_3 \bar{w}_0 - \pi_4 y^T \quad [17]$$

If we had allowed for higher order time lags, further changes in g would be required to keep y at y^T.

Thus, to be completely successful, Keynesian stabilisation policy must involve the continuous and sophisticated manipulation of policy instruments. Even if the aim is a more modest one, its achievement will require more than the occasional 'touch on the tiller' and must be based on an understanding of a large number of empirical magnitudes.

This of course does not necessarily imply that Keynesian policies will be destabilising, for if governments are aware of the time lags involved then they can, *in theory*, still find optimal values for g^* and m^*. However, it is not hard to envisage circumstances in which the existence of time lags leads to instability. In the algebraic example above policies had less impact on current income than on subsequent income. Faced with the possibility of a temporary fall in income this period–which might be an election period–the government might be tempted into a policy of fiscal 'overkill'–that is, they might expand their own expenditures more than they otherwise would to ensure that the election does not take place in a slump. The effects such a policy has on income in subsequent periods may, if the initial policy change is difficult to reverse, imply a larger boom in later periods than would otherwise have occurred. Thus the existence of time lags may amplify the volatility in the economic system arising from other factors.

The second and more serious problem is that certain key relationships are not understood with sufficient precision. Two recent examples of this from the UK economy concern the consumption function and the demand for money function.

The ratio of private sector savings to income rose sharply from 11.9 per cent in 1973 to 14.4 in 1974, 15.0 in 1975 and 14.6 per cent in 1976, even though real income dropped sharply below trend during the years 1974–76. Existing theories of consumption expenditure predicted that the opposite would happen. The permanent income hypothesis, for example, predicts that in a recession the savings-to-income ratio should fall, since consumption is a function of permanent income which is less volatile than measured income. Thus one of the key relationships in any model of the economy was badly predicted. Of course, *after it had occurred* a number of studies offered possible reasons for the shift in savings behaviour in this period (see Deaton 1977, Bank of England 1976), but it was not anticipated by the authorities.

A similar type of shift occurred in another much researched

function–the demand for money. Holdings of money (as conventionally defined in the UK) were much greater in the early 1970s than existing estimates of the demand for money function would have indicated. Once again, explanations of this phenomenon were put forward after it occurred but the phenomenon was not predicted, and hence policies were not designed to take this structural shift into account. It is safe to conjecture that shifts are occurring all the time in economic relationships. Sometimes they are trivial, transitory and possibly offset one another; at other times they may be large and persistent. The more important, frequent and unpredicted they are, the greater the implied lack of knowledge of how the economy works and hence the stronger the possibility that government attempts to pursue Keynesian stabilisation policies will destabilise the economy. Friedman (1953) presents an early formal analysis of the conditions under which stabilisation policy destabilises the economy.

Clearly then the case for Keynesian stabilisation policy depends in large measure upon an accurate empirical knowledge of the economic structure. We cannot review here in any detail all the empirical research of the last thirty or forty years, and we have already referred in a previous section to some surveys of that empirical literature. However, it might be instructive to consider one indicator of the current state of knowledge of the economy–the ability to *forecast* the behaviour of the economy. If these forecasts are sufficiently accurate, then our knowledge may well be sufficient for the purpose of fine tuning the economy; if not, then serious problems inevitably arise for any government pursuing stabilisation policies. Of course for the success of Keynesian stabilisation policies the *government's own* ability to forecast the economy is crucial and so we concentrate on the forecasting performance of the official or semi-official models of the UK economy.

To assess such a model's performance we consider two selected types of error: first, the model may make qualitative errors, e.g. predictions that output (for example) will continue to rise when in fact it falls. These are sometimes called turning-point errors. Second, the forecasters may correctly predict a turning point, but make substantial quantitative errors.

According to Kennedy (1969) the model of the National Institute for Economic and Social Research, which was at the time widely regarded as being similar to the then unpublished Treasury model, correctly predicted turning points in the period 1957–67 with the exception of 1962. He concluded that '... the forecasts have done extremely well as qualitative indicators of the rate of economic expansion' (p.41). However, Kennedy also found that the model made potentially serious quantitative errors: 'As regards the use of the forecasts for making policy recommendations, some misgivings must be felt at the mean error for GDP, which at 1.4% is equivalent in size to the effects of some substantial changes in taxes' (p.49).

Ash and Smyth (1973) provide more recent evidence concerning the forecast errors of the models developed by the Treasury and the National Institute. Turning-point errors are split into two types: E_1 represents the proportion of actual turning points that are missed by the forecasters, whilst E_2 is the proportion of forecast turning points that eventually prove spurious. In Table 2.2 the

TABLE 2.2 Turning point errors

	E_1	E_2	Period
Annual forecasts			
Treasury	0.28	0.33	1951–71
NIESR (May)	0.35	0.35	1963–71
Half-yearly			
Treasury	0.30	0.32	1968.1–1971.2
NIESR	0.25	0.28	1967.1–1971.2
LBS	0.39	0.36	1968.1–1971.2

Source: Ash and Smyth (1973)

values for E_1 and E_2 are set out for the two models. Almost one third of actual turning points were missed by the Treasury forecasters, and an equal proportion of turning points turned out to be spurious. Although Ash and Smyth find that the Treasury model forecasts were significantly more accurate than simply extrapolating or averaging past outcomes, they conclude that 'overall there is a tendency to underestimate and often mistime economic fluctuations' (p.263). The reasons for these forecast errors are often difficult to isolate but two types may be distinguished. First, there are errors arising from the model structure itself which would appear even if the values of the exogenous variables were known exactly; second, there are those that arise from incorrect forecasts of exogenous variables.[6] Kennedy found for the period 1959–67 that the National Institute's errors in forecasts of endogenous expenditure were generally *worse* when *actual* rather than 'guessed' exogenous values were included. This indicates that the model structure was mis-specified, for if it were not then the inclusion of the actual exogenous variables in the model would obviously reduce forecast errors. The National Institute's *ex ante* forecast for 1975 (i.e. the forecast taking the National Institute's estimate of exogenous variables) predicted that GDP would rise by 1.8 per cent on the previous year. In fact it fell by 2.8 per cent. The *ex post* forecast for the same year (i.e. the value the model predicts when the actual values of the exogenous variables are used) was – 1.9 per cent. In this case the National Institute forecast missed the turning point because it employed incorrect values of the exogenous variables. By contrast, in 1976, the National Institute's *ex ante* forecast of 2.4 per cent growth in GDP was fairly close to the actual growth rate of 2.2 per cent. However, the *ex post* forecast, using actual exogenous variables, was 5.4 per cent. For this year the evidence suggests that the National Institute model was mis-specified (see Osborn and Teal 1979).

The performance of these large-scale models has made most economists less confident of their ability to predict accurately the future course of the economy and to explain the precise mechanisms through which policy changes have their effects.

Proponents of the reduced form or St Louis approach mentioned in section 3 have come to a similar conclusion. Their results suggest that the timing of the impact on income of monetary and fiscal changes varies across periods in ways which as yet are not understood. The best known statement of this view, at least as far as monetary policy is concerned, is provided by Friedman and Schwartz (1963), who present a mass of evidence to support the idea that *on average* there is for the USA a close relationship between money and nominal income: changes in the rate of growth of the money supply precede changes in the rate of growth of real income by about six to nine months, and they precede a change in the rate of growth of prices by about eighteen to twenty-four months. However, in any individual instance the time lags can be significantly shorter or longer. Friedman (1970) argues that the same long and variable time lags between money and income changes occur in other countries too.

As we mentioned earlier the St Louis approach has produced fewer results in the UK than the USA and less is known about the timing of monetary and fiscal changes from such results. However, certain monetarists, e.g. Laidler (1974), Parkin (1975), and even Friedman (1980), seem to regard the UK economy as subject to the same (variable) lags as the USA. Other economists, e.g. Artis (1978), are less convinced.

It would be misleading to suggest that this drop in confidence has been so great that most economists now believe that our ignorance of the way the economy works rules out the possibility of the successful implementation of Keynesian stabilisation policies. Nevertheless it is probably true to say that experience has made most economists less confident about our understanding of the workings of the economy at the level of detail required if the economy is to be stabilised the way Keynes suggested. And the number of economists who reject the Keynesian approach has probably grown. In the next section we shall discuss an alternative approach to stabilisation, but before doing so we turn briefly to a feature of most economies which we have so far neglected and which has implications for both Keynesian and other approaches to stabilisation policy.

THE OPENNESS OF THE ECONOMY

One deficiency of Keynes's General Theory is that the economy is essentially treated as if it were 'closed', i.e. as if it does not trade with other countries to any significant degree. Most economies are open–trade forms a significant part of national income. This is certainly true of the UK, where for example in 1979 exports accounted for about 30 per cent of gross domestic product. In fact the openness of many industrial economies has been increasing since the Second World War as restrictions on the movements of both goods and financial capital between countries have been gradually reduced. Early extensions of the Keynesian model of a closed economy to incorporate openness concentrated on the current account of the balance of payments (that is the difference between what is earned from exports of goods and services and what is spent on imported goods and services), and largely ignored the capital account–the amount spent by UK residents on the acquisition of foreign financial assets net of the amount spent on the acquisition of UK financial assets by foreigners.[7] Even this limited treatment of openness has some implications for Keynesian stabilisation policy: for example, in such an economy the Keynesian multiplier is likely to be smaller since any increase in income will lead partly to purchases of imports which will directly boost foreign rather than domestic output. See, for example, Robinson (1952) or Kindleberger (1968). But the main implications of openness are best seen when both the current and the capital account are explicitly incorporated in the model. To do this consider an economy which is open and which is operating a fixed exchange rate. We shall assume that the country is small relative to the rest of the world so that the impact of measures taken by its government on the rest of the world can be ignored. Elementary analysis suggests that the current account deficit on the balance of payments will be a function of, amongst other things, the level of domestic income. The higher is real income the more will be spent on imported goods and hence the greater, *ceteris paribus*, the deficit on the current account of the balance of payments.

The overall balance of payments is the sum of the current and capital accounts. The latter, to repeat, measures the difference between the amount spent on the acquisition of foreign financial assets by domestic (e.g. UK) residents and the amount spent on the acquisition of UK financial assets by foreigners. One major determinant of this difference is likely to be the level of the interest rate on domestic securities relative to that in the rest of the world. If the world interest rate is given then the higher the UK interest rate, the smaller the capital account deficit or the larger the capital account surplus.

Given these assumptions, suppose that the economy is in equilibrium at below full employment and that at the going interest rate and level of income the overall balance of payments is zero. Following Keynesian policy prescriptions the government might increase its own expenditure in order to boost output. Unless the IS and LM curves for this economy have certain extreme slopes the initial result will be a rise in output and interest rates. For the closed economy that is the end of the story. But for the open economy there are the implications for the balance of payments to be considered. If international capital is not sensitive to interest rate differentials (i.e. is not 'mobile') then the fact that the economy's interest rate has risen will make little difference to the capital account of the balance of payments, so the effect of the increase in imports caused by the rise in income will dominate. The balance of payments will be in overall deficit. This means that money is flowing out of the country, for UK residents are supplying more pounds to the foreign exchange market in order to acquire foreign currencies with which to buy foreign goods than foreigners are demanding pounds. To meet this imbalance the UK monetary authority is taking in the pounds and releasing foreign exchange from its reserves. Thus the balance of payments deficit involves a loss of foreign exchange reserves by the UK monetary authority and fall in the UK money supply, since holdings of UK money by the UK monetary authority do not count as part of the UK money supply. This fall in the money supply will persist until income has fallen back to a level consistent with an overall balance of payments equilibrium. Of course the monetary authority can sterilise the monetary outflow by carrying out an open market purchase of bonds and thereby prevent the fall back in output. But this it can do only for as long as its holdings of foreign exchange reserves are sufficiently high.

If we had assumed initially that international capital was highly sensitive to interest rate changes then the increase in government expenditure would have produced a balance of payments *surplus* and a tendency for the domestic money supply to *increase*. The effect on output of the rise in government expenditure would then be reinforced rather than offset by resultant monetary flows through the balance of payments.

The same type of analysis can be applied to an increase in the money supply, though here the result is that any domestically generated increase in the money supply will be offset by a balance of payments deficit regardless of the degree of capital mobility. Furthermore the same analysis can be applied to the case of flexible exchange rates, though here the detailed results will differ from those discussed above.

This analysis has a number of important implications, for policies directed towards balance of payments problems, for exchange rate determination, etc. But the main implication for our purpose is that it suggests that the government's ability to manipulate the instruments of policy and the potency of those instruments depend on a range of factors which until now we have ignored; for example, the international mobility of capital, monetary developments in the rest of the world, the government's ability to sterilise monetary flows. Successful Keynesian stabilisation policy requires some knowledge of these factors, and thus the openness of the economy can be seen as adding another dimension of difficulty to the implementation of Keynesian policies. It can also be seen as implying that the scope for a government to manipulate its economy is limited by economic developments in the rest of the world and by international financial arrangements. Recent open economy analysis, for example, has emphasised the degree to which certain prices are determined at a world rather than a country level, and that countries on fixed exchange rates are likely in the long run to have more or less the same inflation rate. The scope for a government to choose its own inflation rate is therefore limited. This limitation on the scope for policy applies not just to Keynesian policy but to other approaches as well. In the next section we discuss the main alternative to Keynesian stabilisation policy.

5. New classical macroeconomics

There are three main ingredients in the alternative approach to stabilisation policy. First, if variations in the government's monetary and fiscal policy are minimised, sharp fluctuations in aggregate demand are unlikely to occur. Second, if they do occur, they will not produce persistently high unemployment or persistently lower output – the economy will tend to correct itself. Third, for reasons discussed in earlier sections, government attempts to correct fluctuations in real output will only make matters worse.

The first stage in the argument relies partly on the empirical evidence discussed above, which suggested that government policies in the Keynesian era had actually destabilised the economy. But it also relies on a broader empirical judgement that major fluctuations in aggregate demand in most economies – both pre and post Keynes – have been primarily due to erratic manipulation of policy by governments and not to volatile private sector demand. For example, the Great

Depression in the USA in the 1930s is blamed on the negligent monetary policy of the Federal Reserve Board (see Friedman and Schwartz 1963. Ch.7). The hyperinflations in Europe this century are blamed on excessive monetary growth engineered or allowed by the relevant Central Bank (see Cagan 1956). To take a more recent example, the major rise in the UK inflation rate in the mid 1970s is blamed on the Heath government's decision to rapidly expand public expenditure and the money supply (see Laidler 1976). If this view of the source of major fluctuations in aggregate demand is accepted, then it follows that stabilisation can best be achieved by minimising variations in government policy instruments. Such an approach to policy is made more attractive if the economy is inherently self-correcting, that is, if in response to aggregate demand shocks, mechanisms within the economy restore the economy to its full employment equilibrium. For in that case, the case for Keynesian stabilisation policy is clearly weakened. In this section we shall look at developments in economic theory which suggest that the economy is self-correcting and possibly rapidly so. We shall not consider in detail the empirical evidence concerning the source of fluctuation in aggregate demand, but refer readers to some major sources of evidence (Friedman and Schwartz 1963, Friedman 1956, Howson 1975, Meiselman 1970). However, we would emphasise that the case for this alternative approach to policy is weakened if the empirical evidence is not taken as suggesting that governments have been the major source of fluctuations in aggregate demand (Tobin 1965).

Before examining the relevant theoretical developments we outline the main characteristics of the new approach to policy we are discussing. The approach maintains that governments should abandon attempts to fine-tune the economy in the traditional Keynesian manner, and instead announce in advance targets for monetary and fiscal policy and concentrate on achieving these targets come what may. More specifically, the government should announce at what rate or rates it intends to expand the money stock over time and should try to achieve those targets regardless of the behaviour of the economy after the policy has been announced. It should also announce levels of government expenditure and tax rates which, if the economy were at full employment, would ensure that government expenditure and receipts were equal. Once these levels had been set they should not be changed in response to the behaviour of the economy.

NATURAL RATE HYPOTHESIS

Having outlined the new approach we consider two fairly recent theoretical developments: the natural rate hypothesis (NRH), and the rational expectations hypothesis (REH). Whilst there are several interpretations of the NRH hypothesis, we shall adopt that version which enables us to use the same framework as that developed above. This interprets the NRH as a hypothesis about the AS curve and is based on Friedman's (1968) statement. Consider again the supply of and demand for labour. In deciding the amount of labour to supply workers are concerned with the real value of their wages, that is the nominal value deflated by the *general* level of prices. Since it is generally costly for workers to renegotiate or reset their nominal wages frequently, the workers will normally negotiate a nominal wage to cover a significant period of time, say a year. Once that nominal wage rate is set it is more or less fixed until the next bargaining period. But since workers are interested in the *real* value of wages, they must, at the time of bargaining, form some *expectation* of the likely value of the price level over the period covered by the contract. The quantity of labour supplied will thus depend (positively we shall assume) on W/P^e, where W is the nominal wage and P^e is the expected value of the price level. If w is the log of W and p^e the log of P^e, a log-linear function will imply that labour supply depends upon $w - p^e$. The supply of labour can thus be drawn as an upward sloping function of the nominal wage for a given value of p^e. One such curve is shown in Fig. 2.10 and is drawn on the assumption that $P^e = P_0$ (or $p^e = p_0$). If the expected price level rose to (say) $P^e = P_1$, where $P_1 = 2P_0$ (or $p_1 = \log(2) + p_0$) then the new supply of labour curve would be drawn as in Fig. 2.10 where the gap between the two curves is log (2).

The demand for labour, as before, is treated as a negative function of the real wage though here the 'real wage' that is important for the producer is the nominal wage deflated by the price of the good he produces. Once again, it could be argued that the firm has to form some expectation of the price at which it can sell its good and hence the crucial variable is W/P^e_f, or in logs, $w - p^e_f$ where P^e_f is the price which the firm expects to get for its product. To simplify matters we shall assume that there are no relative price changes and that firms form accurate expectations about the price of their good. These assumptions allow us to write $P^e_f = P$ at all times, where P is the actual general price level. The main justification for this assumption is, as Friedman has argued, that firms 'are more directly con- about the price of the products they are producing and far better informed about that' (Friedman 1976: 223). To simplify, we assume *no* forecast errors by firms. The demand for labour can thus be drawn as before as a negative function of the nominal wage for any given price level. One such curve is shown in Fig. 2.10 on the assumption that $p = p_0$. If $p = \log(2) + p_0$ (i.e. prices were twice as high), then the demand for labour curve would shift up by log(2) in the diagram to the one labelled $p = p_1$.

Using Fig. 2.10 we can establish the following points. First, if the price level is p_0 and if workers correctly anticipate this price level, employment will be L_n.[8] Associated with this level of employment there will (with the production function) be a level of output supplied, y_n. Similarly if the price level was p_1 and workers anticipated it so that $p^e = p_1$, then although the nominal wage would be higher than before (w_1 rather than w_0), the level of employment would remain at L_n, and level of output at y_n. Diagramatically, this is because *both* curves have shifted up by the same amount and hence intersect at the same points as measured along the horizontal axis. The values of L and y at which expectations are correct (i.e. L_n and y_n) are termed respectively the *natural* levels of employment and output. (Associated with them, *ceteris paribus*, will be a natural rate of unemployment.) An aggregate supply curve drawn on the assumption of correct expectations would be vertical at y_n. Such a curve is shown in Fig. 2.11 and labelled $p^e = p$.

The second point to be established from Fig. 2.10 is that incorrect expectations imply deviations from the natural rate of employment and output and will therefore cause real output supplied to be higher or lower than y_n. For example, assume that workers expect a price level of p_0 when the actual price level is higher at p_1. Then clearly from Fig. 2.10 the level of employment will be L_1 and the level of output supplied y_1. The reason for this is that firms correctly–given our assumptions–anticipate the rise in price and bid up nominal wages in order to attract more workers. Workers, whose expectations do not adjust, interpret the higher nominal wage offers as implying a higher *real wage*. They therefore willingly supply more labour at the higher nominal wage. Supply and demand are equated by a higher nominal wage of w_2 which is seen by the employer as a drop in the real wage since p has risen by more than w, but which is seen by the workers as a rise since w has risen and p^e has not. As a result of this unanticipated (on the part of workers) price rise, more output is produced. On the basis of the preceding analysis a short run AS can be constructed. This plots the quantity of output produced against the price level, holding workers' expectations of the price level as given. It should be clear that if the actual price level is above the one workers expect, output supplied will be above y^n; if the price level is below what is expected, output will be below y^n. It follows that the short run AS curve is upward sloping and cuts the long run AS curve (drawn for $p^e = p_0$) at that price level at which workers' expectations are fixed. Thus the short-run aggregate supply curve drawn for $p^e = p_0$ cuts the vertical AS curve at p_0. If p^e equalled p_1 the short-run supply curve would cut the long-run vertical supply curve at p_1.

This analysis of the AS curve in itself weakens the case for Keynesian-type stabilisation policies in two ways. First it implies that government monetary and fiscal policy cannot hope to achieve a level of output permanently above y_n, or at least cannot do so without imposing huge costs on the economy in terms of persistently *accelerating* inflation. The natural level of output is determined by real factors such as the willingness of workers to supply labour, and their productivity. Since the manipulation of monetary and fiscal *aggregates* leaves these real factors unaffected in the long run, the traditional Keynesian approach to monetary and fiscal policy cannot in the longer run achieve a 'better' level of output than y_n. Consider, for example, with the help of Fig. 2.12 an expansion of aggregate demand, either through monetary or fiscal changes. Initially the AD curve is at AD_0 and expectations of the price level are p_0. The economy is therefore in long-run equilibrium at y_n, p_0. If aggregate demand is then shifted to AD_1 and if workers' expectations of the price level remain at p_0, then output will shift to y_1 and the price level to p_1. The source of such a rise in output is that workers have been fooled into thinking that their nominal wage implies a higher real wage than it actually does. This is to be distinguished from the case where workers suffer from 'money illusion'–that is, concern for the money rather than the real value of their wages. If workers did suffer from money illusion a higher price level could boost output permanently; but in the case we are considering the boost can only be temporary. For as workers perceive that prices have risen to p_1, they will incorporate these expectations into the wage bargain, shifting the AS curve up to that labelled $p^e = p_1$. Such a process continues until output is back to y_n and the expansion in AD has been fully reflected in a rise in prices. The actual length of time over

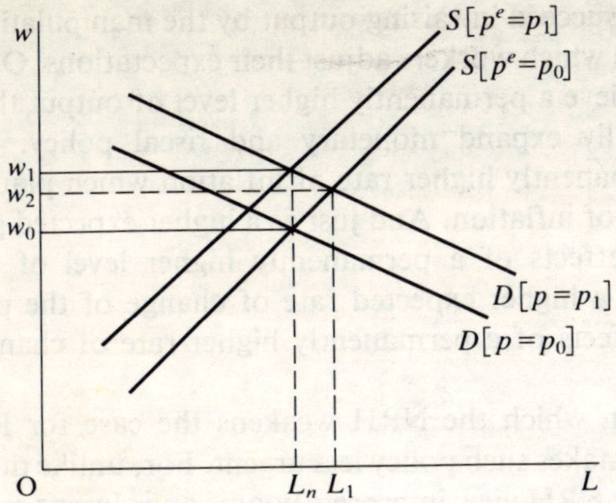

FIG. 2.10 Labour market under natural rate hypothesis

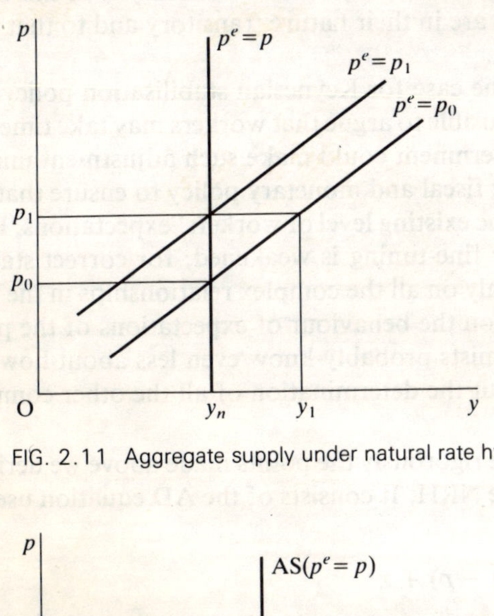

FIG. 2.11 Aggregate supply under natural rate hypothesis

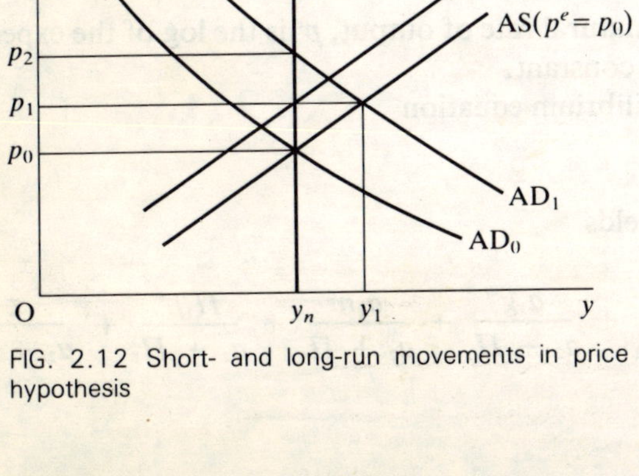

FIG. 2.12 Short- and long-run movements in price and output under natural rate hypothesis

which the government does succeed in raising output by the manipulation of AD depends upon the speed with which workers adjust their expectations. Of course it might be argued that to achieve a permanently higher level of output than y_n the government must continually expand monetary and fiscal policy. But such attempts will lead to a permanently higher rate of inflation which plausibly will raise workers' expected rate of inflation. And just as a higher expected price level frustrates the real output effects of a permanently higher level of aggregate demand, so in the end will a higher expected rate of change of the price level frustrate the real output effects of a permanently higher rate of change of aggregate demand.

The second way in which the NRH weakens the case for Keynesian stabilisation policy is that it makes such policy less urgent. For, unlike the Keynesian view of the economy, the NRH view interprets booms and slumps as resulting from incorrect expectations rather than rigidities. These mistakes in expectations are bound to be corrected over time and hence the economy is in this sense self-correcting: booms and slumps are in their nature transitory and to that extent do not require government action.

This weakening of the case for Keynesian stabilisation policy is hardly fatal though. It is perfectly plausible to argue that workers may take time to adjust their expectations and the government could make such adjustment unnecessary by appropriately manipulating fiscal and monetary policy to ensure that the level of AD is consistent with y_n at the existing level of workers' expectations. However, even on this view the case for fine-tuning is weakened, for correct stabilisation policy is now dependent not only on all the complex relationships in the economy previously discussed, but also on the behaviour of expectations of the price level and its rate of change. Economists probably know even less about how expectations change than they do about the determination of all the other complex relationships in the economy.

To demonstrate more rigorously the points made above we derive below a simple algebraic model of the NRH. It consists of the AD equation used before in section 2:

$$y^d = a_0 + a_1 g + a_2(m - p) + z \quad [18]$$

and an aggregate supply function based on the theory developed above

$$y^s = y_n + \Pi_1 (p - p^e) \quad [19]$$

where y_n is the log of the natural rate of output, p^e is the log of the expected price level, and Π_1 is a positive constant.

Adding the equilibrium equation

$$y^s = y^d \quad [20]$$

and solving for p and y yields

$$p = \frac{a_0}{a_2 + \Pi_1} - \frac{y_n}{a_2 + \Pi_1} + \frac{a_1 g}{a_2 + \Pi_1} + \frac{a_2 m}{a_2 + \Pi_1} + \frac{\Pi_1 p^e}{a_2 + \Pi_1} + \frac{z}{a_2 + \Pi_1} \quad [21]$$

$$y = \frac{\Pi_1 a_0}{a_2 + \Pi_1} + \frac{a_2 y_n}{a_2 + \Pi_1} + \frac{\Pi_1 a_1 g}{a_2 + \Pi_1} + \frac{\Pi_1 a_2 m}{a_2 + \Pi_1} - \frac{\Pi_1 a_2 p^e}{a_2 + \Pi_1} + \frac{\Pi_1 z}{a_2 + \Pi_1} \quad [22]$$

These are of course the short-term solutions for p and y. Defining the long run to be when $p = p^e$, i.e. expectations are correct, allows us to obtain the long-run solutions for p and z as

$$p = \frac{a_0}{a_2} - \frac{y_n}{a_2} + \frac{a_1 g}{a_2} + m + \frac{z}{a_2} \quad [23]$$

$$y = y_n \quad [24]$$

The results derived verbally or diagrammatically above can now be shown more rigorously with the help of equations [18] – [24]. First, as equation [24] shows, the level of output in the long run will be at its natural level, y_n. Second, again in the long run, monetary and fiscal policy changes will not affect the level of output, only the price level. This is demonstrated by the absence of terms in m or g from equation [24] and their presence in equation [23]. Third, equation [22] demonstrates that monetary and fiscal policy changes will affect output in the short run and hence can be used to fine-tune the economy in the short run. For example a negative value for z, i.e. a fall in aggregate demand, will with p^e and everything else remaining constant, cause a fall in price of $z/(a_2 + \Pi_1)$ and a fall in real output of $\Pi_1 z/(a_2 + \Pi_1)$. This fall in real output and price could be offset by a rise in g of $-z/a_1$ or a rise in m of $-z/a_2$ or some combination of monetary and fiscal expansion. Clearly then if such policies could be put into effect swiftly and accurately enough, they would stabilise real output and the price level more efficiently than would a policy which set the growth paths for g and m independently of the exogenous shifts in aggregate demand, i.e. independent of z. However, if the expected level of prices did not remain constant in the face of this negative value for z then these attempts to fine-tune the economy might still make things worse. At the very least the monetary and fiscal policies required to stabilise the economy in the face of a demand shock depend upon the reaction of p^e to that demand shock. Hence the method by which expectations of the price level are formed must be understood for a completely successful policy of fine-tuning the economy to be carried out.

THE RATIONAL EXPECTATIONS HYPOTHESIS

The previous section highlighted the importance for macroeconomic stabilisation policy of the method by which economic agents form their expectations and this has stimulated economists to theorise about how expectations are formed. One theory, which has come recently into prominence, has far-reaching implications for macroeconomic theory and stabilisation policy in particular. This is the 'rational expectations hypothesis' (REH). It is the subject of another survey in this volume and hence we shall concentrate here only on its implications for stabilisation policy. The hypothesis assumes that agents, in forming expectations, act in a fashion implied in other areas of economic analysis, namely as optimisers, assessing the costs and benefits of alternatives. According to the theory economic agents use all available information in forecasting the value of an economic variable. If this information is costless they will form expectations in a manner that is consistent with the actual process by which the variable is determined. This does not imply that forecasters must always be correct, since the value of a variable may be affected by random, unpredictable changes which the forecaster cannot anticipate at the time the forecast is formed. But it does imply that forecast errors will themselves be random and contain no systematic pattern, for otherwise systematic (and therefore predictable) information is not being incorporated into the agent's expectation. For example, a forecasting method which produces forecast errors which alternate regularly in their sign, positive in periods 1, 3, 5, etc., and negative in periods 2, 4, 6, etc., cannot be consistent with rational expectations. For a rational economic agent at time period 3 would be aware from the previous pattern of errors that his forecasting method was about to produce a negative error in period 4. He would therefore adjust his forecast in accordance with the previous pattern, thereby eliminating that pattern.

When applied to the NRH the REH is usually accompanied by some strong and questionable assumptions about the scope and quality of available information. In its strongest form it argues that the parameters of the economy, the a's and Π's of equations [21] and [22] above, are known and to the extent that government monetary and fiscal policy are systematic rather than random, the values of m and g will also be predictable and therefore anticipated. In fact the only variable whose value is unknown in equations [21] and [22] is z, the aggregate demand shock. And even that can be partially predicted if its behaviour is at all systematic. Only if z is wholly random will it be wholly unpredictable. To see the implications of this hypothesis, assume that z is entirely random and that on average its value is zero. Then the systematic predictable component of the price level (p^s) is given by equation [21] as

$$p^s = \frac{a_0}{a_2 + \Pi_1} - \frac{y_n}{a_2 + \Pi_1} + \frac{a_1 g}{a_2 + \Pi_1} + \frac{a_2 m}{a_2 + \Pi_1} + \frac{\Pi_1 p^e}{a_2 + \Pi_1} \qquad [25]$$

Therefore, according to the REH and given our assumption about what information is available, the expected price level will equal this systematic predictable part of the actual price level. Thus

$$p^e = p^s = \frac{a_0}{a_2 + \Pi_1} - \frac{y_n}{a_2 + \Pi_1} + \frac{a_1 g}{a_2 + \Pi_1} + \frac{a_2 m}{a_2 + \Pi_1} + \frac{\Pi_1 p^e}{a_2 + \Pi_1} \qquad [26]$$

Collecting terms in p^e yields the solution for p^e as

$$p^e = \frac{a_0}{a_2} - \frac{y_n}{a_2} + \frac{a_1 g}{a_2} + m \qquad [27]$$

Substituting this expression into equation [22] yields

$$y = y_n + \frac{\Pi_1 z}{a_2 + \Pi_1} \quad [28]$$

The startling feature of equation [28] is that terms in *m* and *g* do not appear. In other words, monetary and fiscal policy changes have no effect on output even in the short run. The reason for this is that any attempt by governments to use fiscal and monetary policy systematically to alter the value of real output will be fully anticipated by rational economic agents and the effects of such policy changes will be totally absorbed by changes in the price level. Only unpredictable, random changes in fiscal and monetary policy which were assumed absent in the example above can change output. But clearly such scope for the effectiveness of fiscal and monetary policy does not allow for Keynesian fine tuning, for the latter requires that *systematic* policy changes, rather than random ones, can affect real output.

The theory of rational expectations has therefore been taken as a strong argument against Keynesian methods of stabilising the economy, not because these methods require more detailed knowledge of the workings of the economy than we possess nor because self-interested politicians are likely to misuse the policy instruments and destabilise the economy, but because such methods are ineffective. If they are employed at all systematically they will be predicted and their effects on real output annulled by price movements.

There is still much controversy surrounding the REH and it is too soon to assess its full importance. This controversy is discussed more fully in another survey and here we confine ourselves to two points. First, the central idea of REH, that economic agents will not typically refrain from using information which allows them to avoid making systematic forecasting errors, does not appear to be a highly objectionable one, especially if it is applied to the medium or long run. To assume that agents will refrain from using such information is not in sympathy with economic theory in general, and to base a macroeconomic policy upon it is foolish. Second, the assumption usually made in REH models that economic agents know the structure of the economy and the method by which government policy is being conducted, and its failure to explain how economic agents learn this structure and policy response, renders the REH unhelpful in considering one of the major current problems facing government policy-makers. This problem is how quickly to move from one policy regime which is generating high inflation to another which would generate, on average, zero inflation. If switches in policy regimes are readily and quickly learnt by economic agents, then the effects on output and employment of a sharp dramatic policy switch will be short lived and therefore more bearable. But if such dramatic changes of regime are not quickly understood, then they may have prolonged and severe effects on output and employment. To the extent that the REH is silent or indistinct on the question of how quickly policy regime switches are assimilated it is unhelpful to policy-makers deciding on how quickly they should attempt to cure inflation.

In fact the REH might best be seen as bolstering and sharpening the policy implications of the NRH: that the economy is self-correcting, possibly rapidly so, and hence Keynesian stabilisation policies are less urgently needed; that attempts to achieve a level of output higher than the natural rate will fail and should therefore not be made; and that governments can contribute to the stabilisation of the economy most by making their own policies as predictable as possible.

A NEW APPROACH TO STABILISATION POLICY

The previous two subsections have outlined the theoretical basis of a different approach to stabilisation policy. We have briefly described this different approach and we can now explain it more fully. Its central theme is that the government macroeconomic policy should be designed with the prime aim of achieving long- or medium-run stability. Direct attempts to achieve short-run stability are considered to have led to even greater instability (for the reasons discussed in section 4). If governments successfully create the conditions for long-run stability, this may well help foster short-run stability, discouraging short-term volatility in private sector spending through its effects on general business confidence. However, such a result should be regarded more as a welcome bonus than the prime aim of policy. In order to create medium- or long-run stability, the government should make its own policy instruments as stable and predictable as possible. If these policy instruments are stable, the medium- and long-term stability of private sector spending (see p.36) and the self-correcting nature of the economy will ensure a tolerable degree of stability for the economy as a whole. This does not imply that there will be no deviations at all of actual variables from their targets. Such deviations are considered unavoidable but likely to be relatively small.[9]

The term 'stability of policy instruments' is a vague one. To make it precise and practical, the proponents of this approach to policy argue that the time paths of the major policy instruments, the money stock and the fiscal policy variables, should be pre-announced for some years in advance and the government should aim to adhere to these time paths as closely as possible. The announcement of such time paths will in itself introduce greater certainty into the economy in that it enables agents to predict what policies the government will be following over the medium term. But if over a shorter period (say six months) the actual time paths of the policy variables diverge from the pre-announced ones, then confidence in the government's ability or resolution to achieve its targets will be lowered and one of the advantages of the new approach will be lost. Hence the argument that the government should aim to achieve its targets even in the short term. This approach to policy implies that the government should not in general alter the target time paths in response to changes in the economy which occur after the setting of the targets. It is in this sense that the new approach to policy is very different from the Keynesian one. For if there is a sharp recession Keynesians will argue for greater government spending, etc.; the proponents of the new approach, however, would argue that no changes in policy instruments should occur as a result of the recession except in so far as they were already allowed for when the target time paths were set. This leads to the question of the precise form of the pre-announced time paths. The most widely-known proposal is that *the rates of growth* of the money stock for the foreseeable future should be pre-announced and that these rates of growth should be those which are consistent with zero inflation or with the gradual elimination of inflation. The setting of the fiscal policy variables should take the form of announcing levels of government expenditure and tax rates which, if the economy was at full employment, would imply that government expenditure and tax receipts were equal. This latter rule is precise enough. Of course it leaves open the question of what the level of government expenditure and tax rates should be, but these are questions which go beyond the boundaries of macroeconomics.

The monetary rule, however, is still somewhat imprecise. Consider the algebraic version of the aggregate supply, aggregate demand model developed earlier in this section. Since the new approach is long term in design, its details are best explained with the use of the long-run version of that model, the key equations of which we repeat here for convenience.

$$y = y_n \qquad [29]$$

$$p = \frac{a_0}{a_2} - \frac{y_n}{a_2} + \frac{a_1 g}{a_2} + m + \frac{z}{a_2} \qquad [30]$$

If, as most proponents of the new approach believe, the long-run value of a_1 is approximately zero and if we treat the value of z (the aggregate demand shock) also as zero, then this second equation can be rewritten as

$$p = \frac{a_0}{a_2} - \frac{y_n}{a_2} + m \qquad [31]$$

Since the value of m is irrelevant for the long-term behaviour of y, its optimal value can be determined solely with reference to its effects on the price level, p. If the aim is to maintain stable prices, i.e. zero inflation with $p = p_{-1}$, then the long-run value of m should be such as to offset any tendency for prices to fall as a result of a rise in the natural level of output. If y_n is rising, as a result of productivity growth and increased labour supply, for example, then more output will be supplied, and hence if aggregate demand remains unchanged, prices will fall. If zero rather than negative inflation is the government's aim, then it needs to boost the money supply and thereby increase aggregate demand so that the increased level of real output will be willingly demanded at the same general price level as before. The required increase in the money supply clearly depends upon the percentage increase in the natural rate of output and certain structural coefficients in the economy. This can readily be seen by lagging equation [32] by one period to get equation [33] and subtracting equation [33] from equation [32] to obtain an expression for the inflation rate:

$$p = \frac{a_0}{a_2} - \frac{y_n}{a_2} + m \qquad [32]$$

$$p_{-1} = \frac{a_0}{a_2} - \frac{y_{n-1}}{a_2} + m_{-1} \qquad [33]$$

$$p - p_{-1} = -\left[\frac{y_n - y_{n-1}}{a_2}\right] + (m - m_{-1}) \qquad [34]$$

If the desired inflation rate is zero and if the estimated rate of growth of the natural level of output is x^* then equation [34] becomes

$$0 = \frac{-x^*}{a_2} + (m - m_{-1}) \qquad [35]$$

Equation [35] suggests that the rate of growth of the money stock $(m - m_{-1})$ should be

$$m - m_{-1} = \frac{x^*}{a_2} \qquad [36]$$

That is, for long-run price stability the growth in the money stock should equal the natural rate of growth of output divided by a coefficient a_2 which, in simple models and given our assumption regarding the importance of fiscal policy, is equivalent to the income elasticity of the demand for money. If, as some empirical evidence suggests, this parameter is unity, then the optimal long-run money supply growth is simply equal to the long-run growth of the natural rate of output, x^*. More generally, if the desired inflation rate is zero the nominal supply of money should be expanded at the same rate as the estimated long-run growth of the demand for real money balances.

The rule for monetary growth can thus be simply stated: if a stable price level is the objective of government, it should allow the money stock to grow at the expected growth rate of the natural level of output. Thus if the government estimates the underlying rate of growth of output to be 3 per cent, and if it estimates the income elasticity of demand for money to be 1.00, it should, if its aim is zero inflation, announce that it will expand the money stock by 3 per cent each year. In line with our previous discussion it should ensure that each quarter or month the annualised monetary growth rate is as near to 3 per cent as is technically possible, and no attempt should be made to let the money stock expand more quickly in periods when a recession is occurring.

There is one important qualification to this rule. The government of an economy in which a fairly high inflation rate is endemic will not in general want to set policy so as to achieve zero inflation in the medium term for, as equation [22] illustrates, if expectations of inflation do not respond rapidly to changes in policy regimes, then the costs of curing inflation quickly may be extremely severe in terms of lost output. Most economists, though not all (see Hayek 1980), argue for a commitment to reduce inflation gradually. In our model this commitment can be seen as a desire to set monetary growth on a path which will not produce inflation of zero in the medium term but will produce inflation which declines gradually each period. For example, if the current inflation rate is 15 per cent, then the aim to reduce it to 12 per cent next period implies, from equation [36], that monetary growth should equal

$$12 + \frac{x^*}{a_2}$$

Next period the monetary growth target should be, say,

$$(12 - 3) + \frac{x^*}{a_2}$$

and so on until inflation has been reduced to zero, when the monetary growth rate can be stabilised at x^*/a_2. In this setting the pre-announced time path for monetary growth should be one of continually declining monetary growth rates. The initial rate would be slightly below the current inflation rate and the final rate would equal the estimated rate of growth of the natural level of output. How quickly the rate of growth declines is a matter for the authorities. Some economists, notably Hayek (1980), favour an abrupt and sharp reduction in monetary growth to non-inflationary levels. Such a policy is not generally favoured by monetarists, since in the absence of sharp accompanying reductions in inflationary expectations it will initially produce a severe slump in economic activity which may prove so great a strain on society that the policy is abandoned. Proponents of this policy answer that a number of the hyperinflations this century have been successfully cured in this abrupt way, and that the alternative, which involves a less severe but probably more prolonged recession, is politically debilitating and is unlikely to be sustained. The problem can clearly be viewed as a problem of intertemporal choice: how much unemployment today is society prepared to accept in order to have less tomorrow? Posed in this way it becomes more of a political question than an economic one.

The major advantages claimed for this new approach to policy are that by binding governments to preannounced policies it will prevent them from manipulating the economy for their own political purposes; in that it does not require detailed knowledge of the short-term working of the economy it is less likely to encourage well-intentioned but destabilising policy changes; and since it makes current and future government policy much clearer and more predictable, it will foster long-run stability in the private sector and possibly short-run stability too.

Its opponents claim that it relies on very optimistic assumptions about the stability of the private sector, in particular private sector spending and the speed with which individuals correct their expectations of prices; and that it is inefficient for it implies that governments should ignore the information on the behaviour of the economy that becomes available as time passes.

It is difficult to assess the strength of these arguments, especially because (unlike the Keynesian approach) the new approach has not been applied extensively. It is true that a number of governments, mainly we suspect as a result of the generally dismal economic performance in the 1970s, have begun at least to pay lip service to the new approach. Thus the USA monetary authority has since 1974 been obliged to announce its target rates of growth for the money stock; a similar though less formal obligation has been accepted by the UK since 1976 and by some other governments. However, the actual rates of monetary growth are frequently different from the specified targets and so the adoption of monetary targets may be little more than cosmetic. Perhaps the government most openly committed to the new approach is the Conservative government of the UK which was elected in May 1979. This commitment is evidenced most clearly by the *Financial Statement and Budget Report 1980–81* in which target rates of growth of the money stock for the years 1980–81 to 1983–84 are published, together with planned government expenditure and tax receipts for the same period. The target rates of growth of the money stock are in line with a gradual deceleration of monetary growth to about 6 per cent in 1983–84, though 'the precise target rate of growth in the intervening years will be decided at the time' (p.16).

Only when the sort of policies favoured by the current UK government have been adopted and employed by a number of countries will we be in a good position to assess the true merits and deficiencies of the new approach to stabilisation policy, and to compare it with the actual performance of the Keynesian approach.

6. Summary and conclusions

Whilst the general aims of macroeconomic policy have changed little in the years since the Second World War, the views of how best to achieve these aims have altered in response both to developments in economic theory and to economic performance. The Keynesian approach to stabilisation policy which has been the dominant influence on policy-makers over the last forty years has become both more sophisticated and less popular. The decline in its popularity, which has been particularly marked since the mid 1960s, is probably mainly due to its apparently poor performance in the last fifteen years or so. But it is also the result of developments in theory which suggest that it may be based on naive views of how the economy works, on the altruism of governments and also on an overly pessimistic view of the strength of the economy's ability to stabilise itself.

These developments not only provide a basis for an attack on Keynesian policies, they also suggest a new approach to policy which advocates a much more limited role for governments. This role consists of announcing some years in advance and achieving targets for the major instruments of macroeconomic policy, and does not include directly attempting to achieve short-term stability. Since this new approach to stabilisation policy has not yet been formally employed for a significant length of time in the major industrial economies, it has not been subject to the same detailed and practical criticisms as has the Keynesian approach.

Notes

1. By 'standard' we distinguish our model from the more recent interpretations of Keynes as a disequilibrium macroeconomist. See Barro and Grossman (1976), Malinvaud (1977), Muellbauer and Portes (1978), and Solow and Stiglitz (1968).

2. The increase in *g* considered here is financed by the issue of bonds. If government bonds affect net wealth, and if net wealth appears as an argument in either the demand for money function or the expenditure function further effects of fiscal policy are possible. The implications of the government budget constraint are beyond the scope of this survey, but readers are referred to Currie (1978) for a survey of the relevant theories.
3. Note here that our assumption of *downward* wage rigidity does not prevent wages from *rising* to clear excess demands.
4. Readers should consult Thompson's survey and Posner (1978) to see the importance of monetary and fiscal variables in some other models of the UK economy.
5. Strictly the equality of instruments and targets, first stressed by Tinbergen (1952), is neither a necessary nor sufficient condition for their achievements. We shall however ignore this problem for the moment.
6. Exogenous variables are variables similar to autonomous expenditure in simple Keynesian models of the economy: their values are not determined by the model itself but do play a crucial role in determining the values of the variables the model does purport to explain. Thus economic forecasters have to make some guess as to the value of these variables and insert that guess into their model before they can make their predictions.
7. Metcalfe (1978) provides a more detailed description of the balance of payments accounts.
8. Note that this alternative approach differs fundamentally from the Keynesian one. Here the labour market *clears* (i.e. the wage adjusts to equate labour supply and demand, given the state of price expectations). By contrast, wage rigidities characterised the Keynesian approach.
9. Friedman (1953, 1959) is the best-known proponent of this new approach. The implications of rational expectations for this approach are developed in Sargent and Wallace (1975).

References

Anderson, L. C. and Carlson, K. (1974) St Louis model revisited, *International Economic Review,* **15**, 305–27.

Anderson, L. C. and Jordan, J. L. (1968) Monetary and fiscal actions: a test of their relative importance in economic stabilisation, *Federal Reserve Bank of St Louis Review,* **50**, 166–83.

Artis, M. J. (1978) Monetary policy, in Blackaby, F.T. (ed.), *British Economic Policy 1960–74,* Cambridge University Press, Cambridge.

Artis, M. J. and Nobay, A. R. (1969) Two aspects of the monetary debate, *National Institute Economic Review,* **49**, 33–51.

Ash, J. C. K. and Smyth, D. J. (1973) *Forecasting the UK Economy*, Saxon House, D.C. Heath Limited, England.

Bank of England (1976) The personal savings ratio, *Bank of England Quarterly Bulletin,* **16**, 53–73.

Barro, R. J. and Grossman, H. I. (1976) *Money, Employment and Inflation,* Cambridge University Press, Cambridge.

Beckerman, W. (ed.) (1972) *The Labour Government's Economic Record 1964–70,* London, Duckworth.

Blackaby, F. T. (ed.) (1979) *British Economic Policy 1960–74,* Cambridge University Press.

Brainard, W. (1967) Uncertainty and the effectiveness of policy, *American Economic Review*, **57**, 411–25.

Bristow, J. A. (1968) Taxation and income stabilisation, *Economic Journal*, **78**, 299–311.

Brittan, S. (1971) *Steering the Economy: The Role of the Treasury*, Penguin Books, Harmondsworth.

Buchanan, J. M. (1978) From private preferences to public philosophy: the development of public choice, *The Economics of Politics*, Institute of Economic Affairs Readings 18.

Cagan, P. (1956) The monetary dynamics of hyperinflations, in Friedman, M. (ed.), *Studies in the Quantity Theory of Money*, Chicago University Press, Chicago.

Chrystal, A. (1979) *Controversies in British Macroeconomics*, Philip Allan, Deddington.

Crossman, R. (1977) *The Diaries of a Cabinet Minister*, 3, Hamish Hamilton, London.

Currie, D. (1978) Macroeconomic policy and government financing: a survey of recent developments, in Artis, M. J. and Nobay, A. R. (eds), *Studies in Contemporary Economic Analysis*, **1**, Croom Helm, London.

Davidson, J. E. H., Hendry, D. F., Srba, F. and Yeo, S. (1978) Econometric modelling of the aggregate time-series relationship between consumers' expenditure and income in the UK, *Economic Journal*, **88**, 661–92.

Deaton, A. S. (1977) Involuntary saving through unanticipated inflation, *American Economic Review*, **67**, 899–910.

Dow, J. C. R. (1964) *Management of the British Economy 1945–60*, Cambridge University Press, Cambridge.

Financial Statement and Budget Report 1980–81, HMSO.

Frey, B. S. and Schneider, F. (1978) A politico-economic model of the UK, *Economic Journal*, **88**, 243–53.

Friedman, M. (1953) The effects of full-employment policy on economic stability: a formal analysis, in his *Essays in Positive Economics*, University of Chicago Press, Chicago.

Friedman, M. (ed.) (1956) *Studies in the Quantity Theory of Money*, Chicago University Press.

Friedman, M. (1959) *A Program for Monetary Stability*, Fordham University Press, New York.

Friedman, M. (1968) The role of monetary policy, *American Economic Review*, **58(1)**, 1–17.

Friedman, M. (1970) *The Counter-Revolution in Monetary Theory*, The Institute of Economic Affairs.

Friedman, M. (1976) *Price Theory*, Aldine Publishing Company, Chicago.

Friedman, M. (1980) Memorandum to the House of Commons Treasury and Civil Service Committee, *Memoranda on Monetary Policy*, Cmnd. 720.

Friedman, M. and Schwartz, A.J. (1963) *A Monetary History of the United States 1867–1960*, Princeton University Press for the National Bureau of Economic Research, Princeton.

Goodhart, C. A. E. and Crockett, A. D. (1970) The importance of money, *Bank of England Quarterly Bulletin*, **10**, 159–98.

Gordon, R. J. (1975) The demand for and supply of inflation, *Journal of Law and Economics*, **18**, 807–36.

Hansen, B. (1969) *Fiscal Policy in Seven Countries 1955–1965*, OECD, Paris.

Hayek, F. (1980) Letter to *The Times*, 5 March.

Howson, S. (1975) *Domestic Monetary Management in Britain 1919–38*, Cambridge University Press, Cambridge.

Kennedy, M. (1969) How well does the National Institute forecast?, *National Institute Economic Review,* **50**, 40–52.

Keran, M. W. (1969) Monetary and fiscal influences on economic activity–the historical evidence, *Federal Reserve Bank of St Louis Review,* **51**, 5–24.

Keynes, J. M. (1936) *The General Theory of Employment, Interest and Money*, Macmillan, London.

Kindleberger, C. (1968) *International Economics*, Irwin, Homewood, Illinois.

Kmenta, J. and Smith, P. E. (1973) Autonomous expenditures versus money supply: an application of dynamic multipliers, *Review of Economics and Statistics,* **55(3)** 299–307.

Laidler, D. E. W. (1974) Brief note on fiscal policy, inflation and the balance of payments, presented to the House of Commons Expenditure Committee, House of Commons *Ninth Report from the Expenditure Committee.*

Laidler, D. E. W. (1976) Inflation in Britain: a monetarist perspective, *American Economic Review,* **66(4)**, 485–500.

Laidler, D. E. W. (1977) *The Demand for Money*, Don Donnelley, New York.

Laury, J. S. E., Lewis, G. R. and Ormerod, P. A. (1978) Properties of macroeconomic models of the UK economy: a comparative study, *National Institute Economic Review,* **83**, 52–72.

Lewis, G. R. and Ormerod, P. A. (1979) Policy simulations and model characteristics, in Cook, S. T. and Jackson, P. M. (eds), *Current Issues in Fiscal Policy*, Martin Robertson, London.

Little, I. M. D. (1962) Fiscal Policy, in Worswick, G. D. N. and Ady, P. H. (eds), *The British Economy in the Nineteen Fifties*, Oxford University Press, London.

Little, I. M. D. (1964) Review of 'The Management of the British Economy 1945–60', *Economic Journal,* **74**, 983–5.

MacMillan Committee (1931) *The Report of the Committee on Finance and Industry*, Cmnd. 3897, HMSO, London.

Malinvaud, E. (1977) *The Theory of Unemployment Reconsidered*, Blackwell, Oxford.

Matthews, K. G. P. and Ormerod, P. A. (1978) St Louis models of the UK economy, *National Institute Economic Review,* **84**, 65–9.

Matthews, R. C. O. (1969) Postwar business cycles in the UK, in Bronfenbrenner, M. (ed.), *Is the Business Cycle Obsolete?*, Wiley, New York.

Meiselman, D. (ed.) (1970) *Varieties of Monetary Experience*, Chicago University Press, Chicago.

Metcalfe, J. S. (1978) The balance of payments, in Prest A. R. and Coppock, D. J. (eds), *The UK Economy: A Manual of Applied Economics* (7th edn), Weidenfeld & Nicolson, London.

Mill, J. S. (1861) Considerations on representative government, in his *Essays on Politics and Society,* **II**, University of Toronto Press, Toronto.

Modigliani, F. (1964) Some empirical tests of monetary management and of rules versus discretion, *Journal of Political Economy,* **72(3)**, 211–45.

Modigliani, F. (1977) The monetarist controversy, or should we forsake stabilisation policies?, *American Economic Review,* **67**, 1–19.

Moseley, P. (1978) Images of the 'floating voter': or the 'political business cycle' revisited, *Political Studies,* **26**, 375–94.

Muellbauer, J. and Portes, R. (1978) Macroeconomic models with quantity rationing, *Economic Journal,* **88**, 788–821.

Musgrave, R. A. and P. B. (1968) Fiscal policy, in Caves, R. *et al., British Economic*

Prospects, Brookings Institution, Washington DC, and George Allen and Unwin, London.

Nordhaus, W. D. (1975) The political business cycle, *Review of Economic Studies,* **42**, 169–90.

Osborn, D. R. and Teal, F. (1979) An assessment and comparison of two NIESR econometric model forecasts, *National Institute Economic Review,* **88**, 50–62.

Parkin, J. M. (1975) Where is Britain's inflation going?, *Lloyds Bank Review,* **117**, 1–13.

Phillips, A. W. (1954) Stabilisation in a closed economy, *Economic Journal,* **64**, 290–323.

Phillips, A. W. (1957) Stabilisation policy and the time form of lagged responses, *Economic Journal,* **67**, 265–77.

Pissarides, C. A. (1980) British government popularity and economic performance, *Economic Journal,* **90**, 569–81.

Poole, W. (1970) Optimal choice of monetary policy instruments in a simple stochastic macro model, *Quarterly Journal of Economics,* **84**, 197–216.

Posner, M. (ed.) (1978) *Demand Management*, Heinemann, London.

Radcliffe Committee (1959) *Report of The Committee on the Working of the Monetary System*, Cmnd. 827, HMSO, London.

Robinson, R. (1952) A graphical analysis of the foreign trade multiplier, *Economic Journal,* **62**, 546–64.

Sargent, T. J. and Wallace, N. (1975) Rational expectations, the optimal monetary instrument and the optimal money supply rule, *Journal of Political Economy,* **83**, 241–54.

Solow, R. M. and Stiglitz, J. E. (1968), Output, employment and wages in the short run, *Quarterly Journal of Economics,* **82**, 537–60.

Taylor, J. B. (1979) Estimation and control of a macroeconomic model with rational expectations, *Econometrica,* **47**, 1267–86.

Theil, H. (1958) *Economic Forecasts and Policy*, North-Holland, Amsterdam.

Theil, H. (1964) *Optimal Decision Rules for Government and Industry*, North-Holland, Amsterdam.

Tinbergen, J. (1952) *On the Theory of Economic Policy*, North-Holland, Amsterdam.

Tobin, J. (1965) The monetary interpretation of history, *American Economic Review,* **55**, 464–85.

Turnovsky, S. J. (1977) *Macroeconomic Analysis and Stabilisation Policy,* Cambridge University Press, Cambridge.

Worswick, G. D. N. (1971) Fiscal policy and stabilisation in Britain, in Cairncross, A. (ed.), *Britain's Economic Prospects Reconsidered*, George Allen and Unwin, London.

CHAPTER THREE

The consumption function

R. Leighton Thomas

1. Introduction: early work on the consumption function

The 'consumption function' is concerned with consumption as theoretically defined–that is, with the sum of consumer expenditures on non-durable goods plus the value of services obtained by consumers from durable goods. Since consumption represents a high proportion of total spending in any economy, an understanding of the factors determining it is of considerable importance.

The notion of a functional relationship between consumption expenditure and disposable income originated in Keynes's *General Theory* (1936), where Keynes suggested a 'consumption function' whereby, as income increases, consumption also increases but by a smaller extent. Keynes advanced, with varying conviction, four basic assumptions concerning the shape of his consumption function:

1. Real consumption is a 'fairly stable' function of real income, i.e. $C = C(Y)$ where C and Y are real consumption and real income respectively.
2. The marginal propensity to consume (MPC) lies between 0 and 1, i.e. $0 < \partial C/\partial Y < 1$.
3. The MPC is less than the average propensity to consume (APC), i.e. $\partial C/\partial Y < C/Y$.
4. as real income rises the MPC falls.

The expression 'fairly stable' was indicative of the fact that factors other than real income, e.g. interest rates, windfall changes in capital values, might also influence real consumption but that in the Keynesian scheme of things the income variable was likely to be of overriding importance. A typical Keynesian consumption function is shown in Fig. 3.1. It should be noted that it is assumption (3) above that ensures that the function has an intercept.

Keynes laid greatest stress on the first two of the above assumptions and these taken together constitute what is nowadays often termed the *Absolute Income Hypothesis* (AIH). In fact, only assumptions (1) and (2) are necessary for much of the analysis (e.g. the familiar multiplier process) in the *General Theory*.

Although Keynes was not specific on the point, consumption,

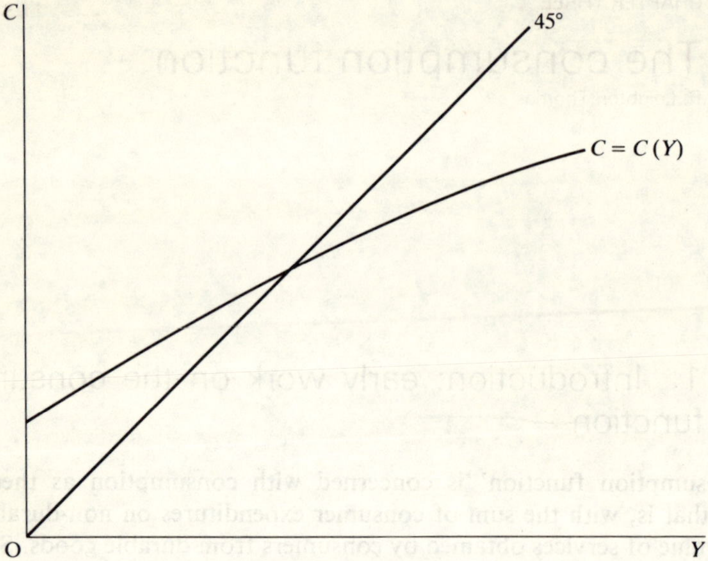

FIG. 3.1 The Keynesian consumption function

nowadays, is generally defined so as to exclude current expenditure on durable goods, including instead the value of services obtained from the total stock of durables. While it is total consumer expenditure which is of most interest from the point of view of economic policy, the determination of durable-good expenditure is complicated by the existence of stocks of durable goods in the hands of consumers, components of which may have lifetimes of twenty years or more.[1] For this reason the theoretical determinants of non-durable and durable expenditure are better considered separately, and nowadays it is also considered essential to treat expenditures on durables separately in empirical work. Indeed many studies concentrate on the demand for particular categories of durable good rather than aggregate expenditure. We do not consider this literature in detail here because it is in many ways separate from that on the consumption function. Moreover, even if total consumer expenditure is most relevant for policy purposes, justification for concentrating on consumption as theoretically defined is provided by the fact that the expenditure component of such consumption forms a large proportion of total consumer spending (in the UK, for example, between 85 and 90 per cent), so that its determination is a matter of importance in its own right.

Little attention was paid in early empirical work to precisely how variables used in estimating consumption functions should be defined. Total real consumer expenditure (i.e. in constant price terms) was frequently used as the consumption variable and 'income' was generally defined simply as real personal disposable income (i.e. net of taxes and insurance contributions, etc.), despite the fact that, as we shall see later, it is possible to argue that a better definition would include retained corporate earnings and capital gains.

Such was the attractive simplicity of the concept of a consumption function that much empirical effort went into checking the validity of the original

Keynesian assumptions. First, aggregate time series data for the short time span of the 1930s were used to estimate the function, using real personal disposable income as the *Y*-variable, and (normally) total real consumer expenditure as the *C*-variable. Second, although Keynes formulated his concept in terms of 'community' income and 'community' consumption, it could equally well be applied to the individual consumer or household, and hence consumption functions were also estimated using budget survey cross-sectional data for given years.

Early conclusions derived from both types of data seemed to support the first three of the Keynesian assumptions listed above, although there appeared little evidence in favour of assumption (4). Thus real consumption did appear to be a stable function of real income, and the shape of this function appeared similar to that shown in Fig. 3.1 although the non-verification of assumption (4) meant that the function seemed approximately linear in form.

Doubts began to arise about this simple form of the consumption function when it was found that if functions fitted to prewar US data were used to forecast post-war levels of consumer expenditure, these functions led to serious underpredictions of such expenditure. A good illustration of this is provided by Davis (1952). Such underpredictions were clearly inconsistent with a 'stable relationship' between income and consumption. Furthermore when the work of Kuznets (1942) and Goldsmith (1955) made available data on aggregate income and consumption from the nineteenth century onwards, it became clear that, for the US at least, as real income rose, the APC did not decline but remained relatively constant at about 0.9, suggesting a 'long run' consumption function which was not only linear but possessed no intercept. Other evidence from cross-sectional data produced at this time (e.g. Brady and Friedman 1947) suggested that, while for any given year a Keynesian type function similar to Fig. 3.1 could adequately describe the data, if data from successive years were employed this function appeared to be shifting upwards over time.

By about 1950 the picture appeared to be that, while long-run time series data suggested a consumption function with no intercept and a constant APC, both short run (ten to fifteen years) time-series and cross-sectional data provided a function with an intercept and for which MPC < APC. This difference could easily be reconciled by maintaining that a 'short-run' Keynesian type function was rising upwards over time (see Fig. 3.2), but this left unexplained the reasons for such a continuous upward shift. Much of the work on the consumption function from this point onwards has been concerned with providing theoretical explanations for these apparent inconsistencies in the results obtained from different types of data.

One of the earliest attempts at reconciling these differences was that by Duesenberry (1949) and Modigliani (1949) who independently developed what has come to be known at the *Relative Income Hypothesis* (RIH).

In Duesenberry's analysis the APC of an individual depends on his percentile position in the income distribution of his associates. This is so because Duesenberry adopts a microeconomic theory substantially different from traditional Hicksian-type demand analysis, and assumes that the individual's utility depends not only on his own level of consumption but also on the consumption levels of his associates. Consumers in the lower percentile of an income distribu-

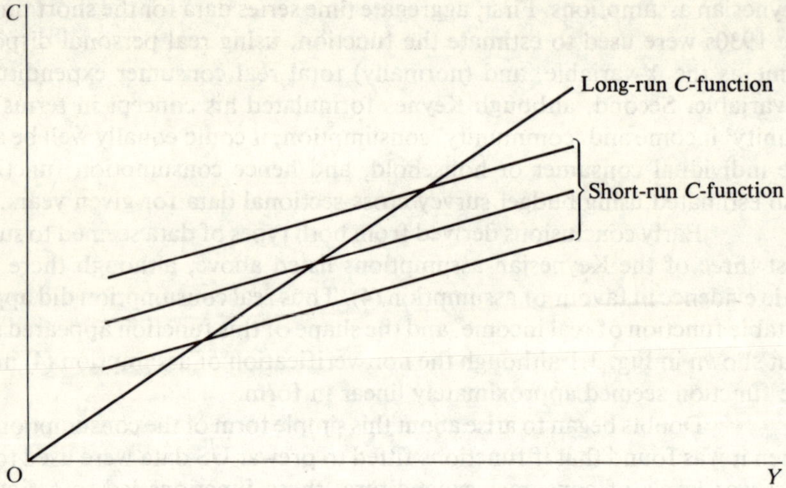

FIG. 3.2 Short- and long-run consumption functions

tion emulate the standards of living of the wealthy and to do so have to spend a larger proportion of their income. This results in a cross-sectional consumption function of typical Keynesian shape with APC declining as income rises. However, Duesenberry's hypothesis also explains the long-run time-series findings. If all incomes increase over time at the same rate, income distribution remains unchanged, each individual's APC therefore remains constant and hence the aggregate APC remains constant. In fact even if individual incomes do not all increase at the same proportionate rate, the aggregate APC will still remain unchanged, because with the income groups defined in percentile terms, for every consumer moving up one percentile there must be another coming down.

A slightly different interpretation of the term 'relative income' is necessary to reconcile the findings of long-run and short-run time-series data. Both Duesenberry and Modigliani suggest that the desire to maintain previous living standards, as well as pure habit, means that the individual's current level of consumption depends not only on the level of his current income but also on the relationship between this level and the previous highest or peak income level. Thus if incomes should fall during a recession, the community in general may regard such a fall as temporary and offset it by consuming a larger proportion of its income in order to keep its living standards intact. The community's APC therefore depends on the ratio between its current income Y_t and its previous income peak Y_0. That is,

$$\frac{C_t}{Y_t} = \alpha_0 + \alpha_1\left(\frac{Y_0}{Y_t}\right) \qquad \alpha_0 > 0 \quad \alpha_1 > 0 \qquad [1]$$

Equation [1] may be rewritten as

$$C_t = \alpha_0 Y_t + \alpha_1 Y_0 \qquad [2]$$

If income were to grow at a constant rate g then $Y_t = (1 + g)\, Y_{t-1}$ and moreover $Y_0 = Y_{t-1}$. Hence equation [2] can then be written as

$$C_t = \left(\alpha_0 + \frac{\alpha_1}{1 + g}\right) Y_t \qquad [3]$$

Since, for most western economies since the beginning of the century, income can in fact be regarded as having grown at a constant rate with only relatively minor cyclical fluctuations, equation [3] suggests that long-run time-series data will present us with a consumption function possessing no intercept and with a constant APC and MPC both equal to $\alpha_0 + \alpha_1/(1 + g)$.

A short-run cyclical fall in income, however, leads to $Y_t < Y_0$ with Y_0 remaining constant until Y_t rises to this level again. Under these circumstances equation [2] can be rewritten as

$$C_t = \alpha_1' + \alpha_0 Y_t \qquad [4]$$

Equation [4] has an intercept $\alpha_1' = \alpha_1 Y_0$ = constant and MPC = α_0. Hence the consumption function obtained from short-run time-series data is of the Keynesian type with an MPC smaller than that obtained from the long-run consumption function given by equation [3].

The relative income reconciliation of long-run and short-run data is illustrated in Fig. 3.3. Suppose the initial level of income is Y_s and that income rises over time until it attains the level Y_0. Consumption rises along the long-run function given by equation [3]. However, if income begins to decline cyclically once it has reached Y_0, then consumption falls back along the shallower short-run curve $C_t = \alpha_1 Y_0 + \alpha_0 Y_t$ as consumers attempt to maintain the living standards achieved with the previous peak income level Y_0. Consumption remains on this curve until income reattains the level Y_0. However, once income (assumed to be growing secularly) exceeds Y_0, consumption again begins to rise along the long-run function. If the next cyclical peak level of income is Y_0' then once income declines from this level, consumption falls back along the new short-run function $C_t = \alpha_1 Y_0' + \alpha_0 Y_t$. Since $Y_0' > Y_0$, this new short-run function has a larger intercept and therefore lies above the previous short-run function. There is therefore a 'ratchet' effect, with the short-run function shifting periodically upwards. A typical scatter of points generated by such a process is shown by the crosses in Fig. 3.3.

One further implication of the RIH may be noted at this point. Equation [3] implies that the larger is the long term growth rate g in an economy, the smaller is the APC. This accords with the observation that countries with the highest growth rates tend to have the largest saving–income ratios. We shall return to this point later.

The RIH reconciliation of short- and long-run time-series data may also be formulated in terms of previous peak consumption rather than previous peak income. Similar short-run and long-run consumption functions are obtained if equation [2] is replaced by $C_t = \alpha_0 Y_t + \alpha_1 C_0$, where C_0 is the previous peak con-

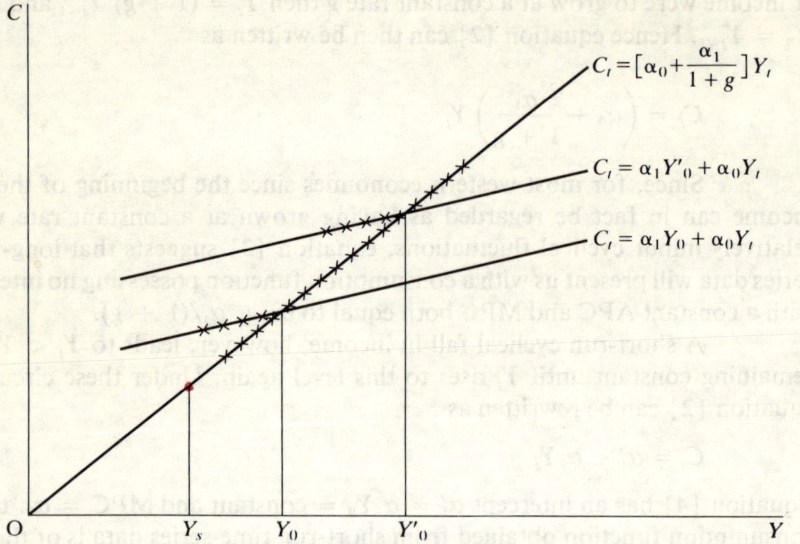

FIG. 3.3 The RIH reconciliation of short- and long-run time series data

sumption level. In an important development, Brown (1952) generalised this approach in his 'habit persistence model' in which he argued that the influence of past consumption is important whether it is above or below the current level. Current consumption therefore always depends on past consumption as well as current income.

$$C_t = \alpha_0 Y_t + \alpha_1 C_{t-1} \qquad [5]$$

If consumption grows over time, the 'short-run' relationship between C_t and Y_t therefore moves continuously upwards. In fact, if consumption grows at a long-run rate g, then since $C_t = (1 + g)C_{t-1}$, a long-run consumption function, again with a constant APC, is obtained. That is,

$$C_t = \left(\frac{\alpha_0}{1 - (\alpha_1/1 + g)} \right) Y_t \qquad [6]$$

2. The normal income hypothesis

As we noted in the previous section, Duesenberry's analysis of the factors determining the proportion of income spent on current consumption is based on a rather unothodox microeconomics. In fact a traditional framework for analysing this problem had been available at least since Fisher (1907).

Consider a consumer faced with the problem of allocating his total resources between consumption in the current period, C_1, and consumption in the next period, C_2, so as to maximise utility derived during the two periods combined. We may express the consumer's preferences through the system of indifference curves shown in Fig. 3.4. If it is assumed that the marginal rate of substitution of

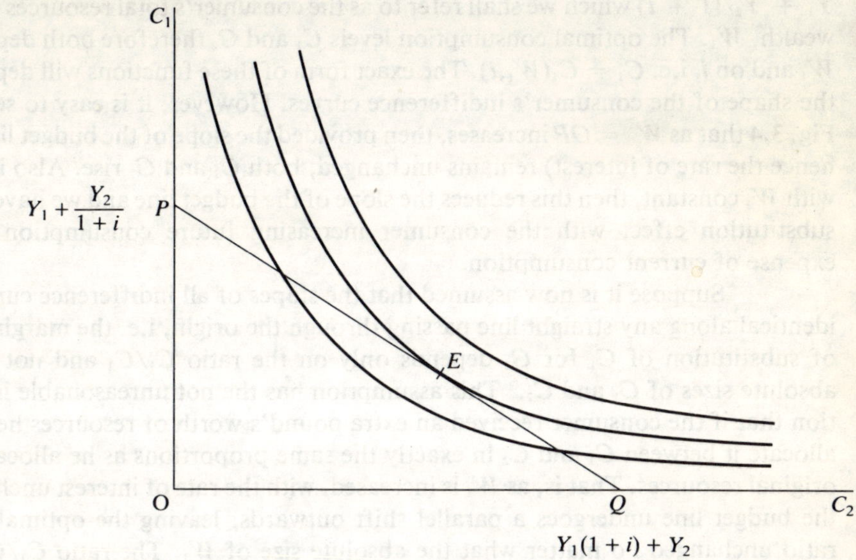

FIG. 3.4 Utility maximisation in the two-period case

current consumption for future (i.e. next period) consumption diminishes as future consumption is substituted for current consumption, then the indifference curves will be convex to the origin.

Suppose the consumer's income (i.e. total receipts) in the current period is Y_1, and in the next period Y_2. If the rate of interest per period is i, then the maximum the consumer can spend on consumption during the current period is $Y_1 + Y_2/(1 + i)$ the sum of his current income plus the maximum loan he could raise and then repay out of his income in the next period. If all resources are consumed in this way during the current period then, obviously, consumption has to be zero in the next period and this behaviour is represented by the point P in Fig. 3.4. At the other extreme, if consumption is zero in the current period then if total resources are to be exhausted, consumption in the next period will be $Y_1(1 + i) + Y_2$ – current period income plus interest earned on it plus income in the next period. This is represented by the point Q in Fig. 3.4. The line PQ represents all possible combinations of C_1 and C_2 that the consumer could choose given that he intends to exhaust all his resources by the end of the next period – it is therefore the consumer's budget constraint.

The consumer will choose the combination of C_1 and C_2 represented by the point E where the budget line is tangential to an indifference curve. Note that, given the indifference map, the position of E and hence the value of current consumption C_1 depends on *both* current *and* future income and also on the rate of interest. It is not possible to derive the AIH from this type of analysis. Indeed, a major criticism of the original Keynesian concept was that it lacked any foundation in orthodox microeconomics.

The position of E depends, in fact, on the slope and height of the budget line PQ. The slope of PQ is $-1/(1 + i)$ while its height depends on the quantity

$Y_1 + Y_2/(1 + i)$ which we shall refer to as the consumer's total resources or total wealth, W_1. The optimal consumption levels C_1 and C_2 therefore both depend on W_1 and on i, i.e. $C_1 = C_1(W_1,i)$. The exact form of these functions will depend on the shape of the consumer's indifference curves. However, it is easy to see from Fig. 3.4 that as $W_1 = OP$ increases, then provided the slope of the budget line (and hence the rate of interest) remains unchanged, both C_1 and C_2 rise. Also if i rises with W_1 constant, then this reduces the slope of the budget line and we have a pure substitution effect with the consumer increasing future consumption at the expense of current consumption.

Suppose it is now assumed that the slopes of all indifference curves are identical along any straight line passing through the origin, i.e. the marginal rate of substitution of C_1 for C_2 depends only on the ratio C_1/C_2 and not on the absolute sizes of C_1 and C_2.[2] This assumption has the not unreasonable implication that if the consumer received an extra pound's worth of resources he would allocate it between C_1 and C_2 in exactly the same proportions as he allocated his original resources. That is, as W_1 is increased, with the rate of interest unchanged, the budget line undergoes a parallel shift outwards, leaving the optimal C_1/C_2 ratio unchanged no matter what the absolute size of W_1. The ratio C_1/C_2 will, however, depend on the rate of interest i and also on the precise form of the consumer's indifference map.

The constancy of C_1/C_2 for a given rate of interest means that C_1 and C_2 are in fact constant proportions of W_1, i.e. $C_1 = \lambda_1 W_1$ and $C_2 = \lambda_2 W_1$ where the λ's are independent of W_1 but dependent on the interest rate and on consumer tastes as represented by his indifference map. (To see this assume $C_1 = \gamma C_2$ and substitute in $W_1 = C_1 + C_2/(1 + i)$).

The usefulness of this not unrealistic special case will become apparent in a moment, but firstly let us consider an even more extreme situation where the rate of interest is zero and where the consumer exhibits an absence of 'time preference proper'. The absence of such time preference implies that each indifference curve is symmetrical about the 45° line passing through the origin as illustrated in Fig. 3.5. This simply means that the consumer is indifferent between, for example, $C_1 = 80$, $C_2 = 40$ and $C_1 = 40$, $C_2 = 80$. The zero interest rate means that the slope of the budget line is -1, and hence that its point of tangency with any indifference curve will always be on the 45° line. Thus C_1 is always equal to C_2 no matter what the size of W_1, and the consumer under these conditions always consumes at the same rate in each period. In Fig. 3.5 $C_1 = \text{OA} = \text{OB} = C_2$. We shall have reason to refer back to this particular case later.

The above two-period analysis was generalised by Modigliani and Brumberg (1954) and formed the basis for their *life-cycle hypothesis* (LCH). It was assumed that households in general plan their lifetime consumption patterns so as to maximise total utility derived during their lifetime. Thus a household of age T maximises a utility function of the form

$$U = U(C_T, C_{T+1}, C_{T+2}, \dots C_L) \qquad [7]$$

where C_j is planned consumption at age j and L is the household's expected age at 'death'. Provided the household intends to just exhaust its total resources by the

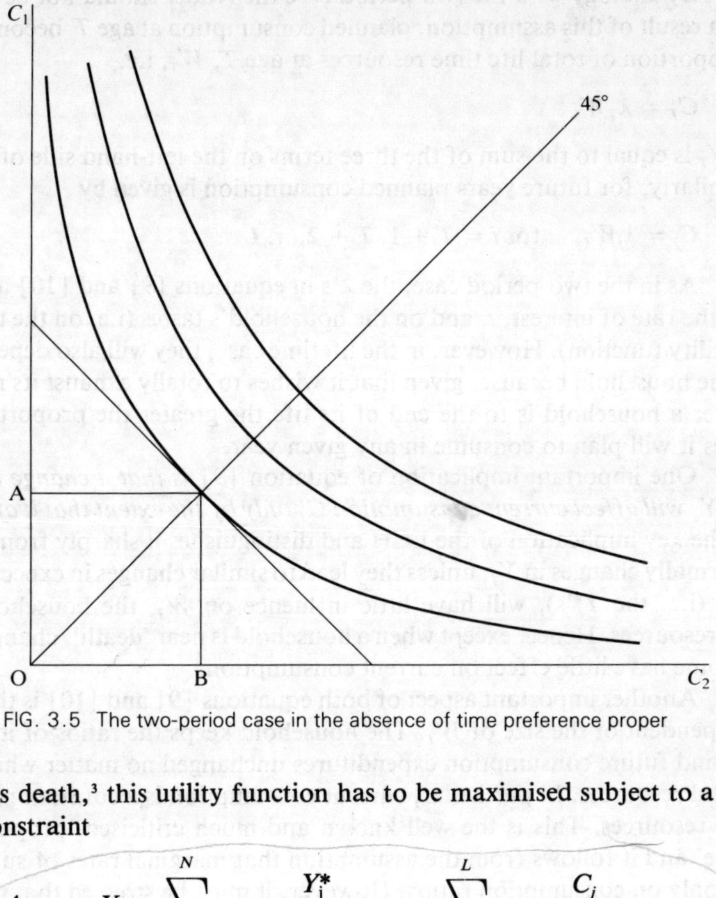

FIG. 3.5 The two-period case in the absence of time preference proper

time of its death,[3] this utility function has to be maximised subject to a lifetime budget constraint

$$A_{T-1} + Y_T + \sum_{j=T+1}^{N} \frac{Y_j^*}{(1+i)^{j-T}} = \sum_{j=T}^{L} \frac{C_j}{(1+i)^{j-T}} \qquad [8]$$

where A_{T-1} represents physical and financial assets at the beginning of the household's Tth year (i.e. its 'non-human wealth'), Y_T is the household's earned or non-property income at age T, Y_j^* its expected earned income at age j, and N is its expected age at retirement. The reader who is unclear why it is earned or non-property income only which enters the budget constraint is referred to Appendix 1 where the constraint is derived for the three-period case.

Modigliani and Brumberg now invoke a simplifying assumption similar to that made above in the simple two-period case. It is assumed that the marginal rate of substitution of consumption in any one year for consumption in any other year is dependent only on the ratio of consumption in those two years and is independent of the absolute levels of consumption in either of the years. In other words, 'if the individual receives an additional dollar's worth of resources he will allocate it to consumption at different times in the same proportion in which he had allocated his resources prior to the addition' (Ando and Modigliani 1963: 56).

By analogy with the two-period case the reader should not be surprised that, as a result of this assumption, planned consumption at age T becomes a constant proportion of total life time resources at age T, W_T, i.e.

$$C_T = \lambda_T W_T \qquad [9]$$

where W_T is equal to the sum of the three terms on the left-hand side of equation [8]. Similarly, for future years planned consumption is given by

$$C_j = \lambda_j W_T \quad \text{for } j = T+1, T+2, \dots L \qquad [10]$$

As in the two-period case, the λ's in equations [9] and [10] are dependent on the rate of interest, i, and on the household's tastes (i.e. on the properties of the utility function). However, in the lifetime case, they will also depend on the age of the household because, given that it wishes to totally exhaust its resources, the nearer a household is to the end of its life the greater the proportion of its resources it will plan to consume in any given year.

One important implication of equation [9] *is that a change in current income Y_T will affect current consumption C_T only by the extent that it affects W_T.* This is the key implication of the LCH and distinguishes it sharply from the AIH since normally changes in Y_T, unless they lead to similar changes in expected future incomes (i.e. the Y_j^*'s), will have little influence on W_T, the household's *total* lifetime resources. Hence, except when a household is near 'death', changes in current income have little effect on current consumption.

Another important aspect of both equations [9] and [10] is that the λ's are independent of the size of W_T. The household keeps the ratios of its planned current and future consumption expenditures unchanged no matter what the size of its total resources. In particular, current consumption is a constant proportion of these resources. This is the well known and much criticised 'proportionality postulate' and it follows from the assumption that marginal rates of substitution depend only on consumption ratios. However, it must be stressed that the convenient proportionality postulate is in no way vital to the central implication of the LCH. As can be seen from the two-period case, the dropping of this assumption would still leave current consumption as a function of *total* lifetime resources although the relationship would no longer be one of proportionality. Hence a change in current income would still only affect current consumption via its probably small effect on W_T. The contrast with the AIH therefore remains.

It is now possible to understand the LCH explanation of the upward shifting short-run aggregate consumption function. Combining equations [9] and [8] gives consumption at age T as

$$C_T = \lambda_T A_{T-1} + \lambda_T Y_T + \lambda_T \sum_{j=T+1}^{N} \frac{Y_j^*}{(1+i)^{j-T}} \qquad [11]$$

Since expected future incomes, i.e. the Y_j^*'s, are likely to be closely dependent on the size of current income Y_T, equation [11] can be regarded as approximately relating consumption at age T to income at age T and to non-human wealth at the beginning of the household's Tth year. For the economy as a whole we can therefore expect an aggregate relationship roughly of the form[4]

$$C_t = \alpha_0 Y_t + \alpha_1 A_{t-1}$$

where C_t and Y_t are aggregate consumption and aggregate non-property income in year t, and A_{t-1} is aggregate non-human wealth at the beginning of year t. If the aggregate consumption function is of this form then, since A_{t-1} rises over time, the 'short-run' relationship between C_t and Y_t (obtained maybe by the ordinary least squares regression of C_t on Y_t with A_{t-1} omitted) will have an intercept and moreover will shift upwards over time as A_{t-1} increases.

Finally consider, as we did for the two-period case, the situation where the interest rate is zero and where there is an absence of 'time preference proper'. As in the two-period case, the household now plans to consume at a constant rate throughout its remaining life span. The time profiles of income and consumption under such conditions are shown in Fig. 3.6 for a typical household. For such a household, income is likely to rise steadily at first until somewhere near the expected age at retirement, N, and decline, possibly quite sharply, afterwards. Consumption in contrast proceeds at a constant rate.

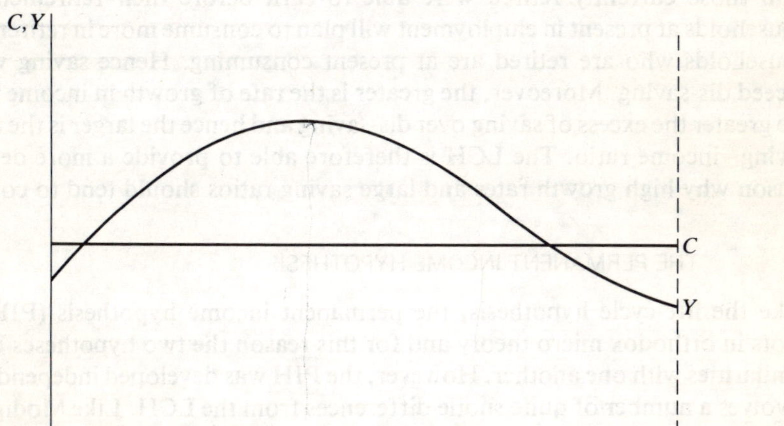

FIG. 3.6 Lifetime profiles of income and consumption

It is clear from Fig. 3.6 that, even with a zero rate of interest and in the absence of time preference proper, a typical household will still borrow and save. Without saving during its 'middle age' and dis-saving during its retirement a household would be restricted to consuming no more and no less than its current income during each year of its life. An important motive for saving in the LCH is therefore *the desire to flatten out the life-time profile of consumption expenditures* and to avoid the restrictions that might be imposed by a varying level of income.

The above behaviour pattern has one important implication for the aggregate saving–income ratio of the economy as a whole. Recall that the RIH was able to provide a possible explanation of why economies with high growth rates tended to have large saving–income ratios. The life-cycle hypothesis is also able to provide such an explanation and the explanation is of a more fundamental nature.

Consider a 'no growth' economy with a constant technology and capital stock and a constant population and age distribution. It is possible to regard a cross-section of such an economy as a series of households each at a different point in its life-cycle. Aggregate saving is hence zero (provided there is no saving for heirs), since the dis-saving of the retired just matches the saving of those who are still working. In a growing economy, however, aggregate saving is positive both because of population growth and because of developing technology. If growth is the result of a growing population with a constant technology, then obviously the larger proportion of younger households means that the saving of the working population will now exceed the dis-saving of the retired. However, even if the population remains constant, a developing technology will lead to rising income per head so that those currently working will earn and expect to earn more than those currently retired were able to earn before their retirement. Hence households at present in employment will plan to consume more in retirement than households who are retired are at present consuming. Hence saving will again exceed dis-saving. Moreover, the greater is the rate of growth in income per head, the greater the excess of saving over dis-saving and hence the larger is the aggregate saving–income ratio. The LCH is therefore able to provide a more deep-seated reason why high growth rates and large saving ratios should tend to coincide.

THE PERMANENT INCOME HYPOTHESIS

Like the life-cycle hypothesis, the permanent income hypothesis (PIH) has its roots in orthodox micro theory and for this reason the two hypotheses bear close similarities with one another. However, the PIH was developed independently and involves a number of quite subtle differences from the LCH. Like Modigliani and Brumberg; Friedman (1957) generalises the two-period model outlined above but the generalisation is to an 'indefinitely long horizon' rather than to a finite life span. Current planned or *permanent* consumption, C^p, depends, as in the two-period model, on current wealth, W, and the rate of interest, i.

$$C^p = q(W, i) \qquad [13]$$

Wealth in the PIH is however defined as the discounted sum of *all* future receipts, including income from non-human assets. Thus wealth in period t is given by

$$W_t = Y_t + \frac{Y_{t+1}}{1+i} + \frac{Y_{t+2}}{(1+i)^2} \dots \qquad [14]$$

where Y_t represents total expected receipts in year t. Notice that in a competitive world of complete certainty the value of non-human assets would exactly reflect the discounted sum of future earnings on them and hence, under these conditions, the Friedman and Modigliani–Brumberg measures of wealth would be the same.

Like the life-cycle theorists, Friedman makes the simplifying assumption that the utility function is homogeneous in all its arguments so that planned or permanent consumption is directly proportional to W. That is, equation [13] becomes

$$C^p = qW \qquad [15]$$

where q is dependent on the consumer's tastes and on the rate of interest.

Friedman now takes the crucial step of introducing the concept of *permanent income*, Y^p. Theoretically, Y^p is the maximum amount a consumer can spend while still maintaining his total wealth W intact. It is therefore the rate of return on wealth, i.e. $Y^p = iW$. This can be most easily seen in terms of the two-period model discussed above. Since initial wealth is W_1, if nothing is consumed in the current period, wealth will grow to $W_1(1 + i)$ by the start of the next period. However, if consumption in the current period is iW_1, then wealth at the start of the next period is W_1 and hence wealth will have been maintained intact. The argument extends of course to the multiperiod case. Equation [15] can now be written as

$$C^p = q\left(\frac{Y^p}{i}\right) = kY^p \quad \text{where } q = ik \qquad [16]$$

Friedman has, in fact, annuitised the wealth concept W, since permanent income Y^p can also be regarded as that level of income which, if received in perpetuity, has a discounted present value exactly equal to W. To see this we solve the following equation for Y^p,

$$W = \frac{Y^p}{1 + i} + \frac{Y^p}{(1 + i)^2} + \frac{Y^p}{(1 + i)^3} \ldots \qquad [17]$$

The right-hand side of [17] is a convergent geometric series with common ratio $1/1 + i$. Its sum to infinity is Y^p/i and hence we obtain $Y^p = iW$ as before.[5]

The replacement of a stock concept (W) by the flow concept (Y^p) does, however, raise one awkward inconsistency. If an individual consumes an amount exactly equal to his permanent income, then by definition his wealth remains unchanged. However, equation [16] implies that a consumer will normally consume less than his permanent income (empirical estimates of k tend to be in the range 0.8–0.9) and hence that wealth will be perpetually increasing. While the annuitisation of wealth and the switch to an implied infinite lifespan can be justified by maintaining that a household attaches as much importance to the consumption of its heirs as to its own consumption, it is difficult to see why it should plan for an ever increasing level of wealth.

The factor of proportionality k in equation [16] depends on household preferences and on the rate of interest. Notice that, unlike the equivalent parameter in the LCH, k does not depend on the age of the household. This is because, in Friedman's model, a household whatever its age acts as if it had an infinite remaining lifespan. Friedman however introduces a further motive for saving: the need, in a world of uncertainty, to accumulate wealth to safeguard against emergencies. Human wealth is less satisfactory than tangible non-human wealth for such a purpose, so the larger the proportion of total wealth held as non-human wealth, the less the consumer feels the need to save and the greater is k. Friedman in fact makes k dependent on w, which is the ratio of non-human wealth to permanent income; for a given interest rate this ratio is directly proportional to the ratio of non-human wealth to total wealth. Thus we have

$$C^p = k(i, w, u)\, Y^p \qquad [18]$$

where u is a portmanteau variable representing the consumer's tastes.

There are obvious similarities between the PIH and the LCH. In both models an increase in current income affects current consumption only to the extent that it influences some key variable–in the PIH the variable is permanent income, in the LCH it is total lifetime resources. For this reason both hypotheses are sometimes referred to as *normal income hypotheses*, normal income being a generic term encompassing both permanent income and lifetime resources.

Both hypotheses make use of the 'proportionality postulate' but in both models this is a convenient rather than a vital assumption. For example, in the PIH, if the assumption of a homogeneous utility function is dropped, C^p still remains a function of W and hence of permanent rather than current income.

There are, however, some distinct but relatively minor differences between the two hypotheses. For example, whereas in the LCH a household is assumed only to plan ahead to the end of its life, in the PIH Friedman's annuitisation of total wealth means that a household believes it has an infinite life, or at least regards the consumption of its heirs as of equal importance as its own consumption. This prevents Friedman drawing any conclusions about the effect of age on the MPC of households. However, under the LCH the closer a household is to 'death' the greater the proportion of any increment in total resources it is likely to spend on current consumption.

The annuitisation of total wealth also means that the stock of non-human assets does not appear explicitly in Friedman's consumption function. Nevertheless, possibly different influences of human and non-human wealth *are* allowed for in the PIH since k, the APC out of permanent income, is made dependent on the ratio between the two. In contrast, as can be seen from equation [11], in the LCH the effect on planned consumption of an extra dollar of resources is the same whether that dollar represents an addition to the stock of a consumer's non-human wealth or whether it represents an addition to the present value of future household non-property income (i.e. an addition to human wealth).

Once an attempt is made to relate the PIH to actual income-consumption data, we immediately face the problem that the theoretical construct 'permanent income' bears little relationship to the current or 'measured income' on which data are available. To get round this problem Friedman considers measured income, Y, as being composed of two components–permanent income Y^p and *transitory in-*

come Y^t. Current or measured consumption C is also divided into permanent consumption C^p and *transitory consumption* C^t. That is,

$$Y = Y^p + Y^t \text{ and } C = C^p + C^t \qquad [19]$$

Empirically, permanent income is that part of its income which the household regards as normal or unfortuitous or expected. This definition is deliberately vague since, according to Friedman (1957), 'the precise line to be drawn between permanent and transitory components is best left to the data themselves, to be whatever seems to correspond to consumer behaviour' (p.23). Thus since, theoretically, permanent or planned consumption depends on permanent income, in practice permanent income must be whatever quantity the consumer sees as determining his planned consumption–in effect permanent income is whatever the consumer thinks it to be! Transitory income is the difference between total measured income and permanent income, and can therefore be roughly regarded as income arising from chance occurrences. Since permanent and planned consumption are synonymous, transitory consumption is to be regarded as unplanned consumption.

In order to give his model predictive power and hence make it capable of contradiction by available data, Friedman makes the following assumptions:

(a) the transitory components of income and consumption are uncorrelated with their respective permanent components;

(b) the transitory component of consumption is uncorrelated with the transitory component of income.

The first of these assumptions is relatively non-controversial and appears to follow from the definition of a transitory component. If Y^t were correlated with Y^p it could hardly be regarded as transitory. Assumption (b), however, is clearly more controversial, since it implies that any unexpected receipt of income will not be spent on unplanned consumption–an implication which is obviously debatable. Friedman defends it in two ways. First, saving has often been regarded as a residual in economics–merely the difference between actual income and planned *and realised* consumption. A consumer who finds his income different to that which he expected usually holds to his consumption plan and saves either more or less than he had planned. Second, Friedman's definition of consumption includes only the flow of services from durable goods and not actual expenditure on such goods. If transitory income is spent on durable goods only then, since this can be classified as unplanned saving rather than unplanned consumption, assumption (b) is made to look much more reasonable. However, as we have already observed, such a definition is less useful from the point of view of economic policy since policy is more concerned with *total* consumers' expenditure. Empirical support for this second justification has been provided more recently by Darby (1972, 1974), who found that, if consumption expenditure is defined so as to exclude spending on durables, then it appears to be far less responsive to changes in transitory income than when it is defined so as to include such spending. Darby's work is discussed in more detail below.

If the definitions (equation [19]) are substituted into the basic underlying relationship $C^p = kY^p$ we obtain

$$C = kY + (C^t - kY^t) \quad [20]$$

Equation [20] can be regarded as a relationship between measured consumption, C, and measured income, Y, but one which contains a 'disturbance' or 'error term', $C^t - kY^t$. The error term, however, is correlated with the right-hand side variable Y since both error term and Y involve transitory income Y^t. Because of this, if an attempt is made to estimate equation [20] by an ordinary least squares regression of C on Y, we are likely to obtain an underestimate of the 'slope coefficient' k. Friedman [6] in fact is able to show that, provided assumptions (a) and (b) above hold, the application of ordinary least squares to equation [20] will yield, for large samples, an estimated slope coefficient

$$b = kP_y \quad \text{where } P_y = \frac{\text{Var } Y^p}{\text{Var } Y^t + \text{Var } Y^p} = \frac{\text{Var } Y^p}{\text{Var } Y} < 1 \quad [21]$$

and, if mean transitory income and mean transitory consumption are zero, an estimated intercept

$$a = k(1 - P_y)\,\bar{Y} \quad [22]$$

where $\bar{Y}$ is the mean value of income in the sample and Var Y^p and Var Y^t are the variances of Y^p and Y^t respectively.

The quantity P_y is the proportion of the total variation in income which is accounted for by variations in its permanent component Y^p. Hence equations [21] and [22] imply that if any proportion of variation in Y is the result of variations in transitory income, we will observe a consumption function with a slope b which is flatter than that of the underlying relationship $C^p = kY^p$ (i.e. $b < k$) and an intercept that is non-zero and positive (i.e. $a > 0$).

Equations [21] and [22] enable the PIH to reconcile the apparently contradictory information provided by long-run and short-run time-series data. Figure 3.7 depicts the time path of income for an economy in the long run, e.g. over a fifty-year period. The broken line traces the path of actual measured income. This typically fluctuates cyclically about the trend path of income which is shown by the secularly growing solid line and which may be taken as describing the long-term growth in permanent income. Had the two lines coincided this would have implied that *aggregate* transitory income was invariably zero (although *individual* consumers may have experienced non-zero transitory incomes). Under such conditions all variations in Y are due to variations in Y^p, so that $P_y = 1$, and we would observe a consumption function of the form $C = kY$. Typically, of course, the dotted and solid lines do not coincide and cyclical fluctuations will occur. However, in the long run such cyclical variations are of minor importance compared with the trend rate of growth, so that variation in Y is dominated by the variation in Y^p and P_y is, hence, still close to unity. Thus we still tend to observe a consumption function without an intercept and with a slope very close to k.

If however we merely consider a ten to fifteen-year period, a different picture emerges. Figure 3.8 represents an enlarged version of the boxed area in Fig. 3.7. For this shorter period, trend movements in income no longer dominate, tran-

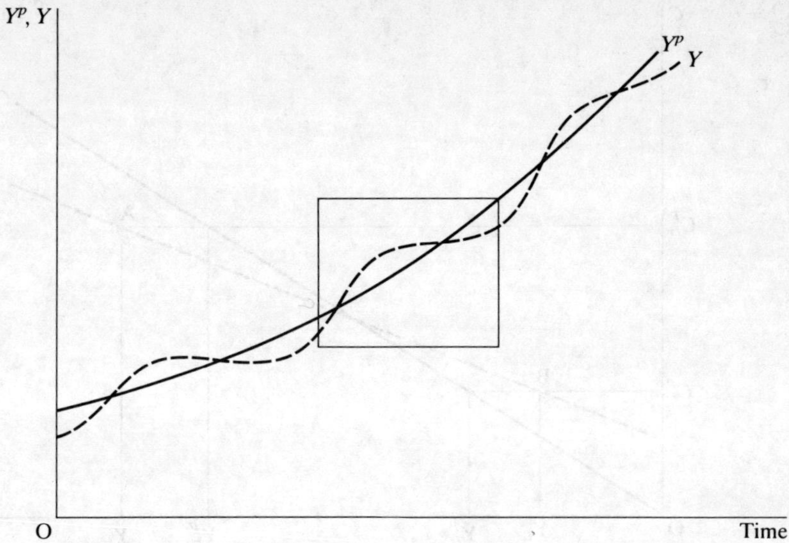

FIG. 3.7 Measured and permanent income in the long run

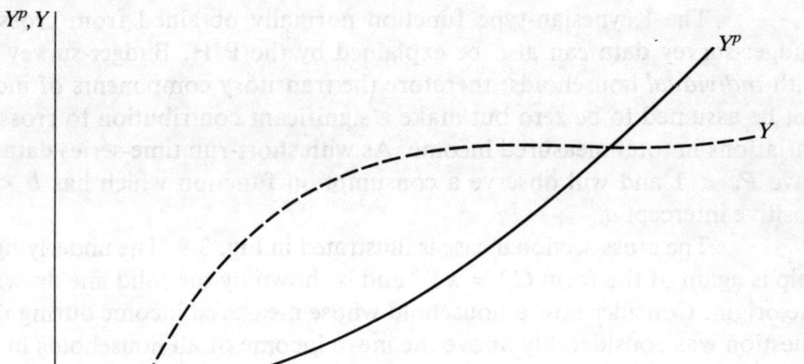

FIG. 3.8 Measured and permanent income in the short run

sitory variations are of much greater relative importance and, hence, P_y is now significantly less than unity. From such 'short-run' data we will therefore observe a consumption function with a shallower slope ($b < k$) than the long-run function and with an intercept ($a > 0$). The PIH (just like the RIH) is therefore able to explain why short-run data provide a Keynesian-type function but long-run data provide a consumption function with a constant APC.

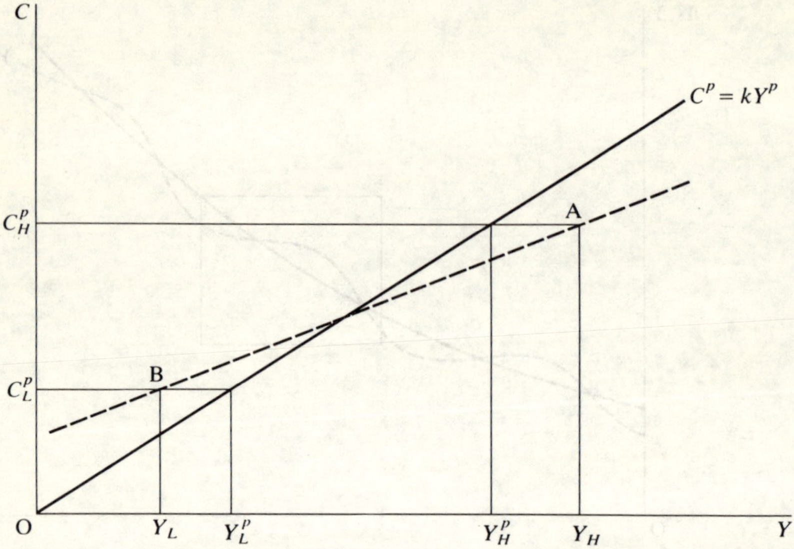

FIG. 3.9 The PIH interpretation of cross-sectional data

The Keynesian-type function normally obtained from cross-sectional budget-survey data can also be explained by the PIH. Budget-survey data deal with *individual* households; therefore the transitory components of income cannot be assumed to be zero but make a significant contribution to cross-sectional variations in total measured income. As with short-run time-series data, then, we have $P_y < 1$ and will observe a consumption function which has $b < k$ and a positive intercept a.

The cross-sectional case is illustrated in Fig. 3.9. The underlying relationship is again of the form $C^p = kY^p$ and is shown by the solid line drawn through the origin. Consider now a household whose measured income during the year in question was considerably above the mean income of all households in the cross-section. Suppose its income was Y_H. Households with high-measured incomes will *on average* have tended to be 'lucky' and will have relatively large positive transitory incomes—this being one of the reasons why they have large measured incomes in the first place. Permanent income, Y^p_H, for such households will therefore be less than measured income Y_H. Since permanent or planned consumption depends on permanent income, a household with permanent income Y^p_H will plan to consume C^p_H. Assuming that plans are on average carried out, such households will tend to provide us with points such as A in the cross-sectional scatter of points representing the measured incomes and consumptions of all households.

Consider now a household with measured income Y_L—considerably lower than the mean cross-sectional income. On average such households will have tended to be 'unlucky' and to have had negative transitory incomes, so that their permanent income, Y^p_L, will be larger than their measured income. Since the planned consumption of households with a permanent income of Y^p_L is C^p_L, such households will tend to provide us with points such as B in the cross-sectional scatter. It should now be clear that if, in the absence of any knowledge of the underlying relationship $C^p = kY^p$, we were to attempt to fit a line to the scatter of points on measured income and measured consumption, we would obtain a line similar to the broken line passing through A and B. That is, we would obtain a consumption function with an intercept and a slope which is shallower than that of the underlying relationship. Thus, despite the 'proportionality' of the basic $C^p = kY^p$ relationship, the PIH suggests that cross-sectional data will provide a function of typical Keynesian shape.

Friedman[7] also shows that a basic equation arising out of the RIH explanation of cross-sectional data can be derived under the PIH. One way of summarising Duesenberry's cross-sectional argument is to express the APC of a household as

$$\frac{C}{Y} = \alpha_0 + \alpha_1 \frac{\bar{Y}}{Y} \qquad \alpha_0 > 0 \quad \alpha_1 > 0 \qquad [1A]$$

where C and Y are household consumption and income and $\bar{Y}$ is the mean income of the household and its associates. Thus, as the income of households rises relative to mean income, i.e. as we move up the income distribution, the APC declines. The above equation can be regarded as the cross-sectional analogue of equation [1].

Under the PIH, we know from equations [21] and [22] that if a consumption function is estimated by ordinary least squares from cross-sectional data, then provided the mean transitory components of income and consumption are zero, the equation obtained can be written as

$$C = k(1 - P_y)\,\bar{Y} + kP_y\,Y$$

Dividing by Y, we then obtain

$$\frac{C}{Y} = kP_y + k(1 - P_y)\frac{\bar{Y}}{Y}$$

an equation identical in form to [1A] obtained under the RIH. Thus the PIH is able to explain a basic empirical relationship of the RIH, and moreover, unlike the RIH, it is also able to tell us something about what determines the size of estimated coefficients in such relationships. Since the PIH implies that in equation [1A] $\alpha_0 = kP_y$ and $\alpha_1 = k(1 - P_y)$, these coefficients clearly depend on the proportion of the total cross-sectional variation in income that is the result of variations in the transitory component. In effect Friedman's hypothesis not only predicts that the cross-sectional consumption function will have an intercept but, unlike the RIH, is also able to make some prediction about the size of this intercept and the slope of the function that will be obtained.

3. Testing the permanent income hypothesis

A major problem that arises when attempts are made to test the PIH, or to estimate equations concerning it, is that the key variables involved – particularly permanent income – are unobservable. Actual data, of course, refer to measured income and not permanent income. This means that, prior to any testing or estimating procedure, some proxy variable for permanent income or some method of estimating it must be found. Unfortunately this means that the validity of any results obtained will depend not only on the appropriateness or otherwise of the PIH, but also on the adequacy of the method used for approximating permanent income.

Friedman suggested, and versions of this method are now almost universally adopted, that for time series data permanent income for period t should be estimated by

$$Y_t^p = \beta Y_t + \beta(1-\beta)Y_{t-1} + \beta(1-\beta)^2 Y_{t-2} \ldots \qquad 0 < \beta < 1 \qquad [23]$$

Equation [23] stresses the 'expected' nature of permanent income, implying that Y^p depends on current and past measured income with consumers giving most weight to their current income and successively declining weight to past incomes. The weights in equation [23] sum to unity and the equation represents what is known as a distributed lag formulation with geometrically declining weights.[8]

Friedman's procedure was to use real per capita US data for 1905–51 to compute alternative time series for Y_t^p, using different values of β and truncating equation [23] after sixteen terms. Measured consumption was then regressed on each such series in turn and a set of estimated equations of the form $\hat{C}_t = a + bY_t^p$ obtained. Friedman found that the closest fit (i.e. highest R^2) was obtained for a value of $\beta = 0.33$. For this equation, the intercept, a, was not significantly different from zero so that the proportionality of the relationship between C^p and Y^p appeared to be confirmed. The estimate of k was $b = 0.88$ but of greater importance was the low value obtained for β. $\beta = 0.33$ suggested that only one third of the total weight used to assess permanent income is attached to current income and, moreover, that over 20 per cent of that weight is attached to income of four or more years ago. Such results, if correct, constituted strong evidence in favour of the permanent income hypothesis over the absolute income hypothesis since the latter implies that $\beta = 1$ and that there is no difference between Y^p and Y. The practical importance of this is that, since from the basic relationship $C^p = kY^p$ and equation [23] the MPC current income is $k\beta$, a low β implies a low MPC. This means low 'impact' values for the various Keynesian multipliers. For example, while the long-run effect on income of an exogenous change in non-consumption expenditure may be large, the time interval necessary for this change to come about will be lengthy and uncertain, and the short-run immediate effects will be much smaller. This has obvious implications for the efficacy of fiscal policy.

The evidence concerning the size of β is not, however, clearcut and has been disputed by other writers. For example, Zellner *et al.* (1965) and particularly, Zellner and Geisel (1970), using US quarterly data, obtain estimates of β which when converted into annual terms are much closer to unity. Furthermore, Wright

(1969), using virtually identical data to Friedman but merely treating wartime years slightly differently, obtains a value for β of 0.8.[9] Such values for β would suggest that the difference between measured and permanent income is nothing like as great as was maintained by Friedman, and that the use of measured income in the consumption function is a much less serious mis-specification that he originally suggested. In contrast, however, Darby (1974) argues that the high values for β obtained by many writers, and to a lesser extent the value obtained by Friedman, are biased upwards, because expenditure on durable goods is commonly included in the consumption variable used for estimating purposes. When allowance is made for this possible bias (by omitting, as far as possible, durable expenditure from the consumption variable or by including transitory income as well as permanent income as a variable in the estimating equation), Darby obtains a value for β as low as 0.1. There is still, then, room for considerable disagreement about the precise size of this coefficient.

It is possible to reformulate Friedman's suggestion for the estimation of permanent income as follows. If equation [23] is multiplied by $1 - \beta$ and lagged one period we obtain

$$(1 - \beta)Y^p_{t-1} = \beta(1 - \beta)Y_{t-1} + \beta(1 - \beta)^2 Y_{t-2} + \beta(1 - \beta)^3 Y_{t-3} \ldots$$

Subtracting this equation from equation [23] eventually yields

$$Y^p_t - Y^p_{t-1} = \beta(Y_t - Y^p_{t-1}) \qquad 0 < \beta < 1 \qquad [24]$$

Equation [24] is an example of what is normally referred to as an *adaptive expectations hypothesis*. From this equation it can be seen that, if current measured income, Y_t, exceeds permanent income in the previous period Y^p_{t-1}, then the estimate of permanent income is adjusted upwards and current permanent income Y^p_t exceeds its previous value. The extent of the upward adjustment depends on the magnitude of β, which is called the 'adjustment coefficient'. The larger is β the greater is the adjustment. At one extreme $\beta = 1$ and adjustment is complete, there being no difference between measured and permanent income; while at the other extreme, $\beta = 0$, no adjustment takes place at all and permanent income remains unchanged regardless of the size of measured income.

It is possible to simplify Friedman's somewhat cumbersome procedure for estimating the consumption function by making use of the so called *Koyck Transformation*. Substituting equation [23] into the basic relationship $C^p_t = kY^p_t$ yields

$$C^p_t = k[\beta Y_t + \beta(1 - \beta)Y_{t-1} + \beta(1 - \beta)^2 Y_{t-2} + \ldots]$$

Lagging this equation by one period and multiplying by $1 - \beta$ yields

$$(1 - \beta)C^p_{t-1} = k[\beta(1 - \beta)Y_{t-1} + \beta(1 - \beta)^2 Y_{t-2} \ldots]$$

Subtracting the second of the above equations from the first eventually leads to

$$C^p_t = k\beta Y_t + (1 - \beta)C^p_{t-1} \qquad [25]$$

an equation no longer involving the unobservable permanent income variable but still containing current and lagged permanent consumption. Finally, by making use of the fact that $C_t^p = C_t - C_t^t$, equation [25] can be rewritten as

$$C_t = k\beta Y_t + (1 - \beta)C_{t-1} + [C_t^t - (1 - \beta)C_{t-1}^t] \qquad [26]$$

Equation [26] can be regarded as an equation expressing current measured consumption as a function of current measured income, lagged measured consumption and an unknown disturbance term, $C_t^t - (1 - \beta)C_{t-1}^t$. Although there are econometric problems involved in the estimation of equation [26] – for example, the disturbance term is correlated with C_{t-1} and if a random disturbance is added to the basic relationship the composite disturbance term in equation [26] is likely to be autocorrelated – the regression of C_t on Y_t and C_{t-1} is a less cumbersome procedure than that originally proposed by Friedman. Estimates of k and β can be obtained from the estimated coefficients on Y_t and C_{t-1},[10] though estimating procedures other than the normal ordinary least squares are necessary because the econometric problems mentioned above lead to bias in the least squares estimators even for large samples. There is, however, a more fundamental problem concerning both Friedman's method and equation [26]. Apart from the unknown disturbance, equation [26] has exactly the same form as equation [5] which was obtained from the habit persistence version of the RIH, i.e. both give C_t as depending on Y_t and C_{t-1}. Moreover, consider a model in which optimal or 'desired' consumption C_t^* depends on current *measured* income, i.e.

$$C_t^* = kY_t \qquad [27]$$

and suppose that actual consumption only partly adjusts to changes in optimal consumption, i.e.

$$C_t - C_{t-1} = \beta(C_t^* - C_{t-1}) \qquad 0 < \beta < 1 \qquad [28]$$

Equations [27] and [28] represent what is commonly called a *partial adjustment hypothesis*. When optimal current consumption, C_t^*, exceeds the actual level of consumption in the previous period, C_{t-1}, current consumption is increased beyond its previous level. However, because of 'habit persistence' the increase in actual consumption is less than the full difference between C_t^* and C_{t-1}. The size of β, again known as an adjustment coefficient, determines the extent to which actual consumption is pushed towards the optimal level. For the extreme $\beta = 1$, adjustment is complete, for the extreme $\beta = 0$, no adjustment takes place at all; in general, the larger is β the greater is the adjustment and presumably the importance of habit persistence. Substituting equation [27] into equation [28] yields

$$C_t = k\beta Y_t + (1 - \beta)C_{t-1} \qquad [29]$$

Except that there are now no problems of least squares bias, equation [29] is identical to equation [26] even as far as the coefficients on the Y_t and C_{t-1} variables are concerned.[11] Yet the interpretation we place on k and the adjustment coefficient β depends crucially on which underlying hypothesis is valid, the PIH or the habit persistence version of the RIH.

The above highlights a major problem with the estimation and testing of consumption functions. The major hypotheses concerning consumer behaviour tend to be formulated in terms of 'unobservable' variables such as 'permanent income', 'desired consumption', etc. Thus, before a consumption function arising out of any of the hypotheses can be estimated or any type of statistical test performed, it is necessary to deduce the implications of the hypothesis for 'observable' variables. Unfortunately these implications tend to be the same whatever the nature of the underlying hypothesis, and this makes it difficult to discriminate between the competing hypotheses using available data. This is particularly true of time-series data where, as illustrated above, entirely different hypotheses often give rise to identical estimating equations. It is less true of cross-sectional data to which we now turn.

Friedman's 1957 book is remarkable for the rigorous way in which the underlying PIH is first developed and then used to generate further testable predictions which may be checked against, usually, cross-sectional data. Unfortunately many of these predictions could also be derived from, for example, the RIH. Moreover, many of Friedman's results could also arise from a less 'extreme' version of the PIH in which C^p depends on Y^p but not necessarily in a proportionate manner, and in which the correlation between transitory income and transitory consumption is merely 'low' rather than zero. As Mayer (1972), particularly, has pointed out, the majority of Friedman's tests are not concerned with the more 'extreme' aspects of his hypothesis, namely the zero correlation between transitory variables and the proportionality postulate.

We describe here two of Friedman's tests which seem to provide support for his hypothesis but not for the RIH.[12] The tests involve both the cross-sectionally estimated MPC, $b = kP_y$ (see equation [21], and the cross-sectionally estimated income elasticity of consumption, measured at the point of sample means, i.e. $E = (\mathrm{d}\hat{C}/\mathrm{d}Y)\,(\bar{Y}/\bar{C}) = b\bar{Y}/\bar{C}$. Notice that, provided the mean transitory components are zero, the estimated income elasticity of consumption is exactly equal to the proportion of the variation in measured income which is the result of variations in permanent income. That is, if $\bar{Y} = \bar{Y}^p$ and $\bar{C} = \bar{C}^p$ then, since $\bar{C}^p = k\bar{Y}^p$ and $b = kP_y$, we have $\bar{C} = k\bar{Y}$ and hence,

$$E = b\left(\frac{\bar{Y}}{\bar{C}}\right) = kP_y\left(\frac{1}{k}\right) = P_y$$

Friedman compares cross-sections of households in which variations in transitory income are likely to be important (i.e. P_y is small) with cross-sections in which transitory variations make little contribution to total variation in income (i.e. P_y is near unity). The PIH predicts that both b and E should be smaller for the first type of cross-section.

Table 3.1 refers to cross-sections of urban and non-farm families, three taken during 'settled' peacetime years and the fourth taken during 1944, an 'unsettled' wartime year when variations in transitory income were presumably most important. As expected, the wartime MPC is considerably lower than the peacetime b's. However, since $b = kP_y$, the lower MPC could have been the result not of a lower P_y but of a lower k = APC, caused by high precautionary savings or maybe supply constraints during the unsettled wartime year. Such a possibility

TABLE 3.1

	1941	1944	1947	1950
Average propensity to consume	**0.92**	**0.82**	**0.92**	**0.91**
Marginal propensity to consume	**0.79**	**0.57**	**0.78**	**0.73**
Income elasticity of consumption	**0.87**	**0.70**	**0.85**	**0.80**

Source: Friedman (1957: 44–5)

could arise whether the PIH was valid or not. In fact, as Table 3.1 shows, the APC was lower in 1944. However, what is impressive is that the income elasticity of consumption, which is independent of the APC, is also definitely lower during 1944. Such a result is exactly as predicted by the PIH but is hard to explain on the basis of the RIH.

Table 3.2 compares a cross-section of 'farm families', the unpredictability of whose occupation suggests a low P_y, with a cross-section of 'non-farm families' who enjoy a more stable occupation. The first figures in the table refer to a 1935–36 cross-section and the second to a 1941 cross-section. Again the results are as predicted by the PIH. The *b*'s and, more significantly, the *E*'s are clearly lower for the farm families.

TABLE 3.2

	Farm		Non-farm	
	1935–36	1941	1935–36	1941
Average propensity to consume	**0.87**	**0.83**	**0.89**	**0.92**
Marginal propensity to consume	**0.57**	**0.57**	**0.73**	**0.79**
Income elasticity of consumption	**0.65**	**0.69**	**0.82**	**0.87**

Source: Friedman (1957: 62)

Another test carried out by Friedman involves the extent of the 'year on year' change in income of a cross-section of consumers.[13] Farm families are classified into those that moved up 4, 3, 2, 1 and 0 'income classes' between 1940 and 1942, an income class being defined as a fixed \$1,000 range of real income. No families actually dropped down such an income class during these years. The point about the classification is that it is effectively a classification by size of transitory income rather than by permanent income. Families with high permanent incomes can be found in any of the five classifications, whereas families with high transitory incomes in 1942 are likely to be found only among those classified as having moved up a large number of income classes. Hence families within each of the five classifications will tend to have similar Y^t's so the Var Y^t (i.e. the variance of Y^t) for each classification should be less than Var Y^t for the full cross-section. However, there is no reason why Var Y^p should be any larger for each classification than for the cross-section as a whole, so that P_y = Var Y^p/(Var Y^t + Var Y^p) can be expected to be larger for the individual classifications. Since the estimated

MPC, b, is equal to kP_y, and there is no reason why k should vary over the classifications, it follows that the b's for each classification should be larger than the overall b. When Friedman, using the 1942 data, regressed measured consumption on measured income for each classification he obtained b's in the range 0.23 to 0.29. Yet when the whole cross-section was used b was as low as 0.15. Again this is as predicted by the PIH and again it is difficult to explain such results on the basis of the RIH.

THE INFLUENCE OF 'WINDFALL GAINS' AND TRANSITORY INCOME

Friedman, in his 1957 book, suggests a series of additional tests of his own hypothesis, one of which involves an attempt to test directly the assumption of a zero correlation between transitory consumption and transitory income. Such tests concentrate on the influence on consumption of 'windfall gains'. We may describe a 'windfall' gain as a payment to a consumer that was completely unexpected, which is not expected to recur and, moreover, does not recur.

A crucial point concerning such windfall gains should be made clear. The consumer who receives a windfall of one dollar *will* normally increase his consumption. There will be no increase in *transitory* consumption but, since the extra dollar is added to the consumer's stock of wealth, there will be an increase in permanent income which is the rate of return on this wealth. Therefore, since $C^p = kY^p$ there will be an increase in permanent consumption equal to k dollars times the rate of return. Only in the exceptional case where the dollar increment in transitory income, today, happens to be matched by the expectation of a reduction in future income, which is such as to leave permanent income unchanged, will the consumer's expenditure remain unchanged. This possibility is effectively ruled out by the description of a windfall gain given above. It follows, then, that the MPC windfalls, while less than the MPC permanent income, is not zero but is equal to kr where r is the rate of return.

The β coefficient obtained from his time-series analysis is regarded by Friedman as an estimate of the rate of return on total wealth. To understand this, consider equation [23]. A dollar increase in current transitory income, Y_t^t, will increase current measured income, Y_t, by the same amount. Hence current permanent income, Y_t^p, will rise by β dollars. But since the extra dollar is initially 'saved' it is added to total wealth, so the increase in permanent income must also equal r dollars. Hence $r = \beta$. Friedman's estimate of β and hence of r was 0.33. It follows that if the MPC permanent income is $k = 0.9$, the MPC windfalls should be $kr = 0.3$.

Thirty-three per cent may seem an inordinately high rate of return, but it must be remembered that this is meant to be the return on a consumer's total wealth including his human assets such as his future earning power. There is no free market in human assets (except in a slave society), so that a consumer's estimate of r cannot be based on existing markets but must be essentially subjective. Friedman has argued that 33 per cent is not an exceptionally high value for such a subjective rate of return and moreover, as noted above, Darby (1974) has provided evidence from US data that the value of β may be as low as 0.1.

An early study of the influence of windfall gains was undertaken by Bodkin (1959), who considered the effect on a group of US 'war veterans' of the receipt of a totally unexpected National Life Insurance Dividend in 1950. Bodkin regressed the non-durable consumption expenditure of such veterans on both their regular income, Y, and the size of the windfall, d, with the following result.

$$\underset{(56.6)}{C = 959.3} + \underset{(0.01)}{0.56Y} + \underset{(0.11)}{0.72d} \qquad R^2 = 0.60$$

Thus the MPC windfalls appeared to be not only greater than that suggested by Friedman but greater even than the MPC regular income – a result that apparently contradicted the PIH. Friedman, however, pointed out that the size of the windfall depended on the length of time the insurance policy involved had been in force, and hence probably on the age of the veteran concerned. Since permanent income also tends to depend on age, the windfall might in fact be acting as a proxy variable for permanent income and this could account for the apparently high MPC windfalls.

In response to Friedman's criticism, Bird and Bodkin (1965) re-examined the problem, including in the above equation extra variables to represent permanent income. Their final results were inconclusive and could be interpreted in terms of either the AIH or the PIH.

A windfalls study that appears to be more in accord with the PIH was that of Kreinin (1961). Kreinin considered German war reparations paid to Israeli consumers during 1957–58 and found that while the marginal propensity to consume these windfalls was low and statistically insignificantly different from zero, the marginal propensity to consume regular income was much higher, being equal to between 0.8 and 0.9. However, even the PIH does not imply that the MPC windfalls should be zero, so that even this study is not in complete agreement with the hypothesis.

Further evidence on the relationship between consumption and windfalls is provided by various US tax experiments carried out in the late 1960s and 1970s. For example, in 1968, during a period of rapid demand-induced inflation, the US Congress imposed a temporary income tax surcharge in an attempt to reduce consumer spending, while in 1975, during the trough of the worst post-war US depression, all consumers received an unexpected tax rebate aimed at stimulating their spending. Since *temporary* tax changes should not have any marked effect on permanent disposable income, it could be argued that on strict theoretical grounds they should have little influence on aggregate consumption. Two points must however be noted. First, since consumers' expenditure includes spending on durable goods (classified as saving under the PIH), it is possible for temporary tax changes to have a significant effect on total spending, via expenditure on durables, even if consumers behave in a manner consistent with the PIH as far as non-durable goods are concerned. Second, even under the normal income hypotheses temporary income gains are *eventually* spent – it is only current consumption which is held to be little influenced by a windfall. Therefore, in considering temporary tax changes, it is necessary to specify the time horizon over which their effect on spending is to be assessed.

Okun (1971), in examining the 1968 surcharge, opened the debate by considering two hypotheses – a 'full effect' hypothesis, in which income is defined as actual disposable income excluding the surcharge, and a 'zero effect' hypothesis in which consumers behave as if the surcharge had not been imposed and was still a part of disposable income. The normal income theories suggest that a 'zero effect' hypothesis should be a closer approximation to reality, provided the horizon considered is sufficiently short. Okun concluded, for both durable goods and even for non-durables, that the surcharge had been successful in curbing expenditure. Springer (1975), however, adopting a similar approach to Okun but using more appropriate estimation and prediction procedures, reached the opposite conclusion: expenditure on both durables and non-durables appeared to be closer to that predicted by the 'zero effect' view.[14]

In considering the 1975 tax rebate, Modigliani and Steindel (1977) found, not surprisingly given the normal income hypothesis, that the apparent effectiveness of the rebate was very much dependent on the time horizon considered. Using a modified version of the LCH, they found that the rebate had very little effect on spending during the first one or two quarters, but that the 'full effect' hypothesis seemed most appropriate when the horizon was extended to six quarters.

Blinder (1981) seeks to quantify the effects of temporary surcharges and rebates. He uses a distributed lag version of the PIH, which distinguishes between temporary tax changes and other income changes on the grounds that the former are known to be of limited duration, and works in terms of total consumer expenditure rather than consumption as theoretically defined, since he is more interested in stabilisation policy than in actually testing the PIH. Blinder concludes that over a one-year horizon a temporary tax increase has little over 50 per cent of the impact of a permanent change of equal magnitude, and that a rebate has only 38 per cent as much impact. Since these effects include changes in spending on durable goods, such figures suggest that temporary tax changes can have little immediate effect on consumption as theoretically defined.

Attempts to assess the influence of transitory income proper on consumption can be made using time-series data. Given any method, similar to Friedman's, for estimating permanent income from such data, it is always possible to derive a series for transitory income by subtracting the permanent income series obtained from the original measured income series. This suggests regressing consumption expenditure not only on permanent income but also on the transitory income variable, estimating an equation of the form

$$C_t = a + bY_t^p + cY_t^t$$

and testing to see whether the coefficient c on the transitory income variable is significantly different from zero, or at least less than that on the permanent income variable.

Darby (1972, 1974) has estimated such equations for post-war US data, using three different definitions of consumption expenditure – expenditure on non-durables, expenditure on non-durables plus clothing and shoes, and expenditure on non-durables, clothing and shoes, and consumer durables. There are two main points of interest in the results. First, as predicted by the PIH, the estimated coefficient of Y_t^t is invariably smaller than that on Y_t^p. Second, the less inclusive the definition of consumption expenditure used, the smaller the size of the coefficient on Y_t^t. For non-durable expenditure only, this coefficient is about one fifth of the size of the Y_t^p coefficient. This is again as expected under the PIH since, because spending on durables is more correctly classified as saving, its exclusion from C_t should reduce the responsiveness of C_t to changes in transitory income.

4. Uncertainty and the wealth hypothesis

In the above descriptions of the various hypotheses of consumer behaviour very little has so far been said about the fact that the typical household inhabits a world in which there is considerable uncertainty about the future. In the life-cycle hypothesis, for example, households in reality cannot know with any degree of certainty the profile of their future lifetime income stream or even predict with any degree of accuracy the date of their 'death'. Under such conditions the process of inter-temporal utility maximisation attributed to the consumer under the normal income hypotheses becomes rather less convincing.[15] The existence of uncertainty also has obvious implications for the workings of the capital market. When a household expects with certainty a steadily rising stream of income receipts then, in a perfect capital market, it can without difficulty arrange to be a net borrower during its early years, repaying the debts incurred out of its higher future income levels. However, when survival is no longer certain and future income levels are unpredictable, the risk of default makes the raising of such loans a far less easy proposition and hence may make the process of 'consumption spreading', as implied by the normal income hypothesis, considerably more difficult. It is true that, in Friedman's version of the hypothesis, some recognition of the existence of uncertainty is made by the introduction of an extra precautionary motive for saving as a buffer for unforeseen contingencies; and capital market imperfections are theoretically allowed for by the inclusion of the ratio of non-human wealth to permanent income as an additional variable determining the APC. However, in empirical versions of the hypothesis this variable usually drops out of the analysis, variation in it either being assumed not to occur over time or being assumed to be counterbalanced by other factors influencing the APC.

A hypothesis which raises to central importance the question of uncertainty has been independently presented by Spiro (1962) and Ball and Drake (1964), and further developed by Clower and Johnson (1968). The central idea behind this 'wealth hypothesis' is that consumers are short-sighted in the face of uncertainty and that 'the principal motive for accumulating assets is not related to some lifetime plan of consumption in any very precise sense but is more satisfactorily thought of in terms of a broad precautionary motive' (Ball and Drake 1964: 65). The consumer, however, is not assumed to be short-sighted to the extent of totally ignoring the future. He safeguards against future uncertainty by accumulating assets, and the more assets he accumulates the 'less worried' about the future the consumer becomes. The future is therefore allowed for in the model without imposing on the consumer the rigorous intertemporal utility maximisation required by the normal income hypotheses.

Formally this idea is presented by assuming that the consumer maximises utility over a relatively short interval and by including, as arguments in his utility function, consumption during this interval, C_t, and non-human wealth at the end of the interval, W_t. Utility is assumed to be an increasing function of both these arguments,[16]

$$U_t = U(C_t, W_t) \qquad [30]$$

The utility function is maximised subject to the budget constraint,

$$W_{t-1} + Y_t = C_t + W_t \qquad [31]$$

where W_{t-1} is the level of non-human wealth at the beginning of the interval and Y_t is the consumer's income during it. These quantities are assumed given during the maximisation process. If the utility function is assumed to be homogeneous in both C_t and W_t then the optimal relationship between C_t and W_t is one of proportionality, i.e. $W_t = hC_t$, where h depends on consumer preferences. Substituting for W_t in the budget constraint then yields a consumption function

$$C_t = \left(\frac{1}{1+h}\right)Y_t + \left(\frac{1}{1+h}\right)W_{t-1} \qquad [32]$$

or, provided the optimal relationship holds for interval $t - 1$,

$$C_t = \left(\frac{1}{1+h}\right)Y_t + \left(\frac{h}{1+h}\right)C_{t-1} \qquad [33]$$

Thus, as with the PIH and the habit persistence version of the RIH, we end up with a formulation which relates consumption to income and to consumption in the previous period. However, under the wealth hypothesis a further prediction is obtained: the coefficients in equation [33] should apparently sum to unity if the hypothesis is valid.

Just like the hypotheses discussed previously, the wealth hypothesis has implications that make it possible to reconcile the conflicting evidence from short- and long-run time-series and cross-sectional data. Suppose that a consumer's income were to grow at a constant rate g so that $Y_t = (1 + g)Y_{t-1}$. We can then rewrite equation [33] as

$$\frac{C_t}{Y_t} = \frac{1}{1+h} + \left(\frac{h}{1+h}\right)\frac{C_{t-1}}{Y_t} = \frac{1}{1+h}\left[\frac{h}{(1+h)(1+g)}\right]\frac{C_{t-1}}{Y_{t-1}} \qquad [34]$$

The 'equilibrium' average propensity to consume, $\overline{\text{APC}}$, can now be obtained by setting $C_t/Y_t = C_{t-1}/Y_{t-1} = \overline{\text{APC}}$ in equation [34]. This yields

$$\overline{\text{APC}} = \frac{1}{1 + h - [h/1+g]} \qquad [35]$$

Equation [35] indicates that the higher the growth rate g, the lower is the equilibrium APC and hence the higher is the equilibrium average propensity to save. With a zero growth rate, i.e. a constant income, saving will eventually fall to zero as the consumer gradually acquires a stock of wealth sufficiently large relative to his income to eliminate the incentive for any further saving.

Equation [35] clearly provides us with another reason why, at the aggregate level, high growth rates tend to be associated with high saving–income ratios. Moreover, the constancy of the APC for long-run time-series data can be attributed to the stability of long-run growth rates in income, while short-term variations in the APC can be explained by cyclical fluctuations in this long-run trend. Finally, the wealth hypothesis is able to explain the typical results obtained from cross-sectional data. Since high-income households tend to be those who in the past have experienced high rates of growth in income, they tend to have low average propensities to consume. Low-income households, however, will tend to have suffered from low rates of income growth and hence will have higher APC's.

Since it was first presented the wealth hypothesis has come under considerable assault both empirically and from a theoretical point of view. Considering the empirical criticism first, one point made especially by Mayer (1972), is that the sum of the coefficients in estimated versions of equation [33] is typically less than the unity predicted by the wealth hypothesis. Using cross-sectional data for both German and Swiss households, Mayer found the sum of the relevant coefficients to be consistently less than unity and similar findings have generally been reported from time-series studies.

A second empirical criticism, advanced particularly by Evans (1967), is that equilibrium APC's obtained by substituting the estimated value of h and the actual long-run growth rate into equation [35] are generally different from the actual APC's holding over the sample period used to estimate h. Hence the wealth hypothesis is held to be inconsistent with available data. However, there appears to be some confusion here over the meaning of the terms 'long run' and 'equilibrium' average propensities to consume. Equation [35] yields the 'equilibrium' APC which would eventually obtain had an economy been growing for some considerable time at a constant rate g. No matter how long the sample period used to estimate a consumption function, it does not follow that such an 'equilibrium' will ever have been reached, so that there is no real reason why the actual average APC obtained from the sample data should square exactly with that yielded by equation [35].

A further and more serious line of attack, also employed by Evans, is to use actual data on wealth and consumption to obtain alternative estimates of h, the optimal ratio between the two. Alternative estimates of the coefficients of Y_t and C_{t-1} in equation [33] can then be obtained and compared with regression estimates obtained in the usual way. For example, US post-war data suggested a value for h of 5.7, which implies that the coefficient on Y_t should be about 0.15. Evans estimated a series of consumption functions with different specifications and invariably found the coefficient on Y_t to be considerably larger than this. Indeed, Ball and Drake in their original work also experienced some difficulty in reconciling their regression estimates with observed wealth–consumption ratios.

Before considering the merits of these empirical criticisms it is necessary to examine some of the conceptual difficulties implicit in the wealth hypothesis as so far presented. First, the model makes no distinction between planned or expected values for variables and actual values for those variables. Since the model was specifically formulated to cope with a world of uncertainty in which plans and expectations are rarely likely to be exactly realised, this seems to be a serious omission. Equation [30] could more appropriately be regarded as defining expected rather than actual utility, and the variables C_t and W_t interpreted as planned consumption and planned end-interval wealth. The optimal relationship $W_t = hC_t$ would then refer to planned but not normally to actual values of these variables. Second, no allowance has yet been made for possible capital gains made during the planning interval on the initial stock of wealth W_{t-1}. If we are dealing with planned or expected magnitudes then the budget constraint (equation [31]) should be formulated as

$$W_{t-1} + Y_t + G_t = C_t + W_t \qquad [36]$$

where G_t represents expected capital gains and Y_t is now expected income during the planning interval. Now, even if G_t is in fact zero, then for the optimal relationship to hold for actual, as well as planned, magnitudes and for the consumption function (equation [33]) to be valid, it is necessary for all consumer plans and expectations to be realised (in particular *actual* capital gains must also be zero). Only then will actual consumption and actual end-interval wealth coincide with their planned values, and hence only then can the substitution $W_{t-1} = hC_{t-1}$ be made in equation [32] to obtain equation [33]. The assumption that all consumer plans and expectations are realised is a big one, and clearly appears to be at variance with the very rationale of the wealth hypothesis, i.e. that consumers operate under conditions of uncertainty.

These problems do not represent a fundamental critique of the wealth hypothesis. The idea of including only current consumption and wealth in the utility function remains attractive and the model could be reformulated to deal with the above conceptual difficulties. Moreover, since the empirical criticisms discussed previously were all based on properties of equation [33], which is likely to be invalid anyway and would have to be dropped from a reformulated wealth hypothesis, it can be seen that these criticisms do not really constitute evidence against the basic underlying hypothesis.

As we have already indicated, a reformulation of the wealth hypothesis must involve the reinterpretation of equation [30] as defining expected rather than actual utility and its maximisation subject to a budget constraint such as equation [36]. This leads to

$$C_t = \left(\frac{1}{1+h}\right)(Y_t + G_t) + \left(\frac{1}{1+h}\right) W_{t-1} \qquad [32A]$$

where, apart from W_{t-1}, all variables are now in planned or expected terms. However, since the substitution $W_{t-1} = hC_{t-1}$ can normally no longer be made, estimation based on equation [32A] rather than on equation [35] requires data on consumer net wealth.

Ball and Drake's use, for estimation purposes, of equation [33] rather than equation [32] was dictated by the fact that, at least for the UK at that time, there existed no reliable time-series data on consumer net wealth. Investigators interested in the influence of non-human wealth on consumption expenditure have in the past generally been forced to rely either on the liquid assets component of total wealth (on which data is available) or to construct wealth series for themselves using data on past savings. Most such studies have tended to conclude that wealth variables do have some influence on consumption. For example, Townend (1976) using quarterly post-war UK data found that the inclusion of a liquid assets variable improved the performance of his equation for non-durable consumption expenditure. Stone in a series of papers (e.g. 1964 and 1974) constructs his own total wealth series for the post-war UK, using a relationship of the form

$$W_t = W_0 + \sum_{i=1}^{t} (Y_i - C_i) \qquad [37]$$

where W_0 represents total consumer wealth in some 'bench-mark' year when this magnitude happens to be known. Although such a series does not reflect the influence of 'revaluations' or capital gains, Stone invariably found variables such as W_t in equation [37] to be important determinants of aggregate consumer expenditure. W_t is in fact interpreted as 'permanent wealth' and Stone concludes that consumption depends on both permanent *and* transitory income, but only on *permanent* wealth. Such a conclusion implies an equilibrium wealth–income ratio which declines as the rate of growth in real income, g, rises and, as does the Ball–Drake model, an equilibrium saving–income ratio which increases as g rises. The existence of this equilibrium wealth–income ratio enables Stone to interpret his model as one in which consumers have 'a notion of a desirable relationship between their income and their wealth which they are constantly trying to realise' (Stone 1964: 81). The motive for saving in his model is the achieving of this desirable relationship.

As noted earlier, non-human wealth plays an important role in the consumption function derived from the life-cycle hypothesis, and in this guise it has been successfully included, notably by Ando and Modigliani (1963), in time-series estimating equations designed to test the LCH using US data. Another well known time-series study involving US data is that of Zellner, Huang and Chau (1965), who consider the influence of wealth by estimating a consumption function of the form

$$C_t = KY_t^p + \alpha(L_{t-1} - L_t^d) \qquad \alpha > 0 \qquad [38]$$

where L_{t-1} is the actual level of wealth at the beginning of the current period and L_t^d is the desired level (assumed proportional to permanent income Y_t^p) during the current period. Thus an 'asset adjustment' process is added to the permanent income model, whereby consumption is either curtailed or expanded depending on whether the desired asset stock exceeds or falls short of the actual stock held by consumers. While in principle L_{t-1} and L_t^d are supposed to refer to total consumer wealth, liquid asset variables are in fact used for estimation purposes, this being justified by the claim that such assets represent the most 'strategic' form of wealth. The authors find the value of α to be about 0.7 and clearly significantly different from zero, a result which supports the hypothesis that an imbalance in non-human wealth holdings affects consumption expenditure. Clearly one need only add the assumption that consumers desire wealth mainly for precautionary motives to be able to interpret these findings as rough evidence in favour of some version of the wealth hypothesis described above.

Recent improvements in the reliability of available data, particularly for the UK, on total consumer wealth mean that it is no longer necessary to construct data series in the Stone manner or to rely solely on the liquid asset component of wealth.[17] Neither is it any longer necessary, when attempting to test the Ball–Drake wealth hypothesis, to rely on the estimation of equation [33]. Attention can now be paid directly to equations such as [32] and [32A]. However, problems arise in the estimation of these equations which are not immediately obvious. If the wealth hypothesis is accepted as a reasonable description of consumer behaviour, then the lag on the wealth variable in equations [32] and [32A] must be regarded as being equal to the length of the 'planning interval' over which the consumer seeks to maximise utility. Just because data is annual, for example, does not mean that the length of the lag should be set equal to exactly one year, so that the estimation of equations [32] and [32A] is not such a simple matter as it might initially seem. Furthermore, there is no reason to suppose that once a consumer has formulated one plan over a given planning period, he should wait until the end of that planning period before formulating a new plan. The wealth hypothesis was designed to apply to an uncertain world in which plans and expectations are almost never realised, and the non-realisation of expectations may lead to a very rapid revision of consumer plans. Thoms (1981) attempts to deal with such problems, developing a model based on equation [32A] which distinguishes between three separate intervals—an 'observation interval' depending on the frequency of the data, a 'planning interval' as described above, and a 'review interval' representing the time between the successive revision of plans.

Similar comments of course apply to equation [33], and in particular to the lag on the consumption variable on the right-hand side of that equation. Yet whenever equation [33] has been estimated as a 'test' of the wealth hypothesis, this lag is invariably set equal to one year for annual data and one quarter for quarterly data. This, then, is a further reason to treat the 'failure' of the wealth hypothesis to pass such tests with scepticism.

THE ROLE OF CAPITAL GAINS

The idea that changes in consumer wealth are, for whatever reason, an important determinant of changes in consumption suggests that we should consider those factors which give rise to changes in wealth. The stock of consumers' assets changes either because of saving decisions or because of market revaluations of assets already in the stock, i.e. capital gains. We have referred to capital gains at a number of points in the present section but have yet to consider the precise ways in which they might influence a consumer's behaviour. Capital gains are an 'accrual' and in this respect are akin to income. It is therefore conceivable that they have a direct effect on consumption similar to that of income, as well as an indirect effect via changes in the level of wealth. If this is the case it may be that the measured income concept appearing in consumption functions would be more appropriately defined if it included at least some component of capital gains. Indeed Darby (1974), in the work mentioned earlier, experimented with alternative measures of income and concluded that adding undistributed corporate profits (as a proxy for net capital gains) to disposable personal income led to improved explanations of post-war US consumer behaviour.

Bhatia (1972), in one of the earliest attempts to consider explicitly the role of capital gains, used annual US data for 1948–64 to test both for a direct 'income type' effect and an indirect effect via wealth. In the income approach capital gains variables invariably proved insignificant, but Bhatia maintained that regression results using the wealth approach suggested capital gains do affect consumption via wealth.

Feldstein and Fane (1973), using annual UK data for 1948–69, provide evidence of a direct effect for capital gains over and above any effect via wealth. Capital gains which result from companies retaining part of their profits are found to have a much greater effect on consumption than gains arising simply from market revaluations. This is to be expected if consumers regard the retaining of earnings by companies in which they have shares as providing a more permanent type of capital gain than those arising out of revaluations.

Feldstein (1973) found the retained earnings component of capital gains to have a similar effect for US data from 1929–66. However, Bhatia (1979) maintains that these findings are the result of the method used by Feldstein to calculate capital gains. Feldstein subtracts personal saving from changes in household wealth–an unreliable method because of deficiencies in data on net wealth and saving. Using alternative estimates of capital gains based on changes in asset-price indices, Bhatia finds no evidence for a direct capital gains effect and again claims detection of a significant indirect effect via wealth. The precise role of capital gains and the most appropriate definition of income therefore remains unclear.[18]

5. Recent studies of the consumption function

During the 1970s considerable attention was given to the possibility that consumers in general may be subject to some form of what is commonly referred to as 'money illusion'. We have implicitly assumed up to this point that, in considering consumer behaviour, both the level and rate of change of prices could be ignored; for example, we have frequently referred to variables such as 'income' or 'wealth' when in fact we mean *real* income or *real* wealth, i.e. income and wealth measured in constant prices. In justification of this attitude, consider the addition of a price variable to a typical LCH estimating equation

$$C_t = \alpha_1 + \alpha_2 Y_t + \alpha_3 W_t + \alpha_4 P_t \quad [39]$$

where C_t, Y_t and W_t are real consumption, real income and real wealth respectively (in per-capita terms if we are estimating an aggregate relationship), and P_t is the index of consumer prices that has been used to deflate each of the other variables. A priori considerations suggest that α_4, the coefficient of P_t in equation [39], should be zero. Any change in the price level, occurring while real income and real wealth remain constant, must imply an equiproportionate change in money income and in money wealth. Economic theory tells us that under these conditions there should be no change in real consumption expenditure–hence α_4 should be zero. A non-zero α_4 implies that consumers are suffering from money illusion. For example, a positive α_4 would mean that a rise in P_t, with Y_t and W_t constant, leads to a rise in real consumption. This would imply that consumers were treating the equiproportionate rises in money income and wealth as if they were rises in the real values of these variables, i.e. they were not noticing the rise in the price level. Similarly, a negative α_4 could be interpreted as meaning that consumers notice the rise in prices but do not notice the equiproportionate rises in money income and money wealth, i.e. they believe that real income and real wealth have fallen and hence reduce their consumption expenditure.

Branson and Klevorick (1969), using US data for 1955–65, estimated a consumption function similar to equation [39] and found that their equivalent of α_4 was significantly greater than zero. They therefore concluded that 'a significant degree of money illusion exists in the aggregate consumption function for the US' (Branson and Klevorick 1969: 846).

Juster and Wachtel (1972) considered the effects of high rates of price *change* on aggregate consumption expenditure. They argue that high rates of price inflation are historically associated with highly variable rates of price inflation so that, provided consumers do not expect similar variability in their money income, future real income will be subject to considerable uncertainty during times of rapid inflation. This leads to greater precautionary saving and hence a lower APC during inflationary periods and Juster and Wachtel provide empirical evidence, again for the US, in support of this hypothesis. Townend (1976) however, using UK data, found that two variables which he used to proxy uncertainty, one relating to expected unemployment and the other constructed from Gallup poll data on price expectations, failed to provide statistical support for the precautionary savings hypothesis.

Deaton (1978) also considers inflation rates but focuses attention on the rate at which inflation accelerates. In Deaton's model a divergence between the actual and expected rates of inflation (likely during times of rapidly accelerating rates of inflation) leads to general price rises being mistaken by consumers for relative price rises and this leads to a decline in the APC. For example, suppose that the past inflation rate has been 10 per cent per annum and that consumers expect this rate to continue. If the actual inflation rate accelerates to 15 per cent, then a consumer about to purchase a particular good is likely to find its price higher than he had expected. Since his expectations are based on the old 10 per cent inflation rate, he fails to realise that all other goods have increased in price to a similar extent, and therefore mistakes a general rise in prices for a relative price rise in the good he is about to purchase. The consumer may therefore revise his expenditure plans and refrain from buying, or at least reduce his purchases of this good. Since all consumers suffer the same experience (although they may not at any point in time be buying the same good), the aggregate average propensity to save therefore rises whenever the inflation rate accelerates, i.e. whenever the expected inflation rate is below the actual rate.

Deaton estimates his model, in which the underlying consumption function is based on the permanent income hypothesis, using quarterly post-war data for both the US and the UK, and does in fact find that changes in the average propensity to save are positively related to the inflation rate. Townend (1976), using UK data only, finds a similar effect for the difference between expected and actual inflation rates. Deaton's results for the US are similar to those of Juster and Wachtel but do not appear to be consistent with those of Branson and Klevorick. If the rate of *change* in the APS increases as the rate of price *change* rises, then consumption *levels* must fall as the price *level* rises. This implies a negative α_4 in equation [39] whereas we have seen that Branson and Klevorick found evidence of money illusion of the opposite kind.

This recent concentration on the possible influence of inflation rates on levels of consumer expenditure reflects concern about a phenomenon common to many industrialised western economies during the 1970s – a general rise in saving–income ratios. For example, in the UK the conventionally defined APS (i.e. personal saving as a proportion of personal disposable income) was roughly 8 per cent throughout the 1960s but rose during the early 1970s to a level of around 14 per cent by 1974, remaining at about this level until 1977 and then rising further to nearly 16 per cent by the end of the decade. It is conceivable that this rise is merely a reflection of the fact that the personal sector in the UK includes not only households but also unincorporated businesses, life assurance funds and non-profit making bodies. While all theories of the consumption function are concerned specifically with private households, it is frequently the case that empirical studies have to deal with data aggregates involving more than just households. However, Armstrong (1979) has provided evidence that, at least for the UK, the rise in the saving–income ratio is still apparent when household saving and income are isolated from the rest of the personal sector,[19] although the timing of increases may have been slightly different.

There is no general agreement on the reasons for rising saving–income ratios. It is obviously tempting to attribute them to the accelerating inflation rates experienced during the 1970s, but the mechanism through which inflation influenced behaviour may not have involved either uncertainty or money illusion. An equally plausible explanation is provided by the effect of inflation in reducing the real value of wealth. Rapidly rising prices seriously affect the real value of that component of a consumer's wealth that is held in assets such as bank deposits which are fixed in money terms. Moreover, to the extent that rises in the price of non-money-fixed assets, such as company or government securities, fail to match the rise in consumer prices (for example, stock market prices generally failed to keep pace with inflation during the 1970s), the non-money-fixed component of a consumer's wealth will decline in real value also. From equation [32] we see that such a decline in real wealth will reduce consumer expenditure at a given level of real income.

This conflict between competing explanations of rising APS's is well illustrated by considering the recent and influential study of UK time-series data by Davidson *et al.* (1978). This very thorough study of post-war quarterly data is directly concerned more with the dynamic inter-relationship between income and non-durable consumption expenditure, that is the precise lag structure that should be placed on the income variables, than with the economic behaviour underlying this relationship. The authors are perturbed by the widely different conclusions reached by previous investigators using essentially similar data, and to highlight this they concentrate on three previous studies–those of Hendry (1974), Ball *et al.* (1975) and Wall *et al.* (1975). Davidson *et al.*'s aim is not only to explain the differences in the conclusions reached in these studies, but also to discover why the research methods of the three investigators led them to these conclusions.

Davidson *et al.* are able to standardise the three competing models in four respects but the major differences in the conclusions originally reached still persist. That is, even when a common sample period with identical seasonally unadjusted data is used, and when the precise functional forms and data transformations employed are also identical, the three studies still appear to lead to different conclusions. Remaining possible reasons for this are the different types of lag structure employed in the three studies and the varying estimating methods and diagnostic or test statistics used.

The above standardisation enables Davidson *et al.* to represent the three competing hypotheses as special cases of a general hypothesis or estimating equation so that it is possible to test, on purely statistical grounds, which provides the best description of the UK relationship between income and consumption expenditure. In the jargon, the competing hypotheses are 'nested' within the general hypothesis. On the basis of goodness of fit and other standard statistical criteria the best of the three models appears to be that of Wall *et al.* which is of the following type:

$$\Delta C_t = \alpha_0 + \alpha_1 \Delta Y_t + \alpha_2 \Delta Y_{t-1} \qquad [40]$$

where ΔC_t and ΔY_t are the quarterly changes in consumption and income respectively. The problem with this statistically preferred relationship is that it has some rather peculiar economic properties. First, it has no static equilibrium solution: even if the level of income were to remain constant indefinitely, in which case $\Delta Y_t = \Delta Y_{t-1} = 0$, then equation [40] implies that consumption expenditure would continue to rise and never itself reach a constant level since, under such conditions, $\Delta C_t = \alpha_0 \neq 0$. Moreover, the equation implies that not only is the adjustment of consumption to any change in income completed inside two quarters, but this adjustment is apparently independent of the extent of any disequilibrium in the *levels* of the variables C_t and Y_t. Normally, when consumption is, say, far below its equilibrium value in relation to income, one would expect the increase in consumption accompanying a given increase in income to be much greater than that which occurs when consumption and income levels are originally well adjusted to one another.

In an attempt to resolve this conflict between statistical and economic criteria, Davidson *et al.* put forward a model of their own. Suppose the 'steady state' or 'equilibrium' relationship between income and consumption is of the following form

$$C_t^* = KY_t^* \qquad [41]$$

where C_t^* and Y_t^* represent 'equilibrium' values of the variables. For example, equation [41] might represent the basic underlying relationship (equation [16]) of the permanent income hypothesis with C_t^* and Y_t^* being permanent consumption and permanent income respectively. Alternatively equation [41] could be interpreted as being identical to equation [27], the equation arising out of the Brown habit persistence model, in which case C_t^* represents 'optimal' consumption and Y_t^* is simply measured income. Taking natural logarithms of equation [41] yields

$$c_t^* = k + y_t^* \qquad [42]$$

where lower case letters represent the logs of the corresponding variables. Actual consumption and income are not, however, usually equal to their equilibrium values, (if c_t and y_t are the logs of actual consumption and income then the 'extent of disequilibrium' is $k + y_t - c_t$), and in practice we normally observe a 'disequilibrium relationship' involving lagged values of c_t and y_t. Davidson *et al.* represent this disequilibrium relationship by

$$c_t = k^* + \beta_1 y_t + \beta_2 y_{t-1} + \alpha c_{t-1} \qquad [43]$$

The steady state or equilibrium solution to equation [43], for a zero growth rate, can be obtained by setting $c_t = c_{t-1} = c_t^*$ and $y_t = y_{t-1} = y_t^*$, and is given by

$$c_t^* = \frac{k^*}{1-\alpha} + \frac{\beta_1 + \beta_2}{1-\alpha} y_t^* \qquad [44]$$

For equation [44] to be consistent with the actual equilibrium solution (equation [42]) we must have $k^* = k(1-\alpha)$ and, more importantly, $\beta_1 + \beta_2 + \alpha = 1$. Imposing these restrictions on the disequilibrium relationship, equation [43] yields

$$c_t = k(1-\alpha) + \beta_1 y_t + \beta_2 y_{t-1} + (1 - \beta_1 - \beta_2) c_{t-1} \qquad [45]$$

or

$$c_t - c_{t-1} = k\gamma + \beta_1 (y_t - y_{t-1}) + \gamma(y_{t-1} - c_{t-1}) \text{ where}$$
$$\gamma = 1 - \alpha = \beta_1 + \beta_2 \qquad [46]$$

Equations [45] and [46] now represent a relationship which in equilibrium yields equation [42].

Equation [46] relates changes in consumption to changes in income as does Wall *et al.*'s estimated equation, but it also includes a 'disequilibrium term', $y_{t-1} - c_{t-1} = -\log(c_{t-1}/y_{t-1})$ so that the change in consumption accompanying a given change in income depends on the previous relationship between the *levels* of consumption and income. For example, if the previous levels of c_t and y_t satisfied the equilibrium relationship, equation [42], then $y_{t-1} - c_{t-1} = -k$ and the change in consumption would be a constant proportion of the change in income. Otherwise the change in consumption will depend, also, on the extent to which previous levels of c_t and y_t depart from their equilibrium relationship.[20]

Davidson *et al.* explain the good statistical performance of Wall *et al.*'s equation, despite its lack of a disequilibrium effect, by pointing out that there is a high degree of collinearity between the constant term in equation [46] and the disequilibrium term. They show that the parameter k in equation [42] depends on the long-run rate of growth in real income and consumption. Since such growth rates remained relatively constant during the sample period used (1958–70), this implies an approximately constant k, and hence from equation [42] that $y_{t-1} - c_{t-1} \approx$ constant. Davidson *et al.* therefore suggest that the constant in Wall *et al.*'s equation was in fact undertaking the role of the required but absent disequilibrium term.

Although they are not particularly concerned with the economic behaviour underlying their statistical relationships, Davidson *et al.* point out that their basic estimating equation [46] can be interpreted in terms of any of the main hypotheses concerning the consumption function. For example, equation [45], although in logarithmic form, is, apart from the additional lagged income variable, identical to the estimating equation $C_t = \alpha Y_t + \beta C_{t-1}$, which, as we have already seen, can be derived from the habit persistence, permanent income or wealth hypotheses.

If equation [46] is to be estimated from quarterly data then the appropriate lag length is four quarters, so that this equation can be rewritten as follows

$$c_t - c_{t-4} = k\gamma + \beta_1 (y_t - y_{t-4}) + \gamma (y_{t-4} - c_{t-4}) \qquad [47]$$

where $c_t - c_{t-4}$ and $y_t - y_{t-4}$ represent annual changes.[21] Davidson *et al.* in fact estimate a slightly generalised form of equation [47] which is

$$c_t - c_{t-4} = k\gamma + \beta_1 (y_t - y_{t-4}) + \delta(y_{t-1} - y_{t-5}) + \gamma(y_{t-4} - c_{t-4}) \qquad [48]$$

which in turn can be written as

$$c_t - c_{t-4} = k\gamma + (\beta_1 + \delta)(y_t - y_{t-4}) - \delta\Delta_1 (y_t - y_{t-4}) + \gamma (y_{t-4} - c_{t-4}) \qquad [49]$$

where $\Delta_1 (y_t - y_{t-4})$ is the quarterly change in the variable $y_t - y_{t-4}$ and therefore represents the extent to which the annual change in income is itself changing.[22]

From an empirical point of view, Davidson *et al.* interpret equation [48] in terms of a simple 'feedback' model whereby consumers plan to spend in any quarter the same as they spent in the same quarter during the previous year (i.e. $C_t = C_{t-4}$), but where this quantity is modified by, first, the extent to which income has changed since that quarter, second, whether that change is itself increasing or decreasing, and finally a feedback from the C/Y ratio of the previous year to ensure coherence with the long-run target outcome, $C_t = kY_t$.

Davidson *et al.* estimate equation [49] without the constant term using UK quarterly data for 1958–70. Data for 1971–75, although available, are used merely for post-sample predictions. The forecasting performance of equation [48] however is poor, consumption levels during 1971–75 being consistently overpredicted. To get round this difficulty the authors consider the effect of the level and rate of change of prices on consumption expenditure. The variables $p_t - p_{t-4}$ and $\Delta_1 (p_t - p_{t-4})$ are therefore added to equation [49], their inclusion being rationalised by reference to the Deaton hypothesis described above. Their final estimating equation therefore has the form

$$c_t - c_{t-4} = (\beta_1 + \delta)(y_t - y_{t-4}) - \delta\Delta_1 (y_t - y_{t-4}) + \gamma(y_{t-4} - c_{t-4})$$
$$+ \mu_1(p_t - p_{t-4}) + \mu_2\Delta_1 (p_t - p_{t-4}) \qquad [50]$$

where $p_t = \log P_t$ and P_t is the implicit consumption deflator (i.e. an index of consumer prices). Both price variables prove statistically significant when the expanded equation [50] is estimated for 1958–70, and Davidson *et al.* are finally able to resolve their forecasting problem since this equation satisfactorily predicts consumption expenditure during 1971–75.

There are, however, a number of slightly worrying aspects concerning the work and some of the conclusions finally reached by Davidson *et al.* First, while their basic equation [47] is rigorously developed by the addition of disequilibrium effects to an underlying equilibrium relationship, this can hardly be said of the inflation effects they are eventually led to include, and one cannot avoid the feeling that these have been rather uncomfortably tagged on at the end in an *ad hoc* attempt to resolve the forecasting problem. Second, it is apparent that when data for 1958–70 only were available and used, the authors felt no necessity to consider inflation effects. It is only the eventual availability of 1971–75 data and the forecasting problem which emerges that seem to lead them to consider the Deaton hypothesis. If consideration of 1958–70 data alone results in the neglect of a mechanism crucially necessary to the explanation of 1971–75 data, it is equally possible that equations estimated from 1958–75 data will lack some aspect equally crucial to the explanation of post-1975 data. In addition, when 1958–70 data only are used, this time with the Deaton effect included, the equation which fits the data best is, in fact, a version of equation [50] which includes a constant term but excludes the disequilibrium term, $y_{t-4} - c_{t-4}$. It is only when the 1971–75 data are included for prediction purposes that an equation without the constant and including the disequilibrium term emerges as clearly the preferred equation on statistical as well as economic grounds. Davidson *et al.* refer to 'an interesting conflict between goodness of fit and parameter stability as a criteria for model selection' (1978: 688).[23] If preferred equations based only on 1958–70 data forecast poorly for 1971–75, how much confidence can there be that the preferred equation based on the full 1958–75 period will forecast adequately for, say, 1976–85? Indeed the specification and lag structure of equation [50] is so complex that it is difficult to believe that it could remain constant over time. The fact that this equation predicts well for 1971–75 is not really particularly impressive since the adequacy of the 1971–75 forecasts was the main criterion used for selecting this specification in the first place. Proper assessment of the forecasting ability of any equation must necessarily wait until it can be tested against data that was not made use of in its formulation.

Finally, although Davidson *et al.* briefly consider the possibility that factors (e.g. a liquid assets effect) other than that suggested by Deaton may be the reason for the importance of the price variable, little time is spent exploring such a possibility. Bean (1978) has shown, quite rigorously, that the importance of the variables $p_t - p_{t-4}$ and $y_{t-4} - c_{t-4}$ in estimated versions of equation [50] can be explained in terms of a classical wealth effect operating via money-fixed assets. Indeed, it can be seen intuitively that the variables $y_{t-4} - c_{t-4}$ and $p_t - p_{t-4}$ can be regarded as representing, respectively, additions to wealth which occur because of saving, and reductions in wealth arising from the fall in the real value of money-fixed assets when prices are rising. Bean in fact demonstrates that the size of the coefficients on these variables is perfectly consistent with this interpretation. Moreover, when Bean adds a Deaton-type variable involving both the actual and expected rates of inflation to his version of Davidson *et al.*'s equation, it proves to be statistically insignificant. Bean therefore concludes that the high saving–income ratios of the 1970s are the result of wealth effects rather than Deaton-type inflation effects. That is, rapid inflation has so reduced the *real* value of those assets held by consumers that are fixed in money terms that this has led to a sharp curtailment of consumption expenditure. The UK treasury model now incorporates an equation of the Davidson *et al.* form although it is interpreted in terms of wealth-type rather than Deaton-type effects for the above reasons.

Once the possibility of a wealth effect is admitted a further point of interest arises. For both statistical and economic reasons Davidson *et al.* suppress the constant term in their equations in favour of the disequilibrium term. However, if the constant term in equation [46], for example, is zero, then provided $\gamma \neq 0$, this implies that $k = 0$ and hence $K = 1$. Thus for zero growth rates, the equilibrium relationship (equation [41]) takes the form $C_t^* = Y_t^*$, i.e. the equilibrium APC is unity. Such a possibility is not normally envisaged in either the Brown habit persistence model or the permanent income hypothesis, but it is perfectly consistent with and indeed a necessary consequence of, the Ball–Drake wealth hypothesis described in the previous section. While the value of Davidson *et al.*'s work in pointing to the necessity of a constructive research strategy is not in doubt, the above considerations suggest that it is far too early to definitely attribute the recent high UK saving–income ratios to inflation effects of the Deaton kind.

6. Conclusions

Taking into account the vast quantity of empirical evidence concerning the consumption function that has been accumulated during the post-war decades, the majority of economists would probably come down in favour of one of the normal income hypotheses as the most likely simple explanation of consumer behaviour. However, all the competing hypotheses are to varying extents intuitively appealing and as we have seen it is no easy task to discriminate between them on empirical grounds. Discrimination is especially difficult with time-series data. For example, the habit persistence model, the PIH and the wealth hypothesis all lead to an estimating equation in which C_t depends on Y_t and C_{t-1}.

Notwithstanding the general agreement over the superiority of the normal income hypotheses, few investigators have been prepared to accept the more extreme aspects of these hypotheses, namely the proportionality postulate and the zero correlation between the transitory components of income and consumption. A typical view is that of Mayer (1972), who has put forward a 'standard income hypothesis' in which, while consumer expenditure depends on permanent income (or total lifetime resources), it does not do so in a proportionate manner, and in which while the correlation between transitory components is 'low' it is certainly not zero. What is generally accepted, however, is that current consumption cannot be explained in terms of current income alone and that past levels of income, for one reason or another, are also important.

An obvious point, but one which is possibly not sufficiently stressed, is that the competing hypotheses should not be regarded as mutually exclusive. For example, the fact that cross-sectionally estimated consumption functions typically have a smaller slope than those obtained from long-run time-series data may be predominantly the result of Friedman type effects, but this does not preclude the possibility that the underlying cross-sectional relationship may still have an intercept because of the effects suggested by Duesenberry. Similarly, there is no reason why the generally accepted importance of past income levels in explaining time-series variations in consumption should not be the result of both permanent income and relative income effects.

In addition the wealth and life-cycle models are by no means irreconcilable. Consider a model in which a household maximises a utility function defined over a given interval, and having as arguments end-interval wealth and consumption during the interval. The wealth hypothesis and the LCH can be regarded as special cases of such a model. If the length of the interval is equal to the remaining lifespan of the household and wealth receives little or no weight in the utility function, then we have the LCH, while if the maximisation interval is very short and the level of wealth is an important source of utility then we have the wealth hypothesis.

A major empirical problem which has recently arisen is that of explaining the general rise in saving–income ratios. Linked with this is the theoretical issue of whether non-human wealth should be explicitly included in the consumption function as in the life-cycle and wealth hypotheses, or whether it should be included in total wealth and this converted into a flow variable as in the permanent income hypothesis. The inclusion of the stock of non-human wealth in estimating equations assists in explaining the recent rise in APS's, since reductions in consumer expenditure could have arisen from attempts by consumers to restore their real asset position when rapid inflation reduced the value of their wealth stock. However, the issue of whether recent high saving–income ratios are the result of such a classical wealth effect, or whether they are more directly caused by accelerating inflation via, for example, some form of Deaton-type money illusion, remains largely unresolved.

Although most of the recent work discussed in this survey has been concerned only with the consumption of non-durables rather than with total consumer expenditure, the empirical work described has some important implications for economic policy-makers. The agreement that consumption cannot be explained by current measured income alone, and that past income levels are, for whatever reason, also important, has had perhaps the most far-reaching consequences. Lower marginal propensities to consume out of current income imply lower impact values for the various government budget multipliers and hence a reduced immediate effectiveness for fiscal policy measures. Such findings have therefore been one of the more significant reasons for the gradually increasing emphasis placed on monetary as opposed to fiscal policy by most western governments during the past twenty years. It should be noted that the debate as to which of the competing hypotheses concerning consumption is 'correct' has little relevance for this conclusion regarding fiscal policy, since all imply a relatively small MPC current income.

The findings concerning windfalls and transitory income, particularly the consequences of the various US tax experiments, have obvious implications. It appears that 'temporary' changes in personal tax rates, provided they have little effect on the permanent income of consumers, have little noticeable influence on total spending. Finally, there seems to be general agreement that some form of relationship exists between saving–income ratios and inflation rates. Whatever the explanation, in all cases the relationship has been detected during periods of mainly rising inflation rates. Whether a similar relationship will hold when inflation rates are falling cannot be certain and this makes the forecasting of future consumption a more than usually difficult task.

Notes

1. Such stocks have an important influence on durable good expenditure and in particular on the speed at which consumers adjust such expenditures to changes in income and prices.
2. Formally this means assuming that the consumer's utility function is homogeneous of some positive degree in both C_1 and C_2.
3. In the full version of the hypothesis, account is taken of the possibility that a household may plan to leave assets to its heirs and a variable representing 'end of life' assets is included in the utility function and also in the budget constraint.
4. Aggregation is in fact formally difficult, mainly because λ_T depends on the age of the household and is therefore unlikely to be independent of Y_T and A_{T-1}.
5. The discounting procedure in equation [17] begins with the current period, in contrast to equation [14]. However, if the length of the period is short this makes little difference; Friedman, for example, originally used a continuous analysis.
6. Friedman (1957: 31–3). The model is, in fact, formally equivalent to what econometricians call an 'errors in variables' model.
7. Friedman (1957: 160–3).
8. Friedman originally formulated Y_t^p as a continuous function of present and past measured income with exponentially declining weights and also built in a factor reflecting *long-run secular growth* in permanent income. However, for estimation with annual data a discrete approximation to the continuous function is used and this discrete approximation involves the geometrically declining weights of equation [23].

9. Although the war years were omitted from Friedman's actual regressions because of distortions to the data, war-time income data are needed to compute post-war values for Y_t^p when using equation [23].
10. Evans (1969), for example, using 1929–62 data, estimates $C_t = 0.280Y_t + 0.676C_{t-1}$. The implied estimates of k and β are 0.86 and 0.325 respectively – very close to those obtained by Friedman, although in this case no allowance is made for secular growth in real income.
11. Also by successively substituting for C_{t-1}, C_{t-2}, C_{t-3}, etc. in equation [29] we eventually obtain the Friedman estimating equation $C_t = k[\beta Y_t + \beta(1-\beta)Y_{t-1} \ldots]$.
12. Lack of space precludes the description of many other tests presented by Friedman. However, the reader is recommended to examine this material himself, particularly for example the test concerning income correlations (Friedman, 1957: 194–5).
13. Friedman (1957:101–2).
14. Springer attributed the difference in results to a combination of three factors. First, *all* Okun's equations were estimated using the full-effect definition of income, whereas it is more appropriate to use a zero-effect definition when estimating an equation which is to be used for prediction purposes using this definition. Second, Okun made no allowances for the residual autocorrelation found in his equations, and finally made no allowance for interest rate effects.
15. More recently attempts have, in fact, been made to extend the LCH to encompass uncertainty, e.g. Merton (1969) and Dreze and Modigliani (1972).
16. We are following here the Ball–Drake formulation of the hypothesis.
17. For example, the Central Statistical Office (1978) has recently published an annual series for UK consumer net wealth far superior to any previously available.
18. Feldstein's findings, if substantiated, have important implications for corporate taxation policy. Traditionally the disposable income variable used in consumption functions includes the dividend component but not the retained earnings component of profits. A switch from dividends to retained earnings (induced by a higher tax rate on dividends) therefore leads to a rise in company saving that is not fully matched by a fall in personal saving so that total private saving rises. However, if income is more correctly defined to include retained earnings, then any switch from dividends to retained earnings leaves consumption and hence total private saving unchanged.
19. Armstrong also makes allowances for 'non-voluntary' saving (e.g. payments to superannuation schemes and net outlays on housing), but the rise in the saving–income ratio remains even when attention is concentrated on 'voluntary' saving.
20. Notice that equation [46] can be written as $c_t - c_{t-1} = \beta_1(y_t - y_{t-1}) + \gamma(k + y_{t-1} - c_{t-1})$, that is the change in consumption depends on the change in income and the extent of disequilibrium in the previous period.
21. It obviously makes greater sense to relate C_t to C_{t-4}, i.e. consumption in the same quarter during the previous year, than to C_{t-1}, consumption during the previous quarter. Remember, Davidson *et al.* are using seasonally unadjusted data.
22. In their paper, Davidson *et al.* use the following notation: $c_t - c_{t-4} = \log C_t - \log C_{t-4}$ is written as $\Delta_4 \log C_t$. Similarly, $y_t - y_{t-4} = \Delta_4 \log Y_t$ so that $\Delta_1(y_t - y_{t-4})$ in equation [49] is written as $\Delta_1\Delta_4 \log Y_t$.
23. Forecasting performance is assessed by a χ^2 test for parameter stability.

References

Ando, A. and Modigliani, F. (1963) The life cycle hypothesis of savings, *American Economic Review,* **53**, 55–84.

Armstrong, A.G. (1979) An analysis of personal saving in the UK, *Manchester School,* **47**, 369–90.

Ball, R.J. and Drake, P.S. (1964) The relationship between aggregate consumption and wealth, *International Economic Review,* **5**, 63–81.

Ball, R.J., Boatwright, B.D., Burns, T., Lobban, P.W.M. and Miller, G.W. (1975) The London Business School quarterly econometric model of the UK economy, in Renton. G.A. (ed), *Modelling the Economy*, Heinemann Educational Books, London.

Bean, C.R. (1978) The determination of consumers expenditure in the UK, *Treasury Working Paper,* **4**.

Bhatia, K.B. (1972) Capital gains and the aggregate consumption function, *American Economic Review,* **62**, 866–79.

Bhatia, K.B. (1979) Corporate taxation, retained earnings and capital formation, *Journal of Public Economics,* **11**, 123–34.

Bird, R. and Bodkin, R.G. (1965) The national service life insurance dividend of 1950 and consumption: a further test of the strict permanent income hypothesis, *Journal of Political Economy,* **73**, 499–515.

Blinder, A.S. (1981) Temporary income taxes and consumer spending, *Journal of Political Economy,* **89**, 22–53.

Bodkin, R.G. (1959) Windfall income and consumption, *American Economic Review,* **49**, 602–14.

Brady, D. and Friedman, R. (1947) Savings and the income distribution, in *Studies in Income and Wealth,* **10**, N.B.E.R., New York.

Branson, W.H. and Klevorick, A.K. (1969) Money illusion and the aggregate consumption function, *American Economic Review,* **59**, 832–49.

Brown, T.M. (1952) Habit persistence and lags in consumer behaviour, *Econometric,* **20**, 355–71.

Central Statistical Office (1978) Personal sector balance sheets, *Economic Trends,* **291**, 97–107.

Clower, R.W. and Johnson, M.B. (1968) Income, wealth and the theory of consumption, in Wolfe, N. (ed), *Value, Capital and Growth*, Edinburgh University Press.

Darby, M.R. (1972) The allocation of transitory income among consumers' assets, *American Economic Review,* **72**, 928–41.

Darby, M.R. (1974) The permanent income theory of consumption – a restatement, *Quarterly Journal of Economics,* **88**, 228–50.

Davidson, J.E.H., Hendry, D.F., Srba, F., Yeo, S. (1978) Econometric modelling of the aggregate time series relationship between consumers' expenditure and income in the UK, *Economic Journal,* **88**, 661–92.

Davis, T.E. (1952) The consumption function as a tool for prediction, *Review of Economics and Statistics,* **34**, 270–7.

Deaton, A. (1978) Involuntary saving through unanticipated inflation, *American Economic Review,* **68**, 899–910.

Dreze, J.H. and Modigliani, F. (1972) Consumption decisions under uncertainty, *Journal of Economic Theory,* **5**, 236–61.

Duesenberry, J.S. (1949) *Income, Savings and the Theory of Consumer Behaviour,* Harvard University Press.

Evans, M.K. (1967) The importance of wealth in the consumption function, *Journal of Political Economy,* **75**, 335–51.

Evans, M.K. (1969) *Macroeconomic Activity*, Harper and Row, New York.

Feldstein, M.S. (1973) Tax incentives, corporate saving and capital accumulation, *Journal of Public Economics,* **5**, 159–71.

Feldstein, M.S. and Fane, G. (1973) Taxes, corporate dividend policy and personal saving: the British postwar experience, *Review of Economics and Statistics,* **55**, 399–411.

Fisher, I. (1907) *The Theory of Interest*, Macmillan, New York.

Friedman, M. (1957) *A Theory of the Consumption Function*, Princeton University Press.

Goldsmith, R.W. (1955) *A Study of Savings in the United States,* Princeton University Press.

Hendry, D.F. (1974) Stochastic specification in an aggregate demand model of the UK, *Econometrica,* **42**, 559–78.

Juster, F.T. and Wachtel, P. (1972) Inflation and the consumer, *Brookings Papers on Economic Activity,* 1972: **1**, 71–114.

Keynes, J.M. (1936) *The General Theory of Employment, Interest and Money,* Macmillan, London.

Kreinin, M. (1961) Windfall income and consumption–additional evidence, *American Economic Review,* **51**, 388–90.

Kuznets, S. (1942) Uses of national income in peace and war, *National Bureau of Economic Research*, Occasional Paper **6**.

Mayer, T. (1972) *Permanent Income, Wealth and Consumption*, University of California Press.

Merton, R.C. (1969) Lifetime portfolio selection under uncertainty: the continuous time case, *Review of Economics and Statistics,* **57**, 247–57.

Modigliani, F. (1949) Fluctuations in the savings–income ratio: a problem in economic forecasting, in *Studies in Income and Wealth,* **11**, N.B.E.R., New York.

Modigliani, F. and Brumberg, R. (1954) Utility analysis and the consumption function: an interpretation of cross-sectional data, in Kurihara, K. (ed.), *Post-Keynesian Economics*, Rutgers University Press.

Modigliani, F. and Steindel, C. (1977) Is a tax rebate an effective tool for stabilisation policy?, *Brookings Papers on Economic Activity*, 1977: **2**, 175–209.

Okun, A.M. (1971) The personal tax surcharge and consumer demand 1968–70, *Brookings Papers on Economic Activity*, 1971: **1**, 167–211.

Spiro, A. (1962) Wealth and the consumption function, *Journal of Political Economy,* **70**, 339–54.

Springer, W.L. (1975) Did the 1968 surcharge really work?, *American Economic Review,* **65**, 644–59.

Stone, R. (1964) Private saving in Britain, past, present and future, *Manchester School,* **32**, 79–112.

Stone, R. (1974) Personal spending and saving in post-war Britain, in Bos, H.C. *et al.* (eds), *Economic Structure and Development*, North-Holland.

Thomas, R.L. (1981) Wealth and aggregate consumption, *Manchester School,* **49**, 129–52.

Townend, J.C. (1976) The personal savings ratio, *Bank of England Quarterly Bulletin,* **16**, 1, 53–61.

Wall, K.D., Preston, A.J., Bray, J.W. and Peston, M.H. (1975) Estimates of a simple control model of the UK economy, in Renton G.A. (ed.), *Modelling the Economy*, Heinemann Education Books, London.

Wright, C. (1969) Estimating permanent income: a note, *Journal of Political Economy,* **77**, 845–50.

Zellner, A. and Geisel (1970) Analysis of distributed lag models with applications to consumption function estimation, *Econometrica,* **38**, 865–88.

Zellner, A., Huang, D.S. and Chou, L.C. (1965) Further analysis of the short-run consumption function with emphasis on the role of liquid assets, *Econometrica,* **33**, 571–81.

Appendix

We derive here the lifetime budget equation [8] for a three-period case. Suppose we have a household in its tenth year ($T = 10$) that intends to retire at the end of its eleventh year ($N = 11$) and expects to die(!) at the end of its twelfth year ($L = 12$). The lifetime budget constraint therefore becomes

$$A_9 + Y_{10} + \frac{Y_{11}}{1 + r} = C_{10} + \frac{C_{11}}{1 + r} + \frac{C_{12}}{(1 + r)^2} \qquad [8A]$$

To derive equation [8A] we make the simplifying assumption that interest on non-human wealth is always paid at the beginning of the year. The household's budget constraint for its *tenth year* is then given by

$$A_9(1 + r) + Y_{10} = C_{10} + A_{10} \qquad [8A1]$$

where Y_{10} represents earned or non-property income only since unearned income is already included in the constraint as A_9r. Similarly, the household's budget constraints for its *eleventh and twelfth years* are given by

$$A_{10}(1 + r) + Y_{11} = C_{11} + A_{11} \qquad [8A2]$$

and

$$A_{11}(1 + r) = C_{12} \qquad [8A3]$$

where Y_{11} is earned income in the eleventh year, $Y_{12} = 0$ since the household has now retired and $A_{12} = 0$ because the household plans to have no resources left at death.

From equation [8A3] we have

$$A_{11} = \frac{C_{12}}{1 + r}$$

Substituting for A_{11} in equation [8A2] yields

$$A_{10} = \frac{C_{11}}{1 + r} + \frac{C_{12}}{(1 + r)^2} - \frac{Y_{11}}{(1 + r)}$$

Substituting for A_{10} in equation [8A1] yields

$$A_9(1 + r) + Y_{10} = C_{10} + \frac{C_{11}}{1 + r} + \frac{C_{12}}{(1 + r)^2} - \frac{Y_{11}}{1 + r}$$

which on rearrangement yields the three-year budget constraint (equation [8A]) provided we interpret A_9 in equation [8A] as *including* interest received during the household's tenth year.[1] Thus, by combining the budget constraints for each separate year, we eventually obtain the lifetime budget constraint.

Note

1. A more consistent formulation of equation [8A] would be

$$A_9 + \frac{Y_{10}}{1 + r} + \frac{Y_{11}}{(1 + r)^2} = \frac{C_{10}}{1 + r} + \frac{C_{11}}{(1 + r)^2} + \frac{C_{12}}{(1 + r)^3}$$

CHAPTER FOUR

Money in UK macro models

W. Neil Thompson

1. Introduction

The purpose of this survey is to consider the structure of the large UK macro models with particular reference to the incorporation of monetary variables. Until recently these models, in the true Keynesian tradition, paid little attention to such factors, and financial variables played only a small role in the determination of real expenditure decisions. Fiscal policy was regarded as the main tool of demand management, and the extent of any potential linkage from financial market conditions to the real economy was often limited to one or two interest rate terms and variables indicating the severity of hire-purchase controls. These financial variables were in turn generally assumed to be exogenous and no attempt was made to model the factors underlying their determination. Accordingly, in these models, the extent of the financial sector often consisted merely of a solitary demand for money equation, and indeed in some models even this basic relationship was not specified. The present generation of models, however, place much more emphasis on monetary variables, and the links between such variables and the real sector are now much stronger. In addition detailed monetary sectors have now been developed in most models in order to endogenise all the key financial variables: the various money and credit aggregates, the structure of interest rates and the exchange rate. Moreover, the respective monetary and real sectors of the models are gradually becoming fully integrated with each other.

These various developments, which reflect the increased use of monetary policy as a tool of economic management, are considered in more detail in this survey. First of all, in section 2, we consider the principal features of the large UK macro models as they have developed over time, and in particular the relationship between these empirical models and the standard theoretical models of textbook macroeconomic analysis. The empirical models are shown in many respects to be merely disaggregated versions of the theoretical models, reflecting the basic Keynesian belief that a detailed allocative knowledge of the workings of the economy is a prerequisite for a full understanding of policy issues. In section 3 the basic Keynesian and monetarist approaches to the transmission mechanism, as applied to both closed and open economies, are considered. It is shown that, although the conventional Keynesian channels of monetary influence, which stress the role of interest rate, wealth and credit availability effects tend to predominate in the models, some aspects of monetarist philosophy are also finding a place in the new generation of macro models. This is particularly the case under a regime of flexible exchange rates. In most models, for instance, the possibility exists of financial variables such as the money supply influencing the exchange rate and hence the level of import prices. This in turn has some effect on the domestic price level and means that there is potentially a direct link between the money supply and the price level. Sections 4 to 7 consider in more detail the main expenditure decisions as they are analysed in the models. The individual links between monetary variables and the different categories of consumption and investment expenditure are discussed in detail, and in each case the findings of the model builders are compared with those of other UK studies of spending behaviour. The domestic and external monetary sectors, as they have been developed in the models, are described in section 8, and in section 9 we take a brief look at the alternative small model approach to macro modelling. This approach is often associated with the monetarist view of the transmission mechanism, and involves a more direct test of the effect of money on national income than is possible in a large disaggregated model. Finally in section 10 we look at the uses of large macro models, and some of the problems which arise in their construction and estimation.

2. The structure of UK macro models

THEORETICAL MACRO MODELS

The most elementary macro model of an economy is the basic Keynesian income-expenditure system. In this model output is determined by the level of real aggregate demand in the economy, comprising consumption, investment, government expenditure and net exports. No consideration is given to supply factors and instead firms are assumed to adjust passively to demand forces. Furthermore no monetary sector is considered, although exogenous financial factors may influence the main expenditure decisions.

An alternative approach is the ISLM framework developed by Hicks (1937) and popularised by Hansen (1953). Here a monetary sector is incorporated into the basic model. This enables the derivation of an LM curve which shows those combinations of the interest rate and income that ensure equilibrium in the money market, given information on the money supply and price level. From the real side of the model an IS curve can be derived which traces out those combinations of income and the rate of interest that satisfy the goods market equilibrium condition, in relation to consumption and investment plans, given values for the level of autonomous government expenditure. The point of intersection of the two curves thus determines the overall equilibrium levels of income and the rate of interest in the model. The original ISLM model assumed a closed economy, but the framework can easily be extended to include a balance of payments sector. This involves the specification of a BB curve which, given information on the income of the rest of the world, the world rate of interest and the relative price level at home compared to that ruling in the rest of the world, represents the locus of values of the interest rate and income at home that ensures balance of payments equilibrium.

Such a framework can be used to analyse the principal characteristics of the open economy under both fixed and floating exchange rate regimes.

The ISLM framework is normally developed on the assumption of constant prices so that all variables are specified in real terms. Changes in the price level are of course permissible, but only if real output is assumed fixed at some level, such as that consistent with full employment. Within the framework it is therefore not easy to allow simultaneous changes in both the price level and real output, and consequently the division of any change in money income between real income and prices cannot readily be analysed. In order to overcome this problem the basic framework can be extended by constructing an aggregate demand curve from the IS and LM curves, and by introducing a supply side into the model.

Supply factors are neglected in the basic ISLM approach since firms are assumed to supply all the output that is demanded of them at the current price level. However, an aggregate supply curve, showing the relationship between the supply of output and the price level, for given values of expected prices, can be derived from an analysis of the labour market in which it is assumed that supply depends on expected prices and demand on actual prices. Using this framework, both short- and long-run aggregate supply curves can be developed. In the short run, when expectations of the price level lag behind actuality, a rise in the general price level will lead to a rise in output supplied, thus generating an upward sloping curve. However, in the long run when expectations have had time to adjust to actual values, price changes will have no effect on output and the aggregate supply curve will be vertical at the natural level of output. Given the nature of the relationship the aggregate supply curve can be reformulated as an expectations-augmented Phillips curve, in which the rate of inflation is related to the deviation of unemployment from its natural level and the expected rate of inflation. The extension of the model, to include supply influences in this way, is often associated with the growing influence of monetarist ideas.[1]

The aggregate demand curve showing the quantity of real output demanded at each price level, for given values of the money supply and autonomous expenditure, can be combined with the aggregate supply curve in order to determine the equilibrium level of output and the general price level in both the short and long run.[2] In addition, the point of intersection of the demand for and supply of labour will determine the money wage rate and the level of employment consistent with different values of the actual price level. Indeed, the level of employment associated with different price levels is implicit in the derivation of the aggregate supply curve because of the relationship which exists between employment and real output via the aggregate production function. The model outlined above can therefore be used to determine output (real income), employment, the money wage rate and the price level. In the following subsection we will attempt to relate this textbook model to the empirical macro models of the UK economy as they have developed since their inception.

EMPIRICAL MACRO MODELS

The models developed by six groups will be considered; The Treasury (HMT), National Institute of Economic and Social Research (NI), London Business School

(LBS), Bank of England (BE), Cambridge Econometrics (CE)[3] and Cambridge Economic Policy Group (CEPG).[4] These are the main UK macro models, although attempts at model building have also been made by the Southampton Econometric Model Building Unit (SEMBU)[5] and some City institutions. All these models have developed since the late 1960s and are used mainly for purposes of forecasting and policy simulation. Thus the models are used either to produce forecasts of the future path of the economy, or else to explore the effects on the endogenous variables of the system of changes in some of the exogenous variables, typically those under the control of the government. Technical manuals exist for all of the models, but because they are undergoing a process of continual revision, experimentation and updating, it is almost impossible to accurately describe the 'present' state of any econometric model. At the time of writing the current versions of the models were described in H.M. Treasury (1980), National Institute of Economic and Social Research (1979), London Business School (1981), Bank of England (1979), Coutts *et al.* (1980) and Barker *et al.* (1980) respectively. Summaries of the principal characteristics of the models at different stages of their development can be found in Hilton and Heathfield (1970), Renton (1975), Posner (1978) and Ormerod (1979a).

The early models were based largely on the Keynesian income-expenditure system, with output demand determined and supply effects largely ignored. The current models are still based on this framework, but now extensive wage-price, and domestic and external monetary sectors have also been developed as the need to model both inflationary forces and the linkages between the financial and real sectors has become more apparent. Accordingly the size of most of the models has risen dramatically since their initial beginnings, reflecting not only the extension of these sectors, but also the desire to find stable empirical relationships for the various expenditure categories; developments which have in turn necessitated a greater degree of disaggregation in the modelling of the different expenditure decisions. The largest model is that of CE where nearly 3,000 equations are specified, although more than half of these are identities. The main characteristics of the CE model can, however, be represented in a much smaller condensed version which comprises only some 24 equations. The current versions of the HMT, BE, LBS, NI and CEPG models have approximately 760, 500, 300, 180 and 90 equations respectively. In comparison, the versions of the models which were current in the early 1970s were much smaller. The LBS and HMT models at that time comprised some 154 and 95 equations respectively, while the NI model was even smaller with only 20 equations.

It is therefore apparent that the degree of disaggregation involved in the specification of these models is much greater than that involved in textbook models, and that this disparity has shown a tendency to increase over time. For example, whereas textbook income-expenditure models normally specify only one basic relationship for each of the main components of aggregate demand, most empirical models disaggregate each expenditure category further. Consumption, for example, is usually disaggregated into its durable and non-durable components, while total private sector investment is divided into non-residential fixed investment, stockbuilding and housebuilding. In addition, separate non-residential fixed investment and stockbuilding equations are generally specified for different sectors of the economy and types of asset. The development of such a detailed structural approach reflects the Keynesian belief that knowledge of allocative detail is vital for the proper understanding of policy processes in a complex world. The precise degree of disaggregation adopted by the different model builders in their description of the main expenditure decisions does, however, vary considerably and this is obviously an important factor in helping to explain the variation in the overall size of the different models. The large size of the CE model, for example, reflects the fact that here an attempt is made to analyse the real sector in terms of a highly disaggregated input-output framework which distinguishes between forty different industry groupings.

In accordance with standard Keynesian practice, the various expenditure decisions are normally specified in real terms, and in most cases the formulations have changed little since the models were first developed. Consumption expenditure, for example, tends to be mainly determined by present and past disposable income and lagged values of consumption, while fixed investment is often modelled in terms of an accelerator function of the change in output. A rather different approach is adopted in the CEPG model where a single equation is estimated for aggregate private sector expenditure. This conglomerate comprises the sum of all personal consumption expenditure and private fixed investment including housebuilding. Although early model versions estimated the equation in real terms it is now estimated in nominal terms in relation to the current and one period lagged values of total private disposable income. Specifying the relationship in this way increases the overall explanatory power of the equation, but makes meaningful interpretation of the individual coefficients more difficult.[6] Implicit in the equation is the belief that all the disposable income of the private sector as a whole is spent on goods and services within a short period of time. This view, which is counter to mainstream Keynesian theory and the findings of the other model builders, is associated with the CEPG belief that the private sector has a small and predictable financial surplus. However, Chrystal (1981) has shown that the sum of the coefficients on the income variables in the expenditure function is likely to be biased towards one because the estimated relationship closely approximates the national income accounting identity. In addition, a separate private fixed investment equation is also specified, in nominal terms, in relation to certain components of private income, rather than the more usual accelerator mechanism. In this way consumption can be determined as the difference between aggregate private expenditure and fixed investment. The CEPG model is also unique in being based on annual data whereas all other models are quarterly. This distinction reflects the fact that the CEPG model has been designed specifically to take a longer term view of economic prospects and policy.

All the models have developed external trade sectors in which equations are specified for different categories of imports and exports. Imports are usually related to internal demand pressures as proxied, for example, by domestic expenditure and output, while exports of manufactures depend on world production or trade. Relative movements of home and foreign prices and costs, which serve as indicators of competitiveness, are also included in both export and import equations.

The level of employment in the models is determined by demand factors; the level of output appears in all the sectoral employment equations, and productivity trends enter in the BE, HMT, LBS and CE models. The level of unemployment is essentially determined from the employment equation and information on the labour supply and participation rate. Generally an exogenous estimate is made of the labour supply, although the 1980 version of the HMT model does specify a labour supply function. In considering the level of unemployment many of the models make a distinction between the total number of unemployed and those who actually register as being unemployed. Given the approach adopted disparities between the demand for and supply of labour are inevitable, and because of this the large macro models are often termed disequilibrium models.[7]

One area where the various model builders have encountered problems is in the specification of wage equations.[8] In particular, the existence of incomes policies, designed to control the growth of wage rates, over much of the period for which the equations are estimated has created difficulties. As a result wage rates or earnings per head have often been taken to be exogenously determined. Early model versions which attempted to incorporate wage equations usually related these to changes in the price level. Attempts were also often made to incorporate labour market pressure of demand effects in the form of Phillips curve relationships, but these met with mixed success.[9] Recent versions of some of the models have been more successful in isolating such effects and in fact the earnings equations of the current HMT, NI and CE models are all based on Phillips curve relationships in their expectations-augmented form. Given the link between wages and prices, the wage equation in this form can be viewed as an aggregate supply curve. Indeed, the consideration of such relationships shows how supply side factors are increasingly being incorporated into the basically demand orientated models, and illustrates to some extent the growing influence of monetarist ideas on the model builders. This is further illustrated by the fact that in the CE model and the 1979 HMT model and coefficients on the inflation term in the Phillips curve relationship are constrained to take the value one. This implies that all expected price increases are passed on to earnings, and is consistent with the monetarist belief that there can be no long-run trade off between inflation and unemployment.

Of the present generation of models the CEPG and BE models come nearest to maintaining the conventional Keynesian approach by attempting to capture the institutional framework of wage determination. Wages are seen as the outcome of a bargaining process between trade unions and employers. In the BE model earnings are modelled in terms of the settlement rates associated with wage rounds, while in the CEPG model trade unions are assumed to attempt to obtain a target level of post-tax real wages.[10] Changes in the level of taxation in fact exert an influence on wages in all of the models in one way or another. Direct taxes influence wages via the retentions ratio, that is the ratio of net to gross earnings, in the HMT, BE and CEPG models, while the link between consumer prices and wage levels that exists in all models ensures that changes in indirect taxation have some effect on wages. The LBS, CE and CEPG also include dummy variables in their various specifications in order to allow for periods of incomes policy. In the HMT and NI models, however, the earnings equation is suspended during periods of incomes policy, and an exogenous estimate is made of the wage adjustments which are required to ensure consistency with the particular norm in force at the time.

Equations are specified for, or exogenous estimates made of, many of the other categories of income received by units in the personal and company sectors. Included here, for example, are items such as rents, interest and dividend payments, grants, profits and the income of the self-employed. Such items find a place in standard modelling procedure because of the need for consistent sectoral income and expenditure accounts.

The treatment of the price equations has changed little since the models were first developed, except for the fact that greater disaggregation has increased the number of relationships specified. A standard Keynesian full-cost approach still predominates in all models, with domestic or consumer prices being determined by mark-up equations on labour costs, import prices and indirect taxes. In addition, labour productivity variables influence prices in the CEPG, NI and BE models. Only in the NI model, where the consumer price equation includes a term in the change in manufacturing output, and in some earlier versions of the LBS model, is there a direct pressure of demand effect on the price level. However, given that earnings are determined by prices in all models, a wage–price spiral is built into each framework, so that pressure of demand effects which influence earnings will also act on the price level. Also, under a regime of floating exchange rates, any increase in the pressure of demand is likely to result in a fall in the exchange rate and consequently a higher import price level in terms of sterling.

Recent versions of the models specify separate price equations for several categories of traded goods such as finished manufactures, basic materials and fuels. Prices of exported manufactures in all cases are influenced both by home costs and the world export prices of competing goods. Except in the case of the LBS model, the prices of imported manufactures are modelled in a similar way and are related to home costs as well as world prices. Thus overseas suppliers, in setting prices for the UK market, are assumed to be affected by the prices of competing UK goods. Only with respect to the price equation for manufactured imports in the LBS model, and the price specifications for imports and exports of fuel, raw materials and non-manufactured goods generally, do world prices alone determine the prices of traded goods in accordance with the 'law of one price'.

Although the volume of government spending on goods and services is largely assumed to be exogenous as in Keynesian theory, other categories of public expenditure are treated endogenously in several of the models. In the HMT, LBS and BE models, for instance, attempts are made to model transfers such as debt interest, certain categories of grants and subsidies, and unemployment and social security payments. The Treasury in particular, because of its concern with forecasting the government's budget position, has increasingly become concerned with modelling these relatively unimportant items, the role of which is largely ignored in economic theory. In addition, all models make some attempt to consider the revenues accruing to the government from the direct and indirect taxes levied on the personal and company sectors. Using the information gained on the income and expenditure flows of the government, the public sector borrowing requirement (PSBR) can be determined.

The early macro models paid little attention to the modelling of monetary variables and the financial side of the economy was generally explained inadequately or left unexplained altogether. Exchange rates, interest rates and the stock of money were normally taken to be exogenously determined; although a demand for money function was specified in some model versions, so that it was possible to rearrange the estimated relationship in order to endogenise the rate of interest.[11] Furthermore, in these early models the linkages between the financial and real sides of the economy were virtually non-existent. One or two interest rates and hire-purchase credit availability terms typically provided the only links between financial markets and the rest of the economy. In recent years this situation has changed markedly, and most model builders have now developed sophisticated domestic and external monetary sectors, and considered the links between the real and financial sectors in more detail. The Treasury, in particular, has devoted a considerable amount of research to the development of a monetary sector. Furthermore, in most cases, these monetary sectors are now fully integrated within the main model rather than being mere appendages. Underlying the development of such sectors lies the desire to provide an explanation for those financial variables, such as exchange rates, interest rates and money and credit aggregates, which play a role in the transmission mechanism of monetary policy.

Unlike the ISLM model, and the monetary sectors of the early models, the current domestic monetary sectors are not based on a simple money demand and money supply framework, but instead are constructed around accounting schemes containing the government budget constraint and the balance sheet identities of the banking and non-bank private sectors. However, as is the case in the ISLM model, decision-making in the models is segmented between real expenditure and dealings in financial assets. Once all the real expenditure decisions have been taken, the financial surpluses and deficits of the various decision-making sectors are assumed to feed into the monetary model creating demands for and supplies of the different financial assets. Explicit demand for money functions are generally not modelled, although narrow money aggregates such as M1 and notes and coin are related to demand variables in some of the models. The broader monetary aggregates, M3 and sterling M3, are assumed, in all cases, to reflect both demand and supply pressures. In the LBS and CEPG models sterling M3 equations are explicitly modelled to illustrate both sets of influences, while in the HMT, BE and NI models the quantity of broad money is determined as a residual which, within the particular framework adopted, ensures consistency among the other financial decisions analysed. In this case the demand and supply factors which influence these other decisions implicitly determine the broad monetary aggregate. The structure of interest rates in the current models is determined either by the operation of market clearing mechanisms in certain financial markets, as in the HMT model, or more usually by the specification of reaction functions which relate the level of rates to the policy goals of the authorities. This latter practice reflects the tendency of the UK authorities to use interest rates rather than the money supply as a direct instrument of policy.

Parallel developments have also taken place in recent years in the modelling of external monetary relations, and now most models attempt to explain the exchange rate. In the HMT and CEPG models this is done within the context of an explicit structural model which considers both the current and capital accounts of the balance of payments, while in the LBS, NI and BE models the exchange rate is modelled more directly.

3. The transmission mechanism of monetary policy in UK macro models

MONETARIST AND KEYNESIAN VIEWS WITHIN THE ISLM FRAMEWORK

The transmission mechanism of monetary policy is the process by which monetary impulses influence the real sector of the economy. Within the closed economy ISLM framework, the effect on income of a change in the money supply depends on the relative interest sensitivity of the demand for money and the demand for goods. In fact, the traditional Keynesian and monetarist transmission mechanisms differ largely in their prior beliefs as to the values taken by these interest rate parameters.[12]

Keynesians tend to stress the high degree of substitutability existing between money and other financial assets, and therefore believe that the demand for money is highly interest elastic. The monetarist position, on the other hand, is to stress the unique attributes of money. They believe that it has no close substitutes in either financial or real assets. In consequence, the interest elasticity of the demand for money balances is felt to be quite low. In the goods market, the traditional Keynesian position questions the influence of interest rates on investment expenditure and rather neglects any possible influence they might have on consumption decisions. This results in a relatively interest inelastic demand for goods function. In contrast, the monetarist position is generally characterised by a much more interest elastic demand for goods function. Translating these views into the ISLM framework, the greater the interest sensitivity of the demand for money function, the flatter is the LM schedule and, *ceteris paribus,* the weaker is the effect of a monetary change on income; the greater the interest sensitivity of investment and consumption expenditures, the flatter is the IS relation and the stronger is the effect of monetary policy.

THE TRANSMISSION MECHANISM—AN ALTERNATIVE APPROACH

The ISLM model is, of course, highly aggregated and considers only three assets: money, bonds and real assets. The transmission mechanism in a closed economy can, however, also be seen in terms of general portfolio adjustment within an extended framework. In this case an open market purchase of bonds by the authorities, which increases the money supply and therefore creates a disequilibrium situation, can be shown to set in motion a process of adjustment back to a position of portfolio equilibrium. This process of monetary transmission can be analysed in terms of the adjustment of the relative rates of return on different kinds of assets, and in addition wealth and credit availability effects may also have a role to play in the mechanism. Goodhart and Crockett (1970) and Park (1972) analyse the Keynesian and monetarist positions within such a framework.

In the Keynesian case the portfolio adjustment process is tempered by the belief that financial assets, particularly of a short-term liquid nature, are close substitutes for money, whereas goods and real assets are not such close substitutes. The Keynesian view is therefore that the initial disequilibrium results in the purchase of money substitutes, that is alternative liquid financial assets, rather than directly in the purchase of goods and physical assets. This process raises the price and hence lowers the yield on these financial assets, and in turn causes further purchases of somewhat less liquid assets further along the liquidity spectrum. Changes in the money supply therefore produce a ripple effect all along the asset spectrum and in this way the portfolio imbalance is spread from market to market. As the process continues a gap opens between the yields available to investors on purchases of real assets and the reduced yield on financial securities, so that a divergence is created between the cost of borrowing or the cost of capital and the return available on capital. In consequence, it becomes profitable for members of the productive sector to reduce their own holdings of financial assets, or to issue new liabilities upon themselves, in order to obtain funds for the purchase of additional real assets. The change in financial asset yields, operating via this portfolio adjustment mechanism, induces investment and real assets are produced. The production of new capital goods, in turn, affects consumers' expenditure via the multiplier. The adjustment of interest rates in this way therefore moves the system to a new equilibrium at a higher level of expenditure.

Among Keynesians there are however alternative views about the range of financial assets which should be considered in the portfolio adjustment system. In particular, Tobin (1969) feels that the adjustment mechanism should include equities as well as bonds. In this way Tobin rejects the traditional Keynesian notion that it is the bond yield which determines the cost of capital for firms. Instead he places emphasis on the equity yield, which in conjunction with the supply price of capital is said to determine the marginal profitability of investment. Thus an expansionary monetary policy, by lowering the yield on equities, creates a discrepancy between the market valuation of real assets (the price of equities) and their costs of production. This discrepancy stimulates investment by providing an incentive for the production of capital goods.

Given their views about the degree of substitution between financial and real assets, however, many Keynesians would question the importance of this channel of influence, regardless of the range of assets considered. Changes in the money supply, they argue, will have smaller and smaller effects on asset rates of return as the adjustment process proceeds along the liquidity spectrum; in consequence, any effect on the production of real assets is likely to be small. Keynesians therefore generally question the importance of any output effects arising from an increase in the money supply.

This view predominates in the majority of macro models. Indeed, interest rate or cost of capital effects on private fixed investment are not included in many models, and those that do allow for such influences have often not been able to identify significant effects. This would appear to be the case regardless of whether the relationship is measured using nominal rates of interest or real rates, that is, the nominal rate adjusted for (expected) inflation. Similarly, most models have found little evidence of any relationship between interest rates and investment in stockbuilding, although such factors do seem to be much more important in influencing private sector investment in housebuilding. In this case however, as we shall see in section 7, there is some doubt as to the way in which interest rates exert their influence. Both the supply of and demand for new housing may depend on the level of interest rates, and in addition relative rates can be used as a proxy for credit-rationing effect.

Wealth effects

The link between consumption and wealth has received considerable attention since Ando and Modigliani (1963) formulated their 'life-cycle' hypothesis of consumer behaviour, and in the modern Keynesian interpretation of the transmission mechanism wealth effects play a major role. Such effects can take a variety of different forms depending on the way in which wealth is defined. In the models the wealth measures used range from a narrow liquidity measure of personal sector asset holdings in the BE model to the much broader wealth aggregates favoured by HMT and CE. This choice between wealth and liquid assets can obviously have important implications for the way in which monetary changes influence consumption. Thus, whereas according to liquidity theories of consumption an increase in personal sector holdings of money balances, occurring as a result of monetary policy, will increase consumption, according to wealth theories this change may well leave consumption unaffected. This is because the overall wealth of the personal sector remains the same if the change in the money supply is brought about by an open market operation involving the exchange of illiquid government bonds for liquid cash or bank deposits in the portfolio of the personal sector.

Traditionally Keynesians have tended to stress the influence of wealth effects operating through the rate of interest. In particular it is alleged that a change in interest rates alters the market value of capital-uncertain assets already held. Keynes called this the windfall effect, although it can also be termed a capital revaluation effect. It is most readily seen with respect to bond holdings, whose value is increased by an expansionary monetary policy which lowers the rate of interest. Such capital revaluation effects can strengthen the impact on economic activity of the portfolio adjustments already referred to by increasing the size of the net portfolios available for allocation. Only the HMT model makes any attempt to take account of this capital revaluation effect. Even here this is a relatively new development as such an effect was only introduced in the 1980 version of the model. Until this departure the traditional view, implicitly taken by UK investigators, has always been that consumers take no account of changes in the valuation of their wealth after making their initial saving. This in turn implies that capital gains and losses have no effect on consumption.

One other type of wealth effect is associated with the work of Pigou (1943). This 'Pigou effect' refers to the process by which a lower price level increases the real value of accumulated personal sector assets, thus inducing an increase in consumption. Similarly, increases in the price level will lower the value of real balances and so reduce consumption. Such effects are to be found in the HMT, LBS and NI models.

Wealth effects, in whatever form, are primarily a measure of the responsiveness of consumption to changes in asset values. They have however largely been ignored in the traditional ISLM analysis. One exception is Silber (1970), who has shown that when wealth effects are considered the IS and LM curves can no longer be considered to be independent. Variations in wealth induced by monetary policy or price level changes will move both curves simultaneously. An increase in the quantity of notes and coin in circulation, or alternatively a reduction in the price level, will cause a rightward shift of both the LM curve and the IS curve. In this way the power of monetary policy is augmented, though there will be a partial offset if the demand for money is also assumed to be a function of wealth.

An extensive debate, summarised in Johnson (1969), exists as to the categories of asset which constitute the economy's stock of net wealth, and this leads to a major problem in the interpretation of wealth effects. In general terms aggregate wealth in the economy can be defined as physical wealth plus any claims held by the private sector which are not offset by corresponding liabilities. For an item to constitute net wealth it must therefore represent an asset to its holders but not a corresponding debt to others. The early debate hinged on the difference between inside and outside money. Inside money is money created against private debt such that the stock of inside money is an asset to those who hold it and a liability to those who issue it. Outside money is money which is an asset to those who hold it, but either not a liability to those who issue it, or else causes any debt that is incurred to be ignored. Bank deposits are inside money while notes and coin issued by the government are outside money. Gurley and Shaw (1960) felt that outside money formed part of net wealth, while inside money did not. Thus only if the increase in the money supply was of the outside variety would net wealth be affected. If all the money created was of the inside variety, the increase in wealth of those who hold the money would merely be cancelled out by the increase in debt of those who issued it, leaving net wealth unchanged. Similarly it was generally believed that other categories of public sector debt, such as government bonds, formed part of net wealth, because the government was deemed to be unconcerned about the resulting rise in the National Debt, while private sector debt did not qualify as net wealth.

This view was challenged by Pesek and Saving (1967) among others, and it is now generally accepted that a more relevant distinction is that between interest-bearing and non-interest-bearing debt, rather than between inside and outside money or private and public sector debt. In particular it is asserted that at the aggregate level only non-interest-bearing debt should be included in the definition of net wealth. Thus non-interest-bearing inside money may be part of net wealth and interest-bearing outside money may not be. Interest-bearing debt is excluded from the definition of wealth because the interest payments on such debt have to be financed in some way. The interest payments on interest-bearing government debt, for example, have to be financed by taxes levied on the private sector. However, to the extent that the individuals who receive the interest payable on government debt are different from those who pay the taxes, the wealth effects may not be completely cancelled out. In this respect Blinder and Solow (1973) place great emphasis on the bond coupon effect, that is the process by which changes in interest receipts affect the property income component of the disposable income of creditor units in the personal sector, and hence their consumption expenditure. Such bond coupon effects exert their influence on expenditure in the opposite direction to the more conventional interest rate effects and are potentially a much more powerful influence on consumption in all the models, particularly in the short term. In fact the conventional interest rate or cost of credit effects on consumption receive scant attention in most models. For units which are net debtors the bond coupon effect will of course serve to reduce real disposable income. Higher interest rates reduce the cash flow of the company sector which is a net debtor, and may in consequence have a depressing effect on investment expenditure. Such effects exist in the current LBS, NI and CEPG models, and in the 1979 version of the HMT model.

Generally in fact, from the point of view of analysing the influence of wealth effects on expenditure, the way in which the economy's stock of wealth is distributed between the various creditor and debtor units of the different sectors will be relevant. Each sector is likely to respond differently to changes in its respective wealth position and here Keynesians, as we have seen, tend to emphasise the effects on consumption of changes in the wealth position of the personal sector. This belief is reflected in the macro models where there tends to be a basic asymmetry within the non-bank private sector between the respective responses of the personal and company sectors to changes in wealth. In all the models wealth effects are confined to the expenditure decisions of the personal sector and no attempt is made to allow for wealth effects of any kind on company sector expenditure decisions. This means that any redistribution of financial indebtedness within the private sector between individuals and companies will have some effect on aggregate demand. Thus while a rise in the price level working through the 'Pigou effect' will lower the real value of company sector liabilities held by the personal sector, and hence depress consumption by individuals, it will not create any offsetting effects on the expenditure decisions of the company sector because no account is taken in the models of the equivalent reduction in the company sector's real burden of indebtedness.

Credit availability effects

A third relevant channel of monetary influence, stressed by Keynesians, operates through credit rationing, which has to take place when interest rates on loans fail to adjust rapidly enough to clear financial markets. The actual availability of funds may then be a much more important factor than their cost in determining many expenditure decisions. Many markets are imperfect in this way and in such situations lenders may be forced to ration credit by various non-price conditions, such as initial deposits and maximum repayment periods in the hire-purchase finance market, and collateral requirements in the bank advances market. Further, the authorities themselves can vary the conditions under which the public can borrow on hire purchase and also impose directives and ceilings on bank advances. This mode of monetary influence is therefore exerted through the supply side of the loanable funds market in contrast to the channels we have previously considered. Credit availability effects are also exerted in a peculiar way in the housing market. Here the deposit and lending rates offered by the building societies are slow to adapt to market rates because of political and social pressures and the costs of change. As a result building society rates are often described as 'sticky'. This is important because, when there is a divergence between building society and market rates, changes may take place in the channels through which funds flow. In consequence, building societies tend to experience large inflows or outflows of deposits according to whether interest rates are falling or rising. This is particularly relevant when rates generally are rising as the building societies are likely to lose deposits to the banks. They may then be forced to ration their mortgage advances with consequent effects in the housing market. The importance of this phenomenon, which is generally known as the 'sticky rate' effect, was emphasised by the Radcliffe Committee (1959), which claimed that the overall liquidity of the economy was a much more important aggregate for policy purposes than the stock of money.

Credit availability effects appear extensively in the different models, particularly in relation to consumer durable and private housebuilding expenditures. In analysing this channel of influence the models therefore concentrate primarily on its effects on the expenditure decisions of the personal sector. The cash flow position of companies could of course equally well be relevant to their fixed investment and stockbuilding decisions, and indeed the CEPG, NI and LBS models do try to take account of such effects by relating investment to liquidity and profitability variables.

As a kind of mixture of the wealth and credit availability effects, financial institutions may also be unwilling to reallocate their portfolios when there has been a severe fall in the prices of the assets they are presently holding, in order to avoid realising capital losses. In such circumstances, institutions may feel irrationally that they are 'locked in' to their present portfolio and as a result are likely to be very cautious about expanding their lending activity. The 'potential' loss of wealth experienced by financial institutions, consequent on the fall in asset prices, therefore results in a lack of available funds to prospective borrowers. Accordingly the personal sector's spending decisions have to be amended. This aspect of the transmission mechanism, the lock-in effect, was also stressed in the Radcliffe Report.

MONETARIST VIEWS

In portfolio adjustment terms, the monetarist interpretation of the transmission mechanism in a closed economy is formally similar to the Keynesian analysis outlined above. However, the range of assets considered in the monetarist transmission mechanism is much greater because money is not regarded as a close substitute for only a small range of financial assets as it is regarded by Keynesians. Instead money is seen as a unique asset which is highly substitutable for all other assets, real and financial, and is therefore no particular substitute for any one of them. Monetarists, as well as Keynesians, believe that changes in the money supply operate through changes in interest rates, but in the monetarist case the range of relevant rates is much greater and includes the implicit rates of return on real assets. When the money supply is changed, monetarists argue that individuals and firms are just as likely to adjust their portfolios by altering their expenditure on capital goods, including consumer durables, as by buying or selling financial assets. Monetarists therefore believe that a rise in the money supply will lead directly to an increase in expenditure. The demand for real assets will rise, not only because of direct substitution of money for these assets, but also because as prices of financial assets are bid up, real assets become a preferable substitute. Prices of existing real assets therefore rise and these, in turn, become expensive relative to newly produced assets. As a consequence, the demand for current output rises and production is expanded. This mechanism, by which a change in the stock of real cash balances in the individual's portfolio has a direct effect upon his demand for commodities, can be termed a real balance effect and is in essence a type of wealth effect.[13] Equilibrium is restored when the excess real money balances have been eliminated and the nominal money supply is just demanded. This, monetarists argue, can occur either through increases in the price level, or real income adjustment, or some combination of both. Less emphasis is therefore placed on the interest rate as the equilibrating force than is the case in the conventional Keynesian transmission mechanism. In fact, monetarists would argue that, although nominal interest rates are initially lowered by increases in the quantity of money, this effect is only temporary. In the longer term they believe that the price effects of the increase in the money supply will shift the LM curve back to the left, so inducing a rise in nominal interest rates. If the money supply is repeatedly increased, anticipated inflation will raise nominal interest rates further so as to leave real interest rates unchanged.

Nevertheless, although monetarists stress both the income and price effects of any increase in the money supply, in contrast to the Keynesian position, their analysis tends to be rather vague as to the precise quantitative effect of such a change on the respective values of the price level and real output. The way in which changes in nominal output are divided between movements in real income and the price level will, of course, be closely related to the shape of the aggregate supply curve. The more orthodox monetarist position, as outlined in Friedman (1970) and Laidler (1978a), asserts that in the short run, with an upward sloping aggregate supply schedule, a change in the money supply will have significant effects on real income and output. In the longer term, however, as the aggregate supply curve approaches the vertical, it is argued that the total effect on output will be quite small and will eventually diminish to zero, so that the adjustment is solely an adjustment of the general price level with real output, as well as real interest rates, eventually unchanged from their initial levels.

On the other hand, the 'rational expectations' monetarists, as exemplified by Sargent and Wallace (1976), believe that only unanticipated changes in the money stock will have any effect on real income in the short run, and that even this effect will disappear in the long run. Changes in the money supply which are expected will have no real effects, and will influence only the price level. This follows because, under the 'rational expectations' hypothesis, any increase in the money supply causes an immediate adjustment in the expected price level so that the short-run aggregate supply curve moves to the left, thus preventing any increase in real output.[14]

The monetarist transmission mechanism would therefore appear to operate through changes in a broad spectrum of asset yields, price level changes and expectational effects which influence both financial and physical assets. Given such views it is obvious that the ISLM model is a particularly inadequate framework for analysis, and indeed many monetarists have rejected the approach. Brunner and Meltzer (1972), for example, developed an alternative monetarist approach to the transmission mechanism which stresses the role of capital goods. In particular, changes in the 'asset', or demand, price of real capital relative to its 'output', or supply, price form a crucial linkage in the transmission process. A distinction is made between financial assets, consumption goods and three categories of capital goods. The first of these comprises capital goods for which there are separate prices for existing stock (through equity prices) and new output. Such goods include plant, machinery and equipment. The second group consists of capital goods for which the price of existing and new stock of comparable quality is the same. Included here are goods such as housing and cars. The third category is made up of goods for which there is no market for existing stock so that a price for new output alone exists. Such goods include certain types of consumer durables. According to Brunner and Meltzer the transmission mechanism operates through wealth and substitution effects across the different goods markets. An increase in the supply of money, for example, will, through portfolio substitutions, lead to an overall increase in the asset prices of all these types of real capital goods. In particular the increase in the equity price relative to the output price for the first type of real capital goods increases the optimal stock of such goods and so accelerates their actual rate of accumulation.[15] Similarly the increase in the asset price of the second type of capital goods stimulates the production of such goods. Furthermore, the rise in the asset prices of real capital and the fall in the rates of return on financial assets raises the market value of wealth, which in turn increases the desired stock of the third category of capital goods and also consumption expenditure.[16] The total effect of the expansionary monetary policy can then be determined as the sum of these different influences.

Money, output and prices

Until recently the main UK macro models have not incorporated any direct effect on total demand, arising in the short term, from changes in real money balances, because they have developed out of the Keynesian tradition of model building and therefore in the main adopt the Keynesian view of the transmission mechanism. Nevertheless increasingly links are appearing in the large UK models between the money supply and particular expenditure decisions, and between money and the price level. In the LBS model, for example, the equations for consumer durable expenditure, non-residential fixed investment and stockholding include money supply variables. In addition, the stock of money is a major component of the more broadly defined liquid asset and wealth variables which appear in most models as a determinant of consumers' expenditure.

The links between money and prices in the models are, as we shall see later in this section, much stronger in the context of an open economy operating under floating exchange rates. Nevertheless, even in a closed economy setting, links do exist in the models between monetary policy and prices, although these tend to be fairly weak because monetary measures are assumed to influence the price level only after the short-run real output and employment adjustments have taken place.

Even then the links between output, or other measures of the pressure of demand, and prices are subject to a further lagged response. A direct link between the two exists only in the NI model where the change in manufacturing output is included in an equation for the consumer price index. In the HMT, CE and NI models links exist through the augmented Phillips curve via unemployment and earnings. Changes in the pressure of demand, measured in terms of unemployment, are assumed to exert an influence on wages and ultimately prices given the lagged interaction between these variables. In the CE model, a 1 per cent increase in the unemployment rate causes a 1.8 per cent reduction in the rate of wage inflation, while in the HMT model the relationship is more complex and depends on the rate of unemployment. The earnings equation of the LBS model also includes a GDP term, but the CEPG and BE models do not incorporate excess demand variables of any form directly into their wage equations. Nevertheless a similar effect can exist indirectly in the BE model because of the influence of demand pressures on overtime working and hence the total wage bill. In the CEPG model wages rise more slowly the faster the growth of output, because workers are assumed to demand nominal wages sufficient to give them a target real post-tax income level, assuming inflation is at last year's rate. If output grew slowly last period, they demand a larger wage rise this period in order to compensate for the slippage below target income.

In most models the link between monetary policy and the level of prices is completed by the influence of wage costs on domestic prices. Prices do not, however, respond either instantaneously or fully to a change in wages. In the HMT model, for example, changes in wage costs take up to 3 quarters to exert their full influence on the domestic price level, with a long-run coefficient of 0.66. In the CE model the response is quicker and larger with 75 per cent of any change in domestic unit costs feeding through into domestic prices. On the whole, however, this link between monetary policy and the price level, relying in the main on pressure of demand effects in the labour market, tends to be rather weak and slow to work.

The 1980 version of the HMT model also emphasises the role of expectations in the labour market as a possible link between money and prices. A relationship is assumed between money supply growth and price expectations, and given the expected inflation term in the wage equation, money supply influences can be transmitted directly to wages and hence prices. This concession to the 'rational expectations' view of monetary policy does not find favour with the other large macro model builders. Rather it is generally associated with the much smaller monetarist models, such as the Liverpool model which is outlined in Minford (1980).

Further links are provided between monetary policy and the price level by the role played by financial variables in certain individual price relations. In particular the prices of new houses in many of the models respond to variations in such variables. New house prices in the BE model, for instance, are related to the real level of loans for house purchase and personal sector 'surplus' liquidity, while in the LBS model such prices are influenced by the mortgage rate. In the HMT model new house prices are influenced by the supply of building society advances; and higher interest rates raise mortgage costs, which are a component of the retail price index.

THE OPEN ECONOMY

To date in our discussion of the transmission mechanism we have implicitly assumed the existence of a closed economy in which there is no trade with the rest of the world. The theory of the transmission mechanism can however easily be extended to the open economy, and studies by Fleming (1962) and Mundell (1962, 1963) have considered the effects of monetary expansion under both fixed and floating exchange rate regimes using the extended ISLM system incorporating a balance of payments sector. The exchange rate regime adopted by the authorities has potentially important implications for the way in which the money supply interacts with other variables. In a small open economy under fixed exchange rates the immediate effect of an increase in the money supply is to lower the rate of interest and raise the level of income. This leads to a deterioration of both the capital and current accounts and moves the economy into a deficit position on its overall balance of payments. In order to finance this deficit importers use domestic currency to buy foreign exchange from the Exchange Equalisation Account. In consequence the foreign exchange reserves decline and domestic money is withdrawn from the system.[17] The money supply falls and ultimately returns to its original level, as do the levels of interest rates and income. Furthermore the greater the degree of capital mobility existing between the home country and the rest of the world, that is the more interest elastic is the BB curve, the quicker this adjustment will take place. Under fixed exchange rates any attempt to increase the money supply is therefore bound to prove ineffectual. Monetary policy is ineffective since the nominal money supply can change through induced reserve changes. Only the volume of domestic credit can be controlled by the authorities.

If the authorities sterilise the impact of external influences on the money supply by increasing the domestic component, they will be able to pursue an independent monetary policy temporarily. However, such a policy will be self defeating because such increases in the domestic money supply will further reduce domestic interest rates, so causing new capital outflows and increasing the need for sterilisation. In such an environment the country's stock of foreign exchange reserves will continue to fall until they are eventually exhausted. Such a policy of sterilisation can therefore allow the authorities to pursue an independent monetary policy only temporarily.

Under floating exchange rates an increase in the money supply will also lower the interest rate and raise income, creating a balance of payments deficit.

However, in this case no outflow of reserves takes place and instead the exchange rate depreciates. The BB curve moves to the right and there is a relative decline, in terms of the domestic currency, in the price of home goods compared to those in the rest of the world. In consequence, competitiveness increases so that exports rise and imports fall. Overall net injections into the economy increase, causing a rightward movement in the IS curve. Equilibrium is re-established at a higher income level and lower interest rate than previously, with the indirect effect on the IS curve augmenting the increase in income. Monetary policy has in this case raised the level of income at the cost of a lower exchange rate. An independent monetary policy is therefore only possible in a small economy under a floating exchange rate regime.[18] Furthermore the potency of monetary policy under such a regime will depend on the degree of capital mobility existing between the home economy and the rest of the world. The more interest elastic is the BB curve, the greater is the effect of a change in the money supply on income.

In Mundell's model prices were assumed to be exogenously determined under both fixed and floating exchange rates. The determination of prices and their relation to the money supply are clarified in the monetary theory of the balance of payments, developed by Johnson (1972) and others.[19] Within this approach, any increase in the domestic money supply above the world rate of monetary expansion is assumed to create a disequilibrium in the money market which has repercussions in the external sector. Under fixed exchange rates a balance of payments deficit is created with consequent reserve losses leading to a reduction in the money supply. This process continues until the deficit has been eliminated and the money supply has returned to its initial level. The monetary expansion and subsequent adjustment cannot, in the small country case, affect the domestic price level which, when converted at the fixed exchange rate, is assumed to equal that existing in the rest of the world, so that purchasing power parity or 'the law of one price' holds between countries. The different countries of the world become one economy tied by completely fixed exchange rates and having one level of prices. This equalisation of world prices is ensured by the operation of a form of international arbitrage between traded goods. The money supply remains an endogenous variable in the presence of a non-tradable goods sector, but in this case the adjustment process will take longer.

Under floating exchange rates countries' relative excess supplies of money determine the exchange rate and not the payments deficit. The money supply and therefore the domestic price level can be independently determined. If the domestic money supply is increased at a faster rate than the world money supply the exchange rate will decline. The immediate effect of this depreciation is to increase the home currency price of imported goods and so improve the competitiveness of the economy. This in turn should influence trade flows and the real economy generally. Monetary policy is therefore potentially very powerful under a floating regime. In time however the domestic price level will respond to the change in import prices and, because earnings are determined partly as a mark up on prices, a wage–price spiral can be set in motion. Export prices will also eventually adjust to this, so that the economy's initial gain in competitiveness, resulting from the fall in the exchange rate, is likely to be eroded, and ultimately disappear.

Any induced change in the exchange rate is therefore likely to have extensive short-run repercussions for the international price and cost competitiveness of the economy. In this way a link is created, under floating exchange rates, between money and prices which is much more direct than that existing in a closed economy or an open economy operating under fixed exchange rates. Several factors influence the speed with which such effects are transmitted throughout the economy and therefore the size and duration of any potential gains in competitiveness. One consideration is the strength of the wage–price feedback. Another factor is the extent to which changes in the exchange rate, and hence import prices in terms of sterling, are absorbed into domestic prices. In most of the models domestic prices and wages do not adjust immediately, or fully, to any change in import prices, but in the CEPG model changes in sterling import prices are passed fully on to domestic prices, and wages in turn adjust to prices, so that any gains in competitiveness are quickly eroded.

Because of the way in which the exchange rate is determined in the different models, there are several distinct ways in which monetary variables can initially influence the exchange rate. Some of these channels are much more direct than others. The LBS, BE and HMT models all assign a role to the money supply in the determination of the exchange rate. In the LBS and BE models, in accord with the monetary theory of exchange rate determination, the equilibrium exchange rate is related to the growth of the money supply relative to that of the demand for money in the UK as compared to the rest of the world. Similarly, in the HMT model capital flows depend on the equilibrium exchange rate, which is also partly determined by money supply growth in the UK relative to that in the rest of the world. In this case the scale of the effects arising from changes in the money supply depends crucially on the weight given to monetary growth in the determination of the equilibrium rate (75 per cent in the 1980 model).

In addition, in the HMT, BE, LBS, CEPG and NI models, monetary policy can also exert an influence on the exchange rate through the effect of changes in interest rates on capital flows. Such effects tend to be particularly important in the short run and are often associated with speculative behaviour. Finally, to the extent that financial variables may influence domestic demand, and hence imports and the current account of the balance of payments, there is yet another channel by which monetary policy can affect the exchange rate and thus import prices in terms of sterling. Such a channel of influence is present in the HMT model since here the long-run value of the exchange rate is assumed to depend on factors such as activity rates which determine the current account of the balance of payments. In addition in the BE and NI models, the level of the exchange rate is related to balance of payments variables, while in the CEPG model the state of the current account influences short-term capital flows and hence the exchange rate.

In the next four sections we consider the main expenditure decisions in more detail and particularly the way in which financial variables exert their influence. In section 8 we then look at the modelling of monetary variables in the domestic and external financial sectors of the different models.

4. Consumption

THE BASIC EQUATIONS

The consumption function plays a key role in any income–expenditure framework and this is reflected in the structure of the various models. In the early versions consumption was analysed as a single aggregate, but now in most cases separate functions are estimated for durable and non-durable goods.[20] Thus, although only one aggregate consumption function is specified in the 1979 NI model, recent research at the National Institute, reported in Cuthbertson (1980) and Bladen-Hovell *et al.* (1982), has been concerned with estimating separate durable and non-durable consumption functions. In addition, many of the models, presumably in an attempt to forecast tax receipts, estimate separate equations for items such as beer, tobacco, wines and spirits, energy, cars and petrol. An extreme position is taken in the CE model where forty-two categories of expenditure are considered, although in the condensed version only one aggregate consumption function is estimated. A different approach is adopted in the CEPG model where consumption is analysed as part of the aggregate private expenditure function; consumption in the model is determined as a residual from the aggregate relation and the specification for private fixed investment. Except for the CEPG model, the different consumption equations estimated in the various macro models are all expressed in real terms. In this form they largely eliminate the possibility of money illusion, although, as we shall see later, price and inflation variables are included in some consumption equations. The equations specified tend to be very general forms which relate consumption to present and past values of income; in this form they are consistent with several different theories of consumer behaviour and therefore open to many alternative interpretations.[21]

In the recent versions of the HMT and LBS models the non-durable consumption functions are based on the methodology developed by Davidson *et al.* (1978). Recent research on consumer behaviour at the National Institute, as reported in Bladen-Hovell *et al.* (1982), has also been concerned with this approach, which is outlined in more detail in the survey by Thomas in this volume. Basically the approach implies that individuals revise their consumption decisions in accordance with changes in the level and growth rate of income over the last four quarters. The higher the rate of growth of income, the lower the increase in consumption for a given level of income. These terms together define the short-run consumption position. This decision is however modified by an 'error feed-back' mechanism which ensures that in dynamic equilibrium consumption is proportional to income in accordance with a long-run target level. In the HMT model a variable measuring the change in the rate of unemployment over the previous year is also to be found in the specification. The rationale for this variable lies in the fact that a rising level of unemployment, by changing expectations, should increase precautionary savings.

Research at the Treasury, reported in Meen (1979a, b), has been concerned with extending the Davidson *et al.* methodology to the analysis of consumer durable expenditure, and this is reflected in the 1980 version of the HMT model. A similar approach is adopted by the LBS, but in the other models consumption of durables is normally analysed in terms of a conventional stock adjustment formulation in which expenditure is determined by the desired stock of durables and the stock already held. If the existing stock of durables is represented by a lagged function of past consumption, such an approach leads to a reduced form in which consumer durable expenditure is related to its own lagged values and the factors determining the desired stock of durables. This type of approach to the modelling of durables is adopted by Bean (1978) and utilised in the 1979 version of the HMT model. The BE model also adopts a similar approach. Here the desired stock of durables is, among other variables, related to permanent non-grant income; it is assumed that all grant income (government transfer payments) is spent on non-durables within three quarters. A similar distinction between the different types of income is made in the 1979 version of the NI model, with the marginal propensity to consume out of grant income being higher than that out of non-grant income. The early versions of the HMT model also disaggregated personal disposable income by source, but the practice was discontinued because it was generally felt that the exercise did not significantly improve the explanatory power of the consumption equations.

FINANCIAL INFLUENCES ON CONSUMPTION

Traditional Keynesian analysis tended to neglect the influence of financial variables on consumption. This is no longer the case and the consumption equations of the main macro models all contain financial effects in one form or another. There are three main ways in which monetary factors can affect consumer demand. First, the stock of wealth held by the community may be an important determinant of consumer demand. Wealth in this case can either be defined broadly to include illiquid financial assets and even physical capital, or else much more narrowly to include only liquid financial assets such as bank and building society deposits. Within the wider definition, capital gains arising from variations in stock and share prices influence the level of wealth and hence consumption. A further distinction can also be made between gross and net asset holdings, the latter involving the deduction of liabilities such as bank borrowing from the gross value. Second, changes in interest rates may exert a general influence, apart from their wealth effects, on the decision to save or consume. Here interest rates are potentially very important, because of the way in which they affect the cost of any borrowing undertaken in order to finance consumption. This mechanism, by which a change in interest rates affects consumption, can be termed a cost of credit effect. Third, credit rationing by financial institutions and its formal reinforcement by official controls can also affect consumption and durable expenditure in particular. We will now consider each of these financial influences in turn.

Wealth effects

Attempts at quantifying the importance of wealth effects on consumption are unfortunately handicapped by the limited nature of the available data. Official quarterly wealth series have only recently become available, and in any case the reliability of these series must be questioned since the measurement of wealth, involving as it does the valuation of assets, is necessarily difficult. In consequence, the role of asset variables, such as wealth or liquid assets, in the consumption function has traditionally been rather neglected by UK investigators. Recently, however, with the development of the new data series, and as greater importance has come to be attached to the role of wealth and liquid assets in influencing consumption decisions, more research has been undertaken in this area. Indeed, empirical evidence for the 1970s as outlined, for example, in Townend (1976) and Bean (1978), would tend to suggest that wealth or liquid asset variables, of one kind or another, have to be incorporated into consumption functions in order to help explain the rise in the savings ratio which occurred during this period. In consequence, most of the consumption equations in the UK macro models now include wealth or liquid asset variables in some form, although there is considerable disagreement over the particular choice of variable.

The BE model closely follows the work of Townend (1976) and includes the real value of persons' net liquid asset holdings in both the durable and non-durable consumption functions. The coefficients on these variables are, in each case, highly significant. Townend found no evidence of any significant role for the additional wealth variables he investigated, such as measures of the real stock of illiquid assets held by the personal sector and variables designed to capture the change in share prices and the rate of increase in house prices. The 1980 version of the LBS model also includes various liquid asset variables, but in the 1981 version these have been omitted from the consumption equations.[22] In addition, although the 1979 version of the NI model does not include any liquid asset variables, recent research at the Institute, as reported in Cuthbertson (1980) and Bladen-Hovell *et al.* (1982), has been concerned with examining the influence on both durable and non-durable consumption of the ratio of the stock of liquid assets to income and other liquid assets variables.

In contrast, research at the Treasury, as outlined in Bean (1978) and Meen (1979a), has been unable to find any empirical support for the view that personal sector liquidity is an important determinant of either durable or non-durable expenditure. Instead broader wealth variables were found to be a much more relevant influence on consumers' expenditure, and so such effects have been incorporated into the recent versions of the HMT model. The 1980 HMT consumer durable expenditure specification and the equation for spending on cars contain variables in real private sector net financial wealth; the CE model also assumes that real personal wealth is a determinant of consumption. In the CE model wealth is measured by the summation of past savings, but in the HMT model the wealth variables are defined in such a way as to take account of revaluations in personal share and bond holdings as well as new savings. The incorporation, in this way, of a link between the market value of stocks and shares and consumption is a relatively new development which is only present in the 1980 listing of the HMT model. It brings the model into line with the Federal Reserve – MIT – University of Pennsylvania (FMP) model of the US economy, which stresses the stock market link between monetary policy and consumer demand. Using this model Modigliani (1975) has reported simulations for the US indicating that interest rate effects which work through consumption, via revaluation effects, are larger and faster than those which work through investment. This result follows because, although investment is more interest elastic than consumption in the model, the latter is a much larger component of total expenditure in the economy. The implication of this approach, that capital gains and losses will have an influence on consumption, is contrary to the earlier conventional wisdom, as outlined in Dow (1964: 283–5). In fact the empirical literature, as surveyed by Thomas in this volume, is rather unclear as to the precise role played by capital gains in influencing consumption.

Other types of wealth effect arise because of the existence in the consumption equations of some models of variables measuring the change or rate of change of prices. In particular the non-durable consumption equations in the LBS and HMT models, and the aggregate consumers' expenditure function in the 1979 version of the NI model include such terms. These variables can be interpreted as measures of a 'Pigou effect', by which a rising price level reduces the real value of money-fixed assets and so reduces consumption. Such variables may therefore represent an implicit wealth effect.[23] Recent research at the National Institute, reported in Cuthbertson (1980) and Bladen-Hovell *et al.* (1982), has also analysed the effects on both durable and non-durable consumption of a combined multiplicative term in the inflation rate and the liquid assets to income ratio. In this form the variable is designed to be a measure of the inflation loss on the outstanding stock of liquid assets. Cuthbertson found, however, that this term was not a significant determinant of durable consumption. Finally, it is worth noting that the consumer durable equation in the 1981 version of the LBS model contains a real money supply variable, defined as sterling M3 adjusted for the distortions arising from the imposition of the 'corset', deflated by a consumer price index. In this form the variable can be broadly interpreted as capturing a real balance effect consistent with the monetarist view of the transmission mechanism.

A variety of 'wealth' variables have therefore been used by UK investigators, largely in an attempt to explain recent trends in consumer spending and particularly the rise in the savings ratio. Unfortunately, in many cases the findings of the different research groups are contradictory and consequently it is difficult to reach a definite conclusion as to which wealth measure is the most appropriate.[24]

Interest rate and credit availability effects

The other potential channels of monetary influence on consumption work through interest rate and availability effects. The traditional view is that interest rate effects are unimportant in determining consumption, and indeed there is little firm evidence that changes in interest rates, apart from their revaluation effects, have any direct influence on overall savings levels and hence consumption. In fact, there is some ambiguity about the direction of the effect to be expected, since the substitution and income effects of a change in interest rates exert opposite influences on savings. Potentially the most important way in which interest rates can directly influence consumption, and particularly durable expenditure, is via their effects on the outstanding quantity of bank advances and hire-purchase finance.

Changes in interest rates alter the cost of obtaining credit and so affect the demand for bank advances and hire-purchase loans. Credit availability effects are also likely to be important in these markets, and there is considerable debate as to whether the cost of credit or the availability channel is the dominant influence on consumer durable expenditure. This is particularly the case within the bank advances market and it is possible that the relative importance of the two channels of influence varies according to the conditions prevailing in the market. Thus in times of excess demand for bank advances, when loans and overdrafts are essentially supply determined, it is likely that cost effects will be of secondary importance to the actual flow of credit in the determination of consumer spending. In periods of excess supply the cost of credit, as represented by the interest rate on advances, is likely to be a more important influence.

In order to take account of these possibilities, Cuthbertson (1980) estimated equations for consumer durable expenditure with weighted nominal interest rate and bank credit flow variables included in the specification. The weights, in turn, varied according to the type and extent of the disequilibrium existing in the advances market.[25] Using this technique Cuthbertson found that both the flow and price of bank advances influenced durable expenditure. In contrast, in an alternative specification in which the price and flow variables were not weighted in this way, he found that the credit flow term dominated the interest rate term.[26] This result in turn supported the findings of Bean (1978) and Meen (1979a) who were also unable to isolate a significant cost of credit effect on consumer durable expenditure. The importance of availability effects as a factor in the determination of consumers' expenditure was also confirmed by the results of Surrey (1970), Hilton and Crossfield (1970) and Townend (1976); only Garganas (1975) has reported any failure to find a significant bank lending effect.

The incorporation of bank lending variables into consumption equations, however, leads to a simultaneity problem, since it is not clear whether changes in the level of advances cause changes in expenditure or vice versa. In order to measure availability effects, and at the same time overcome this problem, an alternative approach would be to include dummy variables in the various consumption equations. In particular, because bank credit to the personal sector has often in the past been regulated by lending requests and advances ceilings, availability effects on expenditure could be tested using dummy variables to represent such controls. Many studies, including Garganas (1975), Spencer (1975) and Artis (1978), have found that such controls have in the past had an effect on the outstanding total of advances; but only Borooah (1978) in an unpublished study has made any attempt, albeit unsuccessfully, to measure availability effects on consumers' expenditure in this way.

As regards the hire-purchase market, empirical studies have concentrated on testing the impact on consumers' expenditure of credit restrictions, measured either in terms of the actual flow of hire-purchase finance or alternatively policy variables which indicate the terms on which credit can be borrowed. Hire purchase instruments have in the past taken two principal forms, a minimum deposit requirement and a maximum repayment period. Among empirical studies, Surrey (1970) adopts the former procedure and regresses total consumers' expenditure against the flow of credit, while Cuthbertson (1980) takes the alternative approach and relates durable consumption to a hire-purchase controls variable. This is defined as

$$\mathrm{HP} = d + [(1-d)]/m$$

where d = the minimum percentage down payment
and m = the maximum monthly repayment period.

Thus credit restrictions are deemed to be tighter when either d increases or m falls.[27] Similar policy measures are incorporated into various consumption equation, as tests of credit availability, by Stone (1964), Hilton and Crossfield (1970), Williams (1972), Allard (1974, 1979) and Townend (1976). Ball and Drake (1963) and Garganas (1975) attempt to take account of both types of measure by estimating a two-stage model: in the first, durable expenditure is related to hire-purchase credit flow variables; in the second, these flows are in turn modelled in terms of income or consumer demand, the level of outstanding debt and the hire-purchase policy instruments.[28] In spite of these different approaches to the analysis of the problem, most studies tend to support the view that changes in the availability of hire-purchase credit have significant effects on consumption; although estimates of the scale of the effect vary considerably. In comparison to availability factors, the influence of interest rates in the hire-purchase market has been rather neglected, but Garganas does find that the volume of new credit is sensitive to changes in interest rates.

In the various UK macro models credit availability effects on consumption are more common than interest rate effects, which appear only in the HMT model. Based on the work of Bean (1978) and Meen (1979 a, b), the HMT model includes a real interest rate variable in both the durable expenditure function and the equation for expenditure on cars. This variable is constructed as the difference between the nominal interest rate on bank loans to the personal sector and the expected rate of increase of consumer prices. The latter is in turn constructed from past actual price changes. In the 1979 model the coefficient on the cost of credit variable in the durables equation is freely estimated and found to be insignificantly different from zero, while in the 1980 model the coefficient is constrained to take a small negative value. The coefficient on the variable in the equation for expenditure on cars is insignificantly different from zero. None of the other models incorporates interest rate effects on consumption, although, as we have seen, research at the National Institute by Cuthbertson (1980) has been concerned with this issue, and in the CEPG model interest rates are a determinant of aggregate private expenditure.

In contrast, most models include credit availability effects in one form or another. As with the partial equilibrium studies, these availability effects are either incorporated via policy variables which capture the effect of changes in hire-purchase regulations, or else by terms in the level of outstanding credit. Hire-purchase policy variables are included in the consumer durable equations of the HMT, BE and LBS models. In the BE and LBS models these proxies are represented by the effective minimum deposit rate for durables. The change in real outstanding hire-purchase debt is seen as a determinant of private sector expenditure in the CEPG model, while in the 1979 NI model the consumption equation involves a variable, expressed in real terms, which is constructed from the change in the outstanding stock of bank loans to the personal sector (excluding those for home purchase) and the change in hire-purchase debt outstanding. In the same vein the durables equation in the BE model includes a variable in mortgage lending by building societies. Such a term implies that spending on durables is positively associated with the turnover in housing, and indeed research at the Bank of England, reported in Davis and Saville (1982), suggests that a substantial part of mortgage lending does not ultimately finance new or improved housing, but is used for other forms of expenditure.

Summary

It is apparent that financial influences on consumption can work in a variety of ways. The relative power of the different effects in the models is, however, not entirely clear. Availability effects, which have traditionally assumed a major role in the transmission mechanism, are still found in most models. Although such effects are potentially strong, their influence is confined largely to expenditure on durables, such as cars and household goods, which represent only a small, but nevertheless volatile, proportion of total consumption. Recently wealth effects have also become an established feature of the models, and although in this case the coefficients on the individual wealth variables are generally very small, the sheer magnitude of wealth, as it is defined in the models, means that such effects are important influences on both durable and non-durable consumption. Finally, although interest rate effects are potentially very strong because of the scale of consumption expenditure relative to the other components of aggregate demand, such effects are either weak or not represented at all in the models. Indeed, in practice interest rates tend to exert their main influence on consumption through the bond coupon effect. Because personal disposable income is defined to include receipts from rent, interest and dividends, higher interest rates increase the income of the personal sector, and so exert a powerful indirect influence on consumption in the opposite direction to the conventional cost of credit effects.

5. Private non-residential fixed investment

THE BASIC EQUATIONS

Private non-residential fixed investment in the models is normally analysed by sector rather than type of asset. The CE, BE and HMT models do, however, give separate consideration to investment in certain types of capital. Investment is of course required both to replace plant and machinery which has been withdrawn from use (replacement investment) and to increase the overall size of the capital stock (net investment). The normal practice is to try to explain both categories and so equations are generally specified for gross investment. With the exception of the CEPG model, the various equations are all specified in real terms. The most disaggregated approach is adopted in the CE model where investment is divided into nine assets and forty industries; although the basic functional form used to explain each category of investment is the same, and only one equation is specified in the condensed version of the model. In the BE model six categories of private non-residential fixed investment are distinguished. Equations are modelled for four of these aggregates: plant and machinery investment in manufacturing industry, plant and machinery investment in distribution and services, industrial buildings and vehicles. The HMT model distinguishes between two main categories: investment in manufacturing and that in other industries. A similar distinction is made in the NI model, while the LBS and CEPG models have one principal aggregate investment relation. All models, apart from that of CEPG, give separate consideration to private investment in housebuilding. Public sector investment is also separately treated and normally assumed to be exogenously determined.

The theoretical basis of most of the fixed investment equations is generally some kind of accelerator relationship, so that investment is typically modelled in terms of lagged output variables. All four BE investment equations, for example, include the change in output lagged up to 16 quarters. In three of these equations terms are included in order to represent replacement investment. In the two equations for plant and machinery investment this influence is captured by lagged capital stock variables, while in the equation for vehicles a distributed lag of earlier investment is used. The LBS and HMT models adopt the Davidson *et al.* (1978) methodology so that investment is determined by differenced output and lagged investment variables, and an 'error correction' mechanism which takes into account the ratio of investment to output. Such a form implies that there is a long-run equilibrium ratio between investment and output, around which fluctuations take place in the short run. The HMT equations are based on the work of Bean (1979, 1981). None of the present versions of the UK models adopts the more general neo-classical investment models, developed by Jorgenson and associates, which are based on the assumption of optimisation by the individual firm.[29] Earlier versions of the LBS model, which were associated with the work of Boatwright and Eaton (1972), did, in fact, utilise this framework, and the FMP model of the US economy is also based on the Jorgenson approach.

INTEREST RATE EFFECTS

The traditional Keynesian view of the transmission mechanism stresses the role of interest rate or cost of capital effects on gross fixed investment. The level of interest rates gives an indication of the cost to the firm of obtaining external funds for investment expenditure, or, alternatively, the income which could be obtained if the internal funds of the firm were used to buy financial assets rather than as a source of finance for investment. The lower is the market rate of interest, the more firms will tend to invest. Nevertheless, most models have found little evidence of any relationship between interest rates and gross fixed investment. Only in the CE model and the equation for non-manufacturing investment in the 1980 HMT model can significant interest rate effects definitely be isolated, and even here these effects are very small. The long-term interest rate is included in the manufacturing investment equation of the 1980 HMT model, but its coefficient is insignificantly different from zero; and the private fixed investment equation in the CEPG model also includes an interest rate term, the importance of which is not stated. None of the other models includes interest rate variables in the investment equations, although in most cases some attempt has been made to isolate such effects. At the National Institute, for example, research reported by Savage (1977) failed to find important interest rate effects on manufacturing investment. In addition, although no interest rate effects are included in the investment equations of the BE model, some ad hoc consideration is given to such influences in forecasting exercises at the Bank.

Most other studies of UK investment behaviour, such as Klein *et al.* (1961), Lund and Holden (1968) and Feldstein and Flemming (1971), tend to support the findings of the main macro model builders in their failure to find consistent and significant financial effects. This would appear to be the case regardless of whether interest rate variables have been incorporated in an ad hoc manner or tested within Jorgenson's neo-classical framework. From the point of view of testing for the effect of interest rates on investment both approaches have drawbacks. The former approach, it is argued, involves a fundamental misspecification because it lacks a sound theoretical base, while Jorgenson's method makes it difficult to isolate the effect of interest rates, because in the neo-classical framework the interest rate is assumed to affect investment demand through a composite user cost of capital variable which also takes into account capital goods prices, capital gains and the tax structure. Interest rates are therefore seen as only one factor in the all-embracing user cost of capital, so that it is very difficult to make pronouncements on the relative influence of interest rates and the other components of the cost of capital. In particular, the elasticity of investment is necessarily the same with respect to all of the components of the cost of capital variable. Feldstein and Flemming depart from the standard Jorgenson framework by relaxing this and other restrictive assumptions within the overall model. Their results indicate that the standard model understates the effect of the tax system on the cost of capital, and overstates the significance of all other items, including interest rates. When an interest rate variable was introduced separately in their equation it was found to have the wrong sign. These findings cast some doubt on the results obtained by Nobay (1970), who showed that the fit of manufacturing investment equations was in some cases improved by the inclusion of a Jorgenson-type cost of capital variable with a lag of 5 quarters.

One of the few early studies outside the Jorgenson framework to find any evidence of significant interest rate effects on investment is that of Hines and Catephores (1970), who found that manufacturing investment was significantly related to the change in, and level of, interest rates with lags of 6 and 7 quarters respectively.

These findings are in marked contrast to those obtained by US investigators. The FMP model, for instance, assigns an important role to interest rate effects; and US partial equilibrium studies, which are summarised in Jorgenson (1971), Fisher and Sheppard (1974) and Savage (1978), have also typically found investment to be responsive to changes in interest rates. Most studies do however seem to find that these effects are slow to work and spread over a number of years: the various studies by Jorgenson and his associates, for example, indicate that the response of investment to changes in the cost of capital reaches a peak somewhere between 6 and 12 quarters after the monetary change. Given that with large capital projects a considerable time is bound to lapse between the initial planning of the project and its implementation, these findings are perhaps not really surprising. Brechling (1974, 1975) has however cast doubt on many of the results obtained by Jorgenson-type models which have attempted to analyse investment behaviour in the US. In particular, he alleges that such models give rise to coefficient estimates which display 'implausible magnitudes, "wrong" signs, large standard errors, and a high degree of sensitivity to minor changes in specification' (Brechling 1974: 482).

Are interest rates important?

Although we know from economic theory that the level of investment expenditure undertaken by the firm should be inversely related to the cost of capital, it is obvious from the above summary that, for the UK at least, this theoretical relationship has generally eluded empirical verification. Of course, the general approach of many studies of investment behaviour has been criticised and this must cast doubt on the validity of their findings. In addition, several more specific reasons have been suggested for the failure of most UK investment studies to identify significant interest rate effects. It may be the case that the relationship between the level of investment and interest rates is non-linear, making its empirical verification difficult: interest rates may, for instance, affect investment decisions only after they have reached a certain level. It is also possible that interest rate effects would become more discernible if investment decisions were analysed in a more disaggregated manner. In particular, it may make more sense to analyse investment decisions according to type of asset as well as sector. This practice has of course been adopted to a limited extent in some of the macro models. Supply constraints could also be masking any influence which changes in interest rates have on the demand for capital goods. Keynesian-type macro models largely ignore supply considerations; yet, as Brechling (1974, 1975) points out, the supply side as well as the demand side of the capital goods market should be analysed explicitly if satisfactory tests concerning the interest sensitivity of investment demand are to be carried out.

There are also statistical problems to consider. Griliches and Wallace (1965) point out that when interest rates are pegged by the authorities, it is necessarily very difficult in an estimated equation to find any systematic relationship between the level of investment and interest rates. This comment is particularly relevant to the situation in the UK where interest rates have for long periods been pegged by the authorities. It also seems probable that if interest rates do affect investment, they do so with considerable lags. Consequently in investigating the relationship it may be the case that studies have not found significant rate effects because they have not correctly specified and estimated the required lagged response.[30] Finally, from an econometric point of view simultaneity problems between investment and explanatory variables such as output are likely to affect the reliability of the individual coefficient estimates obtained, including those of the interest rate variables.

It is quite possible that the interest rate variables used in the estimated investment equations do not provide good measures of the cost of capital. Nominal interest rates are used in most formulations, but it is likely a firm undertaking investment expenditure will be more concerned with the prevailing view of the ex-ante real rate of interest.[31] Nevertheless, because of the difficulties of proxying the expected inflation rate, most studies use the observable nominal rate to test the interest responsiveness of investment expenditure. Bean (1981) estimates an equation which includes both a nominal interest rate term and a Jorgenson-type cost of capital variable specified in real terms. By decomposing the cost of capital he was able to isolate a real interest rate term and thus compare its significance with that of the nominal interest rate variable. He found that the coefficients on both interest rates were negatively signed and significantly different from zero. The main fixed investment equations in the 1979 HMT model each include a cost of capital variable which is a weighted average of the nominal and real long rates of interest. The coefficients on the variables were not freely estimated, but in each case the imposed coefficients implied that a permanent 1 per cent increase in the rate of interest (for a given expectation of inflation) would lead to a reduction in investment expenditure of approximately one-fifth over a period of 14 quarters. In the 1980 version of the model these variables were replaced by nominal interest rate terms. The evidence on the desirability of including real interest rates in investment functions is therefore rather inconclusive. This could reflect the difficulties of obtaining an accurate measure of this rate or it could imply another rate would be more relevant. In fact, research at the Bank of England by Flemming *et al.* (1976) suggests that no single variable, whether a nominal borrowing rate, a real rate or the yield on equities, provides a good measure of the cost of capital. Accordingly the authors construct a general measure of the cost of capital to a company in which equity finance and borrowing rates are considered together, and allowance is made for tax relief. In their definition the cost of capital is estimated as the ratio of real post-tax profits to the market valuation of the capital stock. This latter concept is defined as the sum of companies' financial liabilities, that is, equity, loans, preference shares and bank advances, all valued at market prices. They find that the valuation ratio, the relationship between the cost of capital as defined above and the real rate of return on physical capital, has demonstrated a close, though not very robust, relationship with investment. The valuation ratio is seen as a measure of the divergence between the demand and supply prices of capital goods, the significance of which as a determinant of investment was emphasised by Tobin (1969).

It could also be argued that other factors dominate interest rates in influencing investment. Traditional Keynesian analysis stresses the importance of entrepreneurial expectations and business confidence as determinants of investment. In econometric modelling such variables are difficult to proxy and accordingly tend to have been ignored. Another potentially important factor in influencing investment, the actual availability of funds to firms, is more easily modelled. Such availability factors, as we noted with consumption, can often be a more relevant financial influence on expenditure than the cost of finance. Bank lending policies may, for example, impose external constraints on the availability of funds. Finance can also be generated internally from sources such as retained profits, and profitability and liquidity theories of investment arising from such considerations have a long tradition; see, for example, Junankar (1972: 36–7). The main investment equations in the NI and LBS models include terms in the level of profits, and an additional investment equation specified by the LBS for the personal sector contains a variable representing the net flows of bank lending to the sector.[32] A cash flow variable appears in the investment equation of the CEPG model, and a similar term was included in the manufacturing investment equation of the 1979 HMT model, but following the work of Bean (1979) this was omitted in the 1980 model. Bean incorporated a measure of credit rationing and variables measuring the liquidity position of companies in different investment functions, but with litle success. Few other studies have attempted to gauge the influence of the availability of funds on investment. In a recent UK study, Anderson (1981) found that a liquidity flow variable was a significant determinant of investment expenditure; but the inclusion of liquidity variables in investment functions, even when they are correctly signed and significant, poses a simultaneity problem since it could equally well be argued that firms obtain new finance in anticipation of investment taking place. It is also worth noting that in the main investment function in the LBS model, the money supply (sterling M3, adjusted for 'corset' distortions) is included as the deflator in a GDP variable. The estimated coefficient on the variable is such that increases in the money supply stimulate investment, so that the variable can be interpreted as capturing a real balance effect consistent with the monetarist view of the transmission mechanism.

Finally, as well as the direct channels of monetary influence outlined above, there is also an indirect mechanism by which such factors can affect investment. This arises because financial variables, as we noted in section 4, can influence consumers' expenditure and therefore sales and output, which in turn affect investment.

6. Stockbuilding

THE BASIC EQUATIONS

All the major UK macro models make some attempt to specify equations for stockbuilding, although many of these do not perform particularly well. Indeed, analysing the determinants of stockholding by firms is a problem area, partly because a large element of total inventory investment is unplanned. A stock adjustment mechanism lies at the centre of most stockbuilding specifications in the various models. The desired level of stocks is generally assumed to be dependent on expected output or demand as proxied by lagged output or sales. The most disaggregated approach is adopted in the CE model where two categories of stockbuilding are distinguished for the forty different industry groupings. However, in each case the specification is the same, so that in the condensed version of the model only one stockholding equation is estimated; a basic stock adjustment formulation. The HMT model contains six equations for the several types of stocks held by manufacturers, distributors and others. Within the manufacturing sector separate equations are specified for stocks of materials and fuels, stocks of finished goods and work in progress. For each of these categories, holdings are related to production or sales measures and lagged values of stocks. In the BE model three categories of stocks are distinguished: first, finished goods; second, basic materials, fuels and work in progress; and finally, all other stocks. Stocks of finished goods are modelled in two stages. First, the determinants of changes in such stocks are specified; a reduced form is obtained which relates stockbuilding non-linearly to the deviation of demand, output and profits from their respective trend values, and to the gap between the actual and trend stock-output ratios. In the second stage aggregate stocks of finished goods are allocated among wholesalers, retailers and manufacturing industry. Stocks of basic materials, fuels and work in progress are modelled by means of a specification similar to that used for the first stage of the finished goods equation. In the main the other models adopt a more aggregated approach, although the NI model does distinguish between stockbuilding in manufacturing, distribution and the rest of the economy. Single aggregate stockbuilding equations are specified in the LBS and CEPG models. In all these models stockbuilding is related to output or sales measures, and in most cases also to lagged stockbuilding. The LBS model adopts the methodology developed by Davidson *et al.* (1978), modelling the change in aggregate inventory investment in terms of changes in aggregate demand, lagged stockholding terms and the stock–output ratio; the latter term represents an 'error feedback' mechanism which ensures that in long-run equilibrium a definite stock–output ratio is maintained.

FINANCIAL EFFECTS ON STOCKBUILDING

Although theoretical models of inventory investment behaviour, including Whitin (1957) and Holt *et al.* (1960), suggest that the opportunity cost of holding inventories should be included as a key explanatory variable in any empirical study, little importance is generally attached to financial factors in the stockbuilding equations of the various models, and only the HMT and BE models include interest rate effects. In the HMT model only one stockbuilding equation, that for manufacturers' materials and fuels, includes the interest rate as an explanatory variable, together with the annual change in wholesale prices, whose coefficient is constrained to be equal and opposite in sign to that on the interest rate. Although the coefficient on the rate of interest is negative, it is not significantly different from zero. These results are confirmed by the BE model, where a real interest rate variable, constructed from the nominal three-monthly local authority rate and a price deflator, is assumed to influence the stocks of finished goods held by wholesalers, retailers and manufacturing industry. Only two equations are estimated, and in each case the coefficients on the rate terms are negative; but only in the wholesalers' stocks equation is this effect significant. A similar real interest rate term is also included in the equation modelling the stocks of basic materials, fuels and work in progress, but here again, although the coefficient on the variable displays the expected negative sign, it is not significantly different from zero.

As for other financial influences on stockbuilding, the aggregate finished goods equation of the BE model includes a variable in the change in the exchange rate, apparently to proxy speculative activity, while lagged changes in the real money supply are included in the stockholding equation of the LBS model. These money supply variables, which make a significant contribution to the overall fit of the equation, can be interpreted as capturing some kind of real balance effect consistent with the monetarist interpretation of the transmission mechanism. None of the other model builders incorporates any financial influences into the stockbuilding equations, although attempts have been made at the National Institute, in particular, to isolate such effects.

Overall it would therefore seem that financial variables in general, and interest rates in particular, play a fairly minor role in the determination of stockbuilding in the UK macro models. The few other studies which have attempted to model stockholding behaviour in the UK have also not been able to isolate strong interest rate effects. The most comprehensive study in this respect is that by Trivedi (1970), who analysed the determinants of investment in stocks of raw materials and fuels and of finished goods, separately and in combination, for both the manufacturing sector in aggregate and particular industry groupings within it. Although the equations were in general not well determined, some displayed significant interest rate coefficients of the correct sign; but the actual reduction in stocks consequent on a rise in rates was often subject to a lagged response. Burrows (1971) carried out a study to test the determinants of investment in stocks of finished goods by manufacturers. The interest rate coefficients in these equations were always negatively signed, but because they were never significant at the 5 per cent level of confidence Burrows was sceptical of the influence of interest rates on stockbuilding activity.

There are several possible reasons, as Savage (1978) points out, for the failure of these studies to find consistent interest rate effects. Other factors may dominate interest rates as determinants of inventory investment. In this regard stockbuilding involves costs of storage, obsolescence and deterioration, and these may be more important than interest costs. Other relevant factors are likely to be the prevailing tax allowances on the holding of stocks, which have changed substantially during the 1970s; while expectations, business confidence and the actual availability of credit are all potentially more important influences on stockbuilding than the level of interest rates. Availability factors could exert their influence in two ways. First, firms may require bank loans to finance the holding of stocks, and second, stocks may build up if limited availability of credit to consumers restricts the demand for the firms' products. None of the macro models attempts to take account of such influences, but Trivedi (1970) estimates stockholding specifications which include a variable in the weighted minimum deposit rate on consumer durables bought on hire purchase, and Burrows (1971) tests the significance of the change in bank loans to manufacturers. In both cases, however, the credit availability proxies contributed little to the explanatory power of the estimated equations.

Of course, it may be the case that interest rates are important in influencing stockbuilding behaviour, but that data limitations make the empirical verification of such a relationship very difficult. In comparison to the other components of GDP, stockbuilding data is prone to large measurement errors; and furthermore because the available data does not distinguish between planned and unplanned stock levels, there is no way of knowing the extent to which observable actual changes mirror the planned changes. As a consequence, any role played by interest rates in determining planned stockbuilding may be dominated by unplanned changes arising from factors such as unexpected sales variations.

Studies of inventory investment undertaken in the US, and summarised by Lovell (1964) and Evans (1969), have also traditionally found little evidence of any direct cost effects. Accordingly US studies have tended to ignore, until recently, the possible relationship between stockbuilding and interest rates. However, recent studies by Rubin (1979), Lieberman (1980) and Irvine (1981a, b, c) have found evidence for several different sectors of the economy which suggests that inventory investment is significantly affected by the cost of holding stocks, and that the lag between the change in such costs and the decision to change inventories is very short. These studies have used a variety of financial variables to measure the cost of holding inventories, ranging from nominal and real rates of interest to more sophisticated measures of the cost of capital which take account of additional factors such as the level of taxation. Their findings seem to indicate that it is easier to detect significant opportunity cost effects on inventory investment when a more disaggregated approach is adopted; aggregation bias may therefore have rendered the coefficients of the relationships estimated in previous studies unreliable. Alternatively the use of more recent data periods, extending into the mid- and late-1970s in most cases, when interest rates have varied to a greater extent, may have made it statistically easier to isolate empirical relationships between cost of capital variables and stockbuilding.

7. Private sector investment in housing

THE MECHANISMS OF MONETARY INFLUENCE

There is general agreement that monetary policy has a powerful effect on the housing sector, unlike the other categories of expenditure which we have considered. Uncertainty exists, however, as to the precise way in which it exerts its influence, because monetary conditions, whether in the form of interest rates or credit availability factors, can affect housebuilding through either the demand or supply side of the market.[33]

As regards interest rates, the mortgage rate is obviously likely to be a factor influencing the demand for new houses because the cost of mortgage credit is a large component of the price of purchasing a house. On the supply side, it is quite likely that builders' decisions about the number of houses they construct will depend on the cost of credit. In fact, builders often rely heavily on banks for the finance required for homebuilding.

Availability effects are also likely to be an important influence on housebuilding. On the demand side, these operate through the rationing of mortgages by building societies, particularly when market interest rates generally are rising. The fact that building society rates are 'sticky' and generally lag movements in other rates means that the societies are likely to lose deposits to other financial institutions at such times; until their rates adjust into line with market rates, the building societies may well have to ration mortgages by tightening the non-price conditions under which loans are given.[34] Conversely, when market interest rates generally are falling, flows of funds into building societies should temporarily increase, making mortgages more freely available. On the supply side, advances to builders, typically small firms, are likely to represent high risks for individual banks. In consequence, banks may well give loans to builders a low priority and prefer to lend to other categories of borrower.

Housebuilding in the macro models

Of the large macro models only the CEPG model and the condensed version of the CE model do not specify a separate equation for private investment in housebuilding. The other models are particularly comprehensive in their analysis of the financial influences on housebuilding. In each case both interest rate and credit availability effects are considered, and in order to explain these mechanisms of monetary influence, building society behaviour is often extensively modelled. In each of the HMT, BE and LBS models, for instance, several equations are specified in order to describe building society behaviour. In all cases these include equations for the repayments of principal to the societies, the deposits and shares held and the mortgage advances given.[35]

The HMT and BE models are similar in their approach. In each interest rate effects are found only on the supply side of the housing market. In the HMT model the equation for private investment in dwellings is assumed to depend on the cost to builders of obtaining finance as represented by the short-term rate of interest: an increase in short-term rates reduces the supply of new houses by raising builders' borrowing costs, though the coefficient on the variable is not significantly different from zero. Also included in the specification are current and lagged variables in the price of new houses, relative to the general consumer price level, to represent the expected rate of profit from the building of houses. In the BE model residential investment is assumed to respond positively to movements in the price of new houses relative to a proxy for building costs. Lagged values of the bank advances rate are used to represent the costs of borrowing. The importance of these variables is shown by the fact that their estimated coefficients are highly significant. Although no measures of credit availability are incorporated directly into the housebuilding equations of either model, such effects enter in other ways. In particular both models specify equations for the flow of deposits into building societies. These flows depend partly on interest rates and directly affect mortgage availability. Mortgage advances, in turn, have a direct impact on the level of house prices and hence on the supply of housing investment. In both models therefore the flow of deposits into building societies will influence housing investment and consequently the potential exists for credit availability effects, working through the demand side of the market, to exert an influence.

The treatment of private fixed residential investment in the LBS model has developed from a study by Duffy (1970). In the 1981 version of the model housebuilding is related to private dwelling starts in the present and previous 3 quarters. Housing starts, in turn, are assumed to be a function of variables such as the minimum lending rate (MLR) and the level of house prices relative to the general price level, the estimated coefficients of which display significant supply responses; and demand influences, represented by disposable income relative to the price of new houses and two indicators of the availability of mortgage credit. The first of these variables, mortgage advances by the building societies and local authorities, deflated by the price of new houses, has a coefficient which is not significantly different from zero. The other measure of credit availability is the ratio of the mortgage rate to the minimum lending rate, which is included to capture the availability effects caused by the 'sticky' nature of building society rates as compared to other interest rates. The coefficient on this variable is significant, such that the higher the mortgage rate relative to the MLR, the lower is housing investment.

The housebuilding sector of the NI model has developed from the work of Artis *et al.* (1975). Demand influences on housebuilding have traditionally predominated in the model and this is reflected in the current equation for investment in private dwellings which is related to real disposable income, the price of new houses relative to the consumer price index, the post-tax mortgage rate, the ratio of the annual rate of change of new house prices to the interest rate on local authority debt, and a variable designed to represent the availability of mortgage credit. This term is defined as the ratio of the net increase in building society deposits to the price of new houses, but like the similar term in the LBS model its coefficient is insignificantly different from zero. Of the different variables in the equation only the term measuring the rate of change of new house prices relative to the local authority interest rate displays a supply side response in that the estimated coefficient is positive. The coefficient on the real house price term displays a demand response in that it is negatively signed in contrast to the supply effects assigned to this variable in the HMT, BE and LBS models. The net increase in building society deposits is modelled in terms of the change in the stock of personal financial assets and the relative interest rates on building society deposits and local authority debt. In the NI model an increase in short-term interest rates therefore reduces the demand for new houses, both by raising the cost of mortgage finance and by restricting its availability in the period before the 'sticky' building society borrowing rates are restored to their normal relationship with other short-term rates.

Other studies of housebuilding activity

Outside the macro models there have been several partial equilibrium studies of UK housebuilding behaviour which are summarised in Savage (1978). In common with the HMT, BE and LBS models, most agree that cost effects on the supply side are influential in determining builders' plans as to the number of houses they construct; these interest rate effects appear to exert an immediate influence on housing investment. Such results are in marked contrast to those obtained for non-residential fixed investment which we summarised in section 5. There is, however, some doubt as to the empirical significance of availability factors on the supply side of the housing market since only Duffy (1970) has attempted to test any such relationship, by including the level of bank advances to the construction industry as a determinant of housing starts.

As regards the demand side influences on housebuilding, there is considerable uncertainty as to whether interest rate or credit availability factors are more important. While Duffy, and O'Herlihy and Spencer (1972) assert that building society rationing effects are much more important in influencing the demand for housing than the cost of mortgage advances, Artis *et al.* (1975) and Whitehead (1974) take the opposite view. At first sight it seems difficult to reconcile these different findings. One possible reason for the difference is that in testing for its effect on housing demand different studies have used alternative measures of the availability of mortgage credit. As we have already seen the various macro models use a wide variety of such measures and the same is also true of the partial equilibrium studies of housing investment. The availability proxies include specially constructed rationing dummies in O'Herlihy and Spencer, mortgage advances in Duffy, and the net inflows of funds into building societies in Whitehead.[36] Artis (1978: 292) alleges that the failure to find any significant mortgage rationing effect in the study by Artis *et al.* was due to the mis-specification of the rationing variable, and the failure to make any allowance for a lag between changes in mortgage rationing and the impact on housing investment. He further claimed that in a later study, when rationing was identified with the flow of funds into building societies, a significant mortgage rationing, as well as mortgage rate, effect was discernible.

8. Monetary sectors

In order to endogenise the financial variables which play a role in the transmission mechanism, explicit monetary sectors have been developed in recent years in all models, except that of CE, and even here research is in progress in this area. Both domestic and external monetary sectors are considered, and in most cases these are now fully integrated with the main income-cxpenditure sectors of the models. In these monetary sectors, the various credit and money aggregates, the structure of interest rates and the sterling exchange rate can be determined endogenously, instead of being treated as exogenous as was the case in the early versions of the models.

DOMESTIC MONETARY SECTORS

The money stock

The domestic monetary sectors of the current models are not based on a simple money demand and money supply framework, as is the monetary sector of the ISLM model, and as was an early model of the UK financial system developed by Crouch (1967), but instead tend to be constructed around accounting schemes involving the government budget constraint and the balance sheet identities of the banking and non-bank private sectors. Such an approach was first applied to an analysis of the UK monetary system by Norton (1969). However, as is the case in the ISLM model, and following the approach of Tobin (1969), decision making in the models is segmented between real expenditure and dealings in financial assets. The real expenditure decisions taken in the income-expenditure model generate financial surpluses and deficits for the different sectors of the economy which feed into the monetary model, creating demands for and supplies of the various financial assets.[37]

Of the large macro models, the domestic monetary sector of the HMT model is the most detailed and comes closest to a 'general equilibrium' approach.[38] The basic principles of portfolio theory, as proposed by Brainard and Tobin (1968), are utilised to model the behaviour of six sectors, including the main banking and non-bank private sectors. Functional forms are not however specified for all of the decisions of these sectors because, as Brainard and Tobin illustrated, the balance sheet structure of any sectoral financial model imposes cross-equation constraints on the parameters of the model. Thus equations are normally only specified for $(n-1)$ of the items in the sectoral balance sheet, leaving the form of the nth to be determined as a residual from the appropriate adding-up constraints. In this way each sector's budget constraint is satisfied. Similarly only $(m-1)$ equations are specified for each financial market; the mth sector's demand being determined residually to ensure market clearing.

The non-bank private sector of the model comprises persons, companies, and non-bank financial intermediaries such as the building societies. The net financial wealth of the sector is calculated by adding the effect of capital revaluations, arising from interest rate changes, to the sectoral financial surpluses generated in the income-expenditure model and the existing stock of wealth. Total net wealth is then allocated, as illustrated in Fig. 4.1, between assets such as gilts, national savings and liquid assets. In addition, decisions are also assumed to be taken over the level of bank borrowing and other liability holdings. Of these various decisions, most attention has been paid to the level of bank borrowing and gilt holdings. Bank borrowing is disaggregated into that by persons, companies and non-bank financial intermediaries. A disequilibrium model based on the work of Spencer (1975) is used to explain personal bank advances; the outstanding quantity of advances is a weighted average of both demand and supply variables, where the weights themselves are variable and depend on the degree of market disequilibrium. The demand for advances is related to real income, relative interest rates, the level of borrowing in the previous period, and a variable indicating the expected change in prices, while supply depends on lagged borrowing alone.[39] In the 1980 model these relationships are imposed, but initially the equations were freely estimated, and the supply of advances was also related to dummy variables representing credit controls and the Competition and Credit Control banking reforms. Company borrowing and loans to other financial institutions are each

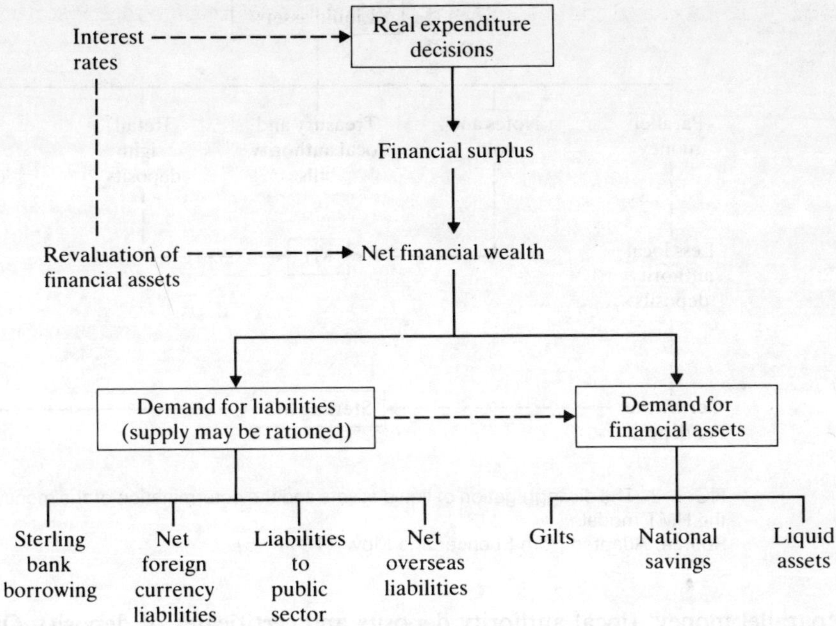

FIG. 4.1 The non-bank private sector decision framework in the HMT model
Source: Adapted from Spencer and Mowl (1978: 4).

modelled by a simpler system in which demand factors dominate. The demand for gilts, in flow terms, is related to gross financial private sector wealth (net wealth plus bank borrowing and other liabilities), relative interest rates, expected capital gains and the market value of gilts already held. The modelling of expected capital gains has posed particular problems and in the 1980 model is taken to depend on current and lagged long rates, the current short rate, the expected change in prices and the ratio of the PSBR to net private sector wealth. Although these relationships are imposed in the 1980 model, evidence has tended to suggest that individuals have regressive interest rate expectations; the higher the level of interest rates and the greater the ex-ante interest rate differential between the long rate and short rate, the greater the capital gains are likely to be. Of the other private sector portfolio decisions, flows into national savings are related to the personal sector's financial surplus, while net foreign currency liabilities and other miscellaneous liabilities are mainly handled judgementally (although some capital flows determined in the external monetary sector are incorporated among the latter). Given this information it is possible to determine non-bank private holdings of liquid assets as a residual from the sectoral budget identity.

A further decision process, illustrated in Fig. 4.2, is then hypothesised in order to allocate the liquid assets aggregate, which largely comprises the items making up the sterling M3 definition of the money stock, among its constituent items. Five categories of asset are distinguished: non-bank holdings of Treasury and local authority bills, notes and coins, retail sight deposits, retail time deposits and

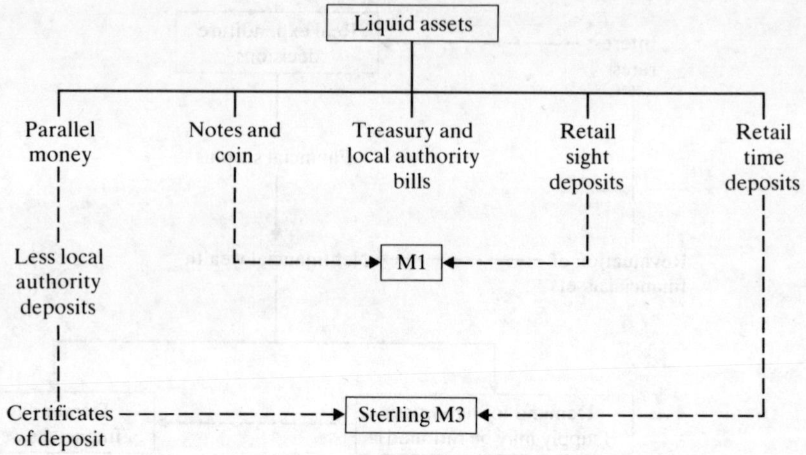

FIG. 4.2 The disaggregation of liquid assets and the determination of the money stock in the HMT model
Source: Adapted from Spencer and Mowl (1978: 5).

'parallel money' (local authority deposits and certificates of deposit). Of these, retail time deposits are treated as the residual asset. Each of the other aggregates is related to demand factors, such as total expenditure and relative interest rates, as well as total liquid assets. This disaggregation enables the narrow money supply aggregate, M1, to be identified as the sum of the notes and coin and retail sight deposit holdings of the private sector. The broad monetary aggregate, sterling M3, can also be obtained by adding public sector sterling bank deposits, which are exogenously determined, and private sector retail time deposit and certificates of deposit holdings to the M1 aggregate. Finally, if exogenously determined non-bank private sector foreign currency deposits are added to sterling M3, the even broader M3 money stock aggregate can be determined.

No explicit demand for money function is therefore modelled. The quantity of money is implicit in the model and is determined as the residual which ensures consistency among the other asset allocation decisions of the non-bank private sector. Nevertheless demand factors do have some influence on the money stock because of the way in which the other portfolio decisions of the non-bank private sector are analysed. Factors such as wealth, income and relative interest rates which affect these other allocation decisions will indirectly exert an influence on money holdings. The practice of specifying functions for all the major asset choice decisions within the non-bank private sector, except the demand for money, contrasts sharply with the approach adopted in the bulk of econometric research into UK private sector financial behaviour, which has concentrated on investigating the demand for money function. In recent years, however, it does appear to have become increasingly difficult to isolate stable demand for money functions, and this may explain the choice of money as the residual. Studies such as Artis and Lewis (1976), for example, have questioned the validity of relating the quantity of money actually observed to income and interest rates, and the interpretation of the result as a demand for money function. Particularly for wider definitions of the money stock, such as M3 and sterling M3, which include certificates of deposit, it seems supply influences arising from the behaviour of banks and government policy actions have a role to play in the determination of the quantity of money.

The analysis of bank behaviour provides the principal vehicle through which supply-side effects on the monetary aggregates are incorporated into the HMT model. Banks are assumed to set interest rates oligopolistically in the retail market, accepting the deposits that are offered to them at these rates. In addition, as mentioned earlier, bank lending to the private sector is modelled as a compromise between demand and supply variables. Given this information, and after allowing for Special Deposit calls, reserve asset requirements and non-deposit liabilities, the other items in the portfolio are allocated in such a way as to reconcile the deposit and loan aggregates, and satisfy the balance sheet requirement.[40] The banks, as illustrated in Fig. 4.3, are assumed to have several possible options: they can issue certificates of deposit, alter net foreign currency liabilities, or else change their holdings of notes and coin, excess reserves, local authority debt and gilts. Within the model the banks are therefore able to engage in both asset and liability side portfolio management, and the ultimate choice among these options is based to a large extent on relative interest rates. Although certificates of deposit

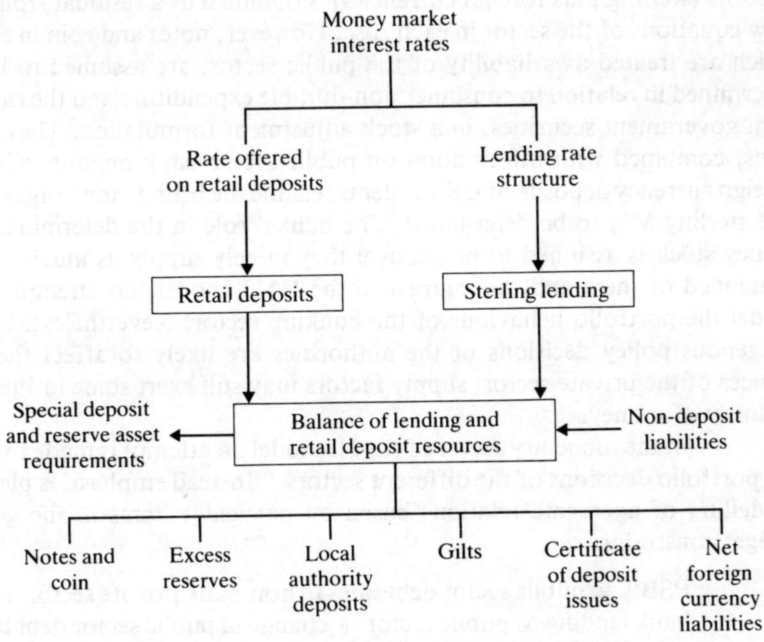

FIG. 4.3 The banks' decision framework in the HMT model
Source: Adapted from Spencer and Mowl (1978: 7).

are treated as the residual, the banks have complete control over their issue and can accordingly exert an independent supply side influence on sterling M3. In particular, the banks' issues of these instruments determine to a large extent the breakdown of private sector holdings of 'parallel money' into certificates of deposit and local authority debt, thereby enabling the stock of sterling M3 to be determined. Given the approach adopted in the model, it is obvious that the quantity of money in existence cannot be viewed as a policy instrument under the direct control of the authorities. Rather, it is determined as the outcome of a series of complex portfolio decisions taken by the other sectors of the economy. Nevertheless, the authorities will have some influence on the stock of money through their ability to manipulate the factors which affect the different portfolio decisions. Of particular relevance here are the interest rate and exchange rate policies adopted by the authorities, and their ability to manipulate the PSBR for monetary purposes, issues to which we shall return later in this section.

A similar approach to the modelling of the monetary sector is adopted in the BE model. However, in this case the non-bank private sector is not treated as one entity; instead separate sectoral accounts are developed for persons, companies, and financial institutions other than the banks. Within the personal sector, equations are specified for various aggregates including net acquisitions of liquid assets, gilt-edged purchases and bank borrowing. Similar flow of funds equations are modelled for the company sector and financial institutions. As in the HMT model no explicit demand for money function is modelled, and the change in bank deposits (sterling plus foreign currencies) is obtained as a residual from the other flow equations of the sector in each case. However, notes and coin in circulation, which are treated as a liability of the public sector, are assumed to be demand determined in relation to consumer non-durable expenditure and the rate on long-term government securities, in a stock adjustment formulation. These specifications, combined with information on public sector bank deposits and the total foreign currency deposits of UK residents, enable the broad money aggregates, M3 and sterling M3, to be determined. The banks' role in the determination of the money stock is assumed to be passive; they merely supply as much money as is demanded of them and, in contrast to the HMT model, no attempt is made to model the portfolio behaviour of the banking sector. Nevertheless, because the exogenous policy decisions of the authorities are likely to affect the portfolio choices of the private sector, supply factors may still exert some influence on the quantity of money.

In the monetary sector of the NI model no attempt is made to explain all the portfolio decisions of the different sectors.[41] Instead emphasis is placed on the modelling of aggregate relations based on particular items in the government budget constraint:

PSBR ≡ public sector debt sales to non-bank private sector + change in bank lending to public sector + change in public sector debt holdings of overseas sector + change in notes and coin in circulation (1)

and the banks' balance sheet:

change in bank deposits of UK residents + change in net other liabilities of banks[42] = change in bank lending to public sector + change in bank lending to non-bank private sector (2)

Substituting these relationships into the money supply identity:

change in M3 = change in bank deposits of UK residents + change in notes and coin in circulation (3)

the following expression is obtained for the determination of the money stock:

change in M3 = PSBR − public sector debt sales to non-bank private sector − change in public sector debt holdings of overseas sector + change in bank lending to non-bank private sector − change in net other liabilities of banks (4)

Of the terms on the right-hand side of this relationship, equations are estimated in the model for both debt sales and bank lending to the non-bank private sector. Total debt sales are disaggregated into two main categories: national savings and a conglomerate comprising British government stocks, local authority debt, public corporation stocks and Treasury bills. Sales of each of these categories of debt are determined by relative interest rates and the net acquisition of financial assets by the sector. Four categories of bank lending to the private sector are distinguished: personal sector loans for house purchase, other personal sector loans, company borrowing and lending to other financial institutions. Equations are estimated for the first three categories, which in each case relate the flow of advances to an economic activity variable, interest rates, the net acquisition of financial assets by the sector, the lagged stock of advances and dummy variables representing lending requests and the Competition and Credit Control regime. Given that the PSBR is determined elsewhere in the model from the income and expenditure flows of the public sector, and borrowing from overseas and banks' net other liabilities are assumed exogenous, it is possible to obtain the change in the M3 money stock as a residual from the accounting relationship developed above.

As is the case in the HMT and BE models, there is therefore no explicit demand function for broad money in the NI model. However, separate demand functions are estimated for notes and coin in circulation, in relation to consumers' expenditure, and for narrow money, or M1, in terms of GDP and the interest rate on local authority deposits. This means that it is in effect only the remaining time deposits component of M3 which is truly a residual. The quantity of such deposits (principally retail time deposits and certificates of deposit) is implicitly determined in the model by exogenous external flows and net other liabilities, and the factors which influence the PSBR and non-bank private sector holdings of government debt, narrow money and bank loans. In this way the determination of the money stock is shown to depend on both demand and supply factors just as in the HMT and BE models. In particular the approach highlights the individual links between the money stock and fiscal policy, debt management operations and bank lending. Furthermore, because the change in the public sector debt holdings of the overseas sector bears a close relationship to the balance for official financing, that is the sum of the current balance and capital flows, the link between balance of payments flows, foreign exchange reserve changes and the money supply is also illustrated. The importance of this link for the determination of the money stock will of course depend on the particular exchange rate regime in force. It is normally assumed that only under fixed exchange rates will the balance of payments position influence the quantity of money in the domestic economy. Under a floating regime, exchange rate adjustments equate inflows and outflows for the domestic economy, so that external factors have no influence on the money stock.[43]

The monetary sector of the LBS model differs from those of the HMT, BE and NI in that the quantity of money is not determined as a residual asset; instead an explicit equation is specified for the rate of change of sterling M3.[44] However, this is not a 'pure' demand for money function since both supply and demand influences are included in the equation. Supply pressures are represented by the stock of public sector debt, the PSBR, the balance for official financing and a Competition and Credit Control dummy. On the demand side, a term in the net acquisition of financial assets by the company sector is included, along with the minimum lending rate (MLR), and the differential between the own rate on sterling M3 and the MLR. Each of the interest rate responses is however small. No equation is modelled for M1 but a stock adjustment formulation is estimated for notes and coin in circulation. This is demand determined in relation to the long rate of interest and the nominal value of non-durable consumption. Sterling deposit accounts held by UK residents can then be determined by subtracting notes and coin holdings from the sterling M3 aggregate. The proportion of these sterling deposits held by the private sector as time deposits is also modelled in relation to its own lagged value, the deposit interest rate and the gross rate of interest on building society shares. Other equations are estimated for personal sector bank borrowing and liquid asset holdings. The flow of bank lending to the personal sector is related to durable consumption expenditure, the tax allowance on loan interest charges and the past level of bank loans.

The CEPG monetary sector is similar to that of the LBS in that an explicit equation is modelled for the money stock; sterling M3 balances are related to a demand variable, GNP, and various supply influences. The latter are measured by bank lending to the public sector and an index of quantitative restrictions on the banking system. No opportunity cost variable is included in the specification. Within the model bank lending to the public sector and currency in circulation are given exogenously, while the balance for official financing and PSBR are determined elsewhere in the model. In consequence sales of public debt to the non-bank private sector can be determined as a residual from the government budget constraint. Finally, an equation is specified for domestic credit expansion (DCE) which corrects the change in the actual money stock for the effect of external transactions.

In the models it is apparent that many important aggregates are determined purely as residuals after the other related allocation decisions have been taken. In this role they ensure consistency within sectoral budget constraints and balance sheet identities. This approach is nevertheless somewhat unsatisfactory since the choice of residual is normally never justified. In addition, the economic implications of treating certain decisions as residuals are unlikely to be particularly meaningful, and we have no way of knowing whether the quantities and functional forms implied for the residual assets in each model are plausible. In the majority of models some component of the money stock is chosen to fulfil this role, and as we have already noted, this is probably because empiricists have recently found it difficult to isolate stable demand for money functions. There is however no guarantee that the economic properties of the implied demand for money functions will be acceptable.[45] The implication, for example, of treating the quantity of time deposits as the residual in the NI model is that changes in public sector borrowing, external flows, and the private sector's demands for bank loans, bond holdings and narrow money will always be entirely accommodated by changes in the demand for time deposits; it is assumed the private sector will always passively agree to hold the quantity of money which is created on the supply side of the monetary system by these various credit flows. In practice, it seems more likely that an increase in private sector loan demand or public sector borrowing, for example, would create a divergence between demand and supply in the money market, which would only disappear if other factors such as interest rates, prices or real income were responsive to the disequilibrium. However, direct links between money and prices or income are not incorporated into the model, and, as we shall see below, only in the HMT model is any attempt made to relate the level of interest rates to a money market clearing mechanism.

The structure of interest rates

Initial attempts at modelling the monetary sector in the different models paid little attention to the various financial flows underlying the determination of the money stock; instead emphasis was placed on the structure of interest rates. The common practice was to specify an equation for one representative rate, normally a short rate, and then use a term structure relationship to determine the long rate. In addition bank deposit and loan rates, and building society mortgage and share rates were modelled in many cases. The representative short rate was generally treated as a policy instrument of the authorities, and modelled in terms of a reaction function which linked its determination to the economic goals of the authorities. In particular, in this respect, external objectives played a major role in the determination of interest rates. Such an approach still predominates in the current models, although increasingly attempts are being made to link the determination of interest rates directly to money aggregates; a development which reflects the changing emphasis of monetary policy.

The most ambitious approach in this respect is that adopted in the HMT model, where the traditional reaction function approach to the determination of interest rates has been abandoned. Here the key short rate, the three-month interbank rate, is set at the level which ensures clearing in the 'parallel money' market. The rate is therefore determined by the behaviour of all agents, including the authorities, who participate in this market. The banks' base and retail deposit rates are set by simple mark-ups in relation to the short rate, while the long rate is given exogenously. As well as treating the short rate as endogenous and solving the model via market clearing conditions, it is however also possible to peg the rate at the level required to attain the target value of sterling M3. If this procedure is adopted the authorities are assumed to clear the market by supplying whatever mix of obligations the other sectors wish to hold.

In the NI model, a more traditional reaction function approach is adopted, although the central short rate, the Treasury bill rate, is related to a 'monetary targets' variable as well as the level of foreign exchange reserves, the visible trade balance and the US Treasury bill rate, which represents the trend in world short-term rates. The 'monetary targets' variable is measured as the difference between the rate of growth of M3 in the previous quarter and the stated target; it takes the value zero when there were no targets and when the rate of growth of the money supply was below the stated ceiling. The long rate, represented by the yield on consols, is linked to the Treasury bill rate by a term structure relationship that includes lagged terms in the change in the inflation rate. Given these equations, and the accounting relationships developed earlier for the NI model, it is possible to solve for the level of interest rates which ensures that gilt sales and bank lending are consistent with a prescribed rate of growth of M3. In this way the Treasury bill rate can be viewed as a policy instrument which enables the authorities to exert influence on the money supply. With the emergence of monetary targets as the main focus of monetary policy, this procedure would seem to be much more sensible than that implied by the specification of more conventional reaction functions. The quantity of money also influences the rate structure in the CEPG model. In this case the MLR, which is used to represent the short rate, is explained by the exogenously determined eurodollar rate (a proxy for the level of world interest rates) and the ratio of bank lending to the public sector to sterling M3 balances. The long rate, the yield on war loan stocks, is modelled in terms of MLR. In the LBS model the authorities are assumed to set MLR from a consideration of exchange rate changes, the inflation rate, and the balance of payments deficit in relation to nominal GDP; the short rate, represented by the Treasury bill rate, and the long rate or yield on consols, are derived as functions of the MLR, with the rate of change of prices an additional determinant of the long rate. In the BE model, the short rate is represented by the rate on three-month deposits with local authorities. The exogenously determined eurodollar rate and beliefs about price expectations are assumed to influence this rate. In addition it is postulated that the rate will tend to fall when foreign exchange reserves increase or upward pressure develops on the exchange rate. The representative long rate, the yield on twenty-year government stocks, is related to the short rate, price expectations and the size of the PSBR relative to GDP.

EXTERNAL MONETARY SECTORS

The central issue in all external monetary sectors is the determination of the exchange rate. The modelling of this relationship is important in most models, for although the exchange rate does not normally appear in the different expenditure functions as a direct determinant of demand, it does affect the relative competitiveness of traded goods, and under a floating regime provides a key link between monetary policy and the price level. A major problem for modelling purposes is that since 1972 the UK has adopted neither a clearly fixed nor a clearly floating regime but has followed a changing set of objectives externally. In consequence the environment in which the exchange rate is determined is often characterised as one of 'dirty floating'.[46] Nevertheless, unlike the early versions of the models which assumed that the exchange rate was determined exogenously, the standard approach now is to make some attempt to estimate exchange rate relationships. Normally it is the effective sterling exchange rate, that is the rate for sterling relative to a weighted average of the exchange rates for other countries, which is modelled. The BE model is slightly different in that it attempts to explain the sterling–dollar rate.

As with the domestic monetary sector, the HMT approach to the modelling of the exchange rate is the most sophisticated.[47] No explicit equation is modelled for the exchange rate; rather movements in the rate are analysed implicitly within a compete structural model of the external sector, involving a consideration of both the current and capital accounts of the balance of payments. The level of the exchange rate in the long run depends mainly on the factors which influence the current account of the balance of payments. It is, for example, likely to reflect trends in relative costs and activity rates between countries. To the extent that financial developments affect the variables which determine the current account balance, the exchange rate will therefore be influenced by monetary variables in the long run. In the short run the exchange rate is assumed to reflect capital account flows, which are deemed to be influenced by interest rate and expectational effects. Several capital flow aggregates are considered, but the main equations are for net short-term flows and overseas investment in the UK private sector. Such flows are modelled in terms of adjustments to equilibrium stocks of assets whose distribution within total assets depends on relative rates of return in the UK as compared to the rest of the world. In this context, rates of return are taken to be affected by relative interest rates, expected changes in exchange rates and, in the case of covered transactions, the cost of forward cover. Short-term flows have proved the most difficult to model; there is, for example, likely to be an element of joint dependence between interest rates and such capital flows. In consequence, the equation for such flows in the 1980 model is imposed rather than freely estimated. Flows are related to movements in short-term covered and uncovered interest rate differentials between the UK and the rest of the world, the change in the expected rate of exchange rate depreciation and a proxy for world wealth which acts as a scale variable. Overseas investment in the UK private sector is related to movements in both short- and long-term uncovered interest rate differentials, and the changes in the expected rate of exchange rate depreciation and world wealth. Because of the way in which these equations are formulated, it is apparent that capital flows respond to changes in interest rates, rather than interest rate levels. A once and for all change in the level of interest rates will have only a transient effect on capital flows. Several of the explanatory variables included in the capital flow equations are also separately modelled. The short-term covered differential is modelled as the difference between the short-term uncovered differential and the cost of forward cover, which is itself determined by the spot and forward exchange rates. The forward exchange rate in turn depends on the expected exchange rate and the short-term uncovered interest rate differential. Exchange rate expectations are related to speculators' estimates of the underlying or equilibrium rate, and the differential between this rate and the actual spot rate. Although an extrapolative element is allowed for in the formation of expectations, the system is stable overall. The concept of purchasing power parity underlies the determination of the equilibrium exchange rate which is modelled in terms of relative competitiveness (as measured by wage costs and prices) and relative money supply growth, adjusted for differences in demand for money growth, between the UK and the rest of the world. In this way changes in the domestic money supply can exert some direct influence on the exchange rate.

The model can be used either to forecast changes in foreign exchange reserves, given an assumed path for the exchange rate, or alternatively to provide forecasts for exchange rates given assumptions about the amount of official intervention in the foreign exchange market. The predictions of the model then reflect the paths of all the variables which determine the current and capital accounts of the balance of payments. In the latter case the exchange rate is determined as the result of a market clearing process in which short-term speculative capital flows play a key role. Movements in the spot rate clear the market by altering the expected returns on the holding of domestic assets relative to those in foreign currencies, and so induce movements in short-term capital. These capital flows are assumed to feed into the domestic monetary model and interact with the domestic flows in order to determine interest rates and the various monetary aggregates. These in turn feed back on to capital flows and the real sector of the model, both directly and via the exchange rate (if it is floating). The capital flows model is therefore an important link between the domestic monetary model and the main income–expenditure model. However, given the difficulties involved in modelling capital flows generally, and items such as exchange rate expectations in particular, the predictions obtained from the model are likely to be subject to wide margins of error.

A similar, but much less detailed, approach is adopted in the CEPG model. Here equations are modelled for flows of both short- and long-term capital. Short-term flows are modelled in relation to the exchange rate-adjusted differential between UK and world interest rates, and the state of the current account of the balance of payments. Long-term inflows and outflows are related to profits in the UK relative to those abroad. Within this framework, and as in the HMT model, the exchange rate can either be regarded as a policy target which is maintained by official intervention in the market, or as a variable which is determined by market clearing.

None of the other model builders attempts to explain the exchange rate in terms of a structural model of the balance of payments. Instead, the exchange rate is modelled more directly. Attempts are, however, made to distinguish between the factors which determine the equilibrium exchange rate and those which cause short-run deviations of the rate from its long-run equilibrium path. Further, in the LBS and BE models, the modelling of the equilibrium exchange rate closely follows the principles associated with the monetary theory of the balance of payments as outlined, for example, in the series of articles in Frenkel and Johnson (1976).

In the LBS model it is assumed that the equilibrium or expected exchange rate moves to equilibrate the demand for and supply of nominal money, given the assumption of purchasing power parity. Thus the equilibrium exchange rate is hypothesised to vary directly with the ratio of world money to domestic money, and inversely with the ratio of world demand for money to domestic demand for money. However, the actual sterling exchange rate, as distinct from its equilibrium rate, may be influenced by other factors, such as capital flows, which exert an influence on the balance of payments. These factors are represented by variables in the change in the PSBR, the change in the sterling balances of the OPEC countries, the sterling value of North Sea oil reserves and movements in the differential between domestic and world short-term interest rates.

In the NI model a single equation based on Batchelor (1977) is used to determine the effective exchange rate. Deviations of the exchange rate from the level required to ensure purchasing power parity, as measured by the ratio of domestic to world wholesale prices, are explained in terms of the deviation one period ago, changes in the covered differential between UK and US interest rates, and the visible trade balance expressed in real terms. The interest rate variables display insignificant coefficients, but are intended to capture the effects of short-term capital movements, while good trade figures, it is argued, should inspire confidence in sterling and encourage capital inflows.

In the BE model it is assumed that the long-term equilibrium path of the sterling–dollar exchange rate is determined by the growth of the money stock relative to the demand for money in the UK compared to the US. Deviations from this equilibrium path are assumed to create pressure on the rate, where pressure is measured as a weighted average of the change in the exchange rate and the change in reserves. A variety of shorter-run factors also exert pressure on the rate, so that overall pressure is related to the deviation of the actual exchange rate from its equilibrium, relative money supply growth in the two countries, the change in the covered interest rate differential, the deviation of the UK current balance from its recent average, relative price inflation between the two countries and the expected change in the exchange rate. A reaction function is then used to distribute the effect of pressure between movements in the sterling–dollar rate and the change in reserves. The mechanism is such that the respective effects on the exchange rate and the level of reserves will depend on the severity of the pressure. Small amounts of pressure, up or down, are reflected almost entirely in day-to-day movements in the exchange rate which are not resisted. Greater amounts of pressure lead to interventions on the part of the authorities, and therefore some change in the reserves, in order to smooth the path of the exchange rate. Finally, extremely strong pressure exerts its effect almost wholly on the exchange rate because reserves cannot change indefinitely. At the same time the level of intervention is influenced by the divergence of reserves from equilibrium, so that a given amount of downward pressure will lead to more intervention the greater is the level of reserves. In addition in the model equations are specified for several categories of capital flow, both short- and long-term. In most cases the different capital flows are seen as adjustments to desired stocks, which depend on interest rates, other monetary influences and confidence factors as proxied by variables in the visible or current balance. Direct private investment overseas is modelled differently and related principally to the level of profits and world activity. A group of short-term flows are used to ensure that the balance for official financing is consistent with the reserve changes determined by the exchange rate-reserves section of the model. The explanatory power of most of the capital flows equations is not however particularly high, and significant interest rate effects are the exception rather than the rule.

9. An alternative approach

The alternative to large-scale macro modelling of the economy is the small model or 'reduced form' approach which we shall briefly consider in this section. This approach is generally associated with monetarist analysis which has traditionally been sceptical of the value of large-scale models as a vehicle for the modelling of the transmission mechanism of monetary policy. As we noted in section 3, monetarists believe in a much wider transmission mechanism than Keynesians, in which the effect of monetary policy is widely spread over all assets. Their view is that the impact of money in particular markets will be small and may in fact not be measurable with any degree of certainty. They therefore feel that, in analysing the determinants of change in the level of aggregate activity, extensive knowledge of allocative detail about the working of financial markets and institutions is of secondary importance and can be disregarded. Consequently they are not concerned with modelling all of the substitute relations between money and the various financial and real assets, as the large-scale models attempt to do. In any case many of the rates of return relevant to monetarist analysis, such as those on real assets, are for the most part implicit yields and hence not observable. Monetarists therefore believe that the Keynesian practice of looking at the relationship between expenditure decisions and recorded market interest rates will result in an underestimation of the overall impact of monetary policy.

For all these reasons therefore monetarists tend to bypass the structure and prefer to emphasise the direct impact of a monetary impulse on aggregate income and prices, rather than the effect of such a change on the individual categories of expenditure like consumption and investment. Such a procedure implies that the relationship between policy instruments and economic activity can be captured in very small scale models, and even in one equation, linking the level of the money supply to the value of national output. This alternative approach to model building is often characterised by its critics as a 'black box' approach because it fails to identify explicitly the transmission mechanism through which money has its effects on the economy. The procedure has also become known as the 'reduced form' approach. This term is somewhat inappropriate as most of the equations considered do not represent true reduced forms of any structural model.

Instead they are often merely relationships between a dependent variable and other variables which may or may not be truly exogenous. In consequence many of these quasi reduced forms are open to alternative interpretations. Nevertheless advocates of this 'reduced form' methodology stress its simplicity in comparison with the alternative model building approach. Large models, they argue, are too intricate to be readily comprehensible, and although the real world is complex, they maintain that it is precisely because of this that we can best attempt to understand it by searching for theories which can explain much with relatively few variables.

'REDUCED FORM' MODELS OF THE UK ECONOMY

Much of the empirical work based on this 'reduced form' methodological approach has been concerned with the US economy, and is particularly associated with the group of economists at the Federal Reserve Bank of St Louis. Studies of the US economy in this tradition have included Friedman and Schwartz (1963), Friedman and Meiselman (1963), Andersen and Jordan (1968) and Andersen and Carlson (1970). As well as testing for the influence of the money supply on the level of economic activity, these studies have also looked at issues such as the relative effectiveness of monetary and fiscal policies, and the lags involved in their operation. In these US studies monetary forces have generally been found to be the dominant influence on economic activity.[48] In contrast, UK studies in a similar vein are much less conclusive on this issue. Crockett (1970) and Walters (1971), for example, have looked at the cyclical fluctuations of money and income in the UK in a similar exercise to that carried out by Friedman and Schwartz for the US economy. Crockett tested the relationship for both narrow and broad money, and found that changes in these aggregates led changes in GDP by 4 and 5 quarters respectively. The association was more marked for narrow money, but in neither case was it particularly strong. Walters found that for post-1945 data a lag of 2 quarters between the change in the money stock and the change in GDP gave rise to the highest positive correlation between the variables.

Barrett and Walters (1966) attempted to replicate the study of Friedman and Meiselman using annual UK data for the period 1878–1963. Their findings did not support the conclusion of Friedman and Meiselman that the effect of money on consumption was larger and more stable than that of autonomous expenditure. Instead their results led them to believe that both autonomous expenditure and the broad stock of money contributed to the determination of consumption. The money supply appeared to have been more important before 1914, whereas autonomous expenditure was correlated more closely with consumption for the inter-war period. They were unable to obtain any meaningful results for the post-1945 period. In another study Walters (1966) attempted to ascertain for different periods the relationship between current and lagged changes in the broad money supply and the change in GNP. Again the overall explanatory power of the equation was found to be low for post-1945 data. Indeed, when quarterly data from 1955 to 1962 was used, Walters found that the money multiplier was actually negative. The results obtained by Goodhart and Crockett (1970), in a similar study using post-1945 data, were more favourable to the role of monetary forces in the UK economy in this period. They experimented with both broad and narrow money aggregates, and used GDP and industrial production as alternative dependent variables. The explanatory power of the equations was generally good.

Artis and Nobay (1969) attempted to replicate the Andersen and Jordan study for the UK, using quarterly data for the period 1958–67, by constructing a number of reduced form equations directly linking GDP with different monetary variables and indicators of fiscal policy. As monetary indicators they tested broad money, narrow money, bank advances and two measures of the monetary base. The measures of fiscal policy used were full employment receipts and expenditures, the full employment budget surplus and an index of discretionary fiscal changes. Of the monetary measures used, the broad money supply was found to be the most promising, but even here the effect on GDP was very small; and overall the results tended to indicate that the impact of fiscal policy was larger, more predictable and faster than that of monetary policy. The explanatory power of most of the Artis and Nobay equations was however poor, and most coefficients were not statistically significant, making the results somewhat unreliable. Nevertheless, their findings are in conflict with those obtained for the US by Andersen and Jordan, who found the money multiplier to be much larger than the fiscal multiplier.

The only UK studies which are able to find a dominant role for monetary policy are those by Keran (1970) and Matthews and Ormerod (1978). Keran, using quarterly data for the period 1953–68, was able to find a significant relationship between narrow money and industrial production, although the overall explanatory power of the equations tested was again low. Matthews and Ormerod specify an equation for the change in GDP in which monetary policy is represented by the monetary base and fiscal policy by the full employment budget deficit. This relation was tested using quarterly data for the period 1964–74. Although many of the individual coefficients are not statistically significant, the results indicate a greater initial response to fiscal policy, but a dominant role for monetary policy over 4 quarters.

Walters (1966) and Tarling and Wilkinson (1977) have investigated the role of the money supply in the determination of prices. Walters found that prices were responsive to changes in the broad money supply during the inter-war years. Tarling and Wilkinson were unable to identify an important relationship between the broad money supply and prices using annual data for 1960–73, but when the period was extended to 1975 a monetary variable with a two-year lag was found to be highly significant. Although the length of this lag is consistent with monetarist theory, the authors prefer a non-monetary explanation of the 1973–75 inflationary experience in terms of rising import prices.

Some problems

Although the results obtained by these studies seem sensitive to the data period, and the particular dependent and independent variables used, the bulk of the evidence obtained does not seem to confirm the existence of a 'reduced form' relationship between money and output or prices in the UK. However, such evidence, even if it existed, would be far from conclusive or indicative of the influence of monetary policy. Paradoxically, the more successful monetary policy is in stabilising income, the smaller is the resultant variation in income and hence the more difficult it is to find a statistical relationship between money and income.

There are several other reasons why the results obtained by these so-called 'reduced form' studies are very suspect.[49] A true reduced form expresses the endogenous variables of the system solely in terms of the exogenous variables. If one or more of the determinants of the dependent variable are not truly exogenous, the coefficient estimates obtained from such an equation are likely to be biased. The money variables used in the 'reduced form' equations must therefore be exogenous, and it is not clear that this is in fact the case. To illustrate this point we must consider the environment in which monetary policy has been conducted in the relatively small open UK economy since 1945. Fixed exchange rates were maintained continuously until 1972, and even after this date the authorities have, at various times, attempted to maintain particular rates of exchange as part of the policy of 'dirty floating'. In addition, for the 1950s and 1960s at least, the authorities generally tried to stabilise the level of interest rates in the economy. Such policies effectively endogenise the money supply; they mean that the money supply will adjust to the demand for money, so that changes in nominal income lead directly to changes in the money supply, thus reversing the direction of causality between the two variables. Indeed, even under a more active policy of 'monetary targeting', as has been pursued in the UK since 1976, demand variables can still exert some influence on the money stock as we saw in the context of the large macro models in section 8.

Related to the issue of exogeneity is the problem of causality. It is obvious that the examination of simple statistical relationships between money incomes and the money supply reveals nothing directly of the mechanism relating the two variables, and so when interpreting 'reduced form' regression results we must be aware of the danger of confusing association and correlation with causality. In an attempt to overcome this problem some studies have investigated the causal relation between money and income in more detail. A causality test was devised for this purpose by Sims (1972). This involved the regression of income on past, current and future values of the money stock, and also the regression of the money stock on past, current and future values of income. The test is based on the principle that if money leads income, the coefficients on the future values of money in the income equation and the coefficients on the lagged values of income in the money equation will be insignificant, while if income leads money the reverse will be true. Using post-1945 US data, Sims found strong evidence that money led income but not the reverse. Similar tests were carried out for the UK by Williams *et al.* (1976) using quarterly data for the period 1958–71. Their results were much less conclusive in that, although they found tentative evidence of a lead of income over money, in contrast to the US results, there was also some evidence of the money supply leading prices.[50] Unfortunately, these tests merely give information on precedence in time, and this is a dangerous indicator of causality. Tobin (1970), for instance, developed a Keynesian model in which the money stock is demand determined and yet the turning points of the rate of change of money lead those of nominal income. Thus evidence of a lag of one variable behind another does not allow any automatic conclusion on causality. In any case, Sims-type tests for causality between money and income are not valid when applied to small open economies operating under (mainly) fixed exchange rates, since in such circumstances the money supply is endogenous. The different results obtained by UK and US studies of the causality relation, and indeed of reduced form studies in general, are therefore probably attributable to the relatively open nature of the UK economy. Because the US economy is much larger and less open, it is possible to exert a greater degree of control on the money supply.

OTHER SMALL MODELS

In an attempt to overcome the problems inherent in applying such closed economy models to the UK, small open economy models have been developed by Jonson (1976) and Laidler and O'Shea (1980), using the basic principles of the monetary approach to the balance of payments. The model of Laidler and O'Shea (see also Laidler 1978b) consists of six equations: a demand for money function, an output equation, an expectations-augmented Phillips curve, expressions determining inflation expectations and the balance of payments, and lastly a money supply identity. Output is demand determined by private expenditure (including net exports) and government spending. Included among the determinants of private expenditure is a disequilibrium money holdings variable, defined as the difference between exogenously determined domestic credit expansion (DCE) and the demand for money. However, when the model was estimated, using quarterly data for the period 1954–70, the coefficient on this variable was found to be insignificant. Instead, disequilibrium money holdings were found to affect the balance of payments position, and hence the balance for official financing and the external component of the money supply. In so far as the quantity of money influences expenditure, the goods involved are therefore either imported, diverted from exports or drawn from existing stocks, rather than being added to current output. In contrast, the results assign an important role to fiscal policy in the determination of real income. The practice of treating DCE as exogenous can of course be criticised. One implication of such an approach is that monetary and fiscal policies are independent of each other; if they were linked via a budget constraint rather different conclusions might emerge. Jonson has estimated a similar model, using annual data for the period 1888–1970, in which account is taken of this relation, so that DCE is determined endogenously as the difference between the budget deficit and the net change in the private sector's bond holdings and bank borrowing. Such an assumption is obviously more realistic, and allows the model to be used to explain the upturns and downturns of the business cycle. Higher budget deficits financed by DCE lead initially to higher levels of output; but after a time balance of payments deficits result, leading to reserve depletions, contractions in the money supply and ultimately losses in output. Alternatively, exchange rate adjustments may take place, so that domestic prices rise relative to world prices.

Other small models, broadly in the monetarist tradition, have been developed for the UK economy by Smith (1977), Melitz and Sterdyniak (1979), Arestis *et al.* (1978) and a group of researchers at the Bank of England. Smith's model involves the specification of equations for aggregate supply, aggregate demand, the price level, the wage bill, unemployment and the current account of the balance of payments. No demand for money function is considered, and the money stock is determined exogenously. Annual data is used to estimate the model over the period 1880–1975. The results indicate a close, long-run relationship between movements in the money stock and the price level, and that current account deficits are also primarily the result of excessive monetary creation; findings which again support the monetarist view that a permanent increase in economic activity cannot be brought about through an expansionary monetary policy.

A small model of the UK monetary sector has been developed by Melitz and Sterdyniak (1979). This model, which is estimated using quarterly data for the period 1962–74, includes equations for the demand for money and the private sector's demands for government debt and bank loans. The properties of the model are analysed under both fixed and floating exchange rate regimes. Given fixed exchange rates, the money stock is treated as demand determined with reserve flows fulfilling the role of residual. Under a floating regime the money stock is assumed to be supply determined, so that any disequilibrium between the demand for and supply of money, given full employment, will bring about an adjustment of the price level.

An attempt to reconcile the 'reduced form' approach to macro modelling with that of the large model-building groups has been made by Arestis *et al.* (1978). A small, ten-equation model is considered, based on the framework developed by Moroney and Mason (1971), in which behavioural relations are specified for consumption, investment, stockbuilding, imports, the long rate of interest and the demand for and supply of money. Such an approach allows explicit consideration to be given to the individual links between money and the different expenditure decisions, while also enabling a reduced form to be derived relating output to government expenditure and the monetary base. The model was estimated for the UK using quarterly data over the period 1956–74, and the results confirm the findings of the majority of UK 'reduced form' studies in assigning a more dominant role to fiscal policy.

Research at the Bank of England, outlined in Coghlan (1979), Hilliard (1980) and Hoffman (1980), has also been concerned with estimating a small structural model of the UK economy using annual data for the period 1950–76. This model, the properties of which are considered by Currie (1982), incorporates behavioural equations for private sector expenditure, exports, imports, prices, private sector capital flows, the long-term rate of interest, private sector acquisition of public sector debt, bank lending and the exchange rate. The money stock is endogenously determined from the accounting identity relating the change in the money supply to gilt sales, bank lending, external influences and the PSBR.[51] A considerable emphasis is placed on the role of monetary forces in the economy, and direct money supply and interest rate effects exert large and powerful influences in the model. Changes in the real money stock and the level of, and change in, interest rates influence the change in private sector expenditure, while the rate of change of prices depends partly on the rate of change of the nominal money stock and the lagged value of the real money stock.

Finally we should note that other small models of the UK economy, such as Attfield *et al.* (1981) and Minford (1980), have been developed in recent years in the 'rational expectations' tradition of monetarist analysis. This approach is considered in more detail in Demery and Duck's survey of rational expectations in this volume.

10. Some final comments

We now return to the subject of large macro models in order to make some final comments on their uses and limitations.[52] Structurally, the various UK models are obviously very similar, and although differences do exist in the modelling of particular relationships, these have, if anything, diminished in recent years as a consensus has emerged over the form of many equations. As far as monetary factors are concerned, all models now incorporate financial variables, in one form or another, in several of the equations explaining private sector expenditure; although their significance in many cases has yet to be demonstrated. Similarly, explicit monetary sectors have now been developed in most models in order to endogenise the exchange rate, the structure of interest rates and the various money and credit aggregates.

In contrast to these developments in model specification, the techniques employed in model estimation have changed little in recent years. Since all the models are intricate non-linear dynamic systems, incorporating in many cases hundreds of endogenous and exogenous variables, complex simultaneous techniques which recognise the interrelationships between different variables would appear to be required for estimation purposes. However, in practice such estimation techniques are largely ignored, and the standard procedure is still to estimate each specification separately using single equation methods which make no allowance for any interdependencies that might exist between different variables. The possible presence of simultaneous equation bias in the estimated relations must therefore cast doubt on the reliability of some of the results obtained by the model builders. Indeed, it is precisely because of such problems, and other related factors such as the collinearity of many of the data series used, that some or all of the coefficients in particular relationships are often imposed rather than freely estimated.

The UK macro models are used mainly for purposes of forecasting and policy simulation. Forecasting refers to the process by which models are used to trace the future path of the economy. Given information about the values taken by the exogenous variables of the system in the future, the estimated relationships in the model can be used to produce forecasts of the main endogenous variables over the same period. All the models are used in this way to produce forecasts of the future path of key aggregates such as consumption, investment, unemployment and inflation. The accuracy of such forecasts is often used as a test of a model's validity. In this context Ash and Smyth (1973) carried out a study into the accuracy of various UK forecasters' predictions. They felt, with few exceptions, that the forecasters' predictions were significantly more accurate than simple extrapolations or averages of past outcomes. Nevertheless, errors in forecasting can arise for a variety of reasons. Specification, data and estimation problems obviously provide some sources of error, but there are also likely to be margins of error associated with the values assigned to the exogenous variables. It is therefore not necessarily valid to assess the respective performance of different models in terms of their relative forecasting records. In fact, in practice, comparisons are made even more difficult because many of the forecasts which are published by the different model-building groups are not pure forecasts obtained from the model, but rather figures which have been adjusted judgementally to take account of special factors, such as strikes or oil price changes, which may be important on particular occasions but which are not incorporated into the formal model specifications.[53]

The validity of the different models is much more easily analysed if consideration is given to their simulation properties. Simulation exercises are used to explore the effects on the endogenous variables of the system of changes in particular exogenous variables, typically policy instruments under the control of the authorities. The procedure is to compare the values taken by key aggregates such as output and unemployment, over a given period after the change in the policy instrument with the values they would have taken over the same period without the change in the policy instrument. Simulations of monetary changes are carried out by Bladen-Hovell *et al.* (1982) who consider the effects of a step increase in the general level of interest rates in the HMT and NI models. In order to compare the effects of monetary policy under both fixed and floating exchange rates the simulation exercise is carried out both with the exchange rate exogenously fixed at historical levels and with the exchange rate endogenously determined within the model. No attempt is made to simulate the effects of a change in the money stock, since it is argued the authorities do not attempt to control the money supply directly in practice but rather attempt to control it indirectly by influencing interest rates. In the HMT model, under fixed exchange rates, the traditional contractionary effects of higher interest rates on private expenditure are shown to be dominated by the stimulus to consumption provided by the bond coupon effect, so that output is actually higher at the end of the simulation period than it would have been without the initial change in interest rates. Under flexible exchange rates, monetary effects are stronger and are transmitted largely through the appreciation of the exchange rate which is induced by the contraction in the money supply consequent on the rise in interest rates. The change in the exchange rate causes a severe deterioration in the competitiveness of home industry so that imports increase and output falls. However, after 12 quarters output begins to recover as consumption responds to the increase in real wealth induced by a falling price level. In the NI model the simulations show that monetary effects are relatively weak under floating as well as fixed exchange rates. Under fixed exchange rates the bond coupon effect is not as strong as in the HMT model, while under floating rates the induced change in the exchange rate does not have the same output effects as in the

HMT model. Other examples of simulated studies of the effects of monetary changes, in the context of the HMT model, include Richardson (1981) and Middleton *et al.* (1981). Richardson examines the speed of response of prices to changes in the money supply induced in different ways, and the magnitudes of the associated effects on the main economic aggregates. Middleton *et al.* describe simulations on the HMT model designed to quantify the relationship between changes in the PSBR and the money supply. Different ways of manipulating the PSBR are considered and the simulations show that the size and even direction of the change in the money stock, and the consequent effects on the key economic aggregates, depends on the source of the change in the PSBR.

No other study has been directly concerned with simulating the effects of monetary changes. Given the initial concern with fiscal policy in the models, the majority of published simulations have attempted to measure the impact of changes in government expenditure and tax revenues. Examples are reported in Renton (1975), Laury *et al.* (1978), Posner (1978), Ormerod (1979a), Lewis and Ormerod (1979), Mowl (1980) and Artis and Miller (1981). However, because of the government budget constraint, fiscal policy changes cannot be considered independently of monetary policy, so that simulations carried out on fiscal instruments have consequences for monetary variables. In most simulations of the effects of increases in public expenditure, for example, a particular monetary stance is normally assumed. This may either involve fixed interest rates and an endogenous money supply, so that the increase in government expenditure is implicitly financed by the increase in the money stock, or it may assume a fixed money supply and endogenous interest rates, so that the increase in expenditure is implicitly financed by sales of bonds. The standard ISLM model suggests that of these two possibilities short-run bond-financed government deficits are less expansionary than money-financed deficits, since bond-financed spending 'crowds out' private expenditure by exerting upward pressure on interest rates. Comparisons of the effects of the two types of debt financing are made in Ormerod for the HMT model and in Laury *et al.* for the HMT, LBS and NI models. These studies tend to find that the output multipliers are low under both types of deficit financing, but particularly so when the money supply is kept constant.

Simulation exercises are subject to many of the same problems that affect a model's forecasting performance. Reported results, for example, indicate that the simulation properties of particular models are very sensitive to minor changes in model specification. Such exercises are, of course, all artificial to a certain extent and should be regarded as illustrating the partial differentials of the current version of the model rather than what would necessarily happen if such policies were pursued continuously over the whole simulation period. Indeed, Lucas (1976) has argued that policy simulations using such models can provide no useful information as to the actual consequences of alternative policies. Problems can arise with such exercises if the estimation period is not relevant to the simulation period. In such circumstances the estimated parameters may not necessarily be applicable to the assumed conditions of the simulation. Indeed, if different policy regimes had been in operation over the sample period the data would have been different and in consequence so would the estimates of the parameter values.

Thus, for example, although cleanly floating exchange rates are assumed in many policy simulation exercises, where these are freely estimated they include the effects of 'dirty floating'. In fact virtually no data are available with which to model the behaviour of the exchange rate under a clean float, and so the estimated parameters are not necessarily applicable to the assumed conditions of the simulation. A similar problem arises in endogenising earnings in simulation exercises when the available data sample includes periods when incomes policies were in force. In these instances it is quite likely that the true parameters will not be fixed, but will vary with each alternative policy. These comments on the validity of simulation exercises form part of the general rational expectations critique of large macro models. Proponents of this approach, which is considered in more detail in Demery and Duck's survey in this volume, criticise macro models because of their failure to model adequately the mechanism by which economic agents form their expectations of future economic variables.

The various UK macro models as they stand are clearly not ideal representations of the workings of the economy. The model builders realise this and are continually seeking to improve the overall specification of their models. Therefore it is only by attempting to establish stable empirical relationships for the key aggregates in the economy that researchers can understand how the economy functions and, more particularly with respect to monetary policy, how financial variables affect the different components of aggregate expenditure. In spite of the limitations of large models the superiority of any alternative approach to macro modelling is yet to be demonstrated.

Notes

1. For a discussion of the place of the expectations-augmented Phillips curve in monetarist analysis, see Laidler (1981).
2. For a fuller analysis of the derivation of the aggregate demand and supply curves, and the relationship between the latter and the expectations-augmented Phillips curve, see Demery and Duck's surveys in this volume.
3. This model is also known as the Cambridge Growth Project.
4. Otherwise known as the New Cambridge School.
5. See, for example, Pearce *et al.* (1976).
6. Chrystal (1979: 96) is particularly critical of this procedure.
7. For an alternative approach to modelling in which market clearing in the labour market is implicitly assumed, see Demery and Duck's survey of rational expectations in this volume.
8. For a discussion of the problems involved in modelling wage equations see Sumner's survey in this volume.
9. Of course pressure of demand effects could always influence the total wage bill, if not the wage rate, by influencing overtime working.
10. One implication of this view of wage determination is that higher levels of unemployment will increase the disparity between actual and target real wages and so stimulate wage demands. This view is, of course, counter to the more conventional pressure of demand effects.

11. This practice has been criticised; see Goodhart (1978: 186–7). Indeed, if the money supply is taken as given and the money market determines the rate of interest, it would be more appropriate to estimate the equation with the rate of interest as the dependent variable. Estimating it the other way round is likely to produce inconsistent results as the error term will be correlated with one of the included explanatory variables which in this case is the rate of interest.
12. In this regard, it is, of course, extremely difficult to produce definitive lists of characteristics which are accepted by all Keynesians and all monetarists respectively. This problem is highlighted by Leijonhufvud (1968), who has drawn a sharp distinction between Keynesian economics and the economics of Keynes.
13. This compares with the transmission mechanism as seen in the ISLM model where substitution is assumed to occur along only one single path from money to bonds and then from bonds to real assets, so that no direct substitution is allowed between money and real assets. Of course if the level of real balances is included as an argument in the expenditure functions then an increase in the money supply will cause a rightward shift of the IS curve, just as for any wealth effect.
14. For a detailed discussion of the 'rational expectations' hypothesis, see Demery and Duck's survey of the subject in this volume.
15. The way in which this process occurs for the first type of capital goods is formally very similar to the transmission mechanism described by Tobin (1969) which we considered earlier.
16. Brunner and Meltzer do not emphasise the interest rate effects on the desired stock of the third category of capital goods, preferring instead to emphasise the wealth effect.
17. For a fuller discussion of the working of the Exchange Equalisation Account, see Dennis (1981: 16–17).
18. It may in fact be possible to operate an independent monetary policy, even under fixed exchange rates, if the small economy assumption is relaxed. A large economy or a reserve currency country can operate such a policy; see Swoboda (1973).
19. Much of the literature on this subject is summarised in a collection of articles in Frenkel and Johnson (1976).
20. Consumer durables are items such as cars, furniture and carpets, while non-durable goods include food and clothing. Non-durable consumption is by far the more important in aggregate terms, accounting for some 90 per cent of total consumer spending, but durable expenditure is more volatile.
21. The relative income approach of Duesenberry (1949) and its development in the habit persistence theory of Brown (1952), the permanent income approach of Friedman (1957) and the life-cycle hypothesis of Ando and Modigliani (1963) can all, for example, be reduced to forms which relate current consumption to current and lagged values of income.
22. In fact in the 1980 version of the LBS model the coefficients on these variables were not found to be significantly different from zero.
23. Deaton (1977) has provided an alternative rationale for the inclusion of inflation variables in consumption functions. For a discussion of his theory, see Thomas's survey in this volume.
24. For an alternative discussion of the role of wealth effects in the determination of consumers' expenditure, see the surveys by Thomas in this volume and by Grice (1981).
25. In this respect, the period up until the early 1970s was generally characterised by excess demand in the advances market, while since that time supply forces have become much more important. See Spencer (1975) and Artis (1978).
26. Cuthbertson, however, also found that a real interest rate variable was a statistically significant determinant of durable expenditure, when it was included in a specification which also involved a liquid assets term but no credit availability variable.

27. In practice changes in *d* dominate the series.
28. In this way some attempt can also be made to overcome the simultaneity problem as to whether changes in consumer debt cause changes in expenditure or vice versa. In particular, joint dependence between the variables can be allowed for if the overall model is estimated using simultaneous equation techniques. Of the two studies, however, only Ball and Drake make any attempt to do this.
29. The basis of the neo-classical theoretical approach is outlined in Jorgenson (1967), while Jorgenson and Stephenson (1967) and Jorgenson *et al.* (1970) provide examples of empirical studies in this tradition.
30. The general issue of lag structures has proved to be a major problem in the empirical analysis of investment behaviour since it was first highlighted by Koyck (1954).
31. Of course, because of the bond coupon effect, even if real rates are low, high nominal interest rates might exert a greater influence on investment by restricting the cash flow of the company sector which is a net debtor.
32. The definition of the personal sector includes unincorporated companies such as partnerships and one-man businesses.
33. Of course, because few houses are built to order, even demand influences on the housing market must ultimately be filtered through the supply side.
34. Such non-price conditions can take a variety of different forms. In particular the building societies often require potential borrowers to have saved with them for a given period and to have a certain level of savings. Also restrictions are usually imposed on the amount lent to borrowers in accord with their present level of income.
35. In the monetary sectors of the models building societies form part of the non-bank private sector, so that their behaviour is analysed separately from that of banking institutions.
36. Of these measures, the use of mortgage advances variables, in particular, involves a simultaneity problem since it is not clear whether increases in mortgage advances create a higher demand for housing, or whether mortgage borrowing merely responds to housebuilding activity.
37. For a discussion of the principles underlying the development of the domestic monetary sectors of the UK models, see Mayers and Savage (1980a).
38. The early research on the HMT monetary model is outlined in Spencer and Mowl (1978). For a more recent description of the model, see Middleton *et al.* (1981).
39. The expected change in prices is, in turn, modelled in terms of the past growth of wage costs, import costs and the money supply relative to output.
40. The reserve asset requirements referred to here were initiated in 1971 as part of the Competition and Credit Control reforms, but ceased to operate in 1981. In the intervening period the banks were required to keep 12½ per cent of their 'eligible liabilities' in a defined group of liquid assets: balances at the Bank of England (1½ per cent of 'eligible liabilities' had to be kept in this asset), call loans to the discount houses, Treasury bills, local authority bills, commercial bills (up to a maximum of 2 per cent of 'eligible liabilities'), government stocks within a year of maturity and company tax reserve certificates. For the purposes of the model however commercial bills are excluded from the definition of reserve assets, and included among bank advances, so that the effective reserve asset ratio is 10½ per cent.
41. The development of the NI monetary model is considered in Savage (1979) and Mayes and Savage (1980b).
42. Net other liabilities of the banks comprise non-deposit liabilities (capital and reserves) and deposits of (less lending to) the overseas sector.
43. In fact, in the UK context, external flows may well affect the money stock, even under a floating regime; see Lomax and Mowl (1978) or Goodhart (1979: 144–8).
44. The sterling M3 series is adjusted for the distortions arising from the imposition of the 'corset'; this was a device used by the authorities to control the growth of interest-bearing bank deposits in the 1970s.

45. The implied form of the demand for money function in the HMT model is investigated in Spencer and Mowl (1978: 37–9), and Middleton *et al.* (1981).
46. For a discussion of some of the problems involved in the modelling of the exchange rate, see Goodhart (1979: 160–6).
47. The early work on the external monetary sector of the HMT model is outlined in Lomax and Denham (1978).
48. See Fisher and Sheppard (1974) for a fuller discussion of the findings of these studies.
49. For a more detailed account of the deficiencies of 'reduced form' studies, see Dennis (1981: 150–9). See also Laidler (1971).
50. For an alternative view of the causality issue, in the context of the UK economy, see Mills and Wood (1978).
51. The form of the implicit demand for money function is considered by Currie (1982: 68–70).
52. Many of the issues raised in this section are considered in more detail in Ormerod (1979b).
53. The methodology of forecasting is outlined in Surrey and Ormerod (1977) and Economic Progress Report (1981), while a recent comparison of the forecasting records of different models is made in National Institute (1981).

References

Allard, R. J. (1974) An economic analysis of the effects of regulating hire purchase, *Government Economic Service Occasional Paper*, **9**, HMSO, London.

Allard, R. J. (1979) Credit restrictions and lag distributions on consumer durables equations, *Applied Economics*, **11**, 171–84.

Andersen, L. C. and Carlson, K. M. (1970) A monetarist model for economic stabilisation, *Federal Reserve Bank of St. Louis Review*, **52**, 7–25.

Andersen, L. C. and Jordan, J. L. (1968) Monetary and fiscal actions: a test of their relative importance in economic stabilisation, *Federal Reserve Bank of St. Louis Review*, **50**, 11–24.

Anderson, G. J. (1981) A new approach to the empirical investigation of investment expenditures, *Economic Journal*, **91**, 88–103.

Ando, A. and Modigliani, F. (1963) The life cycle hypothesis of saving: aggregate implications and tests, *American Economic Review*, **53**, 55–84.

Arestis, P., Frowen, S. F. and Karakitsos, E. (1978) The dynamic impacts of government expenditure and the monetary base on aggregate income: the case of four OECD countries, 1965–74, *Public Finance*, **33**, 1–22.

Artis, M. J. (1978) Monetary policy, Ch.6, pp.258–303, in Blackaby, F. T. (ed.), *British Economic Policy 1960–74*, Cambridge University Press, Cambridge.

Artis, M. J., Kiernan, E. and Whitley, J. D. (1975) The effects of building society behaviour on housing investment, pp.37–60 in Parkin, J. M. and Nobay, A. R. (eds), *Contemporary Issues in Economics*, Manchester University Press, Manchester.

Artis, M. J. and Lewis, M. K. (1976) The demand for money in the UK 1963–73, *Manchester School*, **44**, 147–81.

Artis, M. J. and Miller, M. H. (eds) (1981) *Essays in Fiscal and Monetary Policy*, Oxford University Press, London.

Artis, M. J. and Nobay, A. R. (1969) Two aspects of the monetary debate, *National Institute Economic Review*, **49**, 35–51.

Ash, J. C. K. and Smyth, D. J. (1973) *Forecasting the United Kingdom Economy*, Saxon House, Farnborough.

Attfield, C. L. F., Demery, D. and Duck, N. W. (1981) A quarterly model of unanticipated monetary growth, output and the price level in the UK: 1963–78, *Journal of Monetary Economics*, **8**, 331–50.

Ball, R. J. and Drake, P. S. (1963) The impact of credit control on consumer durable goods spending in the UK 1957–61, *Review of Economic Studies*, **30**, 181–94.

Bank of England (1979) Bank of England model of the UK economy, *Discussion Paper*, **5**.

Barker, T., Borooah, V., van der Ploeg, R. and Winters, A. (1980) The Cambridge multisectoral dynamic model: an instrument for national economic policy analysis, Department of Applied Economics, University of Cambridge.

Barrett, C. R. and Walters, A. A. (1966) The stability of Keynesian and monetary multipliers in the UK, *Review of Economics and Statistics*, **48**, 395–405.

Batchelor, R. A. (1977) Sterling exchange rates 1951–76: a Casselian analysis, *National Institute Economic Review*, **81**, 45–66.

Bean, C. R. (1978) The determination of consumers' expenditure in the UK, *Treasury Working Paper*, **4**.

Bean, C. R. (1979) An econometric model of manufacturing investment in the UK, *Treasury Paper*, AP(79)7.

Bean, C. R. (1981) An econometric model of manufacturing investment in the UK, *Economic Journal*, **91**, 106–21.

Bladen-Hovell, R., Green, C. and Savage, D. (1982) The transmission mechanism of monetary policy in two large-scale models of the UK economy, *Oxford Bulletin of Economics and Statistics*, **44**, 15–29.

Blinder, A. S. and Solow, R. M. (1973) Does fiscal policy matter? *Journal of Public Economics*, **2**, 319–37.

Boatwright, B. D. and Eaton, J. R. (1972) The estimation of investment functions for manufacturing industry in the UK, *Economica*, **39**, 403–18.

Borooah, V. K. (1978) A model of economic behaviour of the personal sector in the United Kingdom: 1963 to 1974, unpublished University of Southampton Ph.D. dissertation.

Brainard, W. C. and Tobin, J. (1968) Pitfalls in financial model building, *American Economic Review*, Papers and Proceedings, **58**, 99–122.

Brechling, F. R. (1974) Monetary policy and neoclassical investment analysis, pp.454–83 in Johnson, H. G. and Nobay, A. R. (eds), *Issues in Monetary Economics*, Oxford University Press, London.

Brechling, F. R. (1975) *Investment and Employment Decisions*, Manchester University Press Manchester.

Brown, T. M. (1952) Habit persistence and lags in consumer behaviour, *Econometrica*, **20**, 355–71.

Brunner, K. and Meltzer, A. H. (1972) Money, debt and economic activity, *Journal of Political Economy*, **80**, 951–77.

Burrows, P. (1971) Explanatory and forecasting models of inventory investment in Britain, *Applied Economics*, **3**, 275–89.

Chrystal, K. A. (1979) *Controversies in British Macroeconomics*, Philip Allan, Oxford.

Chrystal, K. A. (1981) The 'New Cambridge' aggregate expenditure function: the emperor's old clothes?, *Journal of Monetary Economics*, **7**, 395–402.

Coghlan, R. T. (1979) A small monetary model of the UK economy, *Bank of England Discussion Paper*, **3**.

Coutts, K. J., Cripps, T. F., Fetherston, M. J. and Anyadike-Danes, M. K. (1980) CEPG model of the UK economy technical manual, sixth edition, Department of Applied Economics, University of Cambridge.

Crockett, A. D. (1970) Timing relationships between movements of monetary and national income variables, *Bank of England Quarterly Bulletin*, **10**, 459–68.

Crouch, R. L. (1967) A model of the UK's monetary sector, *Econometrica*, **35**, 398–418.

Currie, D. (1982) The long run properties of the Bank of England's small monetary model of the UK economy, *Applied Economics*, **14**, 63–72.

Cuthbertson, K. (1980) The determination of expenditure on consumer durables, *National Institute Economic Review*, **94**, 62–72.

Davidson, J. E. H., Hendry, D. F., Srba, F. and Yeo, S. (1978) Econometric modelling of the aggregate time-series relationship between consumers' expenditure and income in the UK, *Economic Journal*, **88**, 661–92.

Davis, E. P. and Saville, I. D. (1982) Mortgage lending and the housing market, *Bank of England Quarterly Bulletin*, **22**, 390–8.

Deaton, A. S. (1977) Involuntary saving through unanticipated inflation, *American Economic Review*, **67**, 899–910.

Dennis, G. E. J. (1981) *Monetary Economics*, Longman, London.

Dow, J. C. R. (1964) *The Management of the British Economy, 1945–60*, Cambridge University Press, Cambridge.

Duesenberry, J. (1949) *Income, Saving and the Theory of Consumer Behaviour*, Harvard University Press, Cambridge (Mass.).

Duffy, M. (1970) A model of UK private investment in dwellings, *London Graduate School of Business Studies Discussion Paper*, 18.

Economic Progress Report (1981) Forecasting in the Treasury, **134**, H.M. Treasury.

Evans, M. K. (1969) *Macroeconomic Activity: Theory, Forecasting and Control: An Econometric Approach*, Harper and Row, New York.

Feldstein, M. S. and Flemming, J. S. (1971) Tax policy, corporate saving and investment behaviour in Britain, *Review of Economic Studies*, **38**, 415–34.

Fisher, G. R. and Sheppard, D. (1974) Interrelationships between real and monetary variables: some evidence from recent US empirical studies, pp.179–259 in Johnson, H. G. and Nobay, A. R. (eds), *Issues in Monetary Economics*, Oxford University Press, London.

Fleming, J. M. (1962) Domestic financial policies under fixed and floating exchange rates, *IMF Staff Papers*, **9**, 369–79.

Flemming, J. S., Price, L. D. D. and Byers, S. A. (1976) The cost of capital, finance and investment, *Bank of England Quarterly Bulletin*, **16**, 193–205.

Frenkel, J. A. and Johnson, H. G. (1976) *The Monetary Approach to the Balance of Payments*, George Allen and Unwin, London.

Friedman, M. (1957) *A Theory of the Consumption Function,* Princeton University Press, Princeton.

Friedman, M. (1970) The counter-revolution in monetary theory, *Institute of Economic Affairs*, Occasional Paper, **33**.

Friedman, M. and Meiselman, D. I. (1963) The relative stability of monetary velocity and the investment multiplier in the US 1897–1958, pp.165–268, in Commission on money and credit, *Stabilisation Policies*, Prentice-Hall, Englewood Cliffs.

Friedman, M. and Schwartz, A. J. (1963) Money and business cycles, *Review of Economics and Statistics,* **45**, (Suppl.), 32–64.

Garganas, N.C. (1975) An analysis of consumer credit and its effects on purchases of consumer durables, Ch. 19, pp.610–45, in Renton, G. A. (ed.), *Modelling the Economy*, Heinemann, London.

Goodhart, C. A. E. (1978) Monetary policy, Ch. 9, pp.180–90, in Posner, M. (ed.), *Demand Management*, Heinemann, London.

Goodhart, C. A. E. (1979) Money in an open economy, Ch.6, pp.143–67, in Ormerod, P. (ed.), *Economic Modelling*, Heinemann, London.

Goodhart, C. A. E. and Crockett, A. D. (1970) The importance of money, *Bank of England Quarterly Bulletin*, **10**, 159–98.

Grice, J. W. (1981) Wealth effects and expenditure functions: a survey of the empirical evidence, Ch.3. pp.39–65, in Artis, M. J. and Miller, M. H. (eds), *Essays in Fiscal and Monetary Policy*, Oxford University Press, London.

Griliches, Z. and Wallace, N. (1965) The determinants of investment revisited, *International Economic Review*, **6**, 311–29.

Gurley, J. G. and Shaw, E. S. (1960) *Money in a Theory of Finance*, Brookings Institution, Washington.

Hansen, A. H. (1953) *A Guide to Keynes*, McGraw-Hill, New York.

Hicks, J. R. (1937) Mr. Keynes and the Classics, *Econometrica,* **5**, 147–59; reprinted as

Ch.7, pp.126–42, in Hicks, J. R. (1967) *Critical Essays in Monetary Theory*, Oxford University Press, London.

Hilliard, B. C. (1980) The Bank of England small monetary model: recent developments and simulation properties, *Bank of England Discussion Paper*, **13**.

Hilton, K. and Crossfield, D. H. (1970) Short run consumption functions for the UK 1955–66, Ch.3, pp.59–98, in Hilton, K. and Heathfield, D. F. (eds), *The Econometric Study of the United Kingdom*, Macmillan, London.

Hilton, K. and Heathfield, D. F. (eds) (1970) *The Econometric Study of the United Kingdom*, Macmillan, London.

Hines, A. G. and Catephores, G. (1970) Investment in UK manufacturing industry, 1956–67, Ch.8, pp.203–24, in Hilton, K. and Heathfield, D. F. (eds), *The Econometric Study of the United Kingdom*, Macmillan, London.

Hoffman, J. M. (1980) A quarterly small monetary model of the UK economy: preliminary estimation and simulation results, *Bank of England Discussion Paper*, **14**.

Holt, C. C., Modigliani, F., Muth, J. F. and Simon, H. A. (1960) *Planning Production, Inventories and Work Force*, Prentice-Hall, Englewood Cliffs.

Irvine, F. O. (1981a) Merchant wholesaler inventory investment and the cost of capital, *American Economic Review*, Papers and Proceedings, **71**, 23–9.

Irvine, F. O. (1981b) Retail inventory investment and the cost of capital, *American Economic Review*, **71**, 633–48.

Irvine, F. O. (1981c) The influence of capital costs on inventory investment: time-series evidence for a department store, *Quarterly Review of Economics and Business*, **21**, 25–44.

Johnson, H. G. (1969) Inside money, outside money, income, wealth and welfare in monetary theory, *Journal of Money, Credit and Banking*, **1**, 30–45.

Johnson, H. G. (1972) The monetary approach to the balance of payments, Ch.9, pp. 229–49, in his *Further Essays in Monetary Economics*, George Allen and Unwin, London.

Jonson, P. D. (1976) Money and economic activity in the open economy: the United Kingdom, *Journal of Political Economy*, **84**, 979–1012.

Jorgenson, D. W. (1967) The theory of investment behaviour, pp.129–55, in Ferber, R. (ed.), *Determinants of Investment Behaviour*, NBER, New York.

Jorgenson, D. W. (1971) Econometric studies of investment behaviour: a survey, *Journal of Economic Literature*, **9**, 1111–47.

Jorgenson, D. W., Hunter, J. and Nadiri, M. I. (1970) A comparison of alternative econometric models of quarterly investment behaviour, *Econometrica*, **38**, 187–212.

Jorgenson, D. W. and Stephenson, J. A. (1967) Investment behaviour in US manufacturing 1947–60, *Econometrica*, **35**, 169–220.

Junankar, P. N. (1972) *Investment: Theories and Evidence*, Macmillan, London.

Keran, M. W. (1970) Monetary and fiscal influences on economic activity: the foreign experience, *Federal Reserve Bank of St. Louis Review*, **52**, 16–28.

Klein, L. R., Ball, R. J., Hazelwood, A. and Vandome, P. (1961) *An Econometric Model of the United Kingdom*, Basil Blackwell, Oxford.

Koyck, L. M. (1954) *Distributed Lags and Investment Analysis*, North-Holland, Amsterdam.

Laidler, D. E. W. (1971) The influence of money on economic activity: a survey of some current problems, pp.75–135, in Clayton, G., Gilbert, J. and Sedgwick, R. (eds), *Monetary Theory and Monetary Policy in the 1970's*, Oxford University Press, London.

Laidler, D. E. W. (1978a) Money and money income: an essay on the transmission mechanism, *Journal of Monetary Economics*, **4**, 157–91.

Laidler, D. E. W. (1978b) A monetarist viewpoint, Ch.2. pp.35–65, in Posner, M. (ed.), *Demand Management*, Heinemann, London.

Laidler, D. E. W. (1981) Monetarism: an interpretation and an assessment, *Economic Journal*, **91**, 1–28.

Laidler, D. E. W. and O'Shea, P. (1980) An empirical macro model of an open economy under fixed exchange rates: the United Kingdom 1954–70, *Economica*, **47**, 141–58.
Laury, J. S. E., Lewis, G. R. and Ormerod, P. A. (1978) Properties of macroeconomic models of the UK economy: a comparative study, *National Institute Economic Review*, **83**, 52–72.
Leijonhufvud, A. (1968) *On Keynesian Economics and the Economics of Keynes*, Oxford University Press, New York.
Lewis, G. R. and Ormerod, P. A. (1979) Policy simulations and model characteristics, Ch.8, pp.156–82, in Cook, S. T. and Jackson, P. M. (eds), *Current Issues in Fiscal Policy*, Martin Robertson, Oxford.
Lieberman, C. (1980) Inventory demand and cost of capital effects, *Review of Economics and Statistics*, **62**, 348–56.
Lomax, R. and Denham, M. (1978) A financial sector for the Treasury model: Part 2, The model of external capital flows, *Treasury Working Paper*, **8.**
Lomax, R. and Mowl, C. J. (1978) Balance of payments flows and the monetary aggregates in the UK, *Treasury Working Paper*, **5.**
London Business School (1981) Quarterly econometric model of the United Kingdom economy, Econometric Forecasting Unit.
Lovell, M. C. (1964) Determinants of inventory behaviour, pp.177–231, in Denison, E. F. and Klein, L. R. (eds), *Models of Income Determination*, Princeton University Press, Princeton.
Lucas, R. E. (1976) Econometric policy evaluation: a critique, pp.19–46, in Brunner, K. and Meltzer, A. H. (eds), *The Phillips Curve and Labour Markets*, North-Holland, Amsterdam.
Lund, P. J. and Holden, K. (1968) An econometric study of private sector gross fixed capital formation in the UK, 1923–38, *Oxford Economic Papers*, **20**, 56–73.
Matthews, K. G. P. and Ormerod, P. A. (1978) St. Louis models of the UK economy, *National Institute Economic Review*, **84**, 65–9.
Mayes, D. G. and Savage, D. (1980a) The contrast between portfolio theory and econometric models of the UK monetary sector, *National Institute Discussion Paper*, **34.**
Mayes, D. G. and Savage D. (1980b) The structure, performance and simulation properties of the monetary sector of the National Institute macroeconometric model, *National Institute Discussion Paper*, **36.**
Meen, G. (1979a) A model of consumer durables, *Treasury Paper*, UMDG(79)22.
Meen, G. (1979b) More consumer durable equations, *Treasury Paper*, UMDG (79)33.
Melitz, J. and Sterdyniak, H. (1979) An econometric study of the British monetary system, *Economic Journal*, **89**, 874–96.
Middleton, P. E., Mowl, C. J., Odling-Smee, J. C. and Riley, C. J. (1981) Monetary targets and the public sector borrowing requirement, Ch.4, pp.135–75 in Griffiths, B. and Wood, G. E. (eds), *Monetary Targets*, Macmillan, London.
Mills, T. C. and Wood, G. E. (1978) Money-income relationships and the exchange rate regime, *Federal Reserve Bank of St. Louis Review*, **60**, 22–7.
Minford, A. P. L. (1980) A rational expectations model of the UK under fixed and floating exchange rates, pp.293–355, in Brunner, K. and Meltzer, A. H. (eds), *On the State of Macroeconomics*, North-Holland, Amsterdam.
Modigliani, F. (1975) The channels of monetary policy in the Federal Reserve–MIT–University of Pennsylvania econometric model of the US, Ch.9, pp.240–67, in Renton, G. A. (ed.), *Modelling the Economy*, Heinemann, London.
Moroney, J. R. and Mason, J. M. (1971) The dynamic impacts of autonomous expenditures and the monetary base on aggregate income, *Journal of Money, Credit and Banking*, **3**, 793–814.
Mowl, C. (1980) Simulations on the Treasury model, *Treasury Working Paper*, **15.**
Mundell, R. A. (1962) The appropriate use of monetary and fiscal policy under fixed exchange rates, *IMF Staff Papers*, **9**, 70–9.

Mundell, R. A. (1963) Capital mobility and stabilisation policy under fixed and flexible exchange rates, *Canadian Journal of Economics and Political Science*, **29**, 475–85.

National Institute of Economic and Social Research (1979) Listing of the interim NIESR model IV, *Discussion Paper*, **28.**

National Institute of Economic and Social Research (1981) Assessing economic models and economic forecasts, *National Institute Economic Review*, **95**, 21–31.

Nobay, A. R. (1970) Forecasting manufacturing investment–some preliminary results, *National Institute Economic Review*, **52**, 58–66.

Norton, W. E. (1969) Debt management and monetary policy in the United Kingdom, *Economic Journal*, **79**, 475–94.

O'Herlihy, C. St. J. and Spencer, J. E. (1972) Building societies' behaviour, 1955–70, *National Institute Economic Review*, **61**, 40–52.

Ormerod, P. A. (ed.) (1979a) *Economic Modelling*, Heinemann, London.

Ormerod, P. A. (1979b) Theory, policy and macroeconomic models, Ch.7, pp.141–55 in Cook, S. T. and Jackson, P. M. (eds), *Current Issues in Fiscal Policy*, Martin Robertson, Oxford.

Park, Y. C. (1972) Some current issues on the transmission process of monetary policy, *IMF Staff Papers*, **19**, 1–45.

Pearce, I. F., Trivedi, P. K., Stromback, C. T. and Anderson, G. J. (1976) *A Model of Output, Employment, Wages and Prices in the UK*, Cambridge University Press, Cambridge.

Pesek, B. P. and Saving, T. R. (1967) *Money, Wealth and Economic Theory*, Macmillan, New York.

Pigou, A. C. (1943) The classical stationary state, *Economic Journal*, **53**, 343–51.

Posner, M. V. (ed.) (1978) *Demand Management*, Heinemann, London.

Radcliffe Committee (1959) *Report on the Working of the Monetary System*, Cmnd.**827**, HMSO, London.

Renton, G. A. (ed.) (1975) *Modelling the Economy*, Heinemann, London.

Richardson, P. (1981) Money and prices: a simulation study using the Treasury macroeconomic model, *Treasury Working Paper*, **17.**

Rubin, L. S. (1979) Aggregate inventory behaviour: its response to uncertainty and interest rates, *Journal of Post Keynesian Economics*, **2**, 201–11.

Sargent, T. J. and Wallace, N. (1976) Rational expectations and the theory of economic policy, *Journal of Monetary Economics*, **2**, 169–83.

Savage, D. (1977) A comparison of accelerator models of manufacturing investment, *National Institute Discussion Paper*, **9.**

Savage, D. (1978) The channels of monetary influence: a survey of the empirical evidence, *National Institute Economic Review*, **83**, 73–89.

Savage, D. (1979) The monetary sector of the NIESR model: preliminary results, *National Institute Discussion Paper*, **21.**

Silber, W. L. (1970) Fiscal policy in ISLM analysis: a correction, *Journal of Money, Credit and Banking*, **2**, 461–72.

Sims, C. A. (1972) Money, income and causality, *American Economic Review*, **62**, 540–52.

Smith, D. (1977) A monetary model of the British economy 1880–1975, *National Westminster Bank Quarterly Review*, February, 18–32.

Spencer, P. D. (1975) A disequilibrium model of personal sector bank advances 1963–74: some preliminary results, Treasury Paper presented to Oxford Conference of Money Study Group.

Spencer, P. D. and Mowl, C. (1978) A financial sector for the Treasury model: Part 1, The model of the domestic monetary system, *Treasury Working Paper*, **8.**

Stone, R. (1964) Private saving in Britain, past, present and future, *Manchester School*, **32**, 79–112.

Surrey, M. J. C. (1970) Personal income and consumers' expenditure, Ch.4, pp.99–109, in Hilton, K. and Heathfield, D. F. (eds), *The Econometric Study of the United*

Kingdom, Macmillan, London.

Surrey, M. J. C. and Ormerod, P. A. (1977) Formal and informal aspects of forecasting with an econometric model, *National Institute Economic Review*, **81**, 67–71.

Swoboda, A. K. (1973) Monetary policy under fixed exchange rates: effectiveness, the speed of adjustment and proper use, *Economica*, **40**, 136–54.

Tarling, R. and Wilkinson, F. (1977) Inflation and money supply, *Economic Policy Review*, **3**, 56–60.

Tobin, J. (1969) A general equilibrium approach to monetary theory, *Journal of Money, Credit and Banking*, **1**, 15–29.

Tobin, J. (1970) Money and income: post hoc ergo propter hoc?, *Quarterly Journal of Economics*, **84**, 301–17.

Townend, J. C. (1976) The personal saving ratio, *Bank of England Quarterly Bulletin*, **16**, 53–73.

Treasury, H. M. (1980) Macroeconomic model equation and variable listing.

Trevedi, P. K. (1970) Inventory behaviour in UK manufacturing, 1956–67, *Review of Economic Studies*, **37**, 517–36.

Walters, A. A. (1966) Monetary multipliers in the UK 1880–1962, *Oxford Economic Papers*, **18**, 270–83.

Walters, A. A. (1971) Money in Boom and Slump, *Institute of Economic Affairs*, Hobart Paper, **44**.

Whitehead, C. M. E. (1974) *The UK Housing Market: An Econometric Model*, Saxon House, Farnborough.

Whitin, T. M. (1957) *The Theory of Inventory Management*, Princeton University Press, Princeton.

Williams, D., Goodhart, C. A. E. and Gowland, D. (1976) Money, income and causality: the UK experience, *American Economic Review*, **66**, 417–23.

Williams, R. H. (1972) Demand for consumer durables: stock adjustment models and alternative specifications of stock depletion, *Review of Economic Studies*, **39**, 281–95.

CHAPTER FIVE

The history and significance of the Phillips curve

Michael T. Sumner*

1. Introduction

Unemployment and inflation, either separately or in combination, have been the focus of macroeconomics since its birth. Indeed, the problem of explaining the causes of unemployment and of prescribing cures was the reason for the creation of macroeconomics, as distinct from the much older subject of monetary theory which focused on the more established problem of inflation. The apparent success of full-employment policies during the first two post-war decades contributed substantially to the prestige of economics and economists. The subsequent deterioration of western economic performance, in terms of higher unemployment and higher inflation, accounts for a large part of the accompanying disillusion with the subject and its practitioners. Unlike many other dimensions of economic achievement and failure, unemployment and inflation are readily measurable, painful to experience, and therefore of direct and immediate concern to participants in all markets, including the market for votes.

It is hardly surprising that the Phillips curve which relates these two crucial variables has attracted more attention and generated more literature than any other macroeconomic hypothesis. Its parentage, theoretical foundations, empirical validity, and policy implications, not to mention the estimation problems associated with it, have all been the subject of intense and protracted controversy. Its varied history provides an object-lesson in methodology. Its relevance to current policy remains a matter of serious dispute.

The sheer volume of literature on the Phillips curve presents as much a physical as an intellectual challenge. New entrants to this field of enquiry, whether as producers of new knowledge or consumers of the current conventional wisdom, face considerable difficulty in setting contemporary developments in their historical context, and in judging the conformity of or conflict between current and previous results. Valuable innovations and insights are lost in the spate of conventional reports and ideas of ephemeral significance.

The object of this survey is to guide the reader through this morass, to alert him to the major developments and unsolved problems, to indicate the most rewarding primary sources, and to discourage the intellectual equivalent of

* Thanks are due to Bob Millward, Graham Smith and George Zis for comments and discussion.

reinventing the wheel. Its organisation is broadly chronological, but historical ordering is subordinated to intellectual coherence. The main emphasis is placed on theoretical developments and their empirical basis. Most of the evidence discussed relates to the UK and no attempt is made to consider the success of the Phillips curve as an export, but seminal empirical results from other economies are cited. Policy implications are appraised in the final section.

2. Phillips's contribution

Phillips did not describe the construction of the curve which bears his name until 1958, though he had used the same relationship without discussion in his earlier work on the stabilisation of dynamic systems (1954). An immediate puzzle is why the curve was christened thus, for Phillips was certainly not the first economist to postulate a trade-off between unemployment and wage or price inflation.

It is probably an exaggeration to read a Phillips curve into the work of Marx, who asserted that variations in 'the industrial reserve army' of the unemployed determined 'the general movements of wages' but failed to make clear whether the latter denoted their level or rate of change. Fisher (1926), however, was quite explicit in identifying 'a statistical relation between unemployment and price changes', though he viewed causation as running from high inflation to low unemployment, rather than in the opposite direction. Tinbergen (1933) was apparently the first to estimate a Phillips curve of conventional form, for the Netherlands; he contemplated (1951) applying the same relationship in his study of the British trade cycle in the nineteenth century, though he eventually settled on the rate of change of coal prices as the determinant of wage inflation. Klein and Goldberger (1955) included a Phillips curve in their econometric model of the USA. Brown (1955) illustrated the relation between wage change and unemployment graphically. Indeed, long before Philips's article had been written, the dependence of wage inflation on unemployment had been rejected by Dunlop (1938), in favour of a relationship with *changes* in unemployment. If Phillips had made even a tentative foray into the already extensive literature, his celebrated paper might never have been written.

Its extraordinary influence cannot be attributed to either a more fully articulated statement of the theory to be tested or a more sophisticated technique than in some earlier and many contemporary studies. The theoretical foundation of the Phillips curve was simply the hypothesis that the price of a commodity changes at a rate determined by excess demand for it. The labour market was selected for analysis because the unemployment rate is a readily observable proxy for excess demand, but this relationship was casually asserted without elaboration. Other possible influences on wage inflation were mentioned, but not integrated into any explicit model. The procedure for estimating the curve was not fully articulated, but it was certainly unorthodox. Fifty-three original observations on unemployment and wage inflation were reduced to six by averaging the data within successive ranges of unemployment; then two parameters were estimated from four of these averages, and the third was chosen 'by trial and error

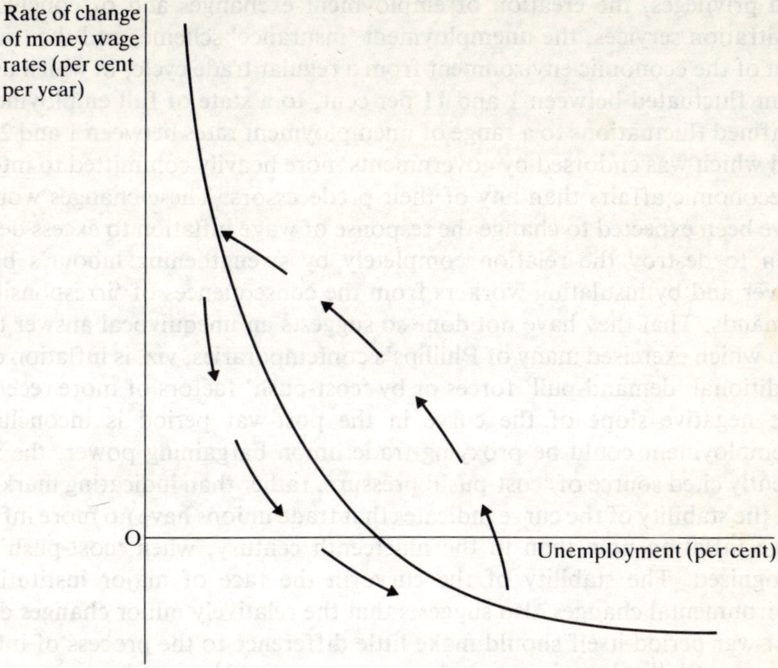

Fig 5.1 The Phillips curve

to make the curve pass as close as possible to the remaining two' [averaged data points] (Phillips 1958: 290) thus producing the characteristic relationship shown in Fig. 5.1. Other influences on wage inflation were not quantified in any way.

Phillips's claim to fame rests on the stability of the relationship he estimated between unemployment and the rate of change of wages. The data used for fitting the curve relate to the period 1861–1913. When that curve was superimposed on a scatter diagram showing the post-Second World War observations, for 1948–57, they were found to lie very close to the curve. Indeed, the Phillips curve, which predicts wage inflation at different unemployment rates on the assumption that the labour market still functions as it did in the nineteenth century, fitted the post-war observations more closely than it fitted the original nineteenth-century data.

This is a remarkable result. Few economic relationships exhibit unchanged parameters over a period of almost a century, even when they are based on a well-developed theory. The Phillips curve was not derived from such a theory, but from an *ad hoc* assumption about the response to disequilibrium. The stability of the Phillips curve was all the more remarkable in that it relates to a market which has experienced major institutional and organisational changes in the interval between the fitting period and the prediction period: changes in the composition of the labour force and the pattern of employment, growth in the membership of trade unions from less than 15 per cent of the labour force before the First World War to over 40 per cent after the Second World War, changes in their legal status and privileges, the creation of employment exchanges and of conciliation and arbitration services, the unemployment 'insurance' scheme, and the transformation of the economic environment from a regular trade cycle, in which unemployment fluctuated between 1 and 11 per cent, to a state of full employment which confined fluctuations to a range of unemployment rates between 1 and 2 per cent, and which was endorsed by governments more heavily committed to intervention in economic affairs than any of their predecessors. These changes would surely have been expected to change the response of wage inflation to excess demand, or even to destroy the relation completely by strengthening labour's bargaining power and by insulating workers from the consequences of 'irresponsible' wage demands. That they have not done so suggests an unequivocal answer to a question which exercised many of Phillips's contemporaries, viz. is inflation caused by traditional 'demand-pull' forces or by 'cost-push' factors of more recent origin? The negative slope of the curve in the post-war period is inconclusive, for unemployment could be proxying trade union bargaining power, the most frequently cited source of 'cost-push' pressure, rather than indicating market forces; but the stability of the curve indicates that trade unions have no more influence on wage inflation now than in the nineteenth century, when 'cost-push' was not recognised. The stability of the curve in the face of major institutional and environmental changes also suggests that the relatively minor changes during the post-war period itself should make little difference to the process of inflation.

Phillips's major results have been presented here as they appeared in 1958. An empirical relationship based on such slender theoretical foundations and with such far-reaching implications could be expected to generate further study and immediate criticism. Both expectations were amply fulfilled, as subsequent sections of this survey will demonstrate; but it is important that the stark simplicity of Phillips's findings should not be lost in the complexities introduced in the subsequent literature. How easily that can happen is clearly illustrated by a remark by Dow, who worked extensively on the same problem as Phillips at the same time, but who adopted the much more restricted perspective of the post-Second World War period only: 'there is no reason to think that correlations based on a short period of history reflect unchanging fundamental laws: the sensitivity of wages to demand may well vary' (Dow 1964: 356). This *caveat* is indisputably true as a general proposition, especially as economic theory offers no rationale for an unchanging relationship between wage inflation and unemployment; but to ignore evidence of constancy over a long period of history is to ignore a phenomenon which demands further investigation and which has major implications for economic theory and policy.

QUALIFICATIONS

Phillips's earliest critics fastened on the dubious quality of the wage and unemployment data in the fitting period, the imprecision of any relationship between them, and the hazards of treating them as commensurate with those of the prediction period, as their grounds for dispute. Routh (1959) showed that a variety of plausible, or at least defensible, adjustments to the nineteenth century data produced a variety of curves relating wage inflation to unemployment. These results were described as 'significantly different', yet the most striking visual feature of the alternative curves charted by Routh (p.311) is the 'important similarities' which he acknowledged in passing rather than the 'important differences' which he discussed in minute detail.

It is certainly true that the scatter of observations on wage change and unemployment in Phillips's data was widely dispersed. His aggregation of the raw data into six composite points can easily mislead the careless reader, but a cursory glance at his scatter diagram is sufficient to confirm another early criticism: 'granted that unemployment may play *some* part in the causal chain, in this region there is still a very great deal left to explain' (Knowles and Winsten 1959: 118). Phillips himself was unable to provide any estimate of the goodness of fit of his curve to the data; contemporary computing limitations accounted for both this omission and his construction of the curve from the six composite data points. An application of modern methods of numerical analysis to Phillips's raw data by Gilbert (1976) confirmed the accuracy of Phillips's idiosyncratic method of estimating the parameters of his curve; but it also showed that the curve 'explained' only about 68 per cent of the variance of wage change in the period 1861–1913. By the normal standards of time-series analysis this is an unusually low coefficient of determination. It implies not only that there is ample scope for further study of the pre-1913 data, but also that a tight relationship between unemployment and wage change is hardly to be anticipated in other periods.

Having drawn attention to the variability of the data around the Phillips curve, Knowles and Winsten (1959) conclude their critique by questioning the value of the exercise on more general grounds:

> even if we felt confident of having achieved a 'complete' explanation of wage movements in the past, we should still really be no nearer to an iron law of wage determination. We should no doubt have come to understand several causal chains, and the strength and importance of their links. But any of these observed links may, over the course of time, weaken or break because of changes in behaviour or institutional structure . . . Indeed, one reason for analysing historical data is precisely to discover which links are important and which of these are the most susceptible of modification (p.320)

It would be difficult to find a clearer explanation of the significance of Phillips's work. The link he established between the two variables of central concern is certainly not rigid, but it does seem to have survived changes in institutional structure and therefore to suggest an impressive degree of stability in behaviour. It would be easier to predict the future, and perhaps to control the present, if the link were firmer; but the continued existence of any link is no less remarkable on account of its variability.

The degree to which the link has survived the passage of time is a separate question. Phillips's dramatic discovery that the observations for 1948–57 lay on the curve exaggerates the stability of the relationship by ignoring changes in the method of recording data. Routh (1959) pointed out that pre-1913 unemployment rates were calculated by expressing the number of unemployed members of those trade unions which operated unemployment funds as a proportion of their total membership. In contrast, the post-war unemployment rates express the number registered as unemployed as a proportion of the total labour force. Salary-earners are less prone to unemployment than wage-earners, and are less inclined to register if they do experience unemployment, but are included in the denominator of the unemployment rate. Hence the change in the method of measurement understates post-1948 unemployment in relation to pre-1913 levels, by perhaps one-eighth according to Routh. In consequence the apparent stability of the Phillips curve is undermined: 'The appropriate adjustment [to post-1948 unemployment rates] would have the effect of moving the points shown in Professor Phillips's figures ... to the right, ... dislodging [them] from the hyperbola' (Routh 1959:307). To terminate the argument at this point is, however, highly unsatisfactory, for the crucial question of how far the Phillips curve has shifted vertically remains unanswered. This vacuum was filled by Lipsey (1962), who applied Routh's suggested correction to the post-war unemployment rates and obtained a predicted mean wage increase of 3.2 per cent per annum in 1948–58, compared with an actual mean increase of 5.2 per cent. The prediction error could be interpreted as indicating the significance of changing institutions; but for reasons to be discussed in a later section, it sets an implausibly high upper bound on the importance of institutional change.

The final qualification is not specific to the work of Phillips but applies to the entire literature on wage inflation, whatever causal mechanism is postulated. As noted already, the labour market is a natural testing-ground for the hypothesis that inflation is caused by excess demand because in the presence of excess demand the unemployment rate is pushed down to unusually low levels; measurable proxies for excess demand are less easily found in other markets, especially over the long periods used in Phillips's analysis. Other proxies do exist or can be constructed for other markets and for shorter periods, however, so intrinsic significance should not be attached either to the unemployment rate or to the labour market.

The availability of additional data in the post-war period means that alternative proxies can be constructed for excess demand in the labour market itself. Whether it is useful to do so is essentially an empirical question which admits of no general answer. Changes in the composition of the US labour force induced Perry (1970) to construct an unemployment series which weighted individuals according to their sex and work-experience. In Canada recent analyses have recorded better results using an index of vacancies rather than unemployment as their proxy for excess demand (Christofides *et al.* 1980). Dow and Dicks-Mireaux (1958) used the difference between unfilled vacancies and unemployment in their study of post-war British wage determination, though the biases which they detected in each of the component series prevent the straightforward interpretation of this difference as a natural measure of excess demand in the sense of having a zero origin. Other alternatives offered in the literature include voluntary quits (Eagley 1965), and the sum of labour hoarding, itself proxied using deviations of average labour productivity from trend, and registered unemployment (Taylor 1972). The range of possibilities is extensive, and in the study of relatively short time-series the choice can make a considerable difference to the statistical outcome. There is no evidence, however, that one proxy performs consistently better than all the others, and the importance of the choice appears to diminish as the period of study is lengthened; some illustrations will be considered later. For the longest periods there is little or no choice.

The concentration on wages in inflation studies is explicable in terms of data availability, but it is often misinterpreted as signifying a pre-eminent role for the labour market in causing inflation. It is then a very short step to the apparent policy implication that a cure for inflation requires a change in the institutional arrangements for wage-fixing, in the form of an incomes policy, simultaneous negotiations on all wages and salaries to avoid 'leap-frogging', compulsory arbitration, or some other panacea favoured by contemporary pundits.

Phillips's analysis and its subsequent extensions constitute only one element in the explanation of inflation. A complete theory requires consideration of the sources of excess demand, and of its effects on other markets. The explanation of excess demand involves issues like the relative importance of monetary and fiscal policy, the relative importance of the public, private and overseas sectors as sources of disturbance, and the propagation of these shocks through multiplier and accelerator mechanisms. Phillips's analysis of the labour market can be combined with the simple assumption that prices of goods are set by adding a fixed mark-up to labour costs; or the mark-up may be treated as a variable which is itself determined by excess demand in the goods market, proxied by the relationship between sales and some measure of potential output. In a small open economy which maintains fixed exchange rates with the rest of the world, the price of tradeable goods is fixed by commodity arbitrage; the Phillips curve for the domestic labour market is then part of the mechanism which determines relative supplies of tradeable and non-tradeable goods, and hence the balance of payments (Duck and Zis 1979). Thus, even if the Phillips curve provided a complete model of wage change, it would be only a part of the theory of inflation. In fact, however, neither Phillips nor later students regarded excess demand as the sole determinant of wage changes.

LOOPS

Phillips thought it 'possible that a second factor influencing the rate of change of money wage rates might be the rate of change of the demand for labour, and so of unemployment' (Phillips 1958: 283). His method of fitting the curve to only six composite data points, each corresponding to an interval of unemployment, obscured this second relationship: 'Since each interval includes years in which unemployment was increasing and years in which it was decreasing the effect of changing unemployment on the rate of change of wage rates tends to be cancelled out by this averaging' (Phillips 1958: 290).

When annual data for each of the '6½ fairly regular trade cycles' of 1861–1913 were compared with the curve, however, the influence of the rate of change of unemployment was immediately apparent. There was 'a clear tendency for the rate of change of money wage rates at any given level of unemployment to be above the average for that level of unemployment when unemployment is decreasing during the upswing of a trade cycle and to be below the average for that level of unemployment when unemployment is increasing during the downswing of a trade cycle' (Phillips 1958: 290). In other words, the data formed a series of anti-clockwise loops around the curve, represented by the arrows in Fig. 5.1, when the observations for successive years were joined up.

Phillips's own 'explanation' was simply that 'in a year of rising business activity . . . employers will be bidding more vigorously for the services of labour than they would be in a year during which the average percentage unemployment was the same but the demand for labour was not increasing. Conversely in a year of falling business activity . . .' (Phillips 1958: 283).

Both Knowles and Winsten (1959) and Lipsey (1960) interpret this statement to mean that wage changes depend not only on the current level of excess demand for labour but also on its expected future level, which in turn is related to the current direction of change. As the latter points out, however, this argument cannot rationalise the loops: 'all that happens is that the point attained on the adjustment [Phillips] curve is different than would have been predicted solely on the basis of current demand for final goods' (Lipsey 1960: 21), because more vigorous bidding for labour in anticipation of future scarcity reduces the current unemployment rate as well as raising the current rate of wage increase.

The mystery of the loops deepens when the post-1948 observations are considered, for the direction is reversed. Phillips suggests that a clockwise loop could reflect a lag between unemployment and wage change, which in turn could have been 'caused by the extension of collective bargaining and particularly by the growth of arbitration and conciliation procedures' (Phillips 1958: 293). Sure enough, when unemployment is lagged by the apparently arbitrary figure of seven months, the clockwise loop disappears and almost all the observations for 1948–57 lie on the curve.[1]

The loops around the Phillips curve and its successors have been the subject of several subsequent investigations, and some of the suggested explanations will be reviewed in the following sections. Their status in contemporary literature is no clearer than their direction in Phillips's analysis. Gordon (1980) finds a role for the change in, as well as the level of, excess demand in explaining US (price) inflation; but the rate of change of excess demand has not featured prominently in recent British studies.

PRICE CHANGES

The third and final element in Phillips's explanation of wage changes was the rate of price change. Unlike the other determinants, however, this influence operated with a threshold effect, and was activated only when the rate of increase in money wages determined by competitive bidding for labour was less than the rate of increase in prices. In other words, price changes, which Phillips identified, without explanation, as a 'cost-push' element in the adjustment process, were believed to affect wage inflation only when the real wage would otherwise have fallen. Under more normal circumstances 'the introduction of cost of living adjustments in wage rates will have no effect, for employers will merely be giving under the name of cost of living adjustments part of the wage increases which they would in any case have given as a result of their competitive bidding for labour' (Phillips 1958: 284). Their restricted sphere of operation meant that price increases became an operative influence only after import prices registered an unusually large jump, for instance in 1862 after the outbreak of the American Civil War, and in 1951–52 as delayed consequences of a sterling devaluation and the Korean War. With so few cases for consideration it is scarcely surprising that no attempt was made to quantify the response to price changes above the threshold level.

His treatment of price changes and their consequences was the most unsatisfactory aspect of Phillips's analysis. It was certainly the aspect which attracted most attention in subsequent discussions, in some cases with repercussions of fundamental importance.

THE INTER-WAR YEARS

The comparison between 1861–1913 and 1948–57 has dominated that part of the literature concerned with historical perspective, but the special problems of the intervening period warrant brief consideration.

The war years themselves, periods of intense though hardly 'economic' activity and, in the second episode, of extensive controls, are of limited interest. Most observations lie very close to the Phillips curve. The exceptions are 1914, which appears as a temporary aberration, 1939, which belongs to the inter-war problem, and 1940–41, whose peculiarities Phillips attributes to the behaviour of import prices. The same factor is invoked to account for a wage increase of almost 30 per cent instead of the predicted 2 per cent in 1919, and *declines* of 22 and 19 per cent in 1921 and 1922 respectively, when the automatic cost of living adjustments introduced during the war were still in force.

After this turbulent interlude the labour market returned to a condition which produced fewer visually striking observations on Phillips's scatter diagram, but which was far from normal. Until after the outbreak of the Second World War unemployment fell below 10 per cent only in 1927, and then only fractionally. In the period to 1913 unemployment had exceeded 10 per cent only once. Thus the inter-war experience was sufficiently different from that in the period used for estimating the Phillips curve to provide a very stringent test of its predictive powers.

Initially it performed very satisfactorily. There was little sign of the anti-clockwise loops during the remainder of the 1920s, but the observations clustered closely around the curve. Phillips drew attention to the close correspondence between the average actual rate of wage change in 1925–29 of −0.60 per cent and the average predicted change of −0.56 per cent, and passed the following comment on the folly of returning to the gold standard in 1925 at the pre-war parity:

> Thus the evidence does not support the view . . . that the policy of forcing the price level down failed because of increased resistance to downward movements of wage rates. The actual results obtained, given the levels of unemployment which were held, could have been predicted fairly accurately

> from a study of the pre-war data, if anyone had felt inclined to carry out the necessary analysis (p.295).

The contrary view to which Phillips referred is typified by the belief then held by Robbins (1934), that downward wage rigidity had been exacerbated by the well-intentioned but fundamentally misconceived efforts of the state to alleviate the poverty hitherto associated with unemployment by instituting the dole.

The anticlockwise loops reappeared in the 1930s, but in other respects the rate of change of wages did not accord with Phillips's expectations. In particular, wages rose every year after 1934, even in 1938 when unemployment increased sharply, instead of continuing to fall. Phillips, conceding the existence of a problem, attributed the underpredictions to price increases, in turn caused by domestic agricultural policy rather than import prices, and to 'the extremely uneven geographical distribution of unemployment' (1958: 295). The latter explanation was not elaborated, but it has been developed at length by later students of wage inflation and will be discussed further below. In the meantime, some insight is provided in a contemporary proposal by Meade (1938) to minimise fluctuations by combining the payment of an additional 'credit' to recipients of state transfer payments when unemployment was 'abnormally' high with an additional wage tax when aggregate demand was abnormally high. The intriguing feature of these fiscal adjustment mechanisms, which in this early example of formula flexibility would have been triggered automatically by variations in unemployment, was the 'equilibrium' unemployment rate below which payment of the credit ceased and collection of the additional wage tax started. This was put by Meade at 11 per cent of the labour force, a figure which he regarded as a regrettable reflection of the increase in 'structural' unemployment, manifested in the wide dispersion of unemployment rates across industries and regions.

POLICY IMPLICATIONS

The emphasis of Phillips's paper was analytical rather than prescriptive, but it contained three allusions of potential relevance to policy. One was the passing reference to the distribution of unemployment that was cited in the last section. The second was the equally casual observation that the post-war Labour government's policy of wage restraint offset the substantial 'cost-push' exerted by price increases in 1948, and held the increase in wages conspicuously below the rate predicted by the Phillips curve in 1949. The last and most explicit point was a direct inference from the Phillips curve itself. Assuming an annual productivity growth rate of 2 per cent and no disturbances from import prices, Phillips tentatively concluded that 'if aggregate demand were kept at a value which would maintain a stable level of product prices the associated level of unemployment would be a little under 2½ per cent'. He also appended the warning that '[b]ecause of the strong curvature of the fitted relation in the region of low percentage unemployment, there will be a lower average rate of increase of wage rates if unemployment is held constant at a given level than there will be if unemployment is allowed to fluctuate about that level' (Phillips 1958: 299).

A substantial proportion of the subsequent literature has been concerned with the explicit development of policy towards inflation and unemployment given the constraint of the Phillips curve, and with the possibility of moving it. It would be premature to consider potential policy implications, however, before the positive analyses inspired by Phillips's contribution have been surveyed.

3. The Phillips curve as the basis of a research programme

Phillips's pioneering contribution attracted the attention not only of critics but also of developers, who were quick to see the possibilities of transplanting his analysis to other economies and other periods, and of introducing refinements and extensions. The most influential early developers were Samuelson and Solow (1960), who applied the Phillips curve to the USA and found much less evidence of stability, and Lipsey (1960). The latter was particularly unusual in his concern to provide a less casual theoretical foundation for the Phillips curve. Most of the literature in the decade following publication of Phillips's paper, and much thereafter, concentrated on empirical variations. The major issues are surveyed in this section in ascending order of prominence.

EMPIRICAL REFINEMENTS

The most mundane variation consisted of experiments with alternative measures of the relevant variables. The range of proxies for excess demand was illustrated in the previous section. The measurement of wages also permits an element of choice. The basic alternatives are wage rates, which are typically minima negotiated at national level, and earnings, which include local and plant-level supplements. Both can be expressed in either weekly or hourly terms, and earnings may include or exclude overtime payments at premium rates. Labour costs can be broadened to include salaries as well as wages. Each of these available measures has attracted its adherents, some of whom have defended their chosen alternative with considerable vigour; but except over very short periods nothing of importance hinges on the choice of wage series.

Another minor controversy has raged over the computation of rates of change from a given wage series. Phillips used the first central difference, i.e. half the difference between the 'next' and 'last' value of the wage index, to approximate the 'current' absolute rate of wage change, on the grounds that the inflation rate is in principle a continuous variable on which only discrete observations are available. Few later students of annual data have bothered with this refinement, which had the unfortunate effect of introducing autocorrelation into the residuals (Gilbert 1976); but the availability of more frequent observations for the period since the Second World War has raised a parallel issue. At first sight the most natural method of inferring the inflation rate from (say) a quarterly wage series is to compute the difference between the corresponding quarters of successive years:

annual rates of change accord with conventional habits of thought, and some of the erratic changes between successive quarters are smoothed out. The use of overlapping 4-quarter changes, however, violates the standard assumptions on which ordinary least-squares estimation is based, and hence produces exaggerated estimates of statistical significance. Intuitively, each observation on the inflation rate overlaps (by 75 per cent) both the preceding and following observation, so that serial dependence is introduced into the error structure. Either a different estimation procedure should be adopted or a non-overlapping definition of the inflation rate should be adopted (Wallis 1971; Rowley and Wilton 1973). The latter has been the more popular response.

The final refinement to be mentioned here, though it might more accurately be described as an approximation, is the adoption of a linear 'curve' as the typical functional form in studies of the recent past. The variation in the post-war unemployment data, at least up to the late 1970s, has been too limited to permit discrimination between specific curves and the more robust linear relation between wage inflation and unemployment, and most investigators have adopted the latter.

The evidence for a non-linear relation even in longer periods which exhibit more variability has also been questioned. For example, Griffin (1962) suggested that the hyperbola fitted by Lipsey (1960) for the period 1923–57 was a statistical artefact, produced by estimating a single relationship from two disparate clusters of data as illustrated in Fig. 5.2. The 'unemployment gap' which then separated

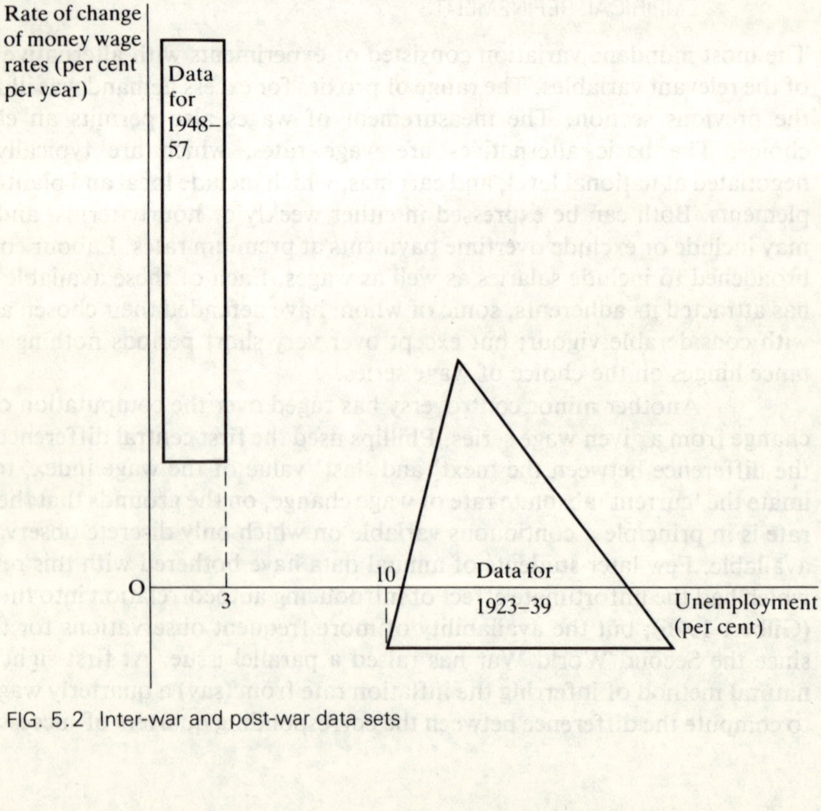

FIG. 5.2 Inter-war and post-war data sets

the inter-war and post-war clusters has, regrettably, been filled in the more recent past; though as subsequent sections will show, the interpretation of the additional information is by no means straightforward.

THEORETICAL DEVELOPMENTS AND THEIR CONSEQUENCES

Most writers on the Phillips curve, both critics and supporters, followed the pattern he had initiated of treating it as an empirical issue. The most conspicuous exception was Lipsey (1960), who provided the theoretical basis for the literature of the ensuing decade. Three features of his analysis are particularly noteworthy.

First, his consideration of the relationship between the rate of change of wages (or any other price) and excess demand indicated two separate channels through which institutional changes, typified by the growth of trade unions in both size and power, could operate. One was by restricting the supply of labour to the market in question; but since the determinant of wage change is proportionate *excess* demand ($\equiv (D - S)/S$, in obvious notation) that influence is already incorporated in Phillips's hypothesis. In other words, the source of excess demand, whether demand shifts, supply shifts or both, is immaterial. Alternatively, 'unions might influence the speed of the dynamic adjustment ... They might, for example, cause a faster increase of wages in response to excess demand and a slower fall in response to excess supply than would otherwise occur' (Lipsey 1960: 17).

He did not develop this line of argument any further, perhaps because his own empirical work 'indicates that the post-1922 experience was of less flexibility of wages in response to excess demand, whether positive or negative, than occurred in the pre-1914 period' (Lipsey 1960: 27). It is clear, however, that any institutional influence on the speed of adjustment to excess demand cannot be captured simply by adding variables to the right-hand side of the Phillips curve. The basic hypothesis linking wage inflation (w) to excess demand (X),

$$w = \theta X,$$

cannot be changed to

$$w = \theta X + \alpha Z,$$

where Z is some measure of institutional forces, because wage inflation could then be positive even with zero or negative excess demand, contrary to the theory supposedly under test. Making the speed of adjustment responsive to institutional factors would imply

$$w = \theta(Z)X.$$

In other words, the additional variable would interact with, and its influence would be conditional on, excess demand. To test the hypothesis suggested by Lipsey would require

$$\frac{\partial \theta}{\partial Z} \gtrless 0 \textit{ as } X \gtrless 0$$

The interested reader is invited to think how that requirement could be fulfilled. The essential point for present purposes is that it could not be done in the standard linear regression procedure. The force of this point will become clear in the next sub-section, when the literature on empirical extensions of the Phillips curve is reviewed.

Lipsey's second major contribution was to provide a rationalisation for the anticlockwise loops around the Phillips curve; though this was relegated to a footnote, no use was made of it in his subsequent analysis, and its implications were presumably not appreciated. The loops were explained in Lipsey's 'footnote' model as an integral component of the relationship between unemployment and excess demand, not as an independent phenomenon requiring separate treatment. The model involves three identities, two behavioural assumptions and some elementary manipulation. Definitionally,

$$\Delta U \equiv Q - H$$

where ΔU is the change in the number unemployed, Q is quits and H is the number of new engagements. Assume quits are a constant proportion of employment, E,

$$Q = \beta E$$

and, simplifying Lipsey's treatment slightly, that new engagements depend on the number of unfilled job vacancies, V,

$$H = \gamma V$$

Then, noting that

$$E \equiv L - U$$

where L is the labour force, rearrangement yields

$$V = \frac{\beta}{\gamma}(L - U) - \frac{1}{\gamma}\Delta U$$

Substituting this expression in the definition of proportionate excess demand,

$$X \equiv \frac{V - U}{L} = \frac{\beta}{\gamma} - \frac{(\beta + \gamma)}{\gamma}\frac{U}{L} - \frac{1}{\gamma}\frac{\Delta U}{L}.$$

Thus in this model the appropriate proxy for excess demand includes not only the unemployment rate (U/L) but also its first difference. If the 'average' relationship between excess demand and the unemployment rate were plotted, the influence of $\Delta U/L$ would be eliminated; but if an individual business cycle were considered, excess demand would exceed the plotted value in the upswing, when unemployment was falling, and conversely in the downswing. The relationship between excess demand and unemployment therefore conforms exactly to the relationship between wage inflation and unemployment in 1861–1913.

The last and most influential component of Lipsey's theoretical analysis concerned the derivation of an aggregate Phillips curve from the relationship be-

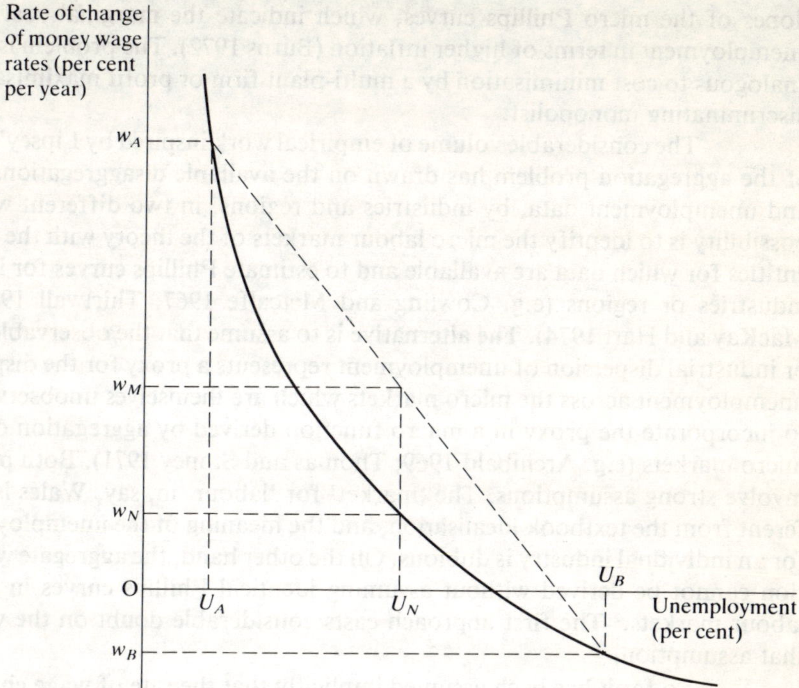

FIG. 5.3 Effects of unemployment dispersion
Note: If national unemployment, at rate U_N, were evenly distributed across individual labour markets, wages would rise at rate w_N; but with the distribution between markets A and B shown in Fig. 5.3, wages rise at an average rate of w_M.

tween wage change and unemployment at the level of the individual labour market. If the micro relation is non-linear but identical in all markets, as assumed by Lipsey, the average rate of change of wages in the economy will depend on the distribution of unemployment across individual labour markets as well as its average level. The significance of unemployment dispersion is illustrated in Fig. 5.3 for the special case where there are two individual markets of equal size. The argument is identical to Phillips's case for minimising the dispersion of unemployment over time. Lipsey, overlooking his own 'footnote' model, suggested that changes in the dispersion of unemployment over the business cycle generated the loops around the Phillips curve, and hence hypothesised that the rate of change of national unemployment was systematically associated with the distribution of unemployment, a hypothesis later rejected by Archibald (1969).

Lipsey's assumption of equal-sized micro labour markets is a matter of convenience only, but the assumption of identical micro Phillips curves is of substantive importance. If it does not hold, it is no longer necessarily true that a reduction in the dispersion of unemployment will shift the macro Phillips curve towards the origin. To minimise the national wage inflation rate for a given national unemployment rate and given relative sizes of the individual labour markets, unemployment should in general be distributed so as to equalise the slopes of the micro Phillips curves, which indicate the marginal cost of lower unemployment in terms of higher inflation (Burns 1972). The problem is formally analogous to cost minimisation by a multi-plant firm or profit maximisation by a discriminating monopolist.

The considerable volume of empirical work inspired by Lipsey's analysis of the aggregation problem has drawn on the available disaggregations of wage and unemployment data, by industries and regions, in two different ways. One possibility is to identify the micro labour markets of the theory with the statistical entities for which data are available and to estimate Phillips curves for individual industries or regions (e.g. Cowling and Metcalfe 1967; Thirlwall 1969, 1970; MacKay and Hart 1974). The alternative is to assume that the observable regional or industrial dispersion of unemployment represents a proxy for the dispersion of unemployment across the micro markets which are themselves unobservable, and to incorporate the proxy in a macro function derived by aggregation over those micro markets (e.g. Archibald 1969; Thomas and Stoney 1971). Both procedures involve strong assumptions. The 'market' for 'labour' in, say, Wales is very different from the textbook idealisation, and the meaning of the unemployment rate for an individual industry is dubious. On the other hand, the aggregate wage equation cannot be derived without assuming identical Phillips curves in the micro labour markets.[2] The first approach casts considerable doubt on the validity of that assumption.

So far it has been assumed implicitly that the rate of wage change in an individual labour market is determined exclusively by excess demand in that market; interaction between markets would then be determined by the geographical and industrial mobility of firms and workers. It need not, however, be assumed that 'spill-overs' are effected solely through market mechanisms. Both empirical procedures have been extended to incorporate wage leadership, which postulates a direct influence of wage inflation in the leading sector(s) on wage movements elsewhere. The practical difficulty, of course, is to identify 'leadership' without resort to circular reasoning. The leader is most frequently defined as the sector with the lowest unemployment rate, but discrimination among alternative criteria has proved difficult.

Early estimates of the effects of unemployment dispersion on the rate of change of wages suggested that policies which succeeded in reducing unemployment disparities would have a substantial impact on inflation (e.g. Archibald 1969). Quite apart from the problems of formulating 'successful' policies and of whether minimising dispersion will also minimise differences among the slopes of the micro Phillips curves, later estimates have produced much smaller estimates of the potential gains, in terms of lower inflation, from effective policies towards the distribution of unemployment, either across regions (Archibald *et al.* 1974) or industries (Thomas 1974).

EMPIRICAL EXTENSIONS

The empirical studies of dispersion were unusual in being grounded fairly closely in an explicit theoretical framework. The philosophy on which much of the literature of the 1960s appears to have been based could be caricatured as the belief that if Phillips could achieve so much success in predicting wage changes with just one explanatory variable, the addition of more explanatory variables would produce even more successful results. Considerable ingenuity was displayed in thinking up new variables for experimental inclusion in estimating equations, rather less in justifying their introduction.

The most persistent of these 'intruders' was the rate of change of prices. This variable, it will be recalled, was invoked by Phillips as a 'cost-push' factor which operated only when real wages would otherwise have fallen. This threshold effect was immediately rejected by Lipsey (1960), who found a small but significant role for price changes in the pre-1913 era, and a substantially larger role thereafter. In both periods price changes influenced wage inflation continuously, like any other variable on the right-hand side of a regression equation. Lipsey's treatment of price inflation was generally adopted in subsequent studies of wage behaviour, though there were periods even after the Second World War when its influence was difficult or impossible to detect (Sumner 1972).

One issue raised by the addition of price changes to the wage equation was the technical problem of estimating simultaneous systems. On any theory of price determination a change in wages would lead to a change in prices. Recognition of this interaction, it might be imagined, would force students of wage inflation to abandon the use of ordinary least squares (OLS), which would produce biased and inconsistent parameter estimates, in favour of an appropriate estimation technique. In fact, however, OLS continued to be widely used, although there were notable exceptions among the earliest studies (e.g. Klein and Ball 1959). One dubious method of circumventing the simultaneity problem was to postulate an arbitrary lag in the effect of price changes on wage inflation, as a means of ruling out contemporaneous feedback by definition. This 'solution' neglected the high serial correlation of post-war price changes, and made specification a matter to be determined in the interests of the econometrician's convenience. A more respectable reason for ignoring the simultaneity problem was that OLS and simultaneous-equation estimators, typically two-stage least squares, produced very similar results in the comparisons conducted by Dicks-Mireaux (1961), the National Board for Prices and Incomes (1968) and Smith (1968). The simultaneity issue was revived in the 1970s, when Godfrey (1971) and Wallis (1971) showed that a controversial assessment of incomes policy by Lipsey and Parkin (1970), and indeed their estimated model of wage and price determination, were very sensitive to the choice of estimation method; but by that stage other problems associated with the role of price changes had become the primary focus of attention.

Price change was the only additional variable to be universally adopted, but many others were offered as determinants of wage change. Many of these were inspired by an attempt to incorporate institutional elements into the analysis, in order to close the gap between descriptions of the labour market and the quasi-competitive model used by Phillips to account for wage inflation. The most persistent search was directed towards a proxy for trade union militancy. The most popular candidate was the change in trade union membership as a proportion of the labour force, a variable introduced by Hines (1964) and further discussed in his subsequent papers (1968, 1969, 1971).[3] In the controversy which ensued both the conceptual basis of this proxy and its statistical contribution to the explanation of wage changes have been attacked (Purdy and Zis 1973, 1974), and defended (Dogas and Hines 1975); the critics had the last word (Purdy and Zis 1976). Some use has also been made of strike activity (e.g. Godfrey 1971) as a proxy for trade union militancy, though it could with equal plausibility be interpreted as an index of employer intransigence. It can be measured in three different ways which are not themselves related in any stable fashion, and the statistical results are in any case weak (Ward and Zis 1974). These and other attempts to isolate the role of trade unions in wage determination are examined more fully in a companion survey by Carline (1984).

Not all the institutional factors which have been alleged to influence wages are presumed to raise their rate of increase. Phillips's reference to wage restraint in 1948–49 has already been noted. The same phenomenon was reported by Klein and Ball (1959), who used a dummy variable, taking a value of unity under Labour and zero under Conservative governments, to capture this 'political factor' in wage determination, and by Dow and Dicks-Mireaux (1958), who constructed a subjective index of trade union 'pushfulness'. Many subsequent investigators have made allowance, usually by including dummy variables, for the attempts made by successive governments during the 1960s and 1970s to restrain wage inflation through persuasion, agreement or statutory decree. Estimates of the success achieved by incomes policies will be examined later.

Finally, a miscellaneous set of additional explanatory variables has been proposed by particular authors. One of the earliest additions was profit, variously measured, which was held to encourage worker demands and to make employers less inclined to resist. Indeed, Kaldor (1959) asserted that Phillips had obtained satisfactory results only because unemployment was proxying the more fundamental influence of profits, a claim which was refuted by Lipsey and Steuer (1961). Profit has continued to feature as an additional variable in some North American wage equations (e.g. Hamermesh 1970; Taylor *et al.* 1972), but it has been generally ignored in later British studies. Other examples from this miscellaneous list include the lagged real wage, proposed by Sargan (1964, 1971) and adopted in several later British investigations (e.g. Dornbusch and Fischer 1980), and productivity change, particularly for the USA (Kuh 1967) and Canada (Vanderkamp 1972).

The additional variables were earlier described as 'intruders', a term coined by Archibald, because the rationale for their inclusion was seldom made explicit. As Lipsey had demonstrated, extra variables cannot simply be appended to the right-hand side of a Phillips curve without violating the theory under test, but his warning went largely unheeded. Archibald *et al.* (1974) reiterate the problem of interpretation posed by the intruders, using as an illustration the addition of productivity by Kuh (1967), which he had attempted to justify by arguing that

> . . . since equilibrium real wages depend on productivity, there is something wrong in the omission of productivity from Phillips' analysis of the rate of change of money wages. This is mistaken. The categories, supply and

> demand, are supposed to provide an exhaustive taxonomy of the factors determining the price of any economic good. Productivity change alters one of them, perhaps both. It therefore alters excess demand, the independent variable of Phillips' disequilibrium model. It is the appearance of productivity (or its rate of change, or departure from trend, etc.) as an additional variable in the fitted linear equation that is inconsistent with theory, unless its role is to improve the proxy measure of excess demand
>
> (Archibald et al. 1974: 117)

Few innovators justified their extensions in these terms. Vanderkamp (1972) was among the exceptions, arguing, like Taylor (1972), that variations in excess demand are initially reflected not inversely in unemployment but directly in productivity, as firms postpone hiring or firing decisions until the permanence of the change in business conditions can be assessed. Innovations of this kind are refinements rather than extensions, in the sense used here.

The more usual justification was the statistical significance of the additional variable. Sargan (1971) was more explicit than most econometricians in arguing that '. . . if the lagged real wage is introduced as a variable into a standard Phillips wage equation it is statistically significant. This is enough to reject models which exclude this variable' (p.52), but this argument was often implicit in other studies which incorporated intruders. One difficulty with it is that the statistical significance of a particular explanatory variable is often found to vary according to the other variables included with it and the time period studied. In this case the significance and even the sign of the lagged real wage in an explanation of wage change are very sensitive to the period chosen (Artis 1981). The problem is not unusual. For example, a cursory inspection of Phillips's scatter diagrams for individual trade cycles suggests that the parameters of a wage-change equation fitted to sub-periods of 1861–1913 would have varied considerably in magnitude and significance. The measured influence of another intruder, strike activity, has been found to be extremely unreliable. Individual cases of statistical significance, or its absence, provide little guidance.

The more serious difficulty is that measurement without theory does not advance understanding. However robust its statistical performance, an intruder which cannot be rationalised merely shifts the problem from the explanation of wage change to the explanation of the intruder. There are two possible rationalisations within the framework considered so far, and a more drastic alternative.

The first possibility is the one mentioned by Archibald *et al.* (1974), that an apparent intruder may serve the purpose of supplementing or even supplanting unemployment as a proxy for excess demand. We have seen already that the rate of change of unemployment and productivity measures can be interpreted in that way. Sargan (1971: 52) speculates that the significance of the lagged real wage might indicate '. . . that the usual measure of unemployment is not a valid measure of the excess supply of labour, and that an equation [containing the lagged real wage] . . . can be derived by considering the interaction of the demand and supply of labour, assuming that both are responsive to the real wage rate'. The dummy variables often used when incomes policies are in operation could similarly be regarded as registering potential breaks in the influence of excess demand.

The second, more remote, possibility is the one mentioned by Lipsey (1960), that the intruders could be capturing variations in the rate of response of wage change to excess demand. Thomas (1974) is one of the few investigators to model this process explicitly, by allowing an industry's wage inflation at a given unemployment rate to depend on its level of unionisation. The Phillips curve pivots, so that at high unemployment rates wages increase more rapidly, or fall more slowly, the greater is the level of unionisation; but at low unemployment rates wage increases are lower in more highly unionised industries, because the bargaining procedure slows down the speed of adjustment.[4] Thomas allows the unemployment rate at which the Phillips curve pivots to be determined by the data, but does not discuss the plausibility of this implicit estimate of the unemployment rate corresponding to zero excess demand. While few students of wage inflation have paid adequate attention to modelling potential influences on the adjustment process, it is possible that the reported significance of some intruders represents an approximation to this kind of mechanism. For example, ignoring the doubts recorded earlier about its adequacy as a proxy for militancy, the rate of change of trade union membership may pick up a significantly positive coefficient even when it is merely added to the Phillips curve, instead of being entered as a variable which modifies the response to excess or deficient demand. Such an approximation would work best, if this interpretation is correct, in periods when excess demand exhibits little variation; but the results should still be improved by selecting a more appropriate functional form. Archibald *et al.* (1974) appear to be unique in reporting some tests which bear on this issue; but so many variations are considered that it is difficult to draw firm inferences from their results.

The more drastic alternative is to regard significant intruders as a reason for rejecting the Phillips model and for constructing a different theoretical framework to account for wage inflation. As long as unemployment continued to play its traditional role in estimated equations, however, there appeared to be little enthusiasm for such a radical departure. Indeed, the theory underlying the Phillips curve became a serious issue only towards the end of the 1960s. When it was questioned, the critics focused not on the superiority of some alternative framework, but on the inconsistency of the Phillips curve with the theory on which it was supposedly based. Evidence on the role of intruders played no part in stimulating the criticism. On the contrary, this evidence was initially interpreted as shielding the developers of the Phillips curve from the theoretical onslaught.

Predictive performance

Before considering the fundamental flaw in the Phillips curve, it is worth digressing briefly to see whether the remarkable predictive achievement recorded by Phillips in 1948–57 was maintained thereafter, and to apply the same test of forecasting beyond the fitting period to some of the equations developed by later investigators.

As the first column of Table 5.1 demonstrates, the Phillips curve continued to predict well up to 1966. The forecasts do not incorporate the adjust-

TABLE 5.1 Forecast errors of wage inflation models (per cent)

	Model			
Year	Phillips (1958)	Lipsey (1960)	Dicks–Mireaux (1961)	Hines (1964)
1958	−1.1	−0.3	—	—
1959	1.2	−2.4	—	—
1960	0.0	−2.4	−1.5	—
1961	1.2	0.3	−1.2	—
1962	−1.6	0.2	0.3	−0.7
1963	−2.5	−2.2	−0.3	−1.9
1964	0.3	−2.3	−2.2	0.6
1965	0.6	−1.0	−1.5	−0.7
1966	1.3	0.3	−1.2	1.1
MAE	1.1	1.4	1.1	1.0

Notes:
1. Forecast error is predicted minus observed rate of change of wages.
2. MAE is mean absolute error.
3. Sources: the forecast errors for the Phillips curve were taken from Kennedy (1972, Table 1.11); the remainder are from Pencavel (1971, Table I), who used Lipsey's equation for 1923–39 and 1948–57, the reduced form of Dicks–Mireaux' two-stage least squares estimates for 1946–59, and Hines's OLS equation for 1949–61.

ment to the post-war unemployment rate suggested by Routh (1959), but that does not affect their comparability with Phillips's own estimates of forecast error. Comparison of the entries in the first column with the remainder of the table indicates that the Phillips curve certainly performed no worse than equations estimated solely or mainly on data for the period since the Second World War. Moreover, the other three equations all include one or more intruders, which on this showing appear to make no contribution to predictive accuracy.

The summary measure of forecast error in the last row of the table is calculated without regard to sign, and therefore conceals an important difference among the competing models. All the later equations display a marked tendency to underpredict the rate of wage increase, whereas the Phillips curve overpredicts more often than not and has the lowest mean algebraic error (taking account of sign) of the four models. The suspicion of systematic error in such a short test of forecasting ability raises serious doubts about the potential of the three later models to predict reliably more than half a century beyond the end of their sample period.

4. The Phillips curve as a mis-specification

Paradoxically, the intruder which proved most difficult to rationalise was the most persistent appendage to the Phillips curve. Phillips's own characterisation of the rate of change of prices as a manifestation of 'cost push' was generally adopted.

This variable was not mentioned at all in the section of Lipsey's paper (1960) devoted to theory, yet in the comparison of results for the nineteenth and twentieth centuries which followed, its regression coefficient was found to have

> increased greatly. . . . This is an extremely interesting change. The face-value interpretation is that the demand and supply model . . . accounts for less of the variations in wage rates in the twentieth century than it did in the nineteenth, while more of the twentieth-century variations can be explained in terms of wages 'chasing' prices or of prices chasing wages
> (Lipsey 1960: 26).

The mere existence of an intruder for which the model provided no explanation, and still more its increasing contribution to the wage equation, must have been embarrassing as well as interesting. To argue, as Lipsey (1962) did, that the post-1948 shift in the Phillips curve (after the Routh correction to unemployment) might be attributable to the increasing importance of cost-of-living adjustments, rather than unspecified institutional changes, is to substitute a named but inexplicable 'cause' for an anonymous one.

The paradoxical element in this story is that the rate of change of prices should never have been classified as an intruder at all. The Phillips curve was inconsistent with the theory on which it was supposedly based. The real problem was neither that the rate of change of prices influenced wage inflation, nor that its role was increasing in importance, but rather that its contribution remained for so long as small as the empirical results suggested.

NOMINAL AND REAL WAGES

Phillips appealed implicitly and Lipsey (1960) explicity to the standard model of a competitive labour market to justify the hypothesised relationship between excess demand for labour and wage change. Yet, as shown in Fig. 5.4, the supply of and demand for labour are represented in that model as functions of the real wage, W/P. When a shift of (say) the labour demand curve generates excess demand at the initial real wage $(W/P)_0$, the new equilibrium $(W/P)_1$ which results can be expressed in terms of the nominal wage only if the price level is known. If the process of wage adjustment is related to unemployment as a proxy for excess demand, then the dependent variable must be defined as the rate of change of *real* wages: using lower-case letters to represent proportional rates of change,

$$w - p = f(U)$$[5]

Alternatively, if the rate of change of nominal wages is the topic of interest, then the hypothesis suggested by the competitive labour market model is

$$w = f(U) + p \qquad [1]$$

The rate of change of money wage rates thus consists of two components: the first reflects disequilibrium between the demand for and supply of labour, the second represents the interdependence between the labour and goods markets. The most important implication of this analysis is that inflation is not solely a disequilibrium

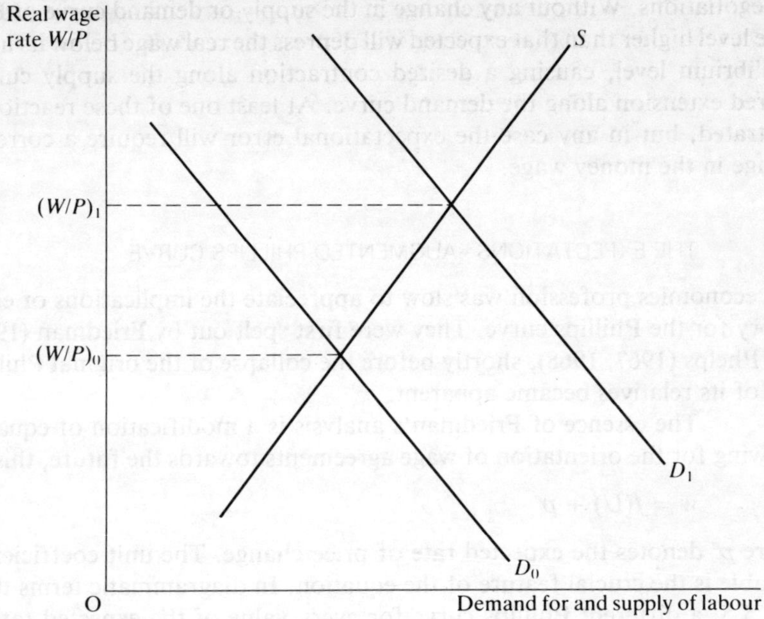

FIG. 5.4 The competitive labour market

phenomenon, for nominal wages and prices can change in tandem without any excess demand for labour.

There is an apparent inconsistency between the elementary theory of the competitive labour market, in which the real wage is determined, and casual observation of wage agreements, which are universally denominated in nominal terms. The inconsistency is, however, superficial. To reconcile the fact that wage bargaining fixes a money wage with the theory of real wage determination, it is necessary only to assume that negotiators take account of the price level when deciding on the number of pounds to be inserted in the pay packet. The interesting question is then: which price level?

The duration of a wage agreement may be fixed, as in North America where the typical contract runs for three years, or it may be unspecified, as in Britain where new negotiations can normally be initiated at any time; but in either case wage bargaining is an essentially forward-looking activity. Negotiations absorb time and resources which could otherwise be devoted to more productive tasks. These transactions costs provide an incentive for the participants to set wages at levels which will not produce a predictable disequilibrium, requiring yet more negotiations, and to incorporate automatic adjustments in explicitly long-term contracts. The objective of avoiding unnecessary transactions costs can only be achieved if wages are set in accordance with the price levels which are expected to prevail in the future, while the agreement is in operation.

Once the nominal wage has been settled, any unanticipated price change will create excess demand or supply, and corresponding pressures for a new round of negotiations. Without any change in the supply or demand curve of Fig. 5.4, a price level higher than that expected will depress the real wage below its unchanged equilibrium level, causing a desired contraction along the supply curve and a desired extension along the demand curve. At least one of these reactions will be frustrated, but in any case the expectational error will require a corresponding change in the money wage.

THE EXPECTATIONS–AUGMENTED PHILLIPS CURVE

The economics profession was slow to appreciate the implications of elementary theory for the Phillips curve. They were first spelt out by Friedman (1966, 1968) and Phelps (1967, 1968), shortly before the collapse of the original Phillips curve and of its relatives became apparent.

The essence of Friedman's analysis is a modification of equation [1]; allowing for the orientation of wage agreements towards the future, this becomes

$$w = f(U) + p^e \qquad [2]$$

where p^e denotes the expected rate of price change. The unit coefficient on this variable is the crucial feature of the equation. In diagrammatic terms there is, in Fig. 5.5, a different Phillips curve for every value of the expected rate of price change. Assume for simplicity that firms set their prices as a mark-up on unit labour costs, and suppose there exists an initial equilibrium at point A: the actual and expected rates of price change are zero, unit labour costs are constant, and nominal and real wages are increasing at the rate of productivity growth (q). There is then a demand expansion which reduces unemployment and increases the rate of wage inflation, so that the economy moves from point A to point B along the curve labelled $p^e = 0$. Wages are now rising at x per cent per period, unit labour costs are no longer constant, and so prices will start to rise. With prices rising (at rate $x - q$ per cent per period) the expectation of price stability embodied in the short-run Phillips curve must sooner or later be revised. When expectations have adjusted fully to this experience of inflation, the relevant Phillips curve will be that labelled $p^e = x - q$, which is derived by displacing the original curve vertically upwards by the change in the expected inflation rate. At any unemployment rate below U_0, however, wages will now rise at a rate in excess of x per cent, and the process of adjustment to changed experience will be repeated. The Phillips curve will continue to shift vertically upwards as long as unemployment remains below U_0, and the actual inflation rate will continue to increase, dragging the anticipated rate upwards with it. The process will be terminated only when unemployment has returned to U_0, at which the acceleration of inflation ceases because the actual and anticipated rates of price change are again equal (e.g. at point C). U_0 is therefore the equilibrium or 'natural' unemployment rate, because only at that rate are expectations consistent with experience. Once reattained it will be maintained, in the absence of further disturbances, with inflation continuing at whatever level was reached while unemployment was below the natural rate. To bring the inflation rate down, unemployment must be held above U_0, so that the process sketched above operates in reverse.

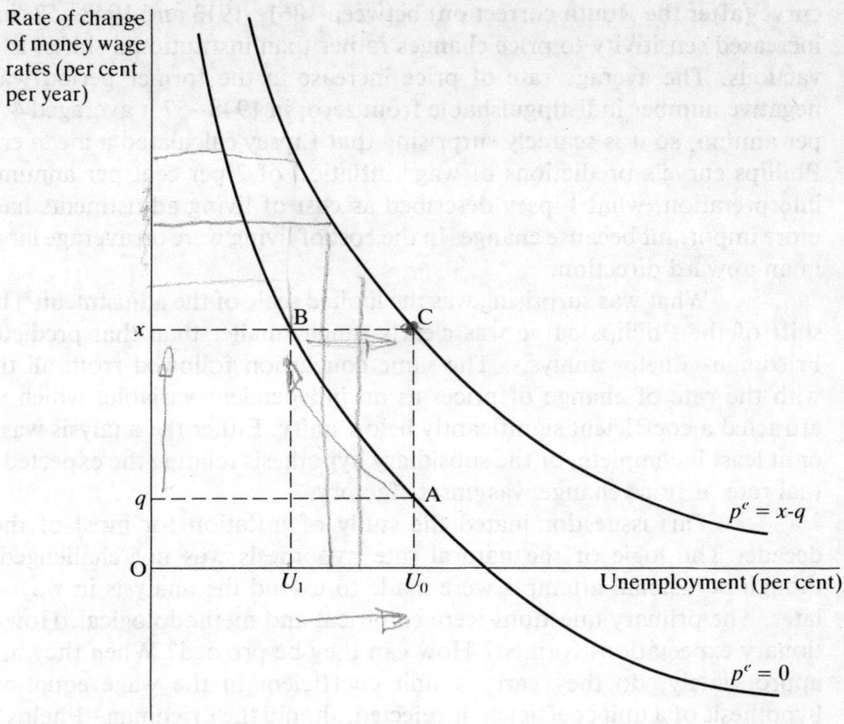

FIG. 5.5 Expectations-augmented Phillips curves

Phelps's version of the expectations-augmented Phillips curve differs from Friedman's in several respects. The most obvious is that the expectational addition is the anticipated rate of change of wages rather than prices, a difference which stems from Phelps's treatment of the representative firm as a dynamic monopsonist, which can increase its labour force only by raising its relative wage sufficiently to offset the imperfect information that characterises the labour market. For present purposes this difference is inessential, for the empirical implications of the two versions are very close, as will be shown below. There is a further contrast between the rigour of Phelps's analysis and the less formal presentation by Friedman; perhaps for that reason the latter's influence has been more evident.

IMPLICATIONS OF THE NATURAL RATE HYPOTHESIS

These reconsiderations of the Phillips curve provided a new perspective on previous studies of wage inflation and a new focus for further exploration. If the actual rate of price change is interpreted as a proxy for its expected value, its robust empirical performance in the studies reported in the 1960s ceases to be an embarrassing case of measurement without theory, and it should not be regarded as an 'intruder'. Lipsey's explanation (1962) for the outward shift of the Phillips curve (after the Routh correction) between 1861–1913 and 1948–57, in terms of increased sensitivity to price changes rather than institutional shifts, is no longer vacuous. The average rate of price increase in the former period was a small negative number indistinguishable from zero; in 1948–57 it averaged 4.7 per cent per annum, so it is scarcely surprising that Lipsey calculated a mean error in the Phillips curve's predictions of wage inflation of 2 per cent per annum. On this interpretation, what Lipsey described as cost of living adjustments had become more important because changes in the cost of living were on average larger and all in an upward direction.

What was surprising was the limited scale of the adjustment. The upward shift of the Phillips curve was clearly much smaller than that predicted by the Friedman–Phelps analysis. The same conclusion followed from all the studies with the rate of change of prices as an independent variable, which invariably attracted a coefficient significantly below unity. Either the analysis was incorrect or at least incomplete, or the subsidiary hypothesis relating the expected to the actual rate of price change was unsatisfactory.

This issue dominated the study of inflation for most of the ensuing decade. The logic of the natural rate hypothesis was not challenged directly, though occasional attempts were made to extend the analysis in ways discussed later. The primary questions were empirical and methodological. How are inflationary expectations formed? How can they be proxied? When they are proxied appropriately, do they carry a unit coefficient in the wage equation? If the hypothesis of a unit coefficient is rejected, should the Friedman–Phelps 'accelerationist' hypothesis or the expectations proxy be rejected?

From this perspective the differences between the formulations of Phelps and Friedman were unimportant, for any reasonable representation of the anticipated rate of wage change would be closely related to the anticipated rate of price change. Another distinctly secondary question was the price index about whose movements expectations were formed. The real value to workers of a given money wage depends on the price index corresponding to their consumption bundle; the real cost to the firm depends on the price received for its output (or strictly, its value-added). At the aggregate level, the relevant deflators correspond to the retail and wholesale (output) price indices respectively. These are separated by the 'wedge' of indirect taxes; and they may change at different rates for other reasons associated with the mechanics of price determination, especially over periods as short as a calendar quarter, which has become the most common unit of time in the study of inflation. These refined distinctions were, however, initially ignored in the search for an answer to the central question: Is there a trade-off between inflation and unemployment in the long run, when expectations accord with actual outcomes?

It would be difficult to exaggerate the importance of that question. Doubts had been expressed by a few earlier writers about the desirability and the feasibility of allowing the post-war creeping inflation to continue. As early as 1955 Robertson, for example, urged the need 'to adopt a reasonable interpretation of the concept of "full employment"' (Robertson 1966: 256), warning that otherwise inflation would accelerate:

> The rush for the band-wagon would set the wagon itself smartly rolling forward . . . . But what that means is that the planned orderly fall in the value of money would be in danger of turning into a land-slide, generating not a comfortable condition of 'full employment' but a hectic and disorderly muddle, which could only be checked, at the cost of much disemployment and distress, by the re-establishment of drastic monetary discipline'
> (Robertson 1966: 252–3).

This and similar warnings fell on deaf ears, perhaps because the analysis underlying their dire predictions was not sufficiently explicit to be tested, except by observing the ultimate collapse; and in the mid-1950s there was little evidence of impending doom. In contrast, the Friedman–Phelps analysis offered clear predictions, for example of accelerating inflation if unemployment were held below the natural rate, which left less to the imagination and which hinged on the result of a single, though far from simple, test. In other respects, however, these newer formulations were similar in their implications to Robertson's warning; specifically, an arbitrarily designated unemployment rate cannot be maintained as the target of full-employment policy without regard to its inflationary consequences.

5. The changing evidence on the long-run trade-off

The title of an article by Rees (1969), 'The Phillips curve as a menu for policy choice', epitomises a common initial reaction to the natural rate hypothesis. The argument can be paraphrased along the following lines. There is clear evidence that price changes influence wage inflation, so the original Phillips curve understates the 'cost' of lower unemployment in terms of inflation in the long run, after allowing for the interaction of wage and price changes. Equally clearly, however, the evidence shows a less than proportionate response of wage inflation to price changes, so it is still possible to trade off the ill effects of inflation and unemployment. As long as that situation prevails, for whatever reason, there is no natural unemployment rate. More formally, if prices are set as a mark-up on unit labour costs, then prices will inflate at the difference between wage change and productivity growth:

$$p = w - q$$

In turn wage inflation depends on unemployment and price changes:

$$w = f(U) + \alpha p$$

Hence by substitution

$$p = \frac{1}{1-\alpha} f(U) - \frac{1}{1-\alpha} q$$

In the Friedman–Phelps analysis of the long run, defined as the period over which expectations are fulfilled, the absence of money illusion implies $\alpha = 1$, and so there is no possibility of trading off unemployment against inflation. As long as the evidence continues to show $\alpha < 1$, however, aggregate demand can be managed so as to maintain the authorities' preferred position on the steep, but not vertical, long-run trade-off.

This pragmatic argument was certainly consistent with the evidence up to the end of the 1960s; but by then the evidence was already changing, and this process continued as new observations accumulated. Simultaneously, the augmented Phillips curve was being estimated on various subsidiary assumptions about the way in which expectations are formed, in an attempt to determine whether the apparent existence of a long-run trade-off was a structural feature or a reflection of imperfectly adjusted expectations. Finally, the changing nature of the evidence, and particularly the 'wage explosion' at the end of the 1960s, stimulated a rash of alternative theories and conjectures about wage determination, most of which denied the existence of a trade-off even in the short run.

THE COLLAPSE OF THE PHILLIPS CURVE

One readily available fragment of evidence was the predictive performance of the original Phillips curve itself. Its distinguished record up to 1966 vanished without trace thereafter. As Table 5.2 demonstrates, the forecasting errors were all much

TABLE 5.2 Forecast errors of wage inflation models (per cent)

Year	Model Phillips (1958)	Marin (1972)
1967	−4.0	−1.3
1968	−5.2	−2.6
1969	−3.8	−2.6
1970	−11.9	−7.2
1971	−11.4	(−6.4)
MAE	7.3	4.0

Notes: See Table 5.1; the prediction of Marin's model for 1971 was calculated from his reported equation.

larger than in the previous period, almost invariably increasing as successive observations were added, and all of the same sign. Wage equations incorporating the rate of price change as an independent variable and fitted to post-war data exhibited a qualitatively similar deficiency in underpredicting wage change from the late 1960s onwards. The remarkable feature of this episode is that as wage inflation more than doubled between the mid-1960s and early 1970s, the unemployment rate also rose and by a similar factor, in direct contradiction to the historical experience encapsulated in the Phillips curve.

This evidence is consistent with two broad alternative interpretations. The first is simply that the Phillips curve broke down and was replaced by some other mechanism, or indeed by no mechanism at all, at least not one susceptible to economic analysis. Wiles's view, that inflation depends on 'what numbers trade union leaders pick out of the air when they make wage claims . . . [which] are entirely subjective' (Wiles 1973: 392), is an extreme example, in which 'less restraint at the bargaining table' ranks along with 'rising crime, sex-and-drug permissiveness, less self-discipline in dress, speech and deportment, less respect for hard work, less religion, loosening of the nuclear family, breakdown of a deferential class structure', as evidence that 'the national character is plainly changing'.

Turvey's more mundane explanation of the wage explosion, in terms of 'strong feelings of social injustice, feelings about the appropriateness of differentials' (Turvey 1971: 200), and Bispham's (1975) appeal to long-delayed recognition of the implications for trade union power of the 1944 White Paper on Employment Policy are less colourful than Wiles's assertions; but they share the characteristic that inflation ceases to be an economic problem, as Turvey frankly admits: 'It is not for the economist to explain these [feelings] unless he is to be more of a polymath than he has been in the past.' Even a polymath, however, would be hard pressed to calibrate feelings of social deprivation or militancy, and to incorporate them in an estimating equation. Thus the 'sociological explanation' of the Phillips curve is not an explanation at all, because it has no predictive power and cannot even account *ex post* for the apparent change in the mechanics of wage determination. There is no hint of why the Phillips curve lasted as long as it did, or of the change in attitudes or the power structure which finally dislodged it when the more conspicuous institutional changes of 1913–48 had apparently failed to do so. There is, perhaps, a presumption that wage determination will not revert to an 'economic' pattern. There is certainly no suggestion that the mysterious change in attitudes would be reversed at some later date; but explicit predictions about the future, even in qualitative form, are even more scarce than explicit accounts of the past.

A replacement for the collapsed Phillips curve need not, as a matter of logical necessity, be as barren as the sociological conjecture concerning the collapse. An ostensibly more promising replacement was suggested by Sargan (1971), who proposed what came to be known as real wage resistance as another possible rationalisation for his finding, noted earlier, that the lagged real wage attracted a significant coefficient when added to a standard wage equation, representing 'the demand of trade unions for a rising real wage rate, and their ability to press for higher wages when the real wage rate for any reason has fallen below its trend line' (Sargan 1971: 52). This suggestion has subsequently been extensively explored by Henry *et al.* (1976), Henry and Ormerod (1978), Sargan (1980), and Henry (1981). The distinguishing characteristic of their estimating equations is the role of discrepancies between target and actual real wages in accounting for wage inflation. The target real wage is represented by a mechanistic time trend; the actual real wage is variously measured as wage rates or earnings, either gross or net of income tax. None of these elaborations has addressed the question of why this new mechanism supplanted the Phillips curve, so to that extent the breakdown remains as mysterious as in the sociological account. Moreover, no guidance has been offered as to what parameter values are consistent with the theory, so it is not clear what would constitute a refutation. It would presumably be unreasonable to expect either the 'trend line' of real wages, which is not explained by any economic process, or the unions' capacity to achieve this target, to be constant over time; but the sensitivity of the reported parameters to small variations in the estimation period, illustrated by a drop in the target growth rate of real wages from about 2.5 per cent per annum in Henry *et al.* (1976) to less than zero in Henry and Ormerod (1978), does seem remarkable. Changes of this magnitude raise the distinct possibility that the real wage equation is merely describing the data, rather than capturing significant features of economic behaviour. Indeed, in the most recent version (Henry 1981) the estimated parameters imply that the process of wage determination is dynamically unstable, i.e. that the inflation rate rises without limit; so it is to be hoped that even the more modest claim of describing the data is unwarranted.

The alternative explanation for the prediction errors of Table 5.2 operates within the framework of the augmented Phillips curve. Both the prolonged success of the original Phillips formulation and the standard result of a less than unit coefficient when actual price change was added, as in equation [1], are interpreted as evidence that inflationary expectations lagged behind experience for substantial periods. In passing, notice that Friedman (1968) inferred from his study of the analogous problem of the adjustment of nominal interest rates to inflation that complete adaptation required two decades; and faster adjustment might reasonably be expected in the financial than in the labour market. The simultaneous increase in inflation and unemployment in the late 1960s and early 1970s is then explained as an adjustment of expectations.

If this expectational argument is to rank as a genuine explanation rather than a mere *ex post* rationalisation, certain conditions must be fulfilled. Minimally, the period of adjustment should not be 'too long', and a simple Phillips curve should reappear if and when inflation stabilises at a higher level. If the actual rate of price change is added to the wage equation, its estimated coefficient should increase towards unity as the estimation period is lengthened to include more of the transitional phase. The timing of the expectational adjustment becomes an additional problem for explanation.

If direct evidence on inflationary expectations could be obtained, the task of evaluating this explanation for the breakdown of the simple Phillips curve would obviously be much more tractable. The expectations-augmented Phillips curve, equation [2], could then be tested directly, and the adjustment of expectations themselves would be observable. In the absence of direct evidence, equation [2] could be tested only as a joint hypothesis, conditional on an assumed mechanism of expectations formation.

An additional possibility, within the same framework, was a shift in the relationship between excess demand for labour and the unemployment proxy. This could not account for all the relevant facts on its own, for it offered no explanation for the predictive performance of the simple Phillips curve up to the mid-1960s, or for the unexpectedly low coefficient on actual price change; but it could be invoked to complement the expectational argument, *provided* that independent evidence could be adduced in support. Such evidence was derived from the observed shift in the historical relation between unemployment and unfilled vacancies, which suggested an increase in the 'frictional' or 'structural' components of unemployment at the same time as the breakdown of the Phillips curve.[6] A given level of unemployment was therefore associated with a higher excess demand for labour in the early 1970s than in the mid-1960s.

The remainder of this section discusses the attempts that have been made to test the expectations-augmented Phillips curve and to assess the role of labour-market disturbances.

PROXIES FOR EXPECTED INFLATION

Testing the expectations-augmented Phillips curve rapidly became a very active field of research. Its attraction to economists is attributable to the significance of its policy implications, the intellectual challenge of reconciling theory with the success of the simple Phillips curve in the past, and the ingenuity required to measure or proxy the expected rate of inflation. Three main approaches to that problem are found in the literature: the first dates from the late 1960s but the others did not emerge until the mid-1970s. All of them eventually yielded the same conclusion, that the expectations-augmented Phillips curve is consistent with the evidence. There is a 'natural' rate of unemployment, at which the expected and actual rates of inflation are equal and which therefore constitutes an equilibrium. An attempt to maintain a different unemployment rate will generate disequilibrium and successive shifts of the nominal Phillips curve. In other words there is a whole family of Phillips curves, each associated with a particular anticipated inflation rate and vertically displaced from any other by the difference between those anticipated inflation rates.

Historical experience

The dominant approach has been to assume that expectations are determined by experience, and can therefore be proxied by some combination of current and past rates of price increase. The wage equations which incorporated the actual rate of inflation can be interpreted as a particularly simple variant of this hypothesis.

A less restrictive assumption is that expectations are formed adaptively, changing in response to new experience but in a slower and smoother fashion than they would if only the most recent experience were taken into account. This assumption, which underlies most time-series studies of the permanent income hypothesis,[7] was first applied to the expected inflation rate by Cagan (1956) in his study of the demand for money during hyperinflations. It is most readily understood as a hypothesis about learning from errors:

$$p^e - p^e_{-1} = \lambda (p - p^e_{-1}) \qquad 0 < \lambda < 1$$

The agent is here portrayed as revising his expectation of the future inflation rate by some fraction of his most recently observed error. Equivalently, the expected inflation rate is a weighted average of the current actual and previously expected rates of price change,

$$p^e = \lambda p + (1 - \lambda)p^e_{-1} \qquad [3]$$

or a geometrically-declining weighted average of the current and all previous inflation rates,

$$p^e = \lambda p + \lambda(1-\lambda)p_{-1} + (1-\lambda)^2 p_{-2} + \ldots \qquad [4]$$

Adaptive expectations can be incorporated in a standard wage equation, of the form

$$w = f(U) + \alpha p^e, \qquad [5]$$

in either of two ways. Equation [4] can be used to generate a set of inflation anticipations, each conditional on an assumed value of λ and starting sufficiently far back in time that the initially assumed value of the expected inflation rate has a negligible influence on the results. Equation [5] can then be estimated (over a shorter period) using each of the generated series in turn to test the hypothesis $\alpha = 1$ and to determine which assumed value of λ gives the best fit to the data. Alternatively, substitute equation [3] in equation [5]; lag equation [5] by one period and multiply throughout by $(1 - \lambda)$; then subtract the second of these equations from the first, and rearrange as

$$w = f(U) - (1-\lambda)f(U_{-1}) + \alpha p + (1-\lambda)w_{-1} \qquad [6]$$

This 'Koyck transformation' eliminates the unobservable expectations variable and permits estimation of a single value of λ, but at the cost of new estimation problems. Equation [6] is non-linear in the parameters, and therefore cannot be estimated by OLS: there are three variables with only two independent coefficients, for the product of the coefficients on the lagged dependent variable and on current unemployment equals (minus) the coefficient on lagged unemployment. In addition, the Koyck transformation affects the error term as well as the systematic part of the equation. If the error in equation [5] is random, as it should be if the expectations-augmented Phillips curve is to be deemed satisfactory, then the error in equation [6] will be serially correlated; and autocorrelated errors in an equation which contains a lagged dependent variable lead to biased and inconsistent estimates of the parameters. Nevertheless, the second method of estimation proved more popular, despite the reservations expressed (e.g. Henry 1974) about the adequacy of the estimation methods employed.

The first applications of the adaptive expectations hypothesis to both the UK (e.g. Parkin 1970) and USA (e.g. Gordon 1971) produced results which were inconsistent with the natural rate hypothesis, for the estimated value of α in equation [6] remained significantly below unity. The implied long-run trade-off between inflation and unemployment did not, however, survive for long, as Gordon reports: 'The gradual acceleration of inflation during 1966–70 caused the computer to yield ever higher values of α as the passage of time provided additional observations until finally . . . tests with a sample period including early 1971 were unable to reject statistically the hypothesis that $\alpha = 1$' (Gordon 1976: 193). He cites his own work (Gordon 1972), in which a more general formulation than adaptive expectations was employed, in support.

The changing evidence strongly suggests some kind of threshold effect in the response to anticipated inflation, and this theme was pursued in several investigations. Sumner (1972) showed that British wage inflation in the 1950s was consistent with a threshold hypothesis, such that actual rates of price change below 2 per cent per annum registered no impact on wage adjustments. Thomas (1974) inferred a more complicated form of non-linear relationship between wage and price inflation in the 1960s; his results indicated that 'price effects are non-existent for rates of price change below about 4.5 per cent, but are experienced by all industries [or markets] for rates of price change above 7.5 per cent'. In the intermediate range, the proportion of markets exhibiting price effects is a linear function of the inflation rate. Furthermore, '[w]hen price effects are evident the coefficient on the price change variable is very close to unity' (Thomas 1974: 249). These results were unaffected by the choice between the adaptive expectations hypothesis and the simpler assumption that the actual rate proxies the anticipated inflation rate. A non-linear response to price changes has also been investigated in Canada by Vanderkamp (1972), who could not reject the natural rate hypothesis that α in his version of equation [6] equalled unity, expecially when the equation included a variable recording the number of quarters in which inflation had exceeded the threshold of 2 per cent during the preceding four years.

Solow (1969), who reported an early but severely criticised refutation of the natural rate hypothesis using adaptive expectations in the price equation,[8] suggested a possible rationale for a threshold effect when he spelt out the 'message' of his results:

> whatever may be true of Latin-American-size inflations or even smaller perfectly steady inflations, under the conditions that really matter–irregular price increases with an order to magnitude of a few percent a year–there is a trade-off between the speed of price increase and the real state of the economy. It is less favourable in the long run than it is at first. It may not be 'permanent'; but it lasts long enough for me (Solow 1969: 17).

If such idyllic conditions had persisted the hypothesis that $\alpha = 1$ might have continued to be rejected; but an annual inflation rate above some critical level, which he puts around 10 per cent,[9] 'will eventually become built into expectations just as the [natural rate] hypothesis describes' (Solow 1969: 15). Such a mechanism would account not only for the eventual breakdown of the simple Phillips curve, but also for its long run of reliable predictions, and for the contrast which Lipsey (1960) noted between the price coefficient in 1862–1913, when price changes were on average small and variable in direction, and in 1923–39 and 1948–57, when the trend tilted conspicuously upwards.

The adaptive expectations hypothesis has been the most popular variant of the assumption that anticipations are based solely on the past history of the variable concerned; but it is not the only formulation to be found in the literature. In a paper written in 1966, before the Phillips curve had been augmented by Friedman and Phelps, but published only after a lengthy delay, Brechling (1972) entered the current and two lagged values of actual price change in a wage equation, representing what with the benefit of hindsight can be interpreted as a more flexible version of the 'historically determined expectations' hypothesis. His results for the UK exhibit two particularly interesting features: the sum of the price coefficients is much closer to unity than in other investigations, which typically adopted a more rigid mechanism for generating expectations;[10] and the coefficients do not decline geometrically, or even monotonically, as the adaptive expectations hypothesis presumes. These results raise the intriguing possibility that the disappearance of the long-run trade off might have been detected at an earlier date if a broader perspective on expectations-formation had been adopted. Whatever the verdict on that speculation, there are strong grounds for criticising adaptive expectations as inconsistent with the assumption of rational behaviour.

Rational expectations[11]

The negative aspect of the rationality postulate, viewed as a criticism of the rough and ready assumptions often invoked to link expectations with observable variables for empirical purposes, consists of two elements. One is that agents forming price expectations can draw on a much richer set of information than merely the past behaviour of prices themselves. Economic theory provides models of price determination which indicate the relevant explanatory variables; if their evolution is monitored, better forecasts of inflation will be made at little additional cost in terms of time and trouble. Second, even if attention is confined to the past behaviour of inflation, the way in which the information is used is crucially important. Any particular assumption about the link between past and future prices will lead to systematic, and therefore avoidable, forecasting errors unless the series evolves in a particular manner. To make the same mistake repeatedly would clearly be inconsistent with rational behaviour. Instead, agents will select a method of processing information which produces purely random errors in their forecasts. The adaptive expectations hypothesis does not fulfil that requirement: given the history of inflation, a rational agent would reject the hypothesis precisely because it would yield systematically incorrect predictions (Sargent 1971). It makes little sense to base estimates of the expectations-augmented Phillips curve on such a demonstrably inefficient foundation.

There is a wide gulf between the negative proposition that rational individuals will not persist in formulating expectations in a manner which produces systematic errors, and the much stronger positive proposition that they will select the 'correct' economic model and apply it efficiently. Perhaps for that reason there have been few attempts to construct rational expectations models of wage determination.

One accessible example is by McCallum (1975), who investigated both 'partly' rational expectations, formed using only the history of prices but in an efficient manner, and a model in which price expectations were determined by money supply growth, government spending, output in the UK and USA (as a proxy for foreign aggregate demand), as well as past inflation. He suggested rather tentatively that 'most observers would probably conclude that our findings tend to provide support for the natural rate viewpoint' (McCallum 1975: 65) over the period 1956–71. Interestingly, and in contrast to his US results, he found that the coefficient on price expectations was much closer to unity when they were assumed to be derived from the 'complete' model than in the case of 'partial rationality'. He speculated that the difference in results might reflect 'the greater importance in the UK of trade union and international influences, these more nearly exogenous sources of price change making the extrapolative sort of forecasting (implied by the partly rational assumption) less effective than in the US' (McCallum 1975: 65 fn.18). The basis for the role imputed to trade unions is not clear, but the allusion to international influences is important and will be developed further below. In the interim, notice that this comment illustrates the difficulty, for both those forming expectations and those attempting to model their behaviour, of selecting the 'correct' model.

The rational expectations hypothesis is more plausible the longer the period under scrutiny and the more stable the magnitude whose evolution is to be predicted. It is difficult to believe that agents incur avoidable costs by making avoidable mistakes; but it is equally difficult to believe that radical changes in the behaviour of a series are predicted accurately. Flemming (1976) has suggested a synthesis of rational and adaptive expectations to avoid the strong assumptions underlying the former and the systematic errors of the latter. Expectations are formed adaptively on 'the *lowest-order* difference (or derivative) of the inflation process to have shown no trend in recent years' (Flemming 1976: 62). In the period for which the original Phillips curve was fitted, for example, the *level* of prices exhibited no trend and would therefore have been a 'rational' subject on which to form expectations by some simple rule of thumb. The price level has risen in every year since 1934, however, so that to continue to apply the same rule of thumb in this later period would have been clearly irrational. Once that was recognised, expectations would have undergone a 'gear shift', being formulated thereafter about the *inflation rate*. When the inflation rate began to accelerate perceptibly, a further gear shift to the *change in the inflation rate* took place.

Flemming's synthesis is eminently plausible, but it obviously poses formidable difficulties of implementation. The crucial question concerns the timing of gear shifts: how rapidly are systematic errors perceived? The history of the Phillips curve suggests that there are substantial lags in the adjustment process.

The relevant domain

One of the incidental features of McCallum's results, the marked contrast between the relative performance of 'restricted' and broader measures of rational expectations in Britain and the USA, suggests an important but so far neglected distinction based on susceptibility to international influences. At the extreme, an open economy which is too small to exercise monopolistic or monopsonistic power must trade at exogenously determined world prices. If its exchange rate is fixed, the dominant influence on its inflation rate will be exerted by its trading partners. In those circumstances mechanistic extrapolation of past changes in the domestic price level would be a particularly misleading method of forming expectations of future inflation rates. It would reflect not only past inflation proper, but also any changes in the relative price of tradeable and non-tradeable goods or in their respective weights in the price index, and any changes in the degree of international integration associated with changes in tariffs or transport costs. Indeed, extrapolation could misstate even the direction of change: if purchasing power parity does not hold instantaneously but is approached over a longer period, for the same reasons that conventional demand functions are generally believed to be more elastic in the long than the short run, then a country wishing to maintain fixed exchange rates which inflates faster than its partners in one period must not merely bring its inflation rate into line with the group, but undergo a relative deflation to restore the equilibrium price *level* (e.g. Sumner and Zis 1982). As long as faith in the fixity of exchange rates remains complete, a rational expectation of inflation cannot be formulated on a purely domestic basis. Relative inflation will induce expectations of further moves not in the same but in the opposite direction. The fixed exchange rate system acts as a brake on the development of inflationary expectations in countries which favour expansive policies.

This theme has been developed along several routes. Duck *et al.* (1976) argued that the expectations-augmented Phillips curve should be sought at the international level, among the members of a fixed exchange-rate bloc. For the period 1955–71, when results for individual national economies almost invariably rejected the natural rate hypothesis, they estimated wage and price equations for a group of ten OECD countries in which the point estimate of the coefficient on the proxy for price expectations was close to, and certainly did not differ significantly from, unity. Moreover, these results were insensitive to the choice of proxy from a set of alternatives all derived from the history of inflation; in particular, a simple adaptive expectations scheme did not perform markedly worse that the optimal forecast corresponding to McCallum's 'partly' rational expectation.

The role of international influences was analysed within a national setting by Cross and Laidler (1976), who estimated expectations-augmented price equations for twenty individual countries in periods of exchange rate fixity within 1954–70. The expected inflation rate was assumed to be revised adaptively in response to changes in both domestic and 'world' inflation, and was found to have a coefficient consistent with the predicted value of unity. The consequences of ignoring international influences in national studies of inflation were examined by Parkin and Smith (1976), who showed that the less than unit coefficient on actual or expected price change in UK wage equations was attributable to an inappropriately constructed price index. The weight on foreign inflation, measured by import prices, in the retail price index is determined by the ratio of imports to national income, whereas the weight indicated by explicit derivation of the expectations-augmented Phillips curve depends on the relative sensitivity of excess demand for labour to the real wage and to the ratio of domestic and international prices.

Apart from their direct bearing on the proxy for price expectations and its coefficient, these results also raise important questions about the distribution of excess demand within a fixed exchange-rate bloc, and the balance of payments pattern associated with that distribution. There is an obvious analogy with the regional distribution of activity within a national economy, but there is no supranational authority capable of modifying the distribution generated by market forces in the way national governments have attempted to do by regional policy.

The restraining influence of fixed exchanges on governments that might otherwise have been tempted to pursue the short-run gains of higher output at the long-run cost of higher inflation became progressively weaker during the late 1960s, when changes in exchange rates became more frequent. The restraint disappeared entirely in the early 1970s when the strains on the Bretton Woods exchange-rate system became too severe to be disguised by cosmetic adjustments. A rational agent could reasonably have anticipated a change in government behaviour at that (admittedly imprecisely defined) moment. It would not be surprising, then, if expected inflation rates registered a jump in relation to the actual inflation rates experienced in the past, of the kind suggested by the increasing coefficient on proxies constructed from inflationary history.

Direct measurement

The reader might reasonably have assumed by now that no direct data on inflation anticipations exist, for if they did there would surely be little point in constructing subsidiary hypotheses so as to infer expectations from other variables. In fact that assumption would be incorrect. Direct evidence does exist, but it is limited in its coverage and in most cases requires processing before it can be utilised in econometric studies to represent the *magnitude* of the anticipated inflation rate.

The obvious method of measuring expected inflation is to ask a suitable sample of the population what they expect to happen. That technique has been used on a wide scale, though with the equally obvious reservations attached to any survey; but the question has seldom been posed in quantitative terms. The only quantitative information available for long enough to be usable when the role of expectations first became an issue was the Livingston series, named after its compiler, who initiated a biannual poll of US business economists in 1947. Several other similar series, usually records of household opinions, are now collected in the USA and elsewhere; but the longest of these, collected as part of its Survey of Consumer Finances by the University of Michigan's Survey Research Center, dates only from 1966.

Experiments with the Livingston series have produced mixed results. Turnovsky (1970) pointed out its apparent sluggishness during the 1950s, when inflation ceased to be a serious problem once the Korean disturbance was over; but, in a joint paper with Wachter (1972), he also showed that the series produced a better statistical explanation of US wage behaviour than the standard proxies derived from history. In that study the expectations coefficient remained well below unity, whereas in a parallel study of Canadian wage inflation Turnovsky (1972) reported a much higher coefficient differing insignificantly from unity, and confirmed the natural rate hypothesis using conventional proxies. Although the two economies were thought sufficiently similar to justify transplanting the Livingston expectations series, Turnovsky conjectured that '[t]he major difference between them, of course, is that unlike the United States, Canada is heavily dependent on foreign trade. This tends to make the economy more competitive and hence to make it conform more closely to the neo-classical assumptions' (1972: 16). It should also be recalled that the Canadian exchange rate was allowed to float between 1950 and 1962, and was permitted some degree of variability during the remainder of Turnovsky's sample period. In consequence the anchor for expectations inherent in the fixed rate system never existed in the Canadian case.

Many writers have expressed scepticism about the Livingston series, on the grounds that those whose views are sampled are not representative of those involved in setting wages. The same objection cannot be applied to the qualitative data on the expected direction of price change which have been collected from samples of households and firms in many countries for substantial periods. With considerable ingenuity and some strong assumptions about the distribution of expectations across respondents, methods of deriving a series on the expected rate of inflation have been developed, and applied in the UK to households by Carlson and Parkin (1975) and to firms by Smith (1978). Elsewhere these methods have been applied to household price expectations by de Menil and Bhalla (1975) in the USA and by Knöbl (1974) in West Germany, and to firms' expectations by Danes (1975) in Australia.

Without going into the details of the derivation, it is easy to see intuitively that changes in the mean inflation rate anticipated by the respondents can be inferred from changes in the proportions of the sample expecting prices to rise, fall, and stay the same, respectively.[12] Difficulties arise, however, when responses become uniform, for if everyone always expects prices to rise the qualitative question yields no information. This problem is more acute for households, who are asked about an index of consumer prices, than for firms, who are asked about the selling prices of their own output; some individual prices invariably fall even when the relevant index is rising monotonically. In the period 1961–73 there were only five occasions when the monthly Gallup Poll of UK consumers reported that nobody expected prices to fall (Carlson and Parkin, 1975),[13] although the actual inflation rate was positive throughout. During the 1970s, however, the higher average level and longer experience of inflation must have increased the frequency of occasions when the method would not work.

A second difficulty is that a scaling factor is needed to standardise the series derived by manipulating the survey response.[14] In most applications there is no feasible alternative to assuming a constant scaling factor, such that the actual and expected inflation rates were equal over the sample as a whole. To assume that people are not misled by inflation on average is preferable to imposing the assumption of systematic mistakes; but it excludes the possibility of learning and of 'gear-changes' in response to new developments.

Considerable attention has been devoted to analysing the properties of 'popular price expectations' (de Menil and Bhalla 1975). Carlson and Parkin (1975) examined the relation between their series and past inflation, concluding that 'when inflation is rapid, expectations approximate a second-order error-learning process, whilst when inflation is mild, expectations approximate an autoregressive scheme' (p.137). This distinction suggests a low correlation between the expectations measure derived from surveys and any single transformation of past inflation rates; de Menil and Bhalla show explicitly that the same is true for the USA. The rationality of the Carlson–Parkin series has been considered by Holden and Peel (1977) and Batchelor and Sheriff (1980); both reach a negative conclusion, though their tests have aroused some controversy.

The role of directly measured price expectations in the UK wage equation has been explored by Parkin *et al.* (1976). Their model incorporated a distinction between the price expectations of consumers and firms by defining excess demand for labour as

$$X = D\left(\frac{W}{P_F}\right) - S\left(\frac{W}{P_C}\right),$$

where the subscripts denote the agents concerned. The expected change in excess demand is therefore given by

$$\Delta X^e = -\alpha(w - p_F^e) - \beta(w - p_c^e)$$

where α and β are assumed constant;[15] as usual lower-case letters represent proportionate rates of change and the superscript denotes an expectation. Notice that as the object of the analysis is to determine wage change, this variable requires no superscript. Wage changes are, in fact, assumed to be determined in such a way that current excess demand (X_0) is reduced, given the expected behaviour of prices:

$$\Delta X^e = -\theta X_0.$$

Substituting this behavioural assumption in the previous equation and rearranging, the wage equation is obtained as

$$w = \frac{\theta}{\alpha + \beta} X_0 + \frac{\alpha}{\alpha + \beta} p_F^e + \frac{\beta}{\alpha + \beta} p_c^e.$$

In other words, the rate of change of wages depends on the level of excess demand for labour, and on the rates of price inflation anticipated by both the firms which demand labour and the households who supply it. The predicted sum of the price expectation coefficients is unity, with weights determined by the relative slopes of the demand and supply functions.

In this analysis the real wage differs on the two sides of the labour market, because the price firms expect to receive for their output can change at a different rate than the price households expect to pay for their consumption bundle. There are lags in the process of price adjustment through the successive stages of production and distribution. The costs and benefits of forming expectations may differ systematically.[16]

Firms sell their output in overseas as well as home markets, and consumption goods are imported as well as produced domestically. Firms are concerned with the net price they receive, which excludes any sales tax collected on the government's behalf, whereas households are concerned with the gross price they pay, including any sales tax; hence anticipated changes in fiscal policy will produce a difference between their respective price expectations. This last point can obviously be generalised to include personal income tax and social security contributions as additional sources of divergence between the real wage paid by firms and that received by households.

The equation estimated by Parkin, Sumner and Ward differed from the simplified version derived above by including the expected rates of change of export prices, income tax and social security contributions. Excess demand for labour was proxied by a moving average of unemployment, price expectations by the Carlson–Parkin series for consumers and analogous processes applied to the industrial trends enquiry of the Confederation of British Industry for firms, and fiscal anticipations by actual tax changes. When the model was fitted to data for the period 1956–71 the price expectations variables performed in concert as predicted, with a sum of coefficients which differed insignificantly from unity; though of the individual coefficients, only that on firms' domestic anticipations was well determined. Tax changes, as measured, did not feature significantly, a result which confirms the importance of distinguishing in the short run between actual and anticipated magnitudes. The unemployment coefficient was correctly signed and, when the price constraints were imposed to increase the efficiency of estimation, significant, in marked contrast to contemporary epitaphs for the Phillips curve even in its augmented form.

In a subsequent study Sumner (1978) showed that the sum of the price coefficients remained insignificantly different from unity when the sample period was extended to 1952–74;[17] but he also showed that the partial Phillips curve, holding price anticipations constant, shifted upwards at the end of the 1960s. In turn, that shift was ascribed to an increase in the 'replacement ratio', the relation between unemployment benefit and net earnings while in employment. The method used was to estimate a relationship between unemployment and output relative to trend, the real wage rate and the replacement ratio. This enabled an adjusted unemployment rate to be derived, holding the replacement ratio constant, as a purer measure of excess labour demand. The adjusted unemployment series was then used in expectations-augmented Phillips curves fitted up to 1965 to estimate wage inflation in 1966–74. The estimates, purged of the influence of the replacement ratio and predicated on the natural rate hypothesis, compared closely with actual wage inflation over this period. The mean error was small, and on average the estimated rate of wage inflation was too *high* at a time when underestimation was a much more common problem.

Firms' price anticipations attract a robust and well-determined coefficient in both studies, but a much greater margin of uncertainty surrounds the coefficient on consumer price expectations. The results are certainly incapable of rejecting the natural rate hypothesis for any of the sample periods examined, but they are also consistent with other interpretations. The experience of the later 1970s cannot be used for further tests of the model in its original form because, as noted already, the Carlson–Parkin method of inferring households' expectations becomes increasingly unreliable as the sample proportion expecting a fall in prices vanishes. Recent work by Sumner and Ward (1983), who resort to proxying consumer expectations by the actual rate of change of the retail price index, suggests an alternative explanation of wage inflation during the last two decades. The coefficient on firms' price expectations continues to show little variation over subsections of the period 1961–80, but the proxy for consumer expectations behaves very differently. Up to 1970 its coefficient is indistinguishable from zero and the point estimate is frequently negative; in the 1970s, however, it enters significantly and the sum of the price coefficients is very close to unity. The result for the 1960s is consistent with that of Parkin, Sumner and Ward, because of the low correlation between actual and expected consumer price inflation during that period. Experiments suggest that expectations were brought into line with experience abruptly, through a 'gear-shift' rather than a gradual learning process. There is similar evidence of a change in the role of tax changes, which again make no contribution to the analysis of the 1960s but enter the wage equation as predicted in the 1970s.

After allowance for these adjustments in reactions to tax and price changes, which now appear much more convincingly in the role ascribed to them under the natural rate hypothesis, there is little or nothing left to be explained by a shift in the relation between unemployment and excess demand for labour. The importance that has been attributed to disturbances in the structure of the labour market, for which change in the replacement ratio is only one of the candidate explanations, may therefore have been exaggerated considerably. Whether it will be possible to discriminate between these two explanations and whether there is scope for combining them are among the questions which remain unanswered at present.

SUMMARY

All of the methods used to construct price expectations series, a precondition for testing the natural rate hypothesis, have aroused criticism: they are repectively mechanistic, excessively sophisticated, or place undue weight on casual survey responses and base the processing of these raw data on strong, untestable assumptions. Over short periods they provide radically different accounts of their subject, as evidenced by the low correlations reported by de Menil and Bhalla (1975), who maintained that 'that observation constitutes a damning judgement'. Most importantly, they initially yielded contradictory answers to the fundamental question they were designed to answer: is there a natural rate of unemployment, or does the trade-off between inflation and unemployment exist even in the long run?

Any procedure for inferring the behaviour of a variable which cannot be observed directly will always be subject to some kind of criticism; but the criticisms carry less conviction when the substantive conclusions derived using different procedures are mutually consistent. That condition is fulfilled over a longer horizon, as a result of the increase in the coefficient on expectations proxies based on past experience and the breakdown of money illusion suggested by the declining proportion of survey respondents who expected a fall in prices. The leisurely pace of this evolution, mirrored in the prolonged success of the original Phillips curve under circumstances considerably different from those prevailing at its inception, poses problems for further investigation. In particular, it remains uncertain whether the 'gear shift' resulted from the gradual accumulation of experience, possibly filtered through some psychological threshold, or was precipitated by a shock such as the collapse, over a relatively short period, of the fixed exchange rate system. The significance of questions like these should not be understated, for reasons illustrated in the final section; nevertheless '[t]here is now much less disagreement about the empirical nature of the interaction of real income and inflation: there is a short-run trade-off between inflation and unemployment and it does seem to vanish in the long run' (Laidler 1981: 25).

The change in conventional wisdom is clearly recorded in the succession of conferences of econometric model-builders.[18] The versions used in 1972 (Renton 1975) either incorporated an augmented Phillips curve which exhibited money illusion, illustrated by the coefficient on actual price change of less than a half in the London Business School's wage equation, or, like the National Institute of Economic and Social Research, had abandoned any attempt to model wage inflation. By 1977, '[t]here was much discussion of the relationship between import prices, the general price level, and the wage level, and the alleged property of the British economy that in the recent past the coefficient of wages on prices had been close to unity after a short time-lag' (Posner 1978: 217). At that stage the National Institute had reinstated the augmented Phillips curve, but in a form which imposed a small degree of money illusion. Two years later that illusion was evidently thought to have evaporated, for the reported wage equation exhibited no long-run trade-off. At the same time it was pointed out that '[s]ince the late 1960s the National Institute, in common with other UK forecasters, has experienced difficulty in estimating a stable and satisfactory version of the [wage] equation' (Ormerod 1979: 120–1). Despite this 'difficulty', which may be partly attributable to the absence of any distinction between actual and expected inflation, economic logic and the weight of evidence have proved compelling.

6. Issues and implications

In this final section the policy implications of the literature on the Phillips curve are examined and the major outstanding questions are raised. Since wider considerations are involved than the proximate determinants of inflation which have been the focus of this survey, the objective is limited to a sketch of the issues in their broader context.

POLICY OPTIONS IN THE LONG RUN

Few economists would now accept Rees's (1969) characterisation of the Phillips curve as 'a menu for policy choice' which presents a trade-off between inflation and unemployment even in the long run. The denial of this proposition does not, however, imply that there are no policy choices to be made. Even if the long-run Phillips curve is vertical, the government can exercise a choice of the inflation rate which prevails at the natural unemployment rate.

By definition expectations are fulfilled at the natural unemployment rate, so the inflation under discussion here would be very different in character from anything ever experienced. As a characteristic of long-run equilibrium it would create none of the disappointments and distortions associated with imperfectly anticipated inflation. For that reason the extensive debates among earlier generations of economists on the most desirable path of the general price level can shed little light on the question under discussion here, for their arguments and the qualifications appended to them hinged on 'the great disturbances to contract and expectation, and so to the distribution and creation of real wealth, which follow from any violent exhibition of instability in the value of money' (Robertson 1948: 111). Although amply justified by experience, these considerations are of no relevance to the hypothetical question of how the general price level should behave when its movements are perfectly predicted sufficiently far in advance that no agent is ever locked into a disadvantageous contract.

A perfectly anticipated inflation would 'tax' holdings of non-interest-bearing money balances, generating real revenue for the issuer in amounts determined by the equilibrium stock of real balances and the rates of inflation and growth. It would also impose welfare losses on 'consumers' of money, in amounts determined by the interest elasticity of their demand function. The observable counterparts of these welfare losses are more frequent transactions and the substitution of other stores of value for money.

A welfare-maximising government would take account of two factors in fixing the equilibrium inflation rate. One is the marginal cost of collecting the inflation tax compared with more conventional sources of revenue. This is a complex issue, for variations in the inflation rate affect both the cost of collecting conventional taxes, since rates of specific and progressive taxes must be revised periodically to maintain their intended real values, and also the amount of interest-bearing debt that must be issued in any period, given the levels of government spending, conventional tax revenue, and the public's demand for money at different inflation rates. The second consideration is the possible effects on *real* interest and therefore growth rates exerted by changes in portfolio composition as the demand for real balances varies with the inflation rate.

There is no presumption that the optimal policy would be price stability, still less a rate of *deflation* sufficient to reduce the nominal interest rate to zero, thus equating the private cost of holding money with the negligible social cost of creating it by making entries in bank ledgers (e.g. Friedman 1969). Nevertheless Phelps (1972), who provides a convenient synthesis of the issues, and most subsequent contributors to this arcane branch of the inflation literature argue that optimality is unlikely to involve rapid price changes in either direction.

The question of what rate of perfectly anticipated inflation would be optimal can be dismissed as an issue devoid of any practical relevance, and of secondary importance even under the conditions that must be assumed for the question to have any meaning. The literature does, however, perform the valuable function of emphasising how stringent those conditions are. For that reason Friedman, for example, lays considerably greater stress on the predictability of inflation, which he associates with a fixed monetary rule, than the choice of a particular rule and the corresponding inflation rate. The literature also suggests that even under these stringent conditions, which make the costs of inflation far lower than they are ever likely to be in more realistic situations, the optimal rate is not far removed from zero.

THE SHORT RUN

If expectations are sufficiently inflexible that a trade-off exists, albeit temporarily, the range of options is widened considerably. If, for example, the inflation rate is in equilibrium at a level regarded as higher than the optimum, there is a choice between policies of gradualism, i.e. a small increase in unemployment above the natural rate for an extended period, or a sharper deflation of shorter duration. There is also, of course, the possibility of doing nothing, on the grounds that the perpetual flow of benefits from a reduction in the equilibrium inflation rate represents an inadequate return on the 'investment' in a temporary reduction of output and employment.[19]

The options can be exploited for political as well as more narrowly economic ends. Nordhaus (1975) ascribes the rising trend of the post-war inflation rate to the political business cycle, in which governments expand demand in pursuit of short-run electoral gain at the cost of faster inflation in the post-electoral future.[20] Gordon (1975) has analysed 'the demand and supply of inflation' in terms of the politico-economic pressures on governments to engage in expansionary policies and the factors determining their readiness to respond. As well as the theoretical analyses exemplified by these two papers, there is also a substantial body of empirical work on the relationship between economic performance and political popularity (e.g. Hibbs and Fassbender 1981). In principle at least, the results could be used to derive the iso-vote loci which, together with the constraint of the (or a) Phillips curve, determine the vote-maximising strategy in Nordhaus's analysis; though it is not clear that these initial explorations have yet succeeded in isolating robust relationships.[21]

The scope for and desirability of departing from the natural rate depend on the rate of time discount, the curvature of the short-run trade-off, the speed with which expectations are revised, and the interpretation placed on the augmented Phillips curve itself. The influence of the first two factors is obvious. The lower the weight assigned to the future, the stronger is the temptation to court electoral favour now and the weaker is the incentive to 'buy' lower inflation in the future. The greater the curvature, the less attractive are deviations in either direction, for a given change in unemployment involves larger immediate costs in terms of faster inflation or smaller immediate benefits in terms of slower inflation.

The significance of the way in which expectations are formed follows from the earlier discussion of rationality and the extrapolation of past experience. If, at one extreme, expectations were strictly adaptive, it would be feasible to maintain any unemployment rate desired by the authorities. For example, unemployment could be kept 'unnaturally' low by engineering an accelerating rate of inflation, which would perpetually surprise firms and households by staying ahead of their anticipations. Such a degree of gullibility would be a pathological violation of the rationality postulate, but, as noted already, there is evidence of persistent differences between actual and anticipated inflation for substantial periods. Whether these afford a legitimate case for active government policy depends on the meaning attached to the expectations-augmented Phillips curve.

The tradition implicit in most of the empirical literature on wage determination treats inflation as the response to a disequilibrium between quantities demanded and supplied. Augmenting this response by incorporating anticipations superimposes a separable equilibrium component of inflation, but it does not in itself require any change in the interpretation of the original Phillips curve. The significance of this interpretation is that

> [i]f adjustments in the level (or rate of change) of money wages and prices to aggregate demand shocks are anything other than instantaneous, then markets fail to clear, trade takes place at false prices, and quantity signals, perhaps amplified by multiplier effects, become an integral part of the mechanism whereby monetary changes are transmitted to the behaviour of the price level (Laidler 1981: 13).

There then follows

> the possibility of the economy slipping below its natural rate of output in a short run that may be of considerable duration, [and] the possibility that there exists an appropriate menu of monetary and fiscal policies that might hasten its return to that natural rate without generating any serious costs during the transition (Laidler 1981: 19).

There is, however, a considerable difference between the logical possibility of appropriate intervention and its realisation since governments, however benign their intentions, are not omniscient.

The alternative interpretation inverts the augmented Phillips curve to obtain an aggregate supply curve which relates output (or employment) as dependent variable to the difference between actual and anticipated rates of price (or wage) change. Under that interpretation 'fluctuations in output or employment in response to price level variations represent the voluntary choices of individuals in markets which are continually clearing' (Laidler 1981: 10). Policy could influence those choices only by inducing expectational errors. Under the rationality postulate systematic policy could achieve nothing, for it would be anticipated and offset; and random intervention could hardly make a positive contribution to social welfare. More fundamentally, policy which can operate only by frustrating voluntary choices lacks any justification when applied beyond a very narrow range of specific activities.

The difference between these two interpretations of the expectations-augmented Phillips curve is clearly of fundamental significance for the whole of macroeconomics. It is one facet of a controversy over the role of market clearing which has appeared in various guises during the last two decades, and is still no nearer resolution. The only definite implication is that further discussion is beyond the scope of this survey.

EXPECTATIONS AND CREDIBILITY

The way in which expectations are formed and the speed with which they are revised in response to new information are critically important in determining the costs of deflationary policies directed towards lowering the equilibrium inflation rate. If expectations are based solely on experience, downward shifts of the short-run Phillips curve will take place only after a movement down the initial curve has reduced the actual inflation rate. The adjustment will be less expensive in terms of output temporarily forgone if the authorities can establish their commitment to lower inflation in a way which influences expectations directly. This point has been formalised by Fellner as the credibility hypothesis, which emphasises

> differences between states of the economy in which inconsistent policies lead market participants to form diffuse personal probability distributions with risk allowances playing a large role in their decisionmaking, and states of the economy in which firm and credible policies condition the public's expectations and lead to much more strongly peaked and widely shared personal probability distributions concerning future events (Fellner 1979: 168–9).

Credibility has in part to be earned, and so the costs associated with successive 'doses' of deflation would diminish as the authorities' determination was recognised and incorporated in expectations. Those costs would be even lower if a credible commitment to price stability could be established in advance, by the prior announcement of disinflationary policies.

The announcement of targets for the rate of monetary expansion can be interpreted as an attempt to influence expectations directly. There is some evidence of initial success in the countries where targets were first introduced and declared in advance. In the USA, the proportion of consumers in the Survey Research Center's sample who expected no price increase peaked conspicuously in the first survey taken after Congress had imposed on the Federal Reserve an obligation to announce monetary targets; and in Germany, the anticipated inflation rate inferred from firms' survey responses registered a trough after the Bundesbank's voluntary adoption of public targetry. In neither case was there any other obvious explanation for these developments. These impact effects quickly evaporated, however. In other countries, such as the UK, where targetry was adopted later and without proclamation, no discernible effect even of a transitory character was registered (Sumner 1980).

Another means of reducing the transitional costs of lowering inflation might be the imposition of direct controls, or the negotiation of voluntary agreement, on prices and incomes. If such a policy were credible the mere announcement would lower anticipations; and any initial success in lowering the actual inflation rate would reinforce this impact effect, provided the controls were accompanied by appropriate adjustments in monetary and fiscal policy to maintain the credibility of lower inflation in the longer term. The appeal of controls or persuasion, as an apparently costless method [22] of lowering inflation, has been demonstrated by their repeated application in the UK and elsewhere.

The history of controls is described as 'venerable' by Brittan and Lilley (1977), who trace them back to Babylon 4,000 years ago, before the introduction of currency. Without going quite that far back in time, it will be recalled that Phillips attributed a conspicuous overprediction of wage change in 1949 to the incomes policy then in force. More recent instances of policies which have succeeded in reducing inflation below what it would otherwise have been are, however, difficult to find. The post-war literature up to the early 1970s was surveyed by Parkin *et al.* (1972), who reached a strongly sceptical verdict about the possibility of reducing inflation by this means. Subsequent studies have failed to detect any durable effects on either the process of wage determination itself (e.g. Parkin *et al.* 1976; Sumner 1978), or on anticipated inflation (Carlson and Parkin 1975; Smith 1978). The same conclusion has been reached elsewhere; for example, Frye and Gordon (1981) epitomise their conclusions in the title, 'government intervention in the inflation process: the econometrics of self-inflicted wounds'.

It may be objected that to isolate the effects of direct controls, a model of wage or price determination is needed to predict what would have happened in their absence; therefore, negative conclusions may indicate a mis-specified model rather than policy failure. This argument would, however, require a very special form of mis-specification if it were to be upheld. It is in any case undermined by the fact that students of inflation who use alternatives to the expectations-augmented Phillips curve to generate their counterfactual predictions have been equally unsuccessful in detecting examples of effective controls. Henry and Ormerod (1978) incorporate five dummy variables in their variant of Sargan's 'real wage bargaining' model, to capture the effects of those policies regarded as most likely to have depressed wage inflation during the period 1961–77. Only one of these, the Heath 'freeze' of 1972–3, turned out to be statistically significant during its period of operation; and its effects were more than offset during the ensuing period of catch-up. At best, therefore, direct controls have delayed inflation; but they have failed to establish the credibility required for any lasting effect, whatever the framework in which they are analysed.

THE NATURAL RATE OF UNEMPLOYMENT

The status of the natural unemployment rate is closely related to the alternative interpretations of the augmented Phillips curve sketched earlier. If it represents the outcome of voluntary choices, as under the inverted supply curve interpretation, the magnitude of the natural rate can represent a cause for concern only if those choices are conditioned by inefficient institutions. Attention is then directed towards reform of those institutions rather than the natural rate itself. Under the alternative interpretation the natural rate 'seems . . . to be synonymous with the Keynesian concept of the minimum feasible unemployment rate' (Laidler 1981: 10, n.4). There is nothing intrinsically 'natural' about the concept when it is denied the legitimacy conferred by voluntary choice, hence the alternative label adopted by some writers, the 'non-accelerating inflation rate of unemployment', NAIRU. The semantic difference reflects their conviction that the unemployment associated with equilibrium inflation is largely involuntary. The NAIRU may be affected by social policy expressed in the replacement ratio, which relates unemployment compensation to potential earnings; but this voluntary component is regarded, often implicitly, as quantitatively unimportant.

If the Phillips curve is interpreted as showing the reaction of wages and prices to excess demand, then the natural rate will depend partly on the dispersion of excess demand both over time and across individual markets at a point of time. The influence of geographical and industrial variations in economic activity has already been discussed: '[t]he economy is in perpetual sectoral disequilibrium even when it has settled into a stochastic macro-equilibrium' (Tobin 1972: 10). If the 'macro' Phillips curve is non-linear, then the NAIRU will be higher the greater the variance of excess demand over time (Baily 1978).[23] Tobin regards the asymmetrical response of inflation to equal degrees of excess and deficient demand as

> a structural bias towards inflation. even towards the acceleration of inflation. The structural bias means that inflation stability is not the same thing as equilibrium, that inflation stability generally requires aggregate excess supply in amounts that depend on the severity of the microeconomic and macroeconomic shocks to which the economy is subject, that inflation stability does not have the properties of allocational optimality associated with equilibrium (Tobin 1980: 64)

The policy implication he derives is that conventional demand management directed towards price stability will require 'chronic sacrifice of output and employment unless it is assisted, occasionally or permanently, by direct incomes policies of some kind'. The disappointing feature of this conclusion is the ascientific belief that some kind of incomes policy, as yet undiscovered, will achieve the desired outcome, presumably with negligible side-effects.

The interpretation of the Phillips curve as an inverted supply curve precludes an immediate relationship between the natural rate and the variance of aggregate demand. Instead Friedman (1977) invokes an empirical link between the average level of inflation and its variability, and argues that variable inflation augments the natural rate by increasing uncertainty. One reason is that appropriate economic institutions, such as indexing, are adopted only slowly; and in any case, 'indexation is, even at best, an imperfect substitute for stability of the inflation rate' (Friedman 1977: 26). In addition, variable inflation lowers the efficiency of the price system as a co-ordinating mechanism by confusing the information about relative prices which is conveyed through absolute prices. In contrast to Tobin's argument, these distortions 'will almost certainly be reinforced by legal restrictions on price changes' (p.27), which will only make matters worse. The outcome is 'a positively sloped Phillips curve . . . as a transitional phenomenon that will disappear as economic agents readjust not only their expectations but their institutional and political arrangements to a new reality' (p.23). The conclusion could, however, be expressed more generally as a relation between the natural rate on the one hand and, on the other, the variability of inflation and the degree of adaptation to the uncertainty which it generates. Variability is significant only as an index of unpredictability, for presumably regular fluctuations would be anticipated.

Thus both approaches yield the same policy implications, that the variance of aggregate demand should be minimised, but for very different reasons. Indeed, there is at least a hint in some of the literature inspired by the traditional interpretation of the Phillips curve that unpredictability of inflation was positively desirable, for by hindering the formation of definite expectations it held in abeyance the threat to active demand management posed by the natural rate hypothesis; perhaps Solow (1969) comes nearest to espousing this view, though admittedly the average inflation rate was very different then. The contrast with the inverted supply curve interpretation could scarcely be more striking.

The natural rate can clearly be affected by economic policy, but there is little agreement about the extent of this influence or the way it should be exercised. Perhaps the most contentious issue is the hypothesis that an attempted adjustment towards the natural rate will increase the natural rate itself. The argument, first suggested by Brechling (1968) and recently revived by Hargreaves Heap (1980), is summarised in Tobin's warning against the assumption 'that the natural rate of unemployment is independent of the history of actual unemployment . . . . Labour markets soggy enough to maintain price stability may increase the number of would-be workers who lack the experience to fit them for jobs that become vacant' (Tobin 1972: 17). Despite its long history, no evidence bearing on this hypothesis has yet been presented, and its implications have not been fully worked out. It does, however, demonstrate that the Phillips curve, even in its augmented form, remains as close to the centre of macroeconomic controversy as it has always been.

Notes

1. Before the further adjustment for the change in the method of measuring unemployment discussed above.
2. Thomas (1974) has generalised the standard aggregation procedure by assuming that the parameters of the wage equations for individual industries are themselves functions of some other variable, specifically the extent of trade union membership. It is, of course, necessary to assume that the wage equations for any two industries with equal proportions of trade union membership are identical. No comparable generalisation has been suggested using regional data.
3. There is nothing new in the allegation of trade union interference with the market forces that used to determine wages. At the end of Phillips's fitting period, one observer of the contemporary English labour market was writing that (unofficially translated)

   > It is of great interest to compare changes in the average wage rates of trade-union members with fluctuations in unemployment rates. Unemployment is . . . subject to considerable variation, but this has only a slight effect on wages. . . . This stability of wages despite variations in unemployment emphasises the recent change in the effects of the trade cycle, a change due above all to unionisation
   >
   > (Tugan-Baranowsky 1913: 336–8, passim).

   As in many literary discussions the dimensionality of the variables is not made clear, so it remains uncertain whether Tugan-Baranowsky anticipated Phillips, Hines, both or neither.
4. Compare the hypothesis suggested by Lipsey (1960) that unions 'kink' the Phillips curve, raising the response of wage inflation to excess demand and reducing the response to excess supply.
5. Applying the quotient rule, the time derivative of the real wage is given by

   $$\mathrm{d}/\mathrm{d}t\,(W/P) = \frac{P\cdot \mathrm{d}W/\mathrm{d}t - W\cdot \mathrm{d}P/\mathrm{d}t}{P^2}$$

   The proportionate rate of change of the real wage is therefore

   $$\frac{P}{W}\frac{\mathrm{d}}{\mathrm{d}t}\left(\frac{W}{P}\right) = \frac{\mathrm{d}W/\mathrm{d}t}{W} - \frac{\mathrm{d}P/\mathrm{d}t}{P} = w - p.$$

6. This change in the labour market has been variously attributed to an increase in the 'replacement ratio' of unemployment compensation to net average earnings in employment, an increase in the propensity of the unemployed to register, demographic changes in the structure of the labour force, or shifts in the composition of demand in the product market.
7. See Thomas's survey in this volume.
8. As Laidler (1970) and Vanderkamp (1972) pointed out, Solow's claim to have refuted the natural rate hypothesis was based on a significantly less than unit value of α in an equation of the form

$$p_e = g(w, \ldots) + \alpha p^e,$$

where p^e was constructed using the first method described in the text; however, one of the other arguments of Solow's equation was the rate of wage change, w, shown in g ( ) above, and since this would contain some effect of p^e through the wage equation, examination of α alone was inadequate.
9. This is close to the figure of 8.5 per cent which Solow claimed to have derived from an experiment with a non-linear response to anticipations, and which purports to answer the question: 'at what steady rate of inflation does this [non-linear] trade-off equation behave locally as if the strict expectations hypothesis were true?' (Solow 1969: 17). The expectational variable he used was defined as $(p^e - \bar{p}^e)^2$ with the same sign as $(p^e - \bar{p}^e)$, where the bar denotes the sample mean. This clearly cannot give an answer to the question posed by Solow, for it would take the value of zero at *any* steady rate of inflation.
10. Not surprisingly, in view of the paper's early date, insufficient information was provided for a formal hypothesis test.
11. See Chapter 6 of this volume for fuller discussion of this topic in its broader context.
12. The 'no change' response is interpreted by Carlson and Parkin as signifying an expected rate of price change which differs from zero by less than a psychological threshold of perception.
13. Strictly, that less than 0.5 per cent of the sample expected a fall.
14. The derived series itself is the expected inflation rate divided by the threshold of perception.
15. Formally

$$-\alpha = D'\,()\cdot \frac{W}{P_F} < 0$$

$$\beta = S'\,()\cdot \frac{W}{P_c} > 0$$

where the prime indicates differentiation with respect to time. The parameters α and β will be strictly constant only if the demand for and supply of labour are semi-logarithmic functions of the respective real wage.
16. The typical firm's output is less heterogeneous than the typical consumption bundle, so the costs of forming expectations are likely to differ. On the benefit side, consumers whose income consists wholly or mainly of state transfers have less incentive to form expectations than wage earners, who have some direct influence on wage rates and can in many cases exercise some choice of working hours.
17. Lengthening the estimation period meant that the expectational series had to be supplemented by drawing on actual inflation rates.

18. See Thompson's contribution to this volume for discussion of the general structure of these models.
19. The possibility that the optimal course would be to do nothing arises because the 'optimal' rate of inflation was discussed above, and in the literature, in an atemporal setting, without reference to the initial position of the economy. The superficial contradiction that it may be optimal not to attain the optimum merely reflects the unavoidable neglect of adjustment costs when economic policy is discussed in the abstract.
20. Nordhaus's formulation of the political business cycle assumes a continuing trade-off even in the long run, but little hinges on that assumption.
21. For instance Frey and Schneider (1978) report two popularity functions, differing only in dynamic structure, in which the reductions in the inflation rate required to compensate for an increase in unemployment differ by a factor of almost two, but pass no comment. In a later paper (Frey and Schneider 1981) the inflation rate is replaced in the popularity function by its first difference, with only a parenthetical (and inadequate) comment on the change. Pissarides (1980) sounds a more sceptical note, suggesting that variables recording the economic achievements of governments make little contribution to the forecasting performance of popularity functions.
22. Although controls are directed at the general price level they necessarily operate by influencing particular prices and wages, consequently changing relative prices and hence the allocation of resources. Advocates of controls respond, however, that it takes a myriad 'Harberger triangles', measuring the costs of resource misallocation, to fill an 'Okun gap' between actual and potential output. Whatever the validity of this casually empirical judgement, the main dispute has centred on the effectiveness of controls in attaining their primary target, rather than their unintended side effects.
23. This is the counterpart for the expectations-augmented Phillips curve of Phillips's own inference that the average inflation rate would be higher the greater the variance of unemployment around a given average level. Under the natural rate hypothesis, variability of aggregate demand raises the natural rate itself, not the average inflation rate, because an increase in the latter would destroy the equality of actual and anticipated inflation and thus shift the short-run Phillips curve upwards.

References

Archibald, G. C. (1969) The Phillips curve and the distribution of unemployment, *American Economic Review* (Papers and Proceedings) **59**, 124–34.

Archibald, G. C., Kemmiss, R. and Perkins, J. W. (1974) Excess demand for labour, unemployment and the Phillips curve, in Laidler, D. E. W. and Purdy, D. L. (eds), *Inflation and Labour Markets*, Manchester University Press and University of Toronto Press.

Artis, M. J. (1981) Is there a wage equation?, in Courakis, A. S. (ed.), *Inflation, Depression and Economic Policy in the West*, Mansell, London.

Baily, M. N. (1978) Stabilization policy and private economic behavior, *Brookings Papers on Economic Activity,* **1** : 1978, 11–50.

Batchelor, R. A. and Sheriff, T. D. (1980) Unemployment and unanticipated inflation in postwar Britain, *Economica,* N.S.**47**, 179–92.

Bispham, J. A. (1975) The new Cambridge and monetarist criticisms of conventional policy-making, *National Institute Economic Review,* **74**, 39–55.

Brechling, F. P. R. (1968) The trade-off between inflation and unemployment, *Journal of Political Economy,* **76**, 712–37.

Brechling, F. P. R. (1972) Some empirical evidence on the effectiveness of prices and incomes policies, in Parkin, M. and Sumner M. T. (eds), *Incomes Policy and Inflation,* Manchester University Press and University of Toronto Press.

Brittan, S. and Lilley, P. (1977) *The Delusion of Incomes Policy,* Temple Smith, London.

Brown, A. J. (1955) *The Great Inflation, 1939–1951*, Oxford University Press.

Burns, M. E. (1972) Regional Phillips curves: a further note, *Bulletin of the Oxford University Institute of Statistics,* **34**, 295–307.

Cagan, P. (1956) The monetary dynamics of hyperinflation, in Friedman, M. (ed.), *Studies in the Quantity Theory of Money*, Chicago University Press.

Carline, D. (1984) Trade unions and wages, in Millward, R., Sumner, M. T., and Zis, G. (eds), *Surveys of Labour Economics*, Longman, London.

Carlson, J. A. and Parkin, M. (1975) Inflation expectations, *Economica,* N.S.**42**, 123–38.

Christofides, L., Swidinsky, R. and Wilton, D. (1980) A microeconometric analysis of the Canadian wage determination process, *Economica,* N.S.**47**, 165–78.

Cowling, K. and Metcalf, D. (1967) Wage–unemployment relationships: a regional analysis for the U.K. 1960–1965, *Bulletin of the Oxford University Institute of Economics and Statistics,* **29**, 31–9.

Cross, R. B. and Laidler, D. E. W. (1976) Inflation, excess demand and expectations in fixed exchange rate open economies: some preliminary empirical results, in Parkin, M. and Zis, G. (eds), *Inflation in the World Economy*, Manchester University Press and University of Toronto Press.

Danes, M. (1975) The measurement and explanation of inflationary expectations in Australia, *Australian Economic Papers,* **19**, 75–87.

De Menil, G. and Bhalla, S. S. (1975) Direct measurement of popular price expectations, *American Economic Review,* **65**, 169–80.

Dicks-Mireaux, L. A. (1961) The inter-relationship between cost and price changes, 1945–1959: a study of inflation in postwar Britain, *Oxford Economic Papers,* N.S.**13**, 267–92.

Dogas, D. and Hines, A. G. (1975) Trade unions and wage inflation in the UK: a critique of Purdy and Zis, *Applied Economics,* **7**, 195–211.

Dornbusch, R. and Fischer, S. (1980) Sterling and the external balance, in Caves, R. E. and Krause, L. B. (eds), *Britain's Economic Performance*, The Brookings Institution, Washington D.C.

Dow, J. C. R. (1964) *The Management of the British Economy*, Cambridge University Press.

Dow, J. C. R. and Dicks-Mireaux, L. A. (1958) The excess demand for labour, *Oxford Economic Papers,* N.S.**10**, 1–33.

Duck, N. W., Parkin, M., Rose, D. and Zis, G. (1976) The determination of the rate of change of wages and prices in the fixed exchange rate world economy: 1956–1970, in Parkin, M. and Zis, G. (eds), *Inflation in the World Economy*, Manchester University Press.

Duck, N. W. and Zis, G. (1979) The natural rate hypothesis, policy rules, and fixed exchange rates, *Oxford Economic Papers,* N.S.**31**, 36–46.

Dunlop, J. T. (1938) The movement of real and money wage rates, *Economic Journal,* **48**, 413–34.

Eagly, R. V. (1965) Market power as an intervening mechanism in Phillips curve analysis, *Economica,* N.S.**32**, 48–64.

Fellner, W. (1979) The credibility effect and rational expectations, *Brookings Papers on Economic Activity,* 1979 : **1**, 167–78.

Fisher, I. (1926) A statistical relation between unemployment and price changes, *International Labor Review,* **13**, 185–92; reprinted in *Journal of Political Economy,* **81**, 496–502.

Flemming, J. (1976) *Inflation*, Oxford University Press.

Frey, B. S. and Schneider, F. (1978) A politico-economic model of the United Kingdom, *Economic Journal,* **88**, 243–53.

Frey, B. S. and Schneider, F. (1981) A politico-economic model of the UK: new estimates and predictions, *Economic Journal,* **91**, 737–40.

Friedman, M. (1966) The case against the case against guideposts: comments, in Schultz, G. P. and Aliber, R. Z. (eds), *Guidelines, Informal Controls, and the Market Place: Policy Choices in a Full Employment Economy*, University of Chicago Press.

Friedman, M. (1968) The role of monetary policy, *American Economic Review,* **58**, 1–17.

Friedman, M. (1969) *The Optimum Quantity of Money*, Aldine, Chicago, Illinois.

Friedman, M. (1977) *Inflation and Unemployment: The New Dimension of Politics,* Institute for Economic Affairs (Occasional Paper 51), London.

Frye, J. F. and Gordon, R. J. (1981) Government intervention in the inflation process: the econometrics of self-inflicted wounds, *American Economic Review* (Papers and Proceedings), **71**, 288–94.

Gilbert, C. L. (1976) The original Phillips curve estimates, *Economica*, N.S.**43**, 51–7.

Godfrey, L. (1971) The Phillips curve: incomes policy and trade union effects, in Johnson, H. G. and Nobay, A. R. (eds), *The Current Inflation*, Macmillan, London.

Gordon, R. J. (1971) Inflation in recession and recovery, *Brookings Papers on Economic Activity* 1971: **1**, 105–58.

Gordon, R. J. (1972) Wage-price controls and the shifting Phillips curve, *Brookings Papers on Economic Activity,* 1972: **2**, 385–421.

Gordon, R. J. (1975) The demand for and supply of inflation, *Journal of Law and Economics,* **18**, 807–36.

Gordon, R. J. (1976) Recent developments in the theory of inflation and unemployment, *Journal of Monetary Economics,* **2**, 185–220.

Gordon, R. J. (1980) A consistent characterization of a near-century of US price behavior, *American Economic Review* (Papers and Proceedings), **70**, 243–9.

Griffin, K. B. (1962) A note on wages, prices and unemployment, *Bulletin of the Oxford University Institute of Economics and Statistics,* **24**, 379–85.

Hamermesh, D. S. (1970) Wage bargains, threshold effects, and the Phillips curve, *Quarterly Journal of Economics,* **84**, 501–17.

Hargreaves Heap, S. P. (1980) Choosing the wrong 'natural' rate: accelerating inflation or decelerating employment and growth, *Economic Journal,* **90**, 611–20.

Henry, S. G. B. (1974) The Koyck transformation and adaptive expectations: a note, *Economica,* N.S.**41**, 79–80.

Henry, S. G. B. (1981) Incomes policy and aggregate pay, in Fallick, J. L. and Elliott, R. F. (eds), *Incomes Policies, Inflation and Relative Pay*, Allen and Unwin, London.

Henry, S. G. B. and Ormerod, P. A. (1978) Incomes policies and wage inflation: empirical evidence for the UK 1961–1977, *National Institute Economic Review,* **85**, 31–9.

Henry, S. G. B., Sawyer, M. C. and Smith, P. (1976) Models of inflation in the United Kingdom: an evaluation, *National Institute Economic Review,* **77**, 60–71.

Hibbs, D. A. and Fassbender, H. (1981) (eds), *Contemporary Political Economy*, North-Holland, Amsterdam.

Hines, A. G. (1964) Trade unions and wage inflation in the United Kingdom, 1893–1961, *Review of Economic Studies,* **31**, 221–52.

Hines, A. G. (1968) Unemployment and the rate of change of money wage rates in the United Kingdom 1862–1963: a reappraisal, *Review of Economics and Statistics,* **50**, 60–7.

Hines, A. G. (1969) Wage inflation in the United Kingdom 1948–1962: a disaggregated study, *Economic Journal,* **79**, 66–89.

Hines, A. G. (1971) The determinants of the rate of change of money wage rates and the effectiveness of incomes policy, in Johnson, H. G. and Nobay, A. R. (eds), *The Current Inflation*, Macmillan, London.

Holden, K. and Peel, D. A. (1977) An empirical investigation of inflationary expectations, *Oxford Bulletin of Economics and Statistics,* **39**, 291–9.

Kaldor, N. (1959) Economic growth and the problem of inflation, *Economica,* N.S.**26**, 212–26 and 287–98.

Kennedy, M. C. (1972) The economy as a whole, in Prest, A. R. and Coppock, D. J. (eds), *The UK Economy: A Manual of Applied Economics* (4th edition), Weidenfeld and Nicolson, London.

Klein, L. R. and Ball, R. J. (1959) Some econometrics of the determination of the absolute level of wages and prices, *Economic Journal,* **69**, 465–82.

Klein, L. R. and Goldberger, A. S. (1955) *An Econometric Model of the United States 1929–1952,* North-Holland, Amsterdam.

Knöbl, A. (1974) Price expectations and actual price behaviour in Germany, *IMF Staff Papers,* **21**, 83–100.

Knowles, K. G. J. C. and Winsten, C. B. (1959) Can the level of unemployment explain changes in wages?, *Bulletin of the Oxford University Institute of Economics and Statistics,* **21**, 113–20.

Kuh, E. (1967) A productivity theory of wage levels—an alternative to the Phillips curve, *Review of Economic Studies,* **34**, 333–60.

Laidler, D. E. W. (1970) Discussion of recent developments in monetary theory, in Croome, D. R. and Johnson, H. G. (eds), *Money in Britain 1959–1969,* Oxford University Press.

Laidler, D. E. W. (1981) Monetarism: an interpretation and an assessment, *Economic Journal,* **91**, 1–28.

Lipsey, R. G. (1960) The relationship between unemployment and the rate of change of money wage rates in the UK, 1862–1957: a further analysis, *Economica,* N.S.**27**, 1–31.

Lipsey, R. G. (1962) Can there be a valid theory of wages? *Advancement of Science,* **19**, 105–12; reprinted in McCormick, B. J. and Smith, E. O. (eds), *The Labour Market*, Penguin, Harmondsworth; and in Smyth, R. L. (ed.), *Essays in Modern Economic Development 1947–1967*, Duckworth, London.

Lipsey, R. G. and Parkin, M. (1970) Incomes policy: a reappraisal, *Economica,* N.S.**37**, 115–38.

Lipsey, R. G. and Steuer, M. D. (1961) The relation between profits and wage rates, *Economica,* N.S.**28**, 137–55.

MacKay, D. I. and Hart, R. A. (1974) Wage inflation and the Phillips relationship, *Manchester School,* **42**, 136–61.

Marin, A. (1972) The Phillips curve (born 1958—died ?), *The Three Banks Review,* **96**, 28–42.

McCallum, B. T. (1975) Rational expectations and the natural rate hypothesis: some evidence for the United Kingdom, *Manchester School,* **43**, 55–67.

Meade, J. E. (1938) *Consumers' Credits and Unemployment*, Oxford University Press.

National Board for Prices and Incomes (1968) *Third General Report,* Cmnd **3715**, HMSO, London.

Nordhaus, W. D. (1975) The political business cycle, *Review of Economic Studies,* **42**, 169–90.

Ormerod, P. (1979) The National Institute model of the UK economy: some current problems, in Ormerod, P. (ed.), *Economic Modelling*, Heinemann, London.

Parkin, M. (1970) Incomes policy: some further results on the rate of change of money wages, *Economica,* N.S.**37**, 386–401.

Parkin, M. and Smith, G. W. (1976) Inflationary expectations and the long-run trade-off between inflation and unemployment in open economies, in Parkin, M. and Zis, G. (eds), *Inflation in Open Economies*, Manchester University Press and University of Toronto Press.

Parkin, M., Sumner, M. T. and Jones, R. A. (1972) A survey of the econometric evidence of the effects of incomes policy on the rate of inflation, in Parkin, M. and Sumner, M. T. (eds), *Incomes Policy and Inflation*, Manchester University Press and University of Toronto Press.

Parkin, M., Sumner, M. T. and Ward, R. (1976) The effects of excess demand, generalized expectations and wage-price controls on wage inflation in the UK: 1956–71, in Brunner, K. and Meltzer, A. H. (eds), *The Economics of Price and Wage Controls*, Carnegie-Rochester Conference Series on Public Policy, 2, North-Holland, Amsterdam.

Pencavel, J. H. (1971) A note on the comparative predictive performance of wage inflation models of the British economy, *Economic Journal,* **81**, 113–9.

Perry, G. L. (1970) Changing labor markets and inflation, *Brookings Papers on Economic Activity,* 1970: **3**, 411–41.

Phelps, E. S. (1967) Phillips curves, expectations of inflation and optimal unemployment over time, *Economica,* N.S.**34**, 254–81.

Phelps, E. S. (1968) Money wage dynamics and labor market equilibrium, *Journal of Political Economy*, **76**, 678–711.

Phelps, E. S. (1972) *Inflation Policy and Unemployment Theory*, Macmillan, London.

Phillips, A. W. (1954) Stabilisation policy in a closed economy, *Economic Journal,* **64**, 290–323.

Phillips, A. W. (1958) The relationship between unemployment and the rate of change of money wage rates in the UK, 1861–1957, *Economica,* N.S.**25**, 283–99.

Pissarides, C. A. (1980) British government popularity and economic performance, *Economic Journal,* **90**, 569–81.

Posner, M. V. (1978) The search for common ground, in Posner, M. V. (ed.), *Demand Management,* Heinemann, London.

Purdy, D. L. and Zis, G. (1973) Trade unions and wage inflation in the UK: a reappraisal, in Parkin, M. (ed.), *Essays in Modern Economics*, Longman, London.

Purdy, D. L. and Zis, G. (1974) On the concept and measurement of trade union militancy, in Laidler, D. E. W. and Purdy, D. L. (eds), *Inflation and Labour Markets*, Manchester University Press and University of Toronto Press.

Purdy, D. L. and Zis, G. (1976) Trade unions and wage inflation in the UK: a reply to Dogas and Hines, *Applied Economics,* **8**, 249–65.

Rees, A. (1969) The Phillips curve as a menu for policy choice, *Economica,* N.S.**37**, 227–38.

Renton, G. A. (1975) (ed.), *Modelling the Economy*, Heinemann, London.

Robbins, L. (1934) *The Great Depression*, Macmillan, London.

Robertson, D. H. (1948) *Money* (revised edition), Cambridge Economic Handbooks, Nisbet, Welwyn, and Cambridge University Press.

Robertson, D. H. (1966) Creeping inflation, *Essays in Money and Interest*, Fontana (Collins), London: reprinted from Bulletin of the London and Cambridge Economic Service, *The Times Review of Industry*, 1955.

Routh, G. (1959) The relationship between unemployment and the rate of change of money wage rates in the UK, 1861–1957: a comment, *Economica*, N.S.**26**, 299–315.

Rowley, J. C. R. and Wilton, D. A. (1973) Quarterly models of wage determination: some new efficient estimates, *American Economic Review*, **63**, 380–9.

Samuelson, P. A. and Solow, R. M. (1960) Analytical aspects of anti-inflation policy, *American Economic Review*, (Papers and Proceedings), **50**, 177–94.

Sargan, J. D. (1964) Wages and prices in the United Kingdom, in Hart, P. E., Mills, G. and Whittaker, J. K. (eds), *Econometric Analysis for National Economic Planning*, Butterworth, London.

Sargan, J. D. (1971) A study of wages and prices in the UK, 1949–1968, in Johnson, H. G. and Nobay, A. R. (eds), *The Current Inflation*, Macmillan, London.

Sargan, J. D. (1980) A model of wage–price inflation, *Review of Economic Studies*, **47**, 97–112.

Sargent, T. J. (1971) A note on the 'accelerationist' controversy, *Journal of Money, Credit and Banking*, **3**, 721–5.

Smith, D. C. (1968) Incomes policy, in Caves, R. E. (ed.), *Britain's Economic Prospects*, The Brookings Institution, Washington D.C., and Allen and Unwin, London.

Smith, G. W. (1978) Producers' price and cost expectations, in Parkin, M. and Sumner, M. T. (eds), *Inflation in the United Kingdom*, Manchester University Press and University of Toronto Press.

Solow, R. M. (1969) *Price Expectations and the Behaviour of the Price Level*, Manchester University Press.

Sumner, M. T. (1972) Aggregate demand, price expectations and the Phillips curve, in Parkin, M. and Sumner, M. T. (eds), *Incomes Policy and Inflation*, Manchester University Press and University of Toronto Press.

Sumner, M. T. (1978) Wage determination, in Parkin, M. and Sumner, M. T. (eds), *Inflation in the United Kingdom*, Manchester University Press and University of Toronto Press.

Sumner, M. T. (1980) The operation of monetary targets, in Brunner, K. and Meltzer, A. H. (eds), *Monetary Institutions and the Policy Process*, Carnegie-Rochester Conference Series on Public Policy, 13, North-Holland, Amsterdam.

Sumner, M. T. and Ward, R. (1983) The Reappearing Phillips curve, *Oxford Economic Papers*, N.S.**35**, Special Issue on Unemployment, 152–66.

Sumner, M. T. and Zis, G. (1982) On the relative bias of flexible exchange rates, in Sumner, M. T. and Zis, G. (eds), *European Monetary Union: Progress and Prospects*, Macmillan, London.

Taylor, J. (1972) Incomes policy, the structure of unemployment and the Phillips curve: the United Kingdom experience, 1953–1970, in Parkin, M. and Sumner, M. T. (eds), *Incomes Policy and Inflation*, Manchester University Press and University of Toronto Press.

Taylor, L. D., Turnovsky, S. J. and Wilson, T. A. (1972) *The Inflationary Process in North American Manufacturing*, Prices and Incomes Commission, Information Canada, Ottawa.

Thirlwall, A. P. (1969) Demand disequilibrium in the labour market and wage rate inflation in the United Kingdom, *Yorkshire Bulletin of Economic and Social Research*, **21**, 65–76.

Thirlwall, A. P. (1970) Regional Phillips curves, *Bulletin of the Oxford Institute of Economics and Statistics,* **32**, 19–32.

Thomas, R. L. (1974) Wage inflation in the UK: a multi-market approach, in Laidler, D. E. W. and Purdy, D. L. (eds.), *Inflation and Labour Markets*, Manchester University Press and University of Toronto Press.

Thomas, R. L. and Stoney, P. J. M. (1971) Unemployment dispersion as a determinant of wage inflation in the United Kingdom 1925–1966, *Manchester School,* **39**, 83–116.

Tinbergen, J. (1933) An economic policy for 1936, reprinted (1959) in his *Selected Papers*, North-Holland, Amsterdam.

Tinbergen, J. (1951) *Business Cycles in the United Kingdom, 1870–1914,* North-Holland, Amsterdam.

Tobin, J. (1972) Inflation and unemployment, *American Economic Review,* **62**, 1–18.

Tobin, J. (1980) Stabilization policy ten years after, *Brookings Papers on Economic Activity,* 1980: **1**, 19–71.

Tugan-Baranowski, M. I. (1913) *Les Crises Industrielles en Angletarre*, Bibliothèque Internationale d'Economie Politique, Paris.

Turnovsky, S. J. (1970) Empirical evidence on the formation of price expectations, *Journal of the American Statistical Association,* **65**, 1441–54.

Turnovsky, S. J. (1972) The expectations hypothesis and the aggregate wage equation: some empirical evidence for Canada, *Economica,* N.S.**39**, 1–17.

Turnovsky, S. J. and Wachter, M. L. (1972) A test of the expectations hypothesis using directly observed wage and price expectations, *Review of Economies and Statistics,* **54**, 47–54.

Turvey, R. (1971) Some features of incomes policy and comments on the current inflation, in Johnson, H. G. and Nobay, A. R. (eds), *The Current Inflation*, Macmillan, London.

Vanderkamp, J. (1972) Wage adjustment, productivity and price change expectations, *Review of Economic Studies,* **39**, 61–72.

Wallis, K. F. (1971) Wages, prices and incomes policies: some comments, *Economica,* N.S.**38**, 304–10.

Ward, R. and Zis, G. (1974) Trade union militancy as an explanation of inflation: an international comparison, Manchester School, **42**, 44–65.

Wiles, P. (1973) Cost inflation and the state of economic theory, *Economic Journal,* **83**, 377–98.

CHAPTER SIX

The macroeconomic implications of the theory of rational expectations

David Demery and Nigel W. Duck

1. Introduction

There are a number of examples in economic theory of models in which the *expectation* held by economic agents of the value of an economic variable affects the actual *equilibrium* value of that variable. For instance, in microeconomic theory there is the well-known cobweb or 'corn-hog' cycle model in which, because of time lags in production, supply in any period is determined by expectations of that period's price formed in the previous period. Since demand is a function of the current price and since the market is assumed to clear, it follows that the expectation of price formed the period before contributes to the determination of the equilibrium or market clearing price of the good this period. Similarly, in macroeconomics, the Keynesian theory of the speculative demand for money makes the demand for money a function of, amongst other things, the expected rate of interest on bonds. A change in the expected interest rate will, *ceteris paribus*, change the demand for money and thereby bring about a new equilibrium interest rate. In conventional IS–LM terms, the change in the expected interest rate shifts the LM curve and produces a new intersection of the IS and LM curves.

More recently the role of expected inflation in determining actual inflation has been shown to be crucial. According to Friedman's (1968) statement of the natural rate of unemployment hypothesis, an increase in aggregate spending of say 10 per cent will, if its effects on inflation are fully anticipated, lead to prices rising by 10 per cent more than they otherwise would have done and no change in the time path of output; but if such effects are not anticipated then the initial impact on prices will be smaller and that on output larger.

In view of these examples–drawn from both micro- and macroeconomics –of the importance of expectations, a crucial and obvious question is: how do people typically form their expectations? To put that question another way: are there general principles which determine how people form their expectations regardless of which variable they are attempting to forecast?

Oddly enough, the development of economic theories about how people form their expectations has been slow, in fact until fairly recently almost non-existent. In place of developing a theory of expectations, economists have tended to use what seemed to them to be plausible 'rules of thumb' about how expectations are formed. So, for example, Keynes treated the expected interest rate on bonds as more or less a constant – a very simple expectation formation mechanism. Other economists have, when dealing with other problems, assumed more sophisticated mechanisms but ones which are nevertheless still difficult to justify by reference to conventional economic theory. The danger with this approach is that rules of thumb are, by their nature, appropriate only for particular circumstances. As long as there exists no theory about why people form their expectations in the way assumed, there is little hope of predicting how people will change their method of forming expectations as circumstances change.

The theory of rational expectations (RE) is an attempt to put the theory of expectations formation on a sounder base. It was originally put forward by Muth (1961) in the context of the corn-hog cycle mentioned above. At its simplest and most general it argues that when forming expectations, economic agents will use all the information available to them. It is a controversial area in modern macroeconomics, both because it assumes that agents possess what many consider to be an unrealistic amount of information, and because its application in macroeconomic theory is thought to have far-reaching implications for macroeconomic policy in particular and for the construction and estimation of macroeconomic models in general. As far as macroeconomic policy is concerned, the theory has been used to undermine orthodox Keynesian stabilisation policies, in which governments use monetary and fiscal policies in an attempt to minimise variations in 'real' variables like output and employment. Since many 'Western' governments have adopted these Keynesian policies in the post-war period, RE offers one explanation of the historical failure of orthodox Keynesian policies. The implications for the construction and estimation of macroeconomic models are that many existing models are seriously flawed and can provide little guide to the likely effects of changes in government policy.

To explain RE and its macroeconomic implications, to understand its attack on other expectation mechanisms and to outline and assess the criticisms levelled against it, we will first develop in section 2 a simple and, we hope, fairly familiar macroeconomic model in which expectations about the price level play an important role. At the end of that section we add to the model an apparently plausible (and certainly popular) mechanism by which expectations of the price level are formed and go on to outline the attack on that mechanism made by RE. In section 3 we state more fully the theory of RE and show the major implications of RE for macroeconomic policy. Section 4 considers the criticisms of RE and the validity of the macroeconomic policy implications usually derived from it. Section 5 considers the importance of RE for the building and estimation of macroeconomic models, and reviews the small but growing body of empirical evidence relevant to the theory of RE as applied to macroeconomics. We complete the survey with a summary and some conclusions.

2. Expectations in macroeconomic models

The model we use is common to many introductory texts in macroeconomics. It consists of two basic relationships: an aggregate demand curve relating the level of aggregate output demanded to the general price level; and an aggregate supply curve relating output supplied to the general price level. Jointly these two relationships determine the equilibrium price level and the level of output or income.

The aggregate demand curve is derived in the standard manner, as summarised in Chapter 2. It can be represented algebraically as:

$$y_t^d = \alpha_0 + \alpha_1 (m_t - p_t) + \alpha_2 g_t \qquad [1]$$

where y_t^d is the natural log of the level of aggregate demand in period t.
m_t is the natural log of the nominal money stock in period t.
g_t is the natural log of the level of real government expenditure in period t.
p_t is the natural log of the general price level in period t.
α_0, α_1 and α_2 are positive constants.

The specification of this relationship as linear in logs is essentially for convenience, the source of which is that the change in the log of a variable is a measure of the proportionate rate of change of that variable. Thus, for example, $p_t - p_{t-1}$ is a measure of the inflation rate.

In the derivation of aggregate supply in Chapter 2 employers were assumed to form correct price expectations but mistakes were made by workers in their expectations. In the derivation of aggregate supply that follows, a more general analysis is introduced in which all suppliers (of goods and labour) may form incorrect aggregate price expectations. The economy can be seen as consisting of a large number of separate markets in each of which price adjusts each period to equate supply and demand. Shifts of demand between markets occur continuously and thus relative prices are always or at least frequently changing. Superimposed on these *relative* price changes there are also *general* price changes due to changes in total demand. Given that information about prices in other markets is limited, an economic agent operating in any one market will find it difficult to tell whether a price rise for the good he produces is due to a relative shift in demand in favour of his good or to a rise in total demand and therefore all prices. Typically, however, a producer will respond differently to changes in his prices when all other prices are changing equally than to a relative price change, for if all prices have risen by the same percentage there is little or no reason for him to supply more output. It makes no difference to him whether his good sells for £1 and other goods on average for £2, or his good sells for £2 and other goods for £4. His real position is unaltered. But if the price rise is a relative one, then it may be worthwhile increasing output since the producer can now acquire other goods on better terms. The degree of response of output to a relative price change may be different depending upon whether the relative change is considered to be permanent or temporary (see Friedman 1976: 207), but the essential point for our purposes is clear enough. Suppliers respond differently to relative and general price changes, but cannot, because of limited information, always distinguish between the two. Hence they may *each* respond to a general rise in the price level as if it represented a relative increase in the price of their particular good. Since all agents are, on average, making the same mistake, aggregate output will rise above what it would have been. Thus a general price rise may well call forth an increase in aggregate supply. For this to happen the general price rise must be unexpected, for if it were not, then each supplier would see the price rise for his good as part of a tendency for all prices to rise and would not alter supply.

On the basis of this analysis we can write an aggregate supply curve in the following form:

$$y_t^s = \beta_0 + \beta_1 (p_t - E_{t-1} p_t) \quad [2]$$

where y_t^s is the log of the quantity of output supplied in period t.
$E_{t-1} p_t$ is the expectation formed at the end of period $t-1$ of the log of the general price level in period t.
β_0, β_1 are both positive constants.

This equation is merely a simple representation of the idea that a rise in the general price level which is unaccompanied by a similar rise in expectations of the price level will lead to a rise in output supplied. But if the actual and expected price levels are the same then output supplied will be equal to some positive number, β_0. We shall call this term β_0, the natural level of output. For simplicity we treat β_0 as a constant though in fact it is unlikely to be. For most economies it will grow over time and may well be influenced by a variety of government policies.

Diagrammatically we can represent this aggregate supply equation as an upward sloping relationship between p and y^s. The higher p, the higher y^s will be for *any given level of* $E_{t-1} p_t$. If p is on the vertical axis then a rise in $E_{t-1} p_t$ will shift the aggregate supply curve vertically upwards by the amount of the rise. Thus in Fig. 6.1 AS_0 is the aggregate supply curve based on $E_{t-1} p_t = p_0$, and AS_1 is the

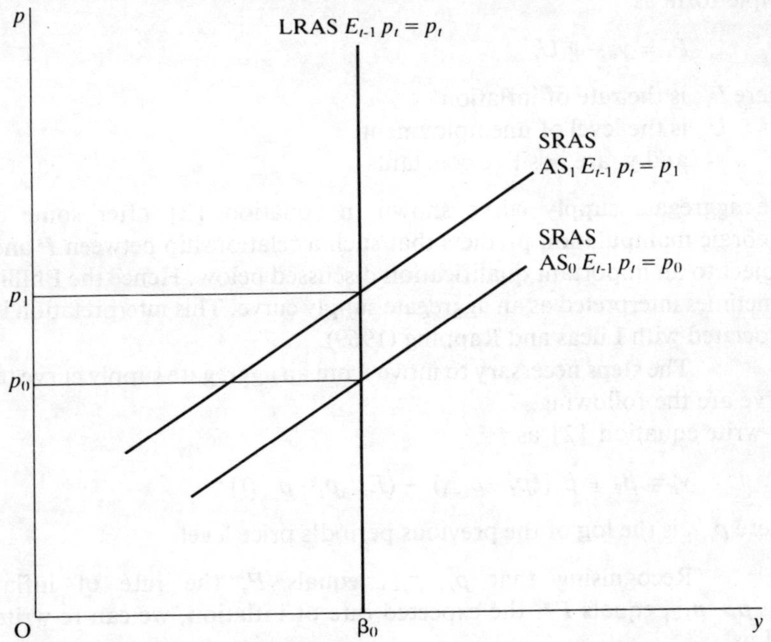

FIG. 6.1 Equilibrium output and price level

aggregate supply curve based on $E_{t-1}p_t = p_t$. The vertical distance between AS_0 and AS_1 at any point is $p_1 - p_0$. The aggregate supply curve we have just derived we shall call the short-run aggregate supply curve. We now define a long-run aggregate supply curve as showing the relationship between price and output supplied when expectations of the price level have had time to adjust so that they are correct: the long-run aggregate supply curve is drawn for $E_{t-1}p_t = p_t$. Clearly from equation [2] it follows that output supplied will be β_0 regardless of the level of prices. This is merely an implication of an earlier assumption: a fully expected price change has *no* effect on the level of output supplied. Diagrammatically the implication is that the long-run aggregate supply curve is vertical. The relationship between the short- and long-run aggregate supply curve is this: the short-run aggregate supply curve cuts the long-run aggregate supply curve at that price level which agents were assumed to be expecting in the construction of the short-run aggregate supply curve. Thus AS_0 cuts the long-run aggregate supply curve at p_0 and hence by assumption the value of $E_{t-1}p_t$ implicit in AS_0 must be p_0; AS_1 cuts the long-run aggregate supply curve at p_1 and hence by assumption the value of $E_{t-1}p_t$ implicit in AS_1 is p_1.

Before combining the aggregate supply and demand curves it might be helpful to show how the aggregate supply curve derived above is related to the Phillips curve. The latter, presented in a famous article by Phillips (1958) and discussed in Chapter 5, represents the idea that there exists a stable negative relationship between wage inflation and the level of unemployment. On the assumption that productivity growth is roughly constant and that price inflation equals wage inflation minus productivity growth, we can re-write the Phillips curve in simple form as

$$\dot{P}_t = \gamma_0 - \gamma_1 U_t \qquad [3]$$

where $\dot{P}_t$ is the rate of inflation
U_t is the level of unemployment
γ_0 and γ_1 are positive constants

The aggregate supply curve shown in equation [2] after some elementary algebraic manipulation predicts that such a relationship between $\dot{P}$ and U exists, subject to an important qualification discussed below. Hence the Phillips curve is sometimes interpreted as an aggregate supply curve. This interpretation is primarily associated with Lucas and Rapping (1969).

The steps necessary to move from an aggregate supply curve to a Phillips curve are the following.
Re-write equation [2] as

$$y_t^s = \beta_0 + \beta_1[(p_t - p_{t-1}) - (E_{t-1}p_t - p_{t-1})] \qquad [4]$$

where p_{t-1} is the log of the previous period's price level.

Recognising that $p_t - p_{t-1}$ equals $\dot{P}$, the rate of inflation, and $E_{t-1}p_t - p_{t-1}$ equals $\dot{P}^e$, the expected rate of inflation, we can re-write equation [4] as

$$y_t^s = \beta_0 + \beta_1(\dot{P} - \dot{P}^e) \qquad [5]$$

Next from Okun's law (see Okun 1970) we might expect there to be a negative relationship between deviations of the actual unemployment rate from its natural level and deviations of the actual level of output supplied from its natural level. We assume a simple form for this relationship:

$$U_t - U_t^N = \gamma_2(y_t^s - \beta_0) \qquad [6]$$

where U_t and U_t^N are the actual and the natural rates of unemployment respectively.
γ_2 is a negative coefficient.

From equation [5] it follows that we can write equation [6] as

$$U_t = U_t^N + \gamma_2\beta_1(\dot{P} - \dot{P}^e) \qquad [7]$$

or

$$\dot{P} = \frac{U_t}{\gamma_2\beta_1} - \frac{U_t^N}{\gamma_2\beta_1} + \dot{P}^e \qquad [8]$$

This relationship is clearly similar to the Phillips curve shown in equation [3]. For equation [8] suggests that since γ_2 is negative and β_1 positive there will be a negative relationship between $\dot{P}$ and U, *provided that expected inflation and the natural rate of unemployment remain constant*. Notice that equation [8] predicts that the Phillips curve will be shifted upwards by increases in expected inflation.

Putting the aggregate supply and demand curves onto the same diagram allows us to determine the equilibrium level of output and the general price level. Since we have two aggregate supply curves – a long run and a short run – we can also distinguish between a long-run and short-run equilibrium.

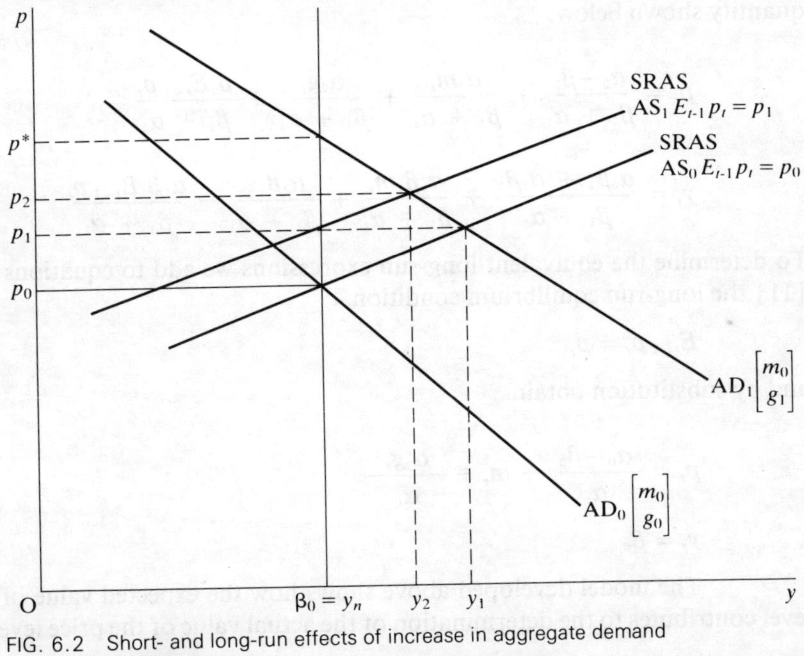

FIG. 6.2 Short- and long-run effects of increase in aggregate demand

If the aggregate demand curve is at AD_0 as in Fig. 6.2, and if $E_{t-1}p_t = p_0$, then a short-run and long-run equilibrium price level of p_0 is determined and output is at its natural level of y_n ($= \beta_0$). The equilibrium is long run in the sense that there are no forces within the system which would lead to any change in the position of any of the curves. If however the AD curve was, because of say an increase in government expenditure from g_0 to g_1, to shift to AD_1, whilst expectations of the price level remained at p_0 then a new equilibrium would be generated. The price level would rise to p_1, and the equilibrium level of output would rise to y_1. But this is a short-run equilibrium only. For the actual price level is now above the expected one, i.e. p_1 as against p_0. Hence one would expect the anticipated price level to rise, eventually to p_1. When it has done so the short-run aggregate supply curve will shift up to cut the long-run AS curve at p_1. The effect of this will be to reduce output and raise price to y_2 and p_2 respectively. The actual price level will still be above the expected one and so once again this new equilibrium will only be a short-run one. The new long-run equilibrium is at p^* and y_n. Here the actual price level is at its expected value and thus output is at its natural level. Notice that if the ultimate effect of the shift in aggregate demand had been fully and immediately anticipated, the short-run aggregate supply curve would immediately have shifted up to cut the long-run AS curve at p^*. The effect of the shift in demand on the general price level would have been to increase it immediately to p^*. There would be no effect on output in this case, even in the short run.

The algebra of these diagrammatic results is given by adding to equations [1] and [2] the equilibrium condition

$$y_t^s = y_t^d \qquad [9]$$

and thereby deriving the two equations for the short-run equilibrium price and quantity shown below.

$$p_t = \frac{\alpha_0 - \beta_0}{\beta_1 + \alpha_1} + \frac{\alpha_1 m_t}{\beta_1 + \alpha_1} + \frac{\alpha_2 g_t}{\beta_1 + \alpha_1} + \frac{\beta_1 E_{t-1} p_t}{\beta_1 + \alpha_1} \qquad [10]$$

$$y_t = \frac{\alpha_0 \beta_1 + \alpha_1 \beta_0}{\beta_1 + \alpha_1} + \frac{\alpha_1 \beta_1 m_t}{\beta_1 + \alpha_1} + \frac{\alpha_2 \beta_1 g_t}{\beta_1 + \alpha_1} - \frac{\alpha_1 \beta_1 E_{t-1} p_t}{\beta_1 + \alpha_1} \qquad [11]$$

To determine the equivalent long-run expressions we add to equations [10] and [11] the long-run equilibrium condition

$$E_{t-1} p_t = p_t \qquad [12]$$

and by substitution obtain

$$p_t = \frac{\alpha_0 - \beta_0}{\alpha_1} + m_t + \frac{\alpha_2 g_t}{\alpha_1} \qquad [13]$$

$$y_t = \beta_0 \qquad [14]$$

The model developed above shows how the expected value of the price level contributes to the determination of the actual value of the price level. But the model is silent on the question of how expectations of the price level are formed. A common, apparently plausible and empirically useful assumption is that such expectations are formed *adaptively*. That is, the expected value of the price level changes by some fraction of previous periods' mistakes. Formally we can write a simple version as

$$E_{t-1}p_t - E_{t-2}p_{t-1} = \lambda(p_{t-1} - E_{t-2}p_{t-1}) \qquad [15]$$

The left-hand side of this equation is the change in the expected value of the price level; the right-hand side is a fraction, λ, of the difference between the previous period's actual price and that which economic agents typically were expecting it to be at the end of period $t-2$.

At first sight this seems quite a plausible idea since it implies that if the price level jumps from, say, 1.00 to 2.00 economic agents gradually 'home in' on the new value. The speed with which they do so depends upon the coefficient λ. If λ is 1.00 then they home in quickly–in fact in one period; if λ is less then the homing-in process is more drawn out.

An additional attractive feature of this expectations formation mechanism is that when it is combined with the AS/AD model it can contribute to an explanation of a common feature of mixed economies: the tendency for them to exhibit cyclical movements in real variables, or booms and slumps. Consider a very simple case of adaptive expectations in which λ assumes a value of 1.00 so that $E_{t-1}p_t = p_{t-1}$; thus the typical forecast of this period's price is that it will equal last period's. Under these assumptions a process similar to the one described in Fig. 6.2 will occur as aggregate demand shifts from AD_0 to AD_1. Output will rise to y_1 and price to p_1. Then output will slowly drop back to its normal level; this process though will be drawn out, and whilst it is occurring output will be above its natural level; that is, the economy will be experiencing a boom. A fall in AD from AD_0 would by a similar sort of argument trace out a slump. Of course the expectations mechanism does not by itself explain the initial shifts in aggregate demand but it does provide one explanation of how, once such shifts occur, they lead to drawn-out booms and slumps. Another explanation might be that expectations are constant whilst those variables affecting the position of the AD curve fluctuate cyclically.

However, that characteristic of adaptive expectations which helps explain booms and slumps is also a weakness which, according to RE is fundamental. To see what this weakness is, consider, with the help of Fig. 6.3, the pattern of errors in forecast brought about by the shift in aggregate demand from AD_0 to AD_1 when the adaptive expectations mechanism developed above (with λ equal to 1.00) is assumed. The initial expectation is $E_0p_1 = p_0$; the actual price level after the shift to AD_1 is p_1 so the forecast error is $p_1 - p_0$. The expectation formed in period 1 of price in period 2 (E_1p_2) is by assumption p_1 since that was the price in period 1. The actual price in period 2 is p_2 so the forecast error is $p_2 - p_1$. Both errors, $p_1 - p_0$ and $p_2 - p_1$, are positive–the actual value is always higher than the expected value. If we considered each step in the process as the price level converges on its new equilibrium p^* then we would observe a continuous string of positive errors, given our assumption about how expectations are formed. This is

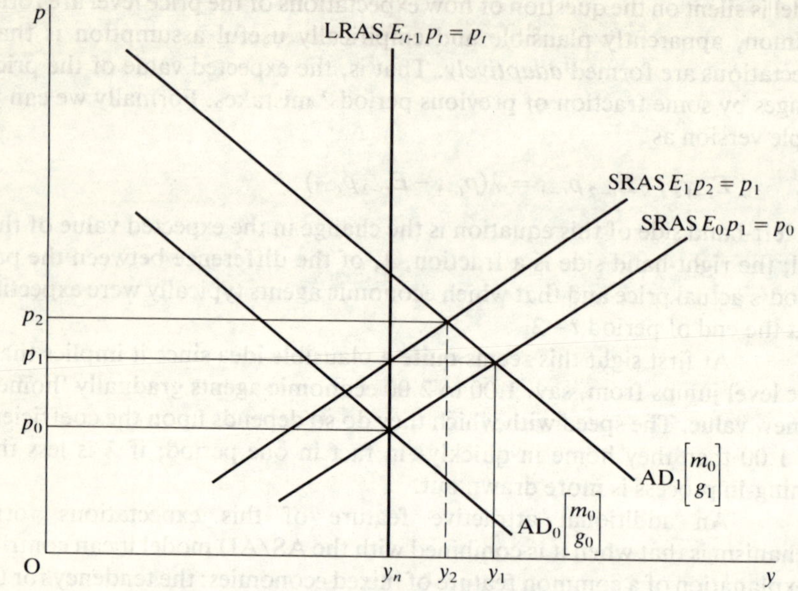

FIG. 6.3 Price and output movements under adaptive expectations

an uncomfortable result, implying as it does that economic agents make systematic errors, i.e. errors which follow an obvious pattern, without this causing them to change their forecasting methods. This seems all the more implausible when it is recognised that economic agents collect information on past errors costlessly–they do so as a side effect of buying goods. Since it is costless, economic theory suggests that economic agents will use it fully to obtain the benefits it brings them in terms of better forecasts. Thus, at the very least, the adaptive expectations mechanism cannot be regarded as stable, for as soon as the systematic pattern of errors it produces becomes clear, the method of forming expectations is likely to change. As a consequence, it may be foolish to frame government monetary and fiscal policy on the assumption that people will persistently form expectations by a stable adaptive mechanism. Consider, for example, a government whose aim is to maintain a high level of output and whose macroeconomic policy consists of a commitment to boost aggregate demand by say 10 per cent every time output reaches y^n. Starting from an initial equilibrium as before aggregate demand rises from AD_0 to AD_1 in Fig. 6.4. If expectations are formed in the simple adaptive way assumed previously then the economy will home in on a new equilibrium of $p_1^*\,y_n$ and of course a systematic pattern of forecast errors will occur. As soon as y^n is reached the government boosts aggregate demand again to say AD_2. If the adaptive expectation mechanism remains unchanged the government will again secure a higher level of output albeit at the expense of a further rise in prices. But it seems unlikely that the expectations mechanism will continue unchanged for long. One possibility is that in the face of continuing rises in prices the expectations mechanism will 'change gear', as Fleming (1976) puts it.[1] In the case at hand people, after the experience of the rise in

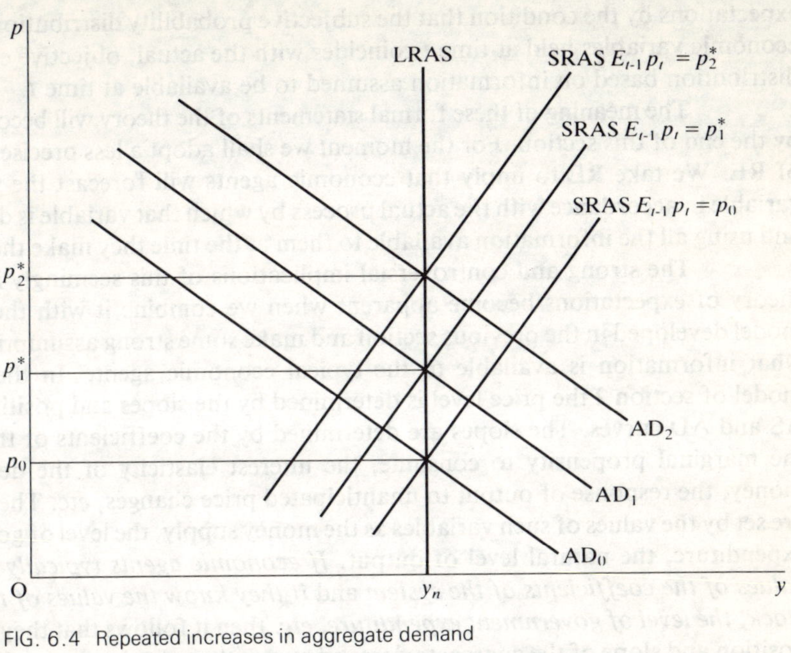

FIG. 6.4 Repeated increases in aggregate demand

prices caused by the shift in aggregate demand from AD_0 to AD_1, may begin to form expectations on the *rate of change* of prices rather than the *level*. If they do then the short-run aggregate supply curve (SRAS $E_{t-1}p_t = p_1^*$) will shift up simultaneously with the shift in aggregate demand from AD_1 to AD_2. The exact size of the shift, and hence the new equilibrium level of output, depends upon how much inflation people anticipate. Alternatively, if economic agents have realised what government policy is and therefore anticipate the position of the new aggregate demand curve AD_2 then they may realise quickly that the price level is going to rise to p_2^*, come to expect that price level immediately and thereby annul the effects on real output of government aggregate demand policies. The RE hypothesis builds on this idea that economic agents will not make mistakes which are systematic and contain easily correctable biases. We turn now to a detailed consideration of the theory of rational expectations.

3. Rational expectations

The theory of RE can be stated in a number of different ways. The concept of RE was formally introduced by Muth (1961), who hypothesised that the mean expectation of firms with respect to a variable, e.g. price, was equal to the prediction that would be made by the relevant and correct economic theory. More generally and more formally, Shiller (1978) has characterised rationally formed expectations of future variables at time t as 'true mathematical expectations of future variables conditional on all variables in the model which are known to the public at time t (p.3). More formally still, Lucas and Prescott (1974) defined rational expectations by the condition that the subjective probability distribution of future economic variables held at time t coincides with the actual, objective conditional distribution based on information assumed to be available at time t.

The meaning of these formal statements of the theory will become clearer by the end of this section. For the moment we shall adopt a less precise statement of RE. We take RE to imply that economic agents will forecast the value of a variable in accordance with the actual process by which that variable is determined and using all the information available to them at the time they make the forecast.

The strong and controversial implications of this seemingly innocuous theory of expectations become apparent when we combine it with the AS–AD model developed in the previous section and make some strong assumptions about what information is available to the typical economic agent.[2] In the AS–AD model of section 2 the price level is determined by the slopes and positions of the AS and AD curves. The slopes are determined by the coefficients of the system: the marginal propensity to consume, the interest elasticity of the demand for money, the response of output to unanticipated price changes, etc. The positions are set by the values of such variables as the money supply, the level of government expenditure, the natural level of output. *If economic agents typically know the values of the coefficients of the system* and *if they know the values of the money stock, the level of government expenditure, etc.* then it follows that they know the position and slope of the aggregate demand curve; they also know the slope of the short-run aggregate supply curve and the position of the long-run aggregate supply curve. With that knowledge the only variable left for them to infer is their own expected price level. But it will only make sense for them to expect a price level, which, together with all their other knowledge, will generate an actual price level equal to the one they are expecting. So, for example, starting from an initial equilibrium of p_0, y_n as shown above in Fig. 6.4 a shift in the aggregate demand curve from AD_0 to AD_1 occurs. Economic agents know the new position of the aggregate demand curve and, of course, the position of the long-run aggregate supply curve. The only sensible price level for them to expect is p_1^*. If they expect any other price level they will *knowingly* make a mistake, which cannot be rational. But if they do form an expectation such that $E_{t-1}p_t = p_t^*$ then, of course, the short-run aggregate supply curve cuts the long-run aggregate supply curve at p_1^*. It follows that the increase in aggregate demand is fully and immediately absorbed by a rise in price. There is no effect on real output. Essentially the assumption of rational expectations has *in this model* made irrelevant the distinction between the short and long run: the 'long-run' result occurs instantly.

The major policy implication is that the government's aggregate demand policies will, if they are known by economic agents, have no effect on real variables like output and unemployment; all their effects will be on the price level. It is this implication more than any other which makes RE so controversial, since it seems to imply that traditional Keynesian stabilisation policy (essentially the manipulation of monetary and fiscal policy to offset changes in private sector demand in pursuance of a target value for a real variable like output) is doomed to failure. For if it is known that because of the state of the economy the government is about to boost aggregate demand, economic agents will anticipate this boost and such anticipations will, as we have seen, neutralise any effect of such a policy on real variables. Therefore, if the policy being pursued by a government (i.e. the 'policy regime') forms part of the information possessed by (i.e. the 'information set' of) economic agents, then policy cannot be used either to achieve a level of output above y_n or to minimise any variation around y_n. RE has therefore been taken as implying support for the sort of approach to macroeconomic aggregate demand policies advocated by, amongst others, Friedman (1959). This emphasises the need for governments to eschew attempts to fine-tune the economy in the traditional Keynesian manner and urges the replacement of such policies by some simple predetermined rules for monetary and fiscal policy. RE has also been taken by some as suggesting that policies to cure inflation may be much quicker acting and less socially harmful than previously thought. For if people form their expectations in accordance with government monetary and fiscal policy then the mere announcement of monetary and fiscal restraint will, provided it is widely believed, reduce inflationary expectations and thereby reduce inflation without any accompanying rise in unemployment or loss of output. Hence RE has been taken to justify quite severe policies of monetary and fiscal contraction to cure inflation–policies which critics of RE consider would have extremely harmful effects on output and unemployment. We shall consider this implication more fully later.

Before looking at the more serious objections to RE as applied to macroeconomics we must first dispel one or two obvious objections. This will allow us to present RE and its policy implications more fully and in the more subtle form in which the RE theorists present them. At the same time, we shall clarify the more formal statements of RE made at the beginning of this section.

The first objection is that the model we have developed above, when combined with RE, suggests that there are *never* any divergencies between actual output and the natural or normal level of output. For such divergencies arise as a result of unanticipated changes in aggregate demand which, under RE and the model as we have specified it, are ruled out. So, given our model and RE, all variations in real output (for example, the Great Depression in the United States) would have to be interpreted as movements in the normal or natural level of output. But even if an explanation for such movements was forthcoming (and it would have to be more convincing than the 'contagious laziness' explanation pilloried by Modigliani 1977), there would still be a problem. For if all movements in real output are due to shifts in the position of the long-run aggregate supply curve, then, as the model developed above shows, prices should rise or rise faster when output falls, and should fall or rise more slowly when output rises. But the evidence from a number of countries suggests very strongly that precisely the opposite happens. Prices and output tend to move together: prices rise faster as output increases and more slowly as output falls. The explanation of movements in real output as the result of shifts in the natural rate would also produce a prediction that interest rates move countercyclically, falling as output rises and rising as output falls. In simple IS–LM terms the fall in the price level caused by the rise in output shifts the LM curve to the right, generating an intersection with the IS curve at a lower interest rate. This prediction, too, is generally refuted by the evidence: interest rates, particularly short-term interest rates, tend to move procyclically. (See Lucas

1977 for a discussion of these empirical regularities.) Thus the model developed above cannot, when combined with RE, provide an explanation for some of the most strongly confirmed empirical regularities in macroeconomics.

The answer to this empirical objection is a simple one. The model developed above was, for simplicity, a *deterministic* one. It is a model in which all the specified relationships were assumed to hold precisely. In the real world such relationships are best viewed as being *stochastic,* ones that are subject to error which we assume to be random with mean or average value of zero. There are a number of reasons why economic relationships might best be treated as stochastic. First, it may be that although we could in theory obtain all the information necessary to explain a variable precisely, in practice the acquisition of such information is impossible, perhaps because the necessary information is not quantifiable. Second, there may be a certain inherent randomness in human behaviour anyway. Whatever the reason for relationships being stochastic in nature, the main implication for our purposes is the same: the aggregate demand curve is best thought of as being subject to random and therefore by definition unpredictable movements. Economic agents can only, even under the assumptions of RE, predict the systematic or non-random movements in aggregate demand. The best prediction that can be made of the value of a random variable at any particular moment is that it will equal its mean value. In our case this value is zero. Thus any non-zero random shift in aggregate demand will have the usual effects of any unanticipated movement in aggregate demand: an unexpected random increase will move the economy up a short-run aggregate supply curve, inducing a simultaneous rise in price and output. The observed data on prices and output are not inconsistent (on the grounds so far specified anyway) with RE and the AS/AD model, so long as that model is viewed as stochastic.

Once the stochastic nature of the model is recognised, the meaning of RE and the implications of RE for macroeconomic policy can be more fully explained. RE does *not* imply that economic agents are always correct in their forecasts, but rather that the forecast errors they make are random with mean zero. Only the systematic movements in, say, aggregate demand can be predicted by rational agents; the random components cannot be. Forecasting errors will therefore occur, but by their nature will be random with mean zero.

Only if a variable is itself free from random influences does RE suggest that economic agents will forecast it with perfect accuracy. In the more general, realistic case where random influences are present, RE suggests that economic agents will be correct only on average; in any single period they can either over- or under-estimate aggregate demand, say, and hence price. Of course the pattern of errors thus produced cannot contain any systematic element and thereby make RE vulnerable to the same objection as that raised against adaptive expectations in the previous section. If such a systematic pattern was present it would be predictable and therefore predicted by rational agents, leaving only the purely random component of the error to influence output and employment.

The implications of RE for macroeconomic policy can also be more fully stated now that the stochastic nature of the economy is recognised. Any systematic linking of a policy instrument (like the money stock or the level of government expenditure) to a variable whose value is known by economic agents (like unemployment in the previous period) will fail to produce any variation of output around its natural rate. If the policy instrument is being determined in this systematic way, the rational economic agent will form his expectation of its value in a way that is consistent with that process and predict it. Any movements of the aggregate demand curve which are due to such systematic movements in government policy will themselves be systematic and therefore predicted. But as we have already shown, such predicted movements of the aggregate demand curve will only affect price and will have no effect on the level of output.

Random movements in policy instruments and therefore the aggregate demand curve still influence the level of output and in the usual way: they produce unanticipated movements in the price level. But there seems little point in a government deliberately introducing randomness into its policy instruments, for such randomness can only by chance push real variables in their desired direction; it is just as likely that it will push them in the wrong direction. Such deliberate introduction of randomness into the behaviour of, say, unemployment is impossible to justify and is certainly not the objective of those who advocate fine-tuning of the economy.

Thus the attack made by RE on the traditional approach to macroeconomic policy and the theoretical support provided by RE for the main alternative strategy of policy by simple predetermined rules both survive the introduction of randomness into the macroeconomic model. Fine-tuning of the economy can at best do no better than policy according to simple rules and might, if it increases the unpredictability of policy instruments, actually make things worse in the sense of increasing the variance of output around its natural rate.

To show these results formally we make use of equations [1], [2], [9]–[14], but introduce a stochastic or random element into the equations. For illustrative purposes we shall assume that the government controls its own expenditure perfectly precisely and announces the level of g_t in period $t-1$ so its value is known. The money stock on the other hand is subject to stochastic change. To be precise we specify the process by which the money stock is determined as follows:

$$m_t = \mu_0 + \mu_1 X_{t-1} + \varepsilon_t \qquad [16]$$

where μ_1 is a row vector of coefficients
μ_0 is a coefficient
X is a vector (or set) of variables whose lagged values influence the current money stock
ε_t is a random error term with mean zero and variance σ^2_ε

This equation is a formal statement that the money stock at time period t is related in a systematic way to a set of predetermined variables, X_{t-1}, plus a random component, ε_t. The variables in X_{t-1} might include unemployment rates, inflation, etc. as well as lagged values of m_t itself. The presence of the former might be taken as being due to government attempts to fine-tune the economy, e.g. increasing the money stock when unemployment is high.

Combining this equation with equations [10] and [11] we obtain the following expressions for p_t and y_t.

$$p_t = \frac{\alpha_0 - \beta_0 + \alpha_1\mu_0}{\beta_1 + \alpha_1} + \frac{\alpha_1\mu_1 X_{t-1}}{\beta_1 + \alpha_1} + \frac{\alpha_2 g_t}{\beta_1 + \alpha_1} + \frac{\beta_1 E_{t-1} p_t}{\beta_1 + \alpha_1} + \frac{\alpha_1 \varepsilon_t}{\beta_1 + \alpha_1} \quad [17]$$

$$y_t = \frac{\alpha_0\beta_1 + \alpha_1\beta_0 + \alpha_1\beta_1\mu_0}{\beta_1 + \alpha_1} + \frac{\alpha_1\beta_1\mu_1 X_{t-1}}{\beta_1 + \alpha_1} + \frac{\alpha_2\beta_1 g_t}{\beta_1 + \alpha_1} - \frac{\alpha_1\beta_1 E_{t-1} p_t}{\beta_1 + \alpha_1} + \frac{\alpha_1\beta_1\varepsilon_t}{\beta_1 + \alpha_1} \quad [18]$$

To explain the more formal statements of RE given at the beginning of this section: equation [17] shows the actual, objective conditional distribution of p_t. It shows how p_t *actually* is determined. The rational expectation of p_t must coincide with it, subject only to the qualification that the actual value of ε_t is unknown. The expected value of ε_t, which is the best guess that can be made, is zero. It follows that under rational expectations

$$E_{t-1} p_t = E_{t-1}\left[\frac{\alpha_0 - \beta_0 + \alpha_1\mu_0}{\beta_1 + \alpha_1} + \frac{\alpha_1\mu_1 X_{t-1}}{\beta_1 + \alpha_1} + \frac{\alpha_2 g_t}{\beta_1 + \alpha_1} + \frac{\beta_1 E_{t-1} p_t}{\beta_1 + \alpha_1}\right] \quad [19]$$

But since the α's and β's and μ's are assumed known; since X_{t-1} and g_t are also assumed to be part of the available information set; and since the expected value of the expected value of a variable, $E_{t-1}(E_{t-1} p_t)$, must equal the expected value of that variable, $E_{t-1} p_t$, we can re-write equation [19] as:

$$E_{t-1} p_t = \frac{\alpha_0 - \beta_0 + \alpha_1\mu_0}{\beta_1 + \alpha_1} + \frac{\alpha_1\mu_1 X_{t-1}}{\beta_1 + \alpha_1} + \frac{\alpha_2 g_t}{\beta_1 + \alpha_1} + \frac{\beta_1 E_{t-1} p_t}{\beta_1 + \alpha_1} \quad [20]$$

Solving this expression for $E_{t-1} p_t$ gives

$$E_{t-1} p_t = \frac{\alpha_0 - \beta_0 + \alpha_1\mu_0}{\alpha_1} + \mu_1 X_{t-1} + \frac{\alpha_2}{\alpha_1} g_t \quad [21]$$

This is the rational expectation of p_t. Substituting this expression back into equations [17] and [18] and solving for p_t and y_t yields

$$p_t = \frac{\alpha_0 - \beta_0 + \alpha_1\mu_0}{\alpha_1} + \mu_1 X_{t-1} + \frac{\alpha_2 g_t}{\alpha_1} + \frac{\alpha_1 \varepsilon_t}{\beta_1 + \alpha_1} \quad [22]$$

$$y_t = \beta_0 + \frac{\alpha_1\beta_1\varepsilon_t}{\beta_1 + \alpha_1} \quad [23]$$

All the implications of RE derived less formally in the text can be illustrated formally from equations [22] and [23].

First, once a stochastic element is introduced into the model output can deviate from its natural level. The extent to which it does so is dependent upon the size of the stochastic error in the money supply process and on the coefficients of the system. For example, the more reponsive aggregate demand is to change in the money stock (i.e. the higher is α_1), or the more responsive aggregate supply is to unanticipated price movements (i.e. the higher is β_1), the greater is the response of real output to a random change in the money stock.

Second, a positive value for ε_t (i.e. a positive monetary 'surprise') causes a positive movement in both p and y, thus making the model consistent with the observed behaviour of p and y over the business cycle. This result follows from the assumption that α_1 and β_1 are both positive, and hence the coefficients attached to ε_t in the p and y equations must both be positive.

Third, although errors in forecasts of the price level do occur, these errors are not systematic but random in nature. This can most readily be seen by subtracting equation [21] from equation [22] to obtain the forecasting error $p_t - E_{t-1}p_t$. It is $\alpha_1\varepsilon_t/(\beta_1 + \alpha_1)$ which, by definition of ε_t, is random. It is also clearly independent of any variable whose value the economic agent is aware of at the time he makes the forecast. This property is sometimes called error orthogonality.

Fourth and more important, the systematic component of the money stock, i.e. that related to X_{t-1}, cannot be used to set a level of real output different from y_n. This is clearly shown by the absence of terms in X_{t-1} from the output equation. Only the random component of the money supply process, ε_t, enters that equation.

A fifth result mentioned in the text–that systematic monetary or fiscal policy cannot influence the *variance of output* around its natural level–is also immediately clear from the absence of terms in X_{t-1} from the output equation.[3]

A second objection frequently voiced against the combination of RE and the sort of macroeconomic model we have put forward is that even in its stochastic form the resulting model cannot explain the tendency for booms and slumps to be drawn out or persistent. More formally, it cannot explain why movements in real variables are *serially correlated*. In section 2 we showed that it was an attractive feature of adaptive expectations that it could, when combined with a suitable macroeconomic model, explain why any initial rise in aggregate demand would cause output to be above its natural rate, not only in the period in which the rise in demand occurs but in subsequent periods too. Since, in the real world, we do tend to observe such serial correlation in real variables like output and employment, it is a necessary feature of any satisfactory model of the macroeconomy that it can account for such movements. As it stands the stochastic AS/AD model developed above cannot be combined with RE to produce a complete model which has this necessary feature. It explains deviations of output from its natural rate as due to random unpredictable shifts in aggregate demand; but in that model these random shifts in aggregate demand will produce similarly random shifts in output. This is clear from equation [23] where the random component of the money stock enters the output equation. So the model as developed so far predicts random, serially uncorrelated movements in real variables, and is therefore at odds with the empirical evidence. However, this criticism can be easily overcome. For as Lucas and Sargent (1978) point out, it is based on a failure to distinguish properly between 'sources of impulses' and 'propagation mechanisms'. It is quite possible to incorporate propagation mechanisms which convert serially uncorrelated or random forecast errors of aggregate demand (the sources of impulses) into serially correlated movements in real output and employment, etc. Indeed, a number of admittedly more complicated macroeconomic models already exist in the literature containing propagation mechanisms which perform just this function. The distinction between sources of impulses and propagation mechanisms is emphasised in a paper by Frisch written in 1933 (see Frisch 1965).

Perhaps the intuitively most appealing mechanism is provided by Blinder and Fischer (1981). In their model an unexpected rise in demand is met partly by greater production and partly by the running down of stocks of goods. If firms have an optimal or desired level of stocks, they will want to replenish them following the run down. To do so they will have to run production at a higher level than they otherwise would. Thus production in some subsequent periods (depending upon how quickly firms rebuild stocks) will be affected by an unexpected one-period rise in demand. The desire to replenish stocks of goods is the 'propagation mechanism' by which a one period (and possibly random) demand surprise is converted into a serially correlated (or drawn out) output response. The incorporation of such a mechanism into our simple macroeconomic model would require a re-writing of the aggregate supply curve to include lagged output terms. For simplicity we ignore this complication in most of what follows. The central point for our purpose is that serially correlated movements in output are quite consistent with RE, provided we assume a slightly more complicated aggregate supply function than the one we have been using. Furthermore, the major policy implications of RE survive the introduction of this more complicated aggregate supply equation.

Other, similar propagation mechanisms are provided by Sargent (1979) and Lucas (1975). The former emphasises the costs to firms of adjusting their stocks of capital and labour rapidly. The presence of these costs makes it optimal for firms to spread out over time their response to the price signals they receive. The Lucas propagation mechanism relies more on lagged information and the impact of 'surprises' on stocks of productive capital carried forward into future periods. To see the importance of the latter consider firms who in the previous period misinterpreted a rise in aggregate demand as a rise in relative demand, and therefore installed more capital to produce more goods. In the current period some of this capital is still with them. They may now realise that they made a mistake; but they might just as well use their increased capital and hence produce in the current and possibly subsequent periods a higher level of output than they otherwise would.

Now that we have considered two objections to RE as applied to macroeconomics, and shown how these objections are countered, thereby presenting the RE macroeconomic model in its more subtle form, we discuss in the next section some more convincing arguments made against RE.

4. Some objections

The objections to RE as applied to macroeconomics are numerous and vary from the obvious (but not, for that reason, necessarily incorrect) to the unavoidably technical and abstruse. They can be discussed under two general headings: the plausibility of the type of economic agent assumed by RE; and the plausibility of the type of macroeconomic model RE requires to produce its more startling results.

THE PLAUSIBILITY OF THE TYPE OF ECONOMIC AGENT ASSUMED BY RE

RE makes two key assumptions about the typical economic agent. First, that they 'rationally' use the information available to them, that is, they exploit information until the marginal cost of acquiring it equals the marginal benefits of improving forecasts. Second, that certain information (i.e. on the structure of the model and the values of certain exogenous variables) is freely available, that is, its marginal cost is zero. The result of these two assumptions is that economic agents use *all* the available information on structure and exogenous variables to make their forecast. Thus RE has to parry two attacks on its view of the typical economic agent: the attack on the assumption of rationality itself, which many have considered a poor foundation for economic analysis; and the attack on the assumed lack of informational constraints, constraints which many feel to be all pervasive in the real world.

The assumption of rationality is made in most of contemporary economic analysis and it is difficult to see how to dispense with it. This is not really the place to enter into a prolonged discussion of its relevance and so we make only one comment. Many individuals – especially in labour markets which play a central role in the relevance of RE for macroeconomic policy – delegate the responsibility for forming expectations to specialists, e.g. union negotiators. The behaviour of such specialists may more closely approximate rationality than that of any individual on whose behalf they act, since the authority of the specialists depends to a certain extent on the inability of others to do better. To make this point, most generally, the theory of RE can be seen as an implication of profit maximisation: if existing forecasting methods are irrational and produce systematic errors then profit opportunities exist for forecasting institutions. These institutions can improve forecasting by removing systematic errors and selling their product, thereby making typical forecasts rational.

The second attack is much more specific and damaging to RE. Of the two types of information which RE assumes the economic agent has – information about the values of exogenous variables and information about the structure of the economy – the latter is perhaps the more difficult to acquire. But the lack of the former can also undermine the macroeconomic implications of RE. Consider as an illustration Fig. 6.5 in which we assume an initial equilibrium with $AD = AD_0$, the short-run aggregate supply curve AS_0 and hence output and the price level at y_n and p_0 respectively. Let the systematic influences on aggregate demand be such as to keep the aggregate demand curve at AD_0, but let there be a random shift (say a

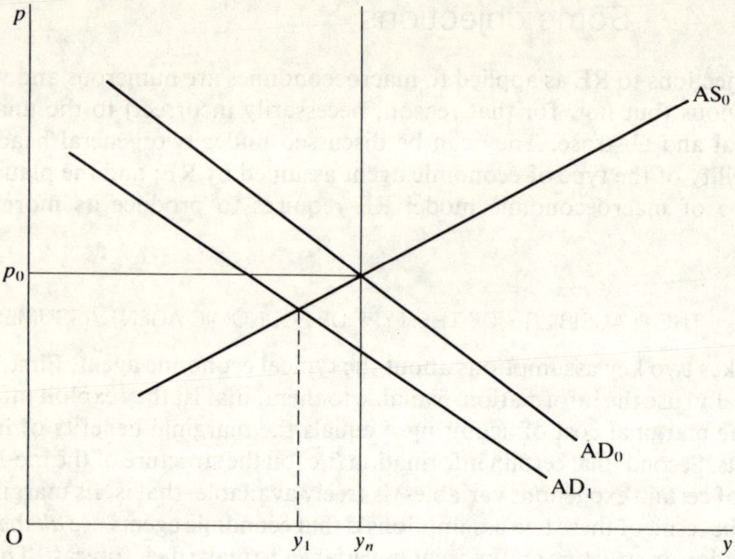

FIG. 6.5 Stabilisation policy with superior information

decrease) in investment expenditure which shifts the aggregate demand curve to AD_1. Since this movement of aggregate demand is random, even if RE is assumed, the movement will not be predicted and hence, *ceteris paribus*, the level of output will fall to y_1. If the government has better information than private economic agents and is aware of this random fall in investment expenditure, then it can act to offset it by, say, increasing the money supply. If it does so successfully then the aggregate demand curve remains at AD_0 and there is no fall in real output. There is nothing in this analysis that is inconsistent with RE. Agents' mistakes are still random and unpredictable: in our example a random overestimate of investment expenditure is offset by a random underprediction of the money stock. Without violating RE we have nevertheless undermined its main implication for macroeconomic policy, for now there is scope for governments to fine-tune the economy. A policy of maintaining the money stock on some predetermined path regardless of new information becoming available (in our example, information about a fall in investment expenditure) is decidedly inferior to one which allows governments in their setting of the money stock to take account of all available information.

To get this result we have only to assume that the government has better information than private economic agents. How sensible is it to make this assumption? Certainly it would seem sensible if the private economic agent is considered as the individual worker or businessman. Most private economic agents defined in that way probably have only the vaguest notion of what a variable like the money supply is, let alone the actual value of its rate of change. If a wider view is taken to mean the private sector as a whole rather than a specific individual who is part of it, then it is perhaps a less sensible assumption. For it is difficult to think of an important set of information to which the government is privy and the private sector of the economy is not. Most government statistics are published soon after collection; the sorts of models used by governments to forecast the economy are available to the private sector of the economy; even changes in government policy, which, clearly, governments will be aware of before anybody else, do not generally come about out of the blue but rather are the result of observable economic and political pressure or developments, and are to that extent not impossible to predict. Thus if each individual in the economy is not aware of each piece of information that it is in fact possible to acquire nevertheless some groups in the economy may be so aware and may, by their ability to sell forecasts based on that information or by acting on behalf of those without it, ensure that the economy reacts as if each individual had the available information. For example, if a trade union which negotiates a wage rate for a group of workers makes use of forecasts of the inflation rate provided by a forecasting firm, then the individual workers in that group may be acting as if they each had information on the money stock,etc. even though if asked none of them would be able to provide that information.

Even in this form the assumption of equal information between governments and the private sector is a strong one at which many would baulk. Ultimately again it is an empirical matter: do theories based on the assumption perform significantly worse than theories which assume asymmetric information? However, even if governments do have better information it does not necessarily follow that this advantageous position should be preserved in the interests of fine-tuning the economy. There is the alternative: publicise the information so that the advantage disappears.

An even more serious problem for the advocates of RE is that of explaining how the typical economic agent or even the private sector of the economy as a whole can know the structure of the economy. As is clear from the stochastic model developed in section 3, to form a rational expectation of the price level the economic agent has to know the values of the parameters α_1 and α_2 and the μ's. Almost all of the theoretical and empirical work on the macroeconomic implications of RE has in fact assumed that economic agents have been operating within a given economy for a sufficiently long time to enable them to have discovered the coefficients which determine its structure. Thus for example Lucas (1977) argues:

> Insofar as business cycles can be viewed as repeated instances of essentially similar events, it will be reasonable . . . to assume [that economic agents'] expectations are rational, that [economic agents] have fairly stable arrangements for collecting and processing information, and that they utilize this information in forecasting the future in a stable way, free of systematic and easily correctable biases (p.15).

This general statement of the case for RE which emphasises the recurrent nature of the events to be predicted has been criticised by B. Friedman (1979) for failing to explain how people came to have the necessary knowledge for the task of making predictions which possess the error orthogonality property mentioned in section 2. To repeat, this property is that the forecast error of say the price level, i.e. $p_t - E_{t-1} p_t$, is independent of any of the information available to people when forming their expectations. Thus, for example, the prediction error is independent of (i.e. orthogonal to) the value of the systematic component of the money stock. If it is not then the available information is not being fully exploited and the expectation is not rational; and as a consequence the policy implications of RE do not necessarily follow.

B. Friedman (1979) introduces one explicit learning method which economic agents might use to gain information about the structure of the economy–ordinary least squares regression using all available information until the latest observation currently available. Agents who use this method to derive estimates of the economy's structure are taking 'full advantage of all available information, in the most efficient way, to yield the minimum variance predictor within the class of all linear unbiased predictors' (B. Friedman 1979: 30). Friedman shows, however, that the orthogonality assumption of RE is not necessarily satisfied in this case. As an illustration consider a variable y, on which expectations are being formed. In reality y is determined solely by the value taken by a variable x together with a random unpredictable component. Thus the true relationship is

$$y_t = \beta x_t + e_t \qquad [24]$$

Agents having information only up to the current period may derive an estimate of β (say b_t) and form an expectation of y_t using this estimate together with information on x_t. Thus

$$E_{t-1} y_t = b_t x_t \qquad [25]$$

from which it follows that

$$y_t - E_{t-1} y_t = (\beta - b_t) x_t + e_t \qquad [26]$$

The left-hand side of this equation defines the prediction error which is independent of the information set, x_t, only if $b_t = \beta$. This means that only if the estimated value of β equals its true value will agents (using efficiently all available information) form expectations such that expectational errors will be independent of the information set. Given *enough* information, obviously the estimate (b_t) will converge to the true value (β), and 'error orthogonality' will be maintained. Friedman (1979) then attacks the application of RE to short-run problems, when convergence of b to β is unlikely: 'Because of the need to assume that economic agents' current . . . estimate b_t has converged to the true β, rational expectations models do not in general address short run phenomena' (p.32). Elaborating on this result Friedman shows that individuals learn more about the true relationship when more information becomes available. Under certain conditions he demonstrates that expectations formed by applying least-squares learning methods 'behave in a way for which the familiar adaptive mechanism may be a useful close approximation' (p.39).

Friedman has raised interesting and important problems for RE: much of the RE literature, by *assuming* that agents know the underlying structure of the economy, begs a very important question. However, Friedman's attack has two important weaknesses. First, it does not demonstrate a case for stabilisation policy in a world where the government is also applying least squares methods as it seeks to understand the economy's structure. It would be fairly straightforward to show that *were the government to have correct information on β*, stabilisation policy would work. But this diverts Friedman's attack to one already considered, viz differential information between government and other economic agents. Second, as Lucas and Sargent argue, knowledge of the true underlying economic structure has been assumed for reasons of simplicity. In principle, at least, equilibrium models of the trade cycle could incorporate learning mechanisms, but 'almost no successful applied work along these lines has come to light' (Lucas and Sargent 1978: 68). The issue is obviously a complicated one, even more so than Friedman's simple case suggests. Agents will not only be trying to derive estimates of β, but also trying to discover whether this relationship is correctly specified (i.e. whether x above, or other variables, x^2, $\log x$, x^{-1}, etc. should be included). Furthermore, one standard case against orthodox Keynesian stabilisation policies has been that governments have such *limited* information that any interventionist exercise is unlikely to be helpful. It must thus be admitted that the role of learning – by the private sector or government – has been difficult to incorporate into either Keynesian or RE macroeconometric models.

The failure to detail a learning mechanism poses a particular problem for the proponents of RE when changes in policy regime occur, for such changes can be sharp. How will the economy respond to a switch in policy regime from one in which the government is expanding the money stock by 20 per cent to one in which with the aim of reducing inflation the government announces that hereafter it will expand the money stock by 3 per cent? Early work on RE was taken by many to imply that such a sudden switch in policy regimes would have the effect of reducing inflation swiftly and cause very little in the way of reduced output or higher unemployment. More recently advocates of RE have denied this implication. Minford for example has argued in the UK context:

> It is quite wrong to suggest that merely 'announcing intentions' will itself establish a credible strategy. The Rational Expectations view of the economy has never made such a suggestion. . . . The RE view does however assert that, once fully believed, new policies will immediately condition expectations of inflation, output growth, etc. However, assessing the speed at which this credibility will be attained is a highly uncertain matter
> (Minford 1980: 131).

The inability of RE to predict what happens when policy regimes are switched and to assess how long it will take for a newly announced policy regime to become credible is a serious weakness for RE, in that it is rendered incapable of being disproved and its status as a scientific theory is thereby reduced. It also, of course, allows the possibility that while economic agents are learning the new policy regime, systematic changes in monetary and fiscal policy can have real effects and can therefore stabilise the economy. Taylor (1975) outlines such a model. In it, systematic monetary policy has no real effects when policy regimes are understood but does have real effects in the transitional period when the policy regime has changed and the new one is not yet understood. Against this advocates of RE can argue that, just as the details of a policy regime can be learnt, so can the conditions for a regime switch. The more such switches occur, the more will agents be sensitive to their likely occurrence. A topical example of this is the concern in the UK about a possible U-turn by the Thatcher government. Proponents of RE might well argue that this awareness of a possible policy regime switch reflects the dramatic switch in regime carried out by a previous Conservative government in 1972. On this argument the main thrust of RE is maintained, though it now applies to a time period sufficiently long for policy regimes and the conditions for switches in them to be understood.

THE PLAUSIBILITY OF RE MACROECONOMIC MODELS

The main objections under this heading are that RE macroeconomic models tend to ignore well-known theoretical results which invalidate their conclusions; that they rely on price flexibility; and that they are always specified (and need to be specified) as linear. We will deal with these objections in turn.

RE models are oversimplified

The first can be illustrated easily enough. It is a standard result in the microeconomics of the utility maximising household that changes in income tax rates might alter labour supply. Hence a tax change, even if it is fully anticipated, may well lead to a different supply of labour and hence a different level of employment and real output. So the RE macroeconomic model, which suggests that only unanticipated fiscal policy will affect output, does so only by ignoring a well-known theoretical result. Similarly, an increase in the rate of growth of the money stock leading to a higher rate of inflation will alter the real rate of return on money holdings whose nominal interest rate is fixed at zero. This change could cause people to desire to hold less money and more capital goods, thereby in the longer run causing a rise in the capital/labour ratio. In simple two-asset (money and capital) models, a higher rate of monetary expansion can thus be associated with a higher level of real output.

These examples show that in more elaborate macroeconomic models, the major policy implications of RE do not seem to hold. However, this type of argument hardly constitutes a serious objection to RE. The point of RE is to show that the usual Keynesian mechanism by which fiscal and monetary policy affects real output and which has formed the basis of attempts to fine-tune the economy is fatally weakened by the assumption of RE. Other, more subtle mechanisms might still exist which allow scope for active government monetary and fiscal policy, though they are as yet poorly established empirically and in any case their existence has not been denied by the main proponents of RE. As Lucas and Sargent (1978) argue:

> The policy implications of equilibrium theories are sometimes caricatured, by friendly as well as unfriendly commentators, as the assertion that 'economic policy does not matter' or 'has no effect'. This implication would certainly startle the neoclassical economists who have successfully applied equilibrium theory to the study of innumerable problems involving important effects of

fiscal policies on resource allocation and income distribution. Our intent is not to reject these accomplishments, but rather to imitate them, or to extend the equilibrium methods which have been applied to many economic problems to cover a phenomena which has so far resisted their application: the business cycle.

Should this intellectual arbitrage prove successful, it will suggest important changes in the way we think about policy. Most fundamentally, it directs attention to the necessity of thinking of policy as the choice of stable 'rules of the game' well understood by economic agents. Only in such a setting will economic theory help us to predict the actions agents will choose to take. Second, this approach suggests that policies which affect behaviour mainly because their consequences cannot be properly diagnosed, such as monetary instability and deficit financing, have the capacity only to disrupt. The deliberate provision of misinformation cannot be used in a systematic way to improve the economic environment (p.70).

RE requires price flexibility

The second objection is to the assumption made in most RE macroeconomic models that prices move to clear markets, i.e. equate supply and demand. This is implicit in our derivation of the aggregate supply curve. Since the time of Keynes, and probably before, economists have felt uncomfortable in making the assumption of price flexibility, especially when considering the labour market. In some markets, the stock market for example, it seems reasonable to assume that prices adjust quickly, even instantaneously, to changes in supply and demand; but in other markets, and the labour market is the obvious example, movements in the relevant price seem a lot more sluggish. Indeed, there is a growing body of work which is beginning to provide a satisfactory theoretical basis for wages in particular being fixed over a significant period of time. And there is also an increasing number of macroeconomic models which assume price and wage inflexibility and consider the 'macroeconomics of disequilibrium'. Both of these developments are beyond the scope of this paper. However, a number of authors have applied RE to a macro model in which for various reasons prices or wages are sticky. Two notable examples of such models are Fischer (1977) and Taylor (1980), both of which introduce stickiness by having wages set for more than one period, whereas aggregate demand changes can occur in each period. The mathematics of these models are complicated; fortunately the general point about price stickiness and its implications for RE can be made with the use of a simple AS/AD diagram.

To keep the analysis as simple as possible assume that prices are, for whatever reasons, set at the beginning of the even-numbered periods, (0, 2, 4, etc.) to cover both the even and subsequent odd period. Thus between periods 0 and 1 the price is fixed, as it is between 2 and 3, etc., but *not* between 1 and 2, 3 and 4, etc.[4] Assume that at the beginning of period 0 the price level expected to prevail in period 0 and 1 is p_0, so that the relevant SRAS curve is the one which is shown in Fig. 6.6. Further assume that the aggregate demand curve happens to be at AD_0 so that the price level is p_0 and the level of output y_n. The price level, p_0, is by assumption now fixed and must remain at p_0 throughout period 1. Firms have agreed or contracted to sell whatever quantity of output is demanded in period 1 at

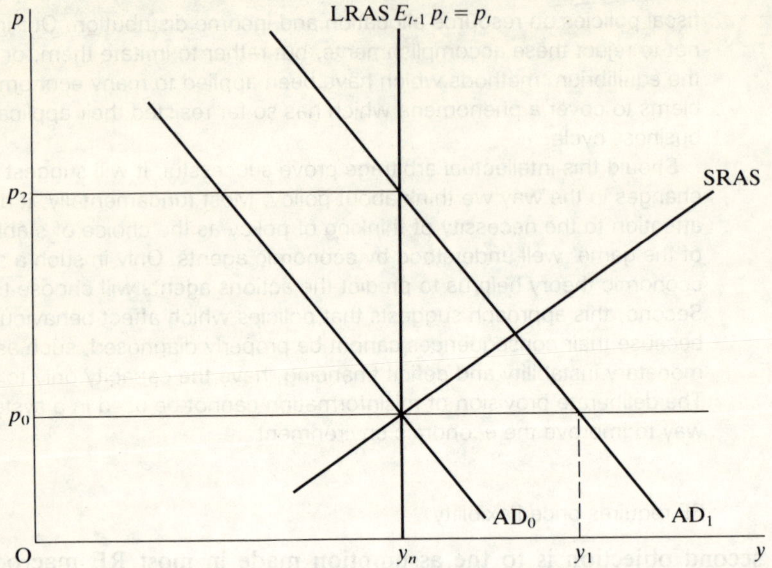

FIG. 6.6 Price stickiness in aggregate supply and demand model

price p_0. The relevant supply curve in period 1 is thus a horizontal line drawn through p_0. It follows that a shift in aggregate demand from AD_0 to AD_1 *even if it is predictable at the end of period 0* will lead to a rise in output to y_1. Of course, if aggregate demand is expected to remain at AD_1 in period 2 a price level of p_2 will be set if RE prevail. But in the meantime the shift in aggregate demand will, because of the stickiness of prices, lead to a rise in output even if that shift is predicted the period before it happens. It follows that within contract periods, i.e. between 0 and 1, or 2 and 3, etc., there is scope for government policy to fine-tune the economy even if RE prevails. In our example the government could reduce its expenditure in period 1, taking account of the information about the future shift in aggregate demand that has become available in period 0. If it thereby totally offsets the rise in demand the aggregate demand curve would remain at AD_0 and the variance of output around its natural level would be minimised. Thus the stickiness of prices provides perhaps some scope for traditional Keynesian policies of fine-tuning the economy even where expectations are rational.

The response of the proponents of RE to this criticism is essentially to question the invariance of the conditions which are somewhat vaguely suggested as being the proximate cause of price inflexibility. These conditions may merely reflect the economic environment–labour contracts, for example, tend to differ across high and low inflation countries; wage bargaining practices change in countries whose inflationary experience changes–and should not therefore be taken as invariant to the type of policy being pursued. If these AD changes are common agents might themselves recognise that it is to their advantage to recontract more frequently. Thus such conditions may be a weak basis on which to erect or re-erect Keynesian fine-tuning. Along these lines Lucas and Sargent (1978) argue:

> So the issue here is really the fundamental one involved in the dispute

> between Keynes and the classical economists: is it adequate to regard certain superficial characteristics of existing wage contracts as given when analysing the consequences of alternative monetary and fiscal regimes? Classical economic theory denies that those characteristics can be taken as given. To understand the implications of long term contracts for monetary policy, one needs a model of the way those contracts are likely to respond to alternative monetary policy regimes. An extension of existing equilibrium models in this direction might well lead to interesting variations, but it seems to us unlikely that major modifications of the implications of these models for monetary and fiscal policy will follow from this (p.65)[5]

It remains a disturbing feature of many Keynesian models that they lack a theoretical rationale for the invariance of the form of nominal contracts across alternative policy regimes. Nevertheless, many Keynesians are content with the simple assertion that the world *is* characterised by rigid nominal contracts, and theories of how the economy works and the ensuing policy implications ought to reflect these features if they are to have any correspondence with reality. Some Keynesians, moreover, argue that the application of RE to models with fixed contracts may even extend the scope for interventionist policies. RE, according to these writers, do not sound the death knell of orthodox interventionist policies, but provide a richer theory of how interventionist policies may work.

The following example is drawn from Buiter (1980) and based in part on recent contributions by Weiss (1980) and Turnovsky (1980). We shall assume that contracts covering period t in the goods and labour markets are drawn up at the end of period $t-1$. The supply function that arises given this assumption might be of the form

$$y_t^* = \beta(p_t - E_{t-1}p_t) + u_t \qquad [27]$$

where y_t^* is the difference between output and its natural rate
and u_t is a random real disturbance.

In contrast, the market for financial assets clears continuously. The demand for money in real terms is assumed to depend on the expected rate of inflation over the period t to $t+1$, together with a random term (e_t) and the departure of income from its natural rate (y_t^*):

$$m_t - p_t = \delta_1 y_t^* - \delta_2\,[E_t p_{t+1} - p_t] + e_t \qquad [28]$$

This model assumes that the markets for goods and labour are quite different from those for financial assets; in this respect, of course, the model might be thought to be 'realistic'.

Combining equations [27] and [28] and solving for the price level we obtain:

$$p_t = \frac{1}{1+\delta_1\beta+\delta_2}m_t + \frac{\delta_1\beta}{1+\delta_1\beta+\delta_2}E_{t-1}p_t + \frac{\delta_2}{1+\delta_1\beta+\delta_2}E_t p_{t+1} - \frac{1}{1+\delta_1\beta+\delta_2}(\delta_1 u_t + e_t) \qquad [29]$$

Taking expectations of equation [29], we can easily derive the price surprise equation:

$$p_t - E_{t-1}p_t = \frac{1}{1+\delta_1\beta+\delta_2}[m_t - E_{t-1}m_t] + \frac{\delta_2}{1+\delta_1\beta+\delta_2}[E_t p_{t+1} - E_{t-1}p_{t+1}]$$

$$- \frac{1}{1+\delta_1\beta+\delta_2}(\delta_1 u_t + e_t) \qquad [30]$$

Now assume that the government determines the money supply exactly and follows the simple deterministic feedback rule:

$$m_t = \mu_1 u_{t-1} + \mu_2 e_{t-1} \qquad [31]$$

Since we define E_{t-1} as the conditional expectation formed at the end of period $t-1$, when u_{t-1} and e_{t-1} are known, it follows from RE that

$$m_t - E_{t-1}m_t = 0 \qquad [32]$$

so that equation [30] may be written

$$p_t - E_{t-1}p_t = \frac{\delta_2}{1+\delta_1\beta+\delta_2}[E_t p_{t+1} - E_{t-1}p_{t+1}] - \frac{1}{1+\delta_1\beta+\delta_2}(\delta_1 u_t + e_t) \qquad [33]$$

This states that the price surprise depends on the 'structural' disturbances (u_t and e_t) and the revision between period $t-1$ and t of the *forward expectation* of price in period $t+1$ as more information becomes available.

From equation [28] we can write

$$p_t = \frac{1}{1+\delta_2}(m_t - \delta_1 y_t^* + \delta_2 E_t p_{t+1} + e_t) \qquad [34]$$

and the following expectations:

$$\begin{cases} E_t p_{t+1} = \dfrac{1}{1+\delta_2}E_t m_{t+1} - \dfrac{\delta_1}{1+\delta_2}E_t y_{t+1}^* + \dfrac{\delta_2}{1+\delta_2}E_t p_{t+2} \\ E_{t-1}p_{t+1} = \dfrac{1}{1+\delta_2}E_{t-1}m_{t+1} - \dfrac{\delta_1}{1+\delta_2}E_{t-1}y_{t+1}^* + \dfrac{\delta_2}{1+\delta_2}E_{t-1}p_{t+2} \end{cases} \qquad [35]$$

Taking the relevant expectations of equation [27] it is easily demonstrated that

$$E_t y_{t+1}^* = \beta E_t p_{t+1} - \beta E_t p_{t+1} = 0 \qquad [36]$$

$$E_{t-1}y_{t+1}^* = \beta E_{t-1}p_{t+1} - \beta E_{t-1}p_{t+1} = 0 \qquad [37]$$

i.e. agents have no expectation at times t and $t-1$ that output will depart from its natural rate at time $t+1$.

We may also note that given the *one period* lagged response of the money supply assumed in equation [31] above, it follows that no new information will become available between periods $t-1$ and t that will lead to change in the rational expectation of p_{t+2}. Therefore, $E_t p_{t+2} = E_{t-1} p_{t+2}$ and we may rewrite equation [35] as

$$E_t p_{t+1} - E_{t-1} p_{t+1} = \frac{1}{1+\delta_2} [E_t m_{t+1} - E_{t-1} m_{t+1}] \qquad [38]$$

Now $E_{t-1} m_{t+1} = \mu_1 E_{t-1} u_t + \mu_2 E_{t-1} e_t = 0$ since u_t and e_t are random variables with zero means. But $E_t m_{t+1} = \mu_1 u_t + \mu_2 e_t$ as both u_t and e_t are known when expectations of m_{t+1} are being formed. Therefore equation [38] may be written as

$$E_t p_{t+1} - E_{t-1} p_{t+1} = \frac{1}{1+\delta_2} [\mu_1 u_t + \mu_2 e_t] \qquad [39]$$

which may be substituted into equation [33] to give:

$$p_t - E_{t-1} p_t = \frac{\delta_2}{(1+\delta_2\beta+\delta_2)(1+\delta_2)} (\mu_1 u_t + \mu_2 e_t) - \frac{1}{1+\delta_1\beta+\delta_2} (\delta_1 u_t - e_t) \qquad [40]$$

If the government could, through the appropriate choice of μ_1 and μ_2, minimise the value of $p_t - E_{t-1} p_t$ in equation [40], it would also minimise y_t^* given equation [27]. By choosing $\mu_1 = \delta_1(1+\delta_2)/\delta_2$ and $\mu_2 = (1+\delta_2)/\delta_2$, the reader can easily verify that the government can eliminate the price surprise altogether (i.e. $p_t = E_{t-1} p_t = 0$). Thus the presence of RE in a 'Keynesian' model actually increases the scope for stabilisation policies. Governments can exploit the rationality of agents to reduce variations in output and employment. This result has been obtained from a fairly simple macro model, with forward expectations entering via the aggregate demand curve, but it does illustrate and emphasise the point that RE, when combined with alternative models, can lead to pro-interventionist conclusions.

RE models are linear

The third objection is that RE macroeconomic models are linear in structure, or at least linear in variables though often non-linear in parameters. The meaning of this distinction can be seen by considering the simply stochastic model in section 2. In equations [22] and [23] each determining variable, m_t, g_t, ε_t, enters those equations in linear form, there are no terms such as m_t^2 or m_t/g_t, etc. Thus the model is said to be linear in variables. Since m_t, g_t, p_t, etc. are defined as logarithms the model is in fact log-linear. The parameters, i.e. the coefficients, α_1, α_2, etc, however do enter in non-linear form: there are expressions such as $\alpha_1/(\alpha_1+\beta_1)$. Thus the model is non-linear in parameters. If in the real world relationships between variables are non-linear then it may well be that the policy implications of RE do not apply. For example, the supply of output might be related to $(p_t - E_{t-1} p_t)^2$ as well as $p_t - E_{t-1} p_t$, in which case the government could affect real variables by deliberately increasing or decreasing the random element in their monetary and fiscal policy. There is in fact no compelling *theoretical* reason for restricting the analysis to linear equations, only issues of analytical tractability and, in applied work, the limitations imposed by existing computer technology.

The problem of estimating non-linear models is beyond the scope of this survey. However, the problems involved in finding solutions to RE models and the need to assume linearity are worth further investigation, if only to explain an unfamiliar method for solving models with RE, first introduced by Lucas and used extensively in the RE literature.

Consider the stochastic model developed in section 2 but modified in three ways. First, in the interest of simplicity, we drop the government expenditure term from equation [1]. Second, assume that the level of aggregate demand at time t is a function of the expected inflation rate. The higher the expected inflation rate over period t to $t + 1$ the more likely economic agents will be to substitute current expenditures in place of future ones. Where p_t refers to the log of the price level at time t, the expected inflation rate over the period t to $t + 1$ formed at the end of period $t-1$ (or equivalently just at the beginning of period t) is $E_{t-1}(p_{t+1} - p_t)$. Third, we assume that X_{t-1} contains only one variable, y_{t-1}. Writing the rest of the model as before, the complete set of equations is as follows

$$y_t^d = \alpha_0 + \alpha_1(m_t - p_t) + \alpha_3 E_{t-1}(p_{t+1} - p_t) \quad [41]$$

$$y_t^s = \beta_0 + \beta_1(p_t - E_{t-1}p_t) \quad [42]$$

$$m_t = \mu_0 + \mu_1 y_{t-1} + \varepsilon_t \quad [43]$$

$$y_t^s = y_t^d \quad [44]$$

Combining equations [41] – [44] and obtaining expressions for p and y gives

$$p_t = \frac{\alpha_0 - \beta_0 + \alpha_1\mu_0}{\alpha_1 + \beta_1} + \frac{\alpha_1\mu_1}{\alpha_1 + \beta_1} y_{t-1} + \frac{\beta_1 - \alpha_3}{\alpha_1 + \beta_1} E_{t-1}p_t + \frac{\alpha_3}{\alpha_1 + \beta_1} E_{t-1}p_{t+1} + \frac{\alpha_1\varepsilon_t}{\alpha_1 + \beta_1} \quad [45]$$

$$y_t = \left[\beta_0 + \frac{\beta_1(\alpha_0 + \beta_0 + \alpha_1\mu_0)}{(\alpha_1 + \beta_1)}\right] + \frac{\beta_1\alpha_1\mu_1}{\alpha_1 + \beta_1} y_{t-1} + \frac{\beta_1(\alpha_1 + \alpha_3)}{\alpha_1 + \beta_1} E_{t-1}p_t + \frac{\beta_1\alpha_3}{\alpha_1 + \beta_1} E_{t-1}p_{t+1} + \frac{\beta_1\alpha_1}{\alpha_1 + \beta_1}\varepsilon_t. \quad [46]$$

In previous versions of this model we have obtained the RE solution for p_t quite simply. We merely assumed that $E_{t-1}p_t$ equalled the non-stochastic component of the equivalent equation to equation [45]. This enabled us, through collecting terms, to obtain a solution for $E_{t-1}p_t$ which we could then substitute back into the equivalent equation to equation [45] and thereby obtain a solution for p_t. By the term 'solution' we mean an expression which explains the determination of

p_t in terms of variables which are exogenous to the model, either in the sense that these variables, like X_{t-1}, are predetermined, or in the sense that their value is determined without reference to any other variable in the model, e.g. ε_t.

This straightforward and familiar technique cannot be applied to equation [46] because of the presence of $E_{t-1}p_{t+1}$. If expectations are rationally formed then, from equation [46], the expectation about p_{t+1} formed at the beginning of period t should be based on the expectation of y_t and the expectation (formed at $t-1$) of the expectation formed at t of the price level in period $t+2$, i.e. $E_{t-1}(E_t(p_{t+2}))$. This latter term, if rationally formed, requires expectations *now* about price levels in period $t+3$ and beyond. This follows simply from the fact that equation [46] contains a term in p_{t+1}. Hence a rational forecast of p_t requires a forecast of p_{t+1} which itself by the same argument requires a forecast of p_{t+2}, etc.

The model based on equations [41] – [46] cannot thus be solved in the normal way. One way of obtaining solutions to this sort of model has been pioneered by Lucas and is known as the method of undetermined coefficients. Given equations [41] – [46] the technique would imply the following steps. First, assume that there exists a solution in the sense that it is possible to express p_t and y_t as functions of the exogenous variables. Since equations [41] – [46] are all linear it seems likely that the solutions will be linear. Write these assumed solutions as

$$p_t = \pi_0 + \pi_1 y_{t-1} + \pi_2 \varepsilon_t \qquad [47]$$

$$y_t = \pi_3 + \pi_4 y_{t-1} + \pi_5 \varepsilon_t \qquad [48]$$

Only terms y_{t-1} and ε_t appear on the right-hand side of these equations since they are the only exogenous variables in this very simple model. $E_{t-1}p_t$ and $E_{t-1}p_{t+1}$ are to be determined within or by the model. The π's are reduced form coefficients, related as we shall see to the structural parameters (α's and β's etc.). If equations [47] and [48] do represent true solutions then if RE applies it follows that

$$E_{t-1}p_t = \pi_0 + \pi_1 y_{t-1} \qquad [49]$$

and

$$E_{t-1}y_t = \pi_3 + \pi_4 y_{t-1} \qquad [50]$$

It also follows that $E_{t-1}p_{t+1}$ can be written as

$$E_{t-1}p_{t+1} = \pi_0 + \pi_1 E_{t-1}y_t \qquad [51]$$

or

$$E_{t-1}p_{t+1} = \pi_0 + \pi_1 [\pi_3 + \pi_4 y_{t-1}] \qquad [52]$$

With the use of equations [41] – [52] we can obtain the solutions we are after. For from equations [42], [47], [48], and [49] it follows that

$$\beta_0 + \beta_1 [\pi_0 + \pi_1 y_{t-1} + \pi_2 \varepsilon_t] - \beta_1 [\pi_0 + \pi_1 y_{t-1}] = \pi_3 + \pi_4 y_{t-1} + \pi_5 \varepsilon_t \qquad [53]$$

i.e.

$$\beta_0 + \beta_1 \pi_2 \varepsilon_t = \pi_3 + \pi_4 y_{t-1} + \pi_5 \varepsilon_t \qquad [54]$$

One solution to this equality is

$$\pi_3 = \beta_0 \quad [55]$$

$$\beta_1\pi_2 = \pi_5 \quad [56]$$

$$\pi_4 = 0 \quad [57]$$

Using equations [41], [43], [47], [48] and [52] we can also obtain

$$\pi_3 + \pi_4 y_{t-1} + \pi_5\varepsilon_t = \alpha_0 + \alpha_1\mu_0 + \alpha_1\mu_1 y_{t-1} + \alpha_1\varepsilon_t - \alpha_1[\pi_0 + \pi_1 y_{t-1} + \pi_2\varepsilon_t] + \alpha_3[\pi_0 + \pi_1[\pi_3 + \pi_4 y_{t-1}]] - \alpha_3[\pi_0 + \pi_1 y_{t-1}] \quad [58]$$

This can be written as

$$\pi_3 + \pi_4 y_{t-1} + \pi_5\varepsilon_t = [\alpha_0 + \alpha_1\mu_0 - \alpha_1\pi_0 + \alpha_3\pi_1\pi_3] + y_{t-1}[\alpha_1\mu_1 - \alpha_1\pi_1 + \alpha_3\pi_1\pi_4 - \alpha_3\pi_1] + \varepsilon_t[\alpha_1 - \alpha_1\pi_2] \quad [59]$$

One solution to this equation is:

$$\pi_3 = \alpha_0 + \alpha_1\mu_0 - \alpha_1\pi_0 + \alpha_3\pi_1\pi_3 \quad [60]$$

$$\pi_4 = \alpha_1\mu_1 - \alpha_1\pi_1 + \alpha_3\pi_1\pi_4 - \alpha_3\pi_1 \quad [61]$$

$$\pi_5 = \alpha_1 - \alpha_1\pi_2 \quad [62]$$

We now have six equations ([55]–[57] and [60]–[62]) to solve for the six π's. It is now a simple matter of substitution to determine the value of the π's as

$$\pi_0 = \frac{\alpha_0 + \alpha_1\mu_0 - \beta_0}{\alpha_1} + \frac{\alpha_3\beta_0\mu_1}{\alpha_1 + \alpha_3} \quad [63]$$

$$\pi_1 = \frac{\alpha_1\mu_1}{\alpha_1 + \alpha_3} \quad [64]$$

$$\pi_2 = \frac{\alpha_1}{\beta_1 + \alpha_1} \quad [65]$$

$$\pi_3 = \beta_0 \quad [66]$$

$$\pi_4 = 0 \quad [67]$$

$$\pi_5 = \frac{\beta_1\alpha_1}{\beta_1 + \alpha_1} \quad [68]$$

Hence by this technique we can write the solutions for p_t and y_t

$$p_t = \frac{\alpha_0 + \alpha_1\mu_0 - \beta_0}{\alpha_1} + \frac{\alpha_3\beta_0\mu_1}{\alpha_1 + \alpha_3} + \frac{\alpha_1\mu_1}{\alpha_1 + \alpha_3} y_{t-1} + \frac{\alpha_1}{\beta_1 + \alpha_1}\varepsilon_t \quad [69]$$

$$y_t = \beta_0 + \frac{\beta_1\alpha_1}{\beta_1 + \alpha_1}\varepsilon_t \quad [70]$$

The solution is derived by assuming that linear solutions exist. If the original equations are non-linear then this assumption is invalid. Even if they are linear the solutions shown in equations [69] and [70] may not be the only possible solutions.

As this example illustrates, the assumption of linearity in RE models is made in order that the problems dealt with can be solved in a relatively simple way. Such simplifying assumptions are commonly made in economics. In Keynesian economics, for example, early estimates of the consumption function assumed a linear relationship between consumption and income because estimation procedures were thereby made simpler. This assumption was made despite the fact that the relationship between consumption and income postulated by Keynes was non-linear. The justification for such simplifying assumptions is usually an empirical one: if they are seriously wrong then the data should reveal it. In the next section we look at the empirical work on RE macroeconomic models.

5. Econometric implications

We mentioned in the introduction that RE has implications not only for macroeconomic policy but also for the estimation of macroeconomic models. In this section we first examine these latter implications; we go on to outline some of the problems associated with setting up refutable hypotheses involving RE; and we end with a review of some of the principal econometric tests of RE.

RE AND ORTHODOX MACROECONOMETRIC MODELS

Until the late 1960s conventional 'Keynesian' macroeconometric models of the UK, USA and other countries were reasonably successful both in tracking the principal macroeconomic aggregates and in forecasting their future values. In the 1970s however two major problems with such models became apparent. First, they proved unable to explain, still less predict, the major macroeconomic phenomenon of the decade: the simultaneous emergence of high levels of unemployment and high rates of inflation. As Lucas and Sargent put it, this was 'econometric failure on a grand scale' (Lucas and Sargent 1978: 57). Second, it became clear that they suffered from parameter instability: estimates of the structural coefficients of the various models, e.g. the marginal propensity to consume, interest elasticity of the demand for money, proved to be significantly different when data from different periods were used.

Lucas (1972b, 1976) has argued that RE provides one possible explanation for the generally unsatisfactory performance of these models. Consider the case where the econometric model builder has, with the use of simple Keynesian theory, assumed and estimated a model of the following form:

$$y_t = \pi_0 + \pi_1 m_t + \pi_2 X_{t-1} \qquad [71]$$

where the π's are coefficients; other notation is as before. Taking the estimated values of the π's as policy *invariant*, that is, unchanging even if government policies on, say, the money stock are different from those pursued over the period for which the model was estimated, the model builder might make predictions about the future course of y on the basis of assumed time paths for m_t and X_{t-1}. He might also recommend one particular time path for m_t (and any of the variables in X_{t-1} which are under the government's control) in order to achieve a desired value for y_t. But what if the model he has estimated, equation [71], is not the result of the simple Keynesian theory assumed by him, but the result of a RE/natural rate model of the type we have discussed? Consider again the stochastic model specified in equations [22] and [23]. We repeat here, for convenience, the RE solution of that model for y_t:

$$y_t = \beta_0 + \frac{\alpha_1 \beta_1 \varepsilon_t}{\beta_1 + \alpha_1} \qquad [23]\ [72]$$

We also repeat the money supply process from which this expression for y_t was partly derived:

$$m_t = \mu_0 + \mu_1 X_{t-1} + \varepsilon_t \qquad [16]\ [73]$$

By substituting for ε_t from equation [73] into equation [72] we can write the expression for y_t as

$$y_t = \beta_0 + \frac{\alpha_1 \beta_1}{\beta_1 + \alpha_1} [m_t - \mu_0 - \mu_1 X_{t-1}] \qquad [74]$$

which can be rewritten as

$$y_t = \beta_0 - \frac{\alpha_1 \beta_1 \mu_0}{\beta_1 + \alpha_1} + \frac{\alpha_1 \beta_1 m_t}{\beta_1 + \alpha_1} - \frac{\alpha_1 \beta_1 \mu_1}{\beta_1 + \alpha_1} X_{t-1} \qquad [75]$$

It should be clear from this equation that it is possible to observe relationships like equation [71] from the data even though the true model is given by equation [75]. It should also be clear that if that is what has happened, then the econometric model builders' estimates of the π's will *not* be policy invariant. For the coefficient attached to X_{t-1}, $-\alpha_1\beta_1\mu_1/(\beta_1 + \alpha_1)$, clearly depends upon the value of μ_1. Similarly, the constant term depends upon μ_0. As a consequence it is not legitimate to recommend different time paths for m_t, i.e. different values for μ_0 and μ_1, and expect the parameters of equation [71] to remain constant. RE can thus explain the instability of conventional macroeconometric models as being the result of failing to recognise the influence of policy changes on parameter estimates.

RE AND OBSERVATIONAL EQUIVALENCE

Given then that the theory of RE has profound implications for the 'orthodox' interpretations of many econometric relationships, how can theories including the assumption of RE be tested empirically? We begin by noting a general problem encountered in any econometric exercise, but one that has particular importance in models with RE. The main aim of empirical research is to formulate alternative theories in a manner that enables the data to adjudicate. This may not always be possible as the following example illustrates. Consider two competing theories about the determinants of real output: a natural rate/RE model (of the type already discussed above) and an 'unnatural rate' theory. The former can be written down in two equations:

$$m_t = \mu_0 + \mu_1 X_{t-1} + \varepsilon_t \qquad [76]$$

$$y_t = \beta_0 + \frac{\alpha_1 \beta_1 \varepsilon_t}{\beta_1 + \alpha_1} + \beta_2 X_{t-1} \qquad [77]$$

The first of these two equations is the familiar money supply equation first introduced in section 2. The second is the RE solution to the stochastic model of section 2 with the extension that the natural rate of output is a function of the same variables as those determining the money supply. Rewriting equation [77] as equation [78] brings out that we are now assuming that the variables in the X_{t-1} vector have two effects on output: a direct one given by the coefficient β_2 and an indirect effect through the influence of X_{t-1} on m_t.

$$y_t = \left[\beta_0 - \frac{\alpha_1 \beta_1 \mu_0}{\beta_1 + \alpha_1}\right] + \frac{\alpha_1 \beta_1 m_t}{\beta_1 + \alpha_1} + X_{t-1}\left[\beta_2 - \frac{\alpha_1 \beta_1 \mu_1}{\beta_1 + \alpha_1}\right] \qquad [78]$$

The econometrician who estimates equation [76] and [78] and who believes they come from the structure we have assumed would interpret the coefficient he estimates on m_t as showing the reaction of output to unanticipated money supply. The coefficient on X_{t-1} in the y equation simply determines the value of β_2 (as μ_1 is determined in equation [76] and $\alpha_1\beta_1/(\beta_1 + \alpha_1)$ is obtained from the estimate of the coefficient on m_t in the y equation).

Now consider an 'unnatural rate' model of the form:

$$m_t = \mu_0 + \mu_1 X_{t-1} + \varepsilon_t \qquad [76]$$

$$y_t = \beta_0 + \beta_1 m_t + \beta_2 X_{t-1} \qquad [79]$$

Here the money stock equation is the same as before but the output equation allows both anticipated and unanticipated monetary growth to affect the level of output. In this case an econometrician who estimates equations [76] and [79] and who believes they come from this unnatural rate theory will interpret the coefficient on m_t in the y equation as the reaction of output to total (anticipated and unanticipated) contemporaneous money supply changes, and the coefficient on X_{t-1} as reflecting the influence of the variables in X_{t-1} on y_t.

There is no way in which an econometrician faced with data series on m_t, X_{t-1} and y_t could distinguish between these theories. The theories clearly have quite different policy implications but the data do not help in this case to say which theory is appropriate. The theories are thus said to be 'observationally equivalent' (see Sargent 1976b, McCallum 1979).

One solution to this problem is to impose restrictions on μ_1 and β_2, which, remember, are both *vectors* of coefficients, not single coefficients. Suppose that economic theory predicts that a set of variables in X, say X_1, affects the monetary authority's decision in setting m_t, but does not directly influence y_t. Another set of variables in X, say X_2, has a direct influence on output, but has no effect on the conduct of monetary policy.

The 'natural rate' theory now becomes:

$$m_t = \mu_0 + \mu_{11} X_{1t-1} + \varepsilon_t \qquad [80]$$

$$y_t = \beta_0 + \frac{\alpha_1\beta_1}{\beta_1 + \alpha_1} m_t - \frac{\alpha_1\beta_1\mu_0}{\beta_1 + \alpha_1} - \frac{\alpha_1\beta_1}{\beta_1 + \alpha_1}\mu_{11} X_{1t-1} + \beta_2 X_{2t-1} \qquad [81]$$

Note that μ_{11} will be estimated as the coefficient on X_{1t-1} in equation [80], and $\alpha_1\beta_1/(1 + \alpha_1)$ is the coefficient on m_t in the estimate of equation [8]. This means that the coefficient on $X_{1\,t-1}$ in equation [81] *should* equal minus the product of the coefficients on $X_{1\,t-1}$ in equation [80]. By contrast, consider the 'unnatural rate' model:

$$m_t = \mu_0 + \mu_{11} X_{1t-1} + \varepsilon_t \qquad [80]$$

$$y_t = \beta_0 + \beta_1 m_t + \beta_2 X_{2t-1} + \beta_3 X_{1t-1} \qquad [82]$$

The 'natural rate' model, given the restrictions assumed, can now be shown to be a special case of equation [82] or, more accurately, equation [81] is 'nested' within equation [82]. Were we to impose the following restrictions on equation [82] the equation would correspond to equation [81]:

$$\beta_3 = -\beta_1 \mu_{11} \qquad [83]$$

In principle, regressions of y_t on m_t, X_{2t-1} and X_{1t-1} could be performed with and without these restrictions, and the results compared statistically in a manner that could throw light on the relative merits of the theories. Of course, as the example shows, the data could only be made 'to adjudicate' by stating *a priori* exclusion restrictions (i.e. the exclusion of X_2 from equation [80] and X_1 from equation [81] other than through $E_{t-1}m_t$). These exclusion restrictions are always used in some form in econometric tests for RE.

EMPIRICAL FINDINGS[6]

The aggregate supply function developed in section 2 was justified by the assumption that economic agents confuse *relative* price changes with general ones. An implication of this assumption, which was pointed out and used as the basis for an empirical test of RE by Lucas, is that the larger are variations in the aggregate price level (or in nominal output, the log of which is defined as $y + p$), the less will rational economic agents respond to any given change in the price level. In an economy with a volatile general price level, agents are more likely to interpret any change in the price of their good as reflecting a general change in prices, rather than a relative price change. Hence they will change their output less in response to a change in prices than will economic agents operating in economies with less volatile prices.

More formally, the greater the *variance* in the aggregate price level (assuming the variance of relative prices constant), the less responsive aggregate supply will be to any given change in price (i.e. the steeper the short-run aggregate supply curve). This means that, if the theory is correct, in countries characterised by considerable variation in overall prices the estimate of the coefficient β_1 in equation [2] will tend to be small relative to those estimated in other countries with smaller variances.

Lucas (1973) estimated supply functions for eighteen countries (using time-series data from 1951 to 1967) and found in general a positive and significant response of real output (y_t) to changes in nominal output ($\Delta y_t + \Delta p_t$, where $\Delta x_t = x_t - x_{t-1}$). In two countries where the aggregate price level (as measured by the change in nominal output) was highly volatile (Argentina and Paraguay), the supply coefficient was essentially zero. This supports the view that 'highly volatile countries' will have steep aggregate supply curves under rational expectations. However, for the remaining sixteen 'less volatile countries', the correlation between the estimated supply coefficients and aggregate price variance was small. Alberro (1981) has extended Lucas's study to fifty countries and came to very similar conclusions. In six 'price volatile countries' (Argentina, Brazil, Chile, Indonesia, Korea and Uruguay), the supply coefficients were low.

In extreme cases of price instability, the supply curve is affected in the way RE predicts; but smaller changes in price level variance do not seem to affect the supply response significantly. There are two weaknesses in Lucas's empirical work that may account for this indistinct result. First, he allows for no change over time in the anticipated rate of change in nominal income. Expectations are rational, but $E_{t-1}(\Delta y_t + \Delta p_t)$ is *assumed* constant. The model is mis-specified if the anticipated rate of change in nominal income has varied over the period examined by Lucas and the estimated supply coefficients may be misleading. Second, by using changes in nominal income ($\Delta y_t + \Delta p_t$) as opposed to the simple inflation rate (Δp_t), Lucas may observe a positive relationship even in cases where y_t and Δp_t are independently determined. This arises because the change in nominal income contains, in part, the dependent variable (y_t) itself.

Sargent (1976c) avoids both criticisms of the Lucas study. Taking the unemployment rate as the dependent variable, he estimated the coefficient on $(p_t - E_{t-1} p_t)$ using quarterly post-war time series data for the US (up to 1973). In order to derive a series on $E_{t-1} p_t$, Sargent assumed RE and regressed p_t on a number of variables dated $t-1$ and earlier. These variables included lagged values of the price level itself, wages, labour supply and unemployment. The fitted values from this 'first stage' regression act as a proxy for $E_{t-1} p_t$. The estimated coefficient on the price surprise in the unemployment equation was found to be negative in sign, relatively small in absolute size but just statistically significant.[7] This model lends some, albeit weak, support for the aggregate supply function assumed above, and to the use of RE in forming expectations. The use of unemployment as the dependent variable may have posed problems due to the well-known secular trends in unemployment in the USA. The tentative nature of Sargent's result is underlined by further estimates of Fair (1979). Fair criticised Sargent for using some 'intruder' variables in forming his proxy for $E_{t-1} p_t$. These variables should not have been used as regressors in Sargent's 'first stage' regression because Sargent's theory does not predict that they will have any influence on the price level. Fair therefore argues that the way in which Sargent generates price expectations is not consistent with his model. On re-estimating the unemployment equation (using as regressors in the first stage only those variables implied by the model to affect the price level), Fair finds that the price surprise is insignificant (and even positive when data for the years 1974–77 are added).

Similar difficulties with the price surprise term in the unemployment equation were encountered by Holden and Peel (1977) when using RE as a basis for expectation formation for a number of countries (UK, Australia, Canada, New Zealand, USA). However, they found that the price surprise term was significant when alternative expectation mechanisms were assumed (e.g. naive, adaptive).

Rather than explain changes in real output or unemployment through changes in the price surprise, a number of recent contributions have examined evidence for equation [72] above, in which the effects of unanticipated monetary growth on output or unemployment are estimated. The most important and influential of these are the two empirical studies of Barro (1977b, 1978b). Barro begins by estimating an equation similar to equations [16] (or [73]). To do this the principal determinants of monetary policy had to be identified over the period under review. Two 'economic determinants' for monetary growth were suggested by Barro: first a measure of government expenditure relative to its 'normal' level (FEDV). When government expenditure is running at a level above trend, methods of finance may be adopted which raise monetary growth. Second, Barro allowed for counter-cyclical monetary policy through the presence of lagged unemployment in the monetary growth equation (U_{t-1}, where $U = \log (UN/1 - UN)$ and UN is the unemployment rate). When unemployment is relatively high, governments may increase monetary growth as part of their stabilisation programmes. For this reason U_{t-1} will enter the money growth equation with a positive sign, as will FEDV_t.

Since agents are assumed to be rational, any systematic relationship of money growth with its determining variables will be included in agents' information sets, and incorporated into their expectations. Only the random components of money growth will be unanticipated. Barro's estimate of the money growth equation (using annual time series data for the USA, 1941–76) is;

$$\begin{aligned}\mathrm{DM}_t = \underset{(0.027)}{0.082} + \underset{(0.14)}{0.41\,\mathrm{DM}_{t-1}} + \underset{(0.12)}{0.21\,\mathrm{DM}_{t-2}} + \underset{(0.016)}{0.072\,\mathrm{FEDV}_t} + \\ \underset{(0.009)}{0.026\,U_{t-1}} + \mathrm{DMR}\end{aligned} \qquad [84]$$

$R^2 = 0.77$ DW = 1.9

(Standard errors in parentheses.)

where $\mathrm{DM}_t = \log \mathrm{M}_t - \log \mathrm{M}_{t-1}$, and M_t is the level of the money supply, M_1 definition.

Taking the residuals from this equation (DMR) to be unanticipated money growth and the fitted value ($\widehat{\mathrm{DM}}_t = \mathrm{DM}_t - \mathrm{DMR}_t$) to represent anticipated monetary growth, Barro tests whether anticipated or unanticipated money growth affects output (in Barro 1978b) or unemployment (in Barro 1977b). If the model underlying equation [72] (above) is correct, then only unanticipated monetary growth will be found to influence the real variables.

Including the current and lagged values of DMR in the output and unemployment equations, Barro derived the following estimates:

$$\begin{aligned}y_t = y_t^N + \underset{(0.21)}{1.04\,\mathrm{DMR}_t} + \underset{(0.22)}{1.21\,\mathrm{DMR}_{t-1}} + \underset{(0.21)}{0.44\,\mathrm{DMR}_{t-2}} + \\ + \underset{(0.16)}{0.26\,\mathrm{DMR}_{t-3}} + \varepsilon_t\end{aligned} \qquad [85]$$

$R^2 = 0.998$ $DW = 1.8$

$$U_t = U_t^N - \underset{(2.1)}{5.8\,\mathrm{DMR}_t} - \underset{(1.9)}{12.1\,\mathrm{DMR}_{t-1}} - \underset{(1.9)}{4.2\,\mathrm{DMR}_{t-2}} + u_t \qquad [86]$$

$R^2 = 0.78$ $DW = 1.96$

where y_t^N and U_t^N are the 'natural' levels of the real variables (explained through the presence of other variables in each equation), and y_t is the logarithm of real output.

It can be seen that unanticipated money has a positive and statistically significant effect on output (with significant lagged effects over two years) and a negative effect on unemployment (with lagged effects again over two years). Moreover, when Barro added to equation [85] current and lagged values for actual monetary growth, he found that 'the hypothesis that actual money growth is irrelevant for output, given the inclusion of unanticipated money growth, is accepted' (Barro 1978b: 557). Similar results were obtained for the unemployment equation. Taken together, these results provide striking support for the model implied by equation [72], and for the relevance of RE itself.[8]

In passing we must note that Barro's empirical test is a joint one: it tests both that monetary surprises alone affect output *and* that expectations are formed rationally. Leiderman (1980) has suggested a way of breaking the joint test into two 'nested' tests. Consider the following simplified version of Barro's model:

$$DM_t = \theta_1 X_{1_{t-1}} + \theta_2 X_{2_{t-1}} + DMR_t \qquad [87]$$

$$y_t = y_t^N + \beta DMR_t + e_t \qquad [88]$$

or

$$y_t = y_t^N + \beta_1 DM_t - \beta_2 D\hat{M}_t + e_t \qquad [89]$$

where $D\hat{M}_t$ is anticipated monetary growth and clearly equation [89] is equivalent to equation [88] with the additional restriction that

$$\beta_2 = \beta_1 = \beta \qquad [90]$$

Leiderman refers to the restriction [90] as 'structural neutrality' as it implies only unanticipated money affects output. It is clear that 'rationality' of expectations implies a further set of restrictions, which can be derived by substituting for DM_t and $D\hat{M}_t$ in equation [89], and identifying $D\hat{M}_t$ with the systematic component of the DM equation. Making these substitutions yields the following output equation:

$$y_t = y_t^N + \pi_0 X_{1_{t-1}} + \pi_1 X_{2_{t-1}} + v_t \qquad [91]$$

where $\pi_0 = \theta_1(\beta_1 - \beta_2)$
$\pi_1 = \theta_2(\beta_1 - \beta_2)$
$v_t = \beta_1 DMR + e_t$

Given the estimates of θ_1 and θ_2 from the DM equation, rational expectations implies restrictions on the coefficients attached to $X_{1_{t-1}}$ and $X_{2_{t-1}}$ in the output equation. These can be written:

$$\frac{\pi_0}{\theta_1} = \frac{\pi_1}{\theta_2} \qquad [92]$$

The 'rational expectations' restriction can be applied by estimating equations [87] and [91], imposing the restriction in equation [92]. Should this restriction be supported by the data, the additional 'structural neutrality' restriction could be imposed (i.e. equation [90]). Leiderman applied this method to Barro's (1977) data, and found that neither RE nor 'structural neutrality' is rejected by the data.

Barro's initial results for the USA using annual data have been corroborated by a number of other studies of a similar nature (and imposing similar exclusion restrictions) but using different data sets. A number of these are listed in Table 6.1. All five studies listed indicated that only the random component of monetary growth (i.e. DMR) affects the level of real output or unemployment. They also find that lagged, as well as current, monetary surprises significantly influence output. Both Barro papers find that the one-year lag on DMR has the largest real impact; the quarterly models of Barro and Rush (for the USA) and

TABLE 6.1

	Data	Real variable	Variables in DM equation	Length of lag on DMR
Barro (1977b)	US Annual 1941–74	Unemployment	(a) lagged DM (b) lagged unemployment (c) Federal expenditure	2 years
Barro (1978b)	US Annual 1941–76	Output	as Barro (1977b)	2–3 years
Barro and Rush (1980)	US Quarterly 1941.1–1978.1	Output Unemployment	as Barro (1977b)	7 quarters
Wogin (1980)	Canadian Annual 1926–72	Unemployment	(a) lagged DM (b) lagged unemployment (c) lagged government expenditure (d) lagged exports	1 year
Attfield *et al.* (1981)	UK Quarterly 1963–78	Output	(a) lagged DM (b) lagged balance of payments (c) central government borrowing requirement	5–6 quarters

Attfield, Demery and Duck (for the UK) suggest peaked effects on the four quarter and five quarter lags respectively, though the evidence for the UK suggests a generally flatter lag distribution compared with a pronounced inverted 'V' distribution for the USA. The summed values of the coefficients on the DMR's in the Barro–Rush model imply a larger response of output to unanticipated monetary growth than that found for the UK. An annual one percentage point increase in DMR in the USA that persists for seven quarters (which is highly unlikely, of course, as DMR is independently and normally distributed by assumption) causes output to rise by just over 2 per cent. The evidence for the UK suggests that an identical increase in DMR that persists for six quarters will increase output by approximately three quarters of one percent.

The empirical evidence thus provides some support for RE, though as yet that support cannot be regarded as anything but highly tentative.

6. Summary and conclusions

The theory of RE assumes that economic agents will fully exploit all the information available to them when forming expectations. If strong assumptions are made about the available information, the theory of RE can be combined with other widely accepted theories in macroeconomics–particularly versions of the natural rate hypothesis–to provide some startling implications, both for the development and estimation of macroeconomic models and for policy formulation and design.

Concerning the development of macroeconomic models, RE has by ruling out one popular explanation of persistent booms and slumps (i.e. the explanation based on serially correlated forecasting errors) forced economic theorists to develop other potentially richer explanations of the same phenomena. Since an explanation of these phenomena is a major aim of macroeconomists the theory of RE has indeed had a revolutionary impact on macroeconomic modelling.

Concerning the estimation of macroeconomic models, RE has brought into question the 'structural nature' of parameter estimates presented in many econometric models. These parameters are, in many cases, not policy invariant, and when they are unstable over time, this may be due to changes in policy responses rather than any underlying changes in economic structure. RE has thus undermined confidence in existing macroeconometric models and emphasised the dangers of using them to assess different policy regimes. The problems established by RE for such models are regarded as 'fatal' (see Lucas and Sargent 1978: 50) by the proponents of RE, who argue that 'modern macroeconomic models are of *no* value in guiding policy, and that this condition will not be remedied by modifications along any line which is currently being pursued' (Lucas and Sargent 1978: 50; original italics.) Even a milder version of this view, which maintains that RE has cast serious doubt on the existing approach to model building and estimation and the use of such models for policy design, implies a major change of direction for macroeconometric model builders.

The policy implications of RE seem to us to be less startling than they are often portrayed as being. In their crude form, these implications are that systematic changes in monetary and fiscal policy will have no effect on real variables even in the short run, and hence an economy experiencing high inflation and high monetary growth would be well advised to cut that monetary growth sharply and quickly. These implications in our view survive neither the failure of RE to specify how a new policy regime comes to be believed nor the apparent existence of a certain inflexibility in prices and wages. In their more sophisticated form (in which the time needed to learn about policy regimes and for the form of wage and price contracts to adjust to policy regimes is stressed), the policy implications of RE are not very different from the implications of other non-RE long-run models. Importantly, RE theories recognise that abrupt changes in policy regime may well have sharp effects on real variables in the short run, even though they leave real variables unaffected in the long run. Hence on the major policy question of how quickly to move from one policy regime which is generating a high level of inflation to one which will generate zero inflation the theory of RE cannot be said *necessarily* to imply that the movement should be rapid. It all depends, as with other expectations formation mechanisms, on a weighing of the short-term costs of lost output and employment against the long-term benefits of reducing inflation.

Whilst the theory of RE has less to say about the transition from one policy regime to another than was at first thought, its attack on continuing Keynesian interventionist policies has been formidable and, in the opinion of some, revolutionary. When governments attempt, using traditional demand management, to stabilise the level of activity on *a regular basis*, their action may be neutralised by the expectations of the private sector. Whether the case for orthodox stabilisation policies has survived this 'revolution' or not, it seems safe to predict that RE will remain a central ingredient of macroeconomic theory.

Notes

1. By changes of gear Flemming strictly means the realisation of people that the variable on which they had been operating adaptively is subject to trend. Gear shifts are further discussed in Sumner's survey.
2. More rigorous macroeconomic RE models appear in Barro (1976, 1978a, 1980), Lucas (1972a, 1975), Lucas and Prescott (1974), McCallum (1978), Sargent (1973). An early attempt to combine a macroeconomic model with ideas similar to RE is given in Walters (1971).
3. These results and their implications are more fully discussed in Barro (1976), Sargent (1976a), Sargent and Wallace (1975), Lucas (1980).
4. The analysis could be made more 'realistic' by allowing different prices to be set in period 0 and 1, etc. whilst retaining the assumption that both the prices are set for two periods; the policy implications that would follow from this assumption would be qualitatively the same as those that follow from our simpler assumption. See Taylor (1980).
5. For fuller discussion of wage/price stickiness see Barro (1977a), Hall (1975), Phelps and Taylor (1977), Poole (1976).
6. In what follows we restrict ourselves to tests of RE models that involve some version of the Lucas supply function. Microeconomic models in general involving RE are ignored, and this includes those studies which examine the validity of the efficient capital market hypothesis. For a useful survey of this literature the reader is referred to Fama (1970).
7. Additional variables in the unemployment equation were a time trend and four lagged unemployment terms.
8. The earlier remarks on observational equivalence are easily illustrated in Barro's test. He assumes that those variables which influence the money supply do not directly affect real output or unemployment. The reader can check that were they all to do so, Barro would be unable to test whether it is only the unanticipated component that affects output or unemployment. In this way Barro uses 'exclusion restrictions' to test the hypothesis. It must be admitted that these restrictions have a 'classical' bias, as they imply that the fiscal variable ($FEDV_t$) does not directly influence output.

References

Alberro, J. (1981) The Lucas hypothesis on the Phillips curve: further international evidence, *Journal of Monetary Economics,* **7**, 239–50.

Attfield, C. L. F., Demery, D. and Duck, N. W. (1981) A quarterly model of unanticipated monetary growth, output and the price level in the UK 1963–1978, *Journal of Monetary Economics,* **8**, 331–50.

Barro, R. J. (1976) Rational expectations and the role of monetary policy, *Journal of Monetary Economics,* **2**, 1–33.

Barro, R. J. (1977a) Long-term contracting, sticky prices, and monetary policy, *Journal of Monetary Economics,* **3**, 305–16.

Barro, R. J. (1977b) Unanticipated money growth and unemployment in the United States, *American Economic Review,* **67**, 101–115.

Barro, R. J. (1978a) A stochastic equilibrium model of an open economy under flexible exchange rates, *Quarterly Journal of Economics,* **92**, 149–64.

Barro, R. J. (1978b) Unanticipated money, output and the price level in the United States, *Journal of Political Economy,* **86**, 549–80.

Barro, R. J. (1980) A capital market in an equilibrium business cycle model, *Econometrica,* **48**, 1393–1417.

Barro, R. J. and Rush, M. (1980) Unanticipated money and economic activity, in Fischer, S. (ed.), *Rational Expectations and Economic Policy*, University of Chicago Press, Chicago.

Blinder, A. A. and Fischer, S. (1981) Inventories, rational expectations and the business cycle, *Journal of Monetary Economics,* **8**, 277–304.

Buiter, W. H. (1980) Money, financial and fiscal policy under rational expectations, *IMF Staff Papers,* **27**, 785–813.

Fair, R. C. (1979) An analysis of the accuracy of four macroeconomic models, *Journal of Political Economy,* **87**, 701–18.

Fama, E. F. (1970) Efficient capital markets: a review of theory and empirical work, *Journal of Finance,* **25**, 383–417.

Fischer, S. (1977) Long-term contracts, rational expectations and the optimal money supply rule, *Journal of Political Economy,* **85**, 191–205.

Flemming, J. (1976) *Inflation*, Oxford University Press, Oxford.

Friedman, B. M. (1979) Optimal expectations and the extreme information assumptions of 'rational expectations' macromodels, *Journal of Monetary Economics,* **5**, 23–42.

Friedman, M. (1959) *A Program for Monetary Stability*, Fordham University Press, New York.

Friedman, M. (1968) The role of monetary policy, *American Economic Review,* **58**, 1–17.

Friedman, M. (1976) *Price Theory*, Aldine Publishing Company, Chicago.

Frisch, R. (1965) Propagation problems and impulse problems in dynamic economics, reprinted in *AEA Readings in Business Cycles*, Gordon, R. A. and Klein, L. R. (eds), George Allen & Unwin, London.

Hall, R. E. (1975) The rigidity of wages and the persistence of unemployment, *Brookings Papers on Economic Activity*, 1975:2, 301–35.

Holden, K. and Peel, D. A. (1977) Unemployment and unanticipated inflation, *European Economic Review,* **10**, 253–71.

Leiderman, L. (1980) Macroeconomic testing of the rational expectations and structural neutrality hypotheses for the United States, *Journal of Monetary Economics,* **6**, 69–82.

Lucas, R. E. (1972a) Expectations and the neutrality of money, *Journal of Economic Theory,* **4**, 103–24.

Lucas, R. E. (1972b) Econometric testing of the natural rate hypothesis, in Eckstein, O. (ed.), *The Econometrics of Price Determination*, Board of Governors of the Federal Reserve System and SSRC, Washington, DC.

Lucas, R.E. (1973) Some international evidence on output-inflation trade-offs, *American Economic Review,* **63**, 326–34.

Lucas, R. E. (1975) An equilibrium model of the business cycle, *Journal of Political Economy,* **83**, 1113–44.

Lucas, R. E. (1976) Econometric policy evaluation: a critique, in Brunner, K. and Meltzer, A. H. (eds), *The Phillips Curve and Labour Markets*, Carnegie-Rochester Conference Series on Public Policy, **1**, North-Holland, Amsterdam.

Lucas, R. E. (1977) Understanding business cycles, in Brunner, K. and Meltzer, A. H. (eds), *Stabilization of the Domestic and International Economy*, Carnegie-Rochester Conference Series on Public Policy, **5**, North-Holland, Amsterdam.

Lucas, R. E. (1980) The role of economic advisor, in Fischer, S. (ed.), *Rational Expectations and Economic Policy*, University of Chicago Press, Chicago.

Lucas, R. E. and Prescott, E. C. (1974) Equilibrium search and unemployment, *Journal of Economic Theory,* **7**, 188–209.

Lucas, R. E. and Rapping, L. (1969) Real wages, employment and inflation, *Journal of Political Economy,* **77**, 721–54.

Lucas, R. E. and Sargent, T. J. (1978) After Keynesian macroeconomics, in *After the Phillips Curve: Persistence of High Inflation and High Unemployment*, Federal Reserve Bank of Boston, Conference Series, **19**.

McCallum, B. T. (1978) Dating, discounting and the robustness of the Lucas-Sargent proposition, *Journal of Monetary Economics,* **4**, 121–30.

McCallum, B. T. (1979) On the observational inequivalence of classical and Keynesian models, *Journal of Political Economy,* **87**, 395–402.

Minford, P. (1980) Memorandum in House of Commons, Treasury and Civil Service Committee, *Memoranda on Monetary Policy,* (No. 720).

Modigliani, F. (1977) The monetarist controversy, or should we forsake stabilization policies?, *American Economic Review,* **67**, 1–19.

Muth, J. F. (1961) Rational expectations and the theory of price movements, *Econometrica,* **29**, 315–35.

Okun, A. (1970) *The Political Economy of Prosperity*, Norton, New York.

Phelps, E. S. and Taylor, J. (1977) Stabilizing powers of monetary policy under rational expectations, *Journal of Political Economy,* **85**, 163–90.

Phillips, A. W. (1958) The relation between unemployment and the rate of change of money wage rates in the United Kingdom, 1861–1957, *Economica,* N.S. **25**, 283–99.

Poole, W. (1976) Rational expectations in the macro model, *Brookings Papers on Economic Activity*, 1976:2, 463–514.

Sargent, T. J. (1973) Rational expectations, the real rate of interest and the natural rate of unemployment, *Brookings Papers on Economic Activity*, 1973:2, 429–72; correction of errors, 1973:3, 799–800.

Sargent, T. J. (1976a) Rational expectations and the theory of economic policy, *Journal of Monetary Economics,* **2**, 169–84.

Sargent, T. J. (1976b) The observational equivalence of natural and unnatural rate theories of macroeconomics, *Journal of Political Economy,* **84**, 631–40.

Sargent, T. J. (1976c) A classical macroeconometric model for the United States, *Journal of Political Economy,* **84**, 207–37.

Sargent, T. J. (1979) *Macroeconomic Theory*, Academic Press, New York.

Sargent, T. J. and Wallace, N. (1975) Rational expectations, the optimal monetary instrument and the optimal money supply rule, *Journal of Political Economy,* **83**, 241–55.

Shiller, R. J. (1978) Rational expectations and the dynamic structure of macroeconomic models: a critical review, *Journal of Monetary Economics,* **4**, 1–44.

Taylor, J. B. (1975) Monetary policy during a transition to rational expectations, *Journal of Political Economy,* **83**, 1009–22.

Taylor, J. B. (1980) Aggregate dynamics and staggered contracts, *Journal of Political Economy,* **88**, 1–23.

Turnovsky, S. J. (1980) The choice of monetary instruments under alternative forms of price expectations, *Manchester School,* **46**, 39–62.

Walters, A. A. (1971) Consistent expectations, distributed lags and the quantity theory, *Economic Journal,* **81**, 273–81.

Weiss, L. (1980) The role for active monetary policy in a rational expectations model, *Journal of Political Economy,* **88**, 221–33.

Wogin, G. (1980) Unemployment and monetary policy under rational expectations: some Canadian evidence, *Journal of Monetary Economics,* **6**, 59–68.

Author index

Subject index